COMING TO MY SENSES

COMING TO MY SENSES

THE AUTOBIOGRAPHY OF A SOCIOLOGIST

GEORGE CASPAR HOMANS

Transaction Books
New Brunswick (U.S.A.) and London (U.K.)

Second printing 1985

Copyright © 1984 by Transaction, Inc.
New Brunswick, New Jersey 08903

Library of Congress Catalog Number: 84-77
ISBN: 0-88738-001-8 (cloth)
Printed in the United States of America

Library of Congress Cataloging in Publication Data

Homans, George Caspar, 1910-
    Coming to my senses.

    Includes index.
    1. Homans, George Caspar, 1910-   . 2. Sociologists
—United States—Biography.   I. Title.
HM22.U6H653 1984   301'.092'4 [B]   84-77
ISBN 0-88738-001-8

To my wife
Nancy Parshall Homans
who bore it bravely

Grau, teurer Freund, ist alle Theorie
Und grün des Lebens goldner Baum.

—Goethe, *Faust*

CONTENTS

ACKNOWLEDGMENTS

The author gratefully acknowledges the following publishers and institutions for permission to use copyrighted and other material:

Massachusetts Historical Society, Abigail Adams Homans's letter to Henry Adams, 27 August 1910. Unpublished ms.

Justice Holmes's letter to Harold Laski, in *Holmes-Laski Letters: The Correspondence of Justice Holmes and Harold J. Laski, 1916-1935.* Cambridge: Harvard University Press, 1953.

A passage in Chapter 10, from George C. Homans, *Sentiments and Activities,* pp. 9-10. New York: The Free Press, a Division of Macmillan Publishing Company, 1962. Copyright © The Free Press.

Chapter 12 was originally a paper, "Sailing with Uncle Charlie," delivered to a meeting of the Massachusetts Historical Society and later published in its *Proceedings* 76 (1964): 55-67. Reprinted, *Atlantic Monthly* 216 (1965): 39-45. Copyright © by George C. Homans.

The excerpt from *The Middle Span,* by George Santayana, is reprinted with the permission of Charles Scribner's Sons. Copyright © 1945 by Charles Scribner's Sons; copyright renewed 1973.

George C. Homans's lines in Chapter 22 are from his poem "The Witch Hazel," in *Harvard Magazine* 72 (1970): 15. Copyright © 1970 by the Harvard Bulletin, Inc.

Abridgements of Chapters 7, 8, 9, 10, 18, 19, 20, and 21 have been previously published in George C. Homans, "Steps to a Theory of Social Behavior," *Theory and Society* 12 (1983): 1-45. Copyright © 1983 by George C. Homans.

PREFACE

What right have I to add another autobiography to the long list, especially when, in *The Education of Henry Adams*,[1] my mother's family produced the greatest of American autobiographies, and she herself in her own autobiography, *Education by Uncles*,[2] proved that she was no slouch at the business. I can only promise that the word "education" will certainly not recur in the title of the present book, even though it is concerned with my education, and that its style will not resemble those of its predecessors. But the question, "Why?" still nags.

I have retired from the academic profession; I have time on my hands; I believe I have still something to say to my colleagues and even to the public, for their social behavior is part of my subject; I should like to try to say this in some form other than the usual treatise, and I enjoy writing, especially about my favorite subject, myself.

If only for reasons of space no autobiography can "tell all": it must be highly selective, and this one is more so than most. Its heart is an effort to describe how over many years I "came to my senses," that is, reached the ideas I now hold about the nature of social science, especially the part theory and explanation play in it. Mine have never been popular ideas, which gives me all the more reason to hammer away at them. The guts, then, of this book is an intellectual autobiography.

But a book that is no more than an intellectual autobiography must tend to boredom, so I have added topics to enliven the subject and to show, by the way, that I was never a wholly disembodied mind. In particular I have added much about my command of small warships, for that provided me with much vivid familiarity with the more elementary forms of social behavior. I have also added some chapters about my own social background and social life. They do not have much to do with the intellect, but a social scientist cannot live on ideas alone: he must batten on the stuff of society itself.

By the same token, I have left out some of the principal ornaments of most autobiographies. I have almost nothing to say about women, for most of us the most central of topics. What today is a book without sex in it? Yet that has made women almost too sensitive a topic. I have almost nothing to say about politics either, though a reader will easily guess what my main political position is. As with sex, almost everything we read today is politicized, and I have little that is even vaguely original to add to the discussion. Less justifiable is my failing to describe the everyday life of the field researcher, though I enjoyed every minute of my own, except writing it up, and much of it was entertaining. I once conducted a splendid interview with a foreman while his pet snapping turtle was roaming at large around the floor of his living room. But since what was important were the ideas that came out of fieldwork, I have had to give up the details of the work itself.

Let me now thank warmly those who have helped me in many different ways in this enterprise: Peter Davison, William B. Goodman, George L. Haskins, Ann Kaplan, Irving Louis Horowitz, my publisher; Louis L. Tucker, Director of the Massachusetts Historical Society; George F. F. Lombard and Abraham Zaleznik of the Harvard Graduate School of Business Administration; Janet Gouldner, Rod Aya, Theda Skocpol, and other editors of *Theory and Society;* above all the able, energetic, and devoted Nellie E. Miller, who prepared the final manuscript.

NOTES

1. Henry Adams, *The Education of Henry Adams* (Boston: Massachusetts Historical Society, 1918).
2. Abigail Adams Homans, *Education by Uncles* (Boston: Houghton Mifflin, 1966).

1

ANCESTORS

Let me waste no time getting myself into the world and placed in it. I was born on 11 August 1910, the eldest child of Robert and Abigail (Adams) Homans, at 164 Beacon Street—the better and "water" side of the street because it looked out over the Charles River Basin—in the Back Bay district of Boston. The house belonged to my paternal grandmother, Helen Amory (Perkins) Homans, and still contained the surgery of her husband, Dr. John Homans, who had died a few years earlier.

My mother, who had just introduced me physically, must introduce me intellectually too. She was one of the nieces of Henry Adams, for whose benefit he liked to pretend he had written *Mont-Saint-Michel and Chartres*.[1] She had written him to announce my arrival; he replied suitably, and she answered his letter with the first description of me and my possible future:

> 164 Beacon Street
> August 27, 1910
>
> Dear Uncle Henry:
>
> It gratified me very much to receive your note—not only as a tribute to my own efforts, but as showing a very proper tendency on your part to recognize the advent of a future Chief Justice into the family. If you could but once see my infant you would appreciate instantly the correctness of my prognostications!! A more hard-featured mite it would be hard to find! His nose has already assumed alarming proportions, while his head is a mass of lumps which will make him look very distinguished when, as a bald old gentleman of eighty odd, he sits upon the bench dispensing justice!!
>
> He is to be named George Caspar for my brother, as the Homans family did not consider that I was the sort of person to produce a good doctor, and so reserved the name [John] for my brother-in-law Jack's benefit. . . .[2]

The Homanses were a locally famous medical family and were well aware of it. The first John Homans in this country had come from Ramsgate, Kent, England. He served for many years in the early

1

eighteenth century as master of a vessel plying between London and Boston. When he had made enough money, he retired from seafaring, bought a farm in Dorchester, now part of Boston, and married a Yankee girl. Their son, the first Dr. John Homans, graduated from Harvard in 1772, tended the wounded on the evening of the battle of Bunker Hill, and then went on to serve through the Revolution as surgeon and adjutant of a dragoon regiment of the Massachusetts Continental Line. Since then the Homanses had produced three successive generations of surgeons, all called John, at least two of them distinguished, if being Professor of Surgery at the Harvard Medical School be a mark of distinction. The latter of the two was my Uncle Jack, to whom my mother's letter refers. He was the discoverer of "Homans' sign," the author of a famous textbook of surgery, and the wittiest of physicians, even at tense moments in the operating room. In due course he did marry and produce a son, also called John, the name reserved for him, who in turn became a physician, but an internist, not a surgeon. Though the eldest of his generation, the family did not allow my father to become a physician, since his name was Robert, not John. He became a lawyer instead.

The Homanses were right. Whether or not my mother could have given birth to a surgeon, it certainly would not have been me. I am sure I have not the proper temperament for the job. I suspect she resented the Homanses making the assumption for her. But then the Homanses would yield the wall to nobody, not even to an Adams.

The father of my Homans grandmother was William Perkins, the son of another William Perkins, who like the first Dr. John Homans had served at Bunker Hill and in the Revolutionary War, but as an artilleryman and not a surgeon. William Perkins II was an India merchant, like so many of the leading Bostonians of his time, that is, someone who owned and operated sailing ships, especially in the Far Eastern trades, and bought and sold their cargoes. His bark *Beverly* holds the record (eighty-five days) for the passage under sail from Boston to Calcutta (the Sand Heads).[3] The flavor of the blue-water trades lingered in my youth in my grandmother's house in the form of an exquisitely carved set of ivory chessmen from India, which we children were sometimes allowed to take out of their box and handle, and in a painting by one of the Roux family, greatest of painters of ship-portraits, of the Perkins ship *Tarquin* entering Havre.

My father used to say that William Perkins stuck to sailing shipping too long, that is, until after the Civil War, when steam, the Suez Canal, and the British superiority in building iron ships made the wooden sailing ships of New England increasingly less profitable. He ought to have shifted his capital, as the wise money had long since done, into cotton mills, railroads, and other products of the Industrial Revolution. He failed to do so, and lost most of it. Yet William Perkins may simply have been interested in other things. He was active in good works in Boston, particularly as president of the Provident Institution for Savings, Boston's oldest savings bank. The early savings banks were not meant to be merely commercial enterprises, but to encourage the deserving poor by providing them with a safe depository for, and a fair return on, their savings however small. His successor at the Provident wrote of William Perkins: "In fact, I have often felt that our friend was too prodigal of his unpaid time. Time is money, and who can compute the fortune he would have accumulated and enjoyed, had he devoted to his own affairs, the time spent in the service of others?"[4] I have inherited little of this trait of my Perkins great-grandfather.

Both of my grandfathers died before I was born, and my Adams grandmother when I was only a year old, so that the only grandparent I can remember is my Homans grandmother, who did not die until I was fourteen. Yet I hold no vivid recollection of her. It was not that I did not visit her often in her second-floor parlor at 164 Beacon Street, looking out over the Charles River, trimmed in golden oak, and dominated by a steel engraving of Rosa Bonheur's *The Horse Fair*. I also stayed with her in her beautiful and spacious country house in Ponkapoag. But all that remains is the impression of a small, plump, rather silent woman dressed in black or grey silk, happy to have me just sitting on her lap.

If I were not to be called John, since I was not of surgical material, why did I receive the rather outlandish name of George Caspar? Since Caspar was one of the three kings that followed the star to the Christ Child at Bethlehem, the name should have been perfectly respectable. Yet throughout my youth I suffered from it because a then famous comic strip had as its nonhero a spineless character called Caspar Milquetoast. As my mother's letter records, she named me after her eldest brother, George Caspar Adams, who died shortly before I was born. She had two other older brothers, Charles Francis and Arthur, but no sister.

Everyone, including my mother, loved George, but he became an alcoholic and drink finally killed him. He himself was named after my mother's grandfather, George Caspar Crowninshield. The Crowninshields include my most romantic, eccentric, and wicked ancestors.[5]

In 1684 there landed in Boston a man calling himself Johannes Kaspar Richter von Kronenscheldt. He claimed to be descended from a long-ennobled family of the kingdom of Saxony; hence his use of the particle *von*. He had come from Germany to Boston by way of England and further affirmed that he was a trained physician. That was all he ever said about himself. My mother always believed that he had fled from Leipzig because he had killed a man in a duel. But when in the nineteenth century his descendants employed genealogists to trace him in the German records, they could find no hint even of his existence. There must have been something profoundly bogus about him. Here was a rare bird to be admitted to the sober Puritan dovecote.

But admitted he was. He settled in Salem, Massachusetts, married a Salem girl, and even made a living practicing medicine. The Yankees, who were never good at pronouncing foreign names, called him "Groun-cell." Later it was Anglicized as Crowninshield. What is more surprising, he became a friend of the most prominent Puritan minister of the time, Cotton Mather, even though Mather admitted he was "a little atheisticall." One may well wonder why Mather was willing to make a friend of anyone who was "atheisticall" at all.

Johannes Kaspar left several sons, who followed the sea. There was nothing much else for Salem boys to do in those days. I am particularly interested in one of his grandsons, George Crowninshield. He too followed the sea, serving among other things as shipmaster for Elias Hasket ("King") Derby. Derby made a great fortune as an operator of privateers during the American Revolution and as a merchant-ship owner before and afterward: he was the first American millionaire. Remember that, according to the international law of the time, it was quite within the rights of a government at war with another to issue to private armed vessels papers entitled "letters of marque and reprisal" authorizing the vessels to capture enemy ships and to sell both the ships and their cargoes—if, of course, they could reach a friendly port. Hence such privateers were often called "letters of marque." While the Homanses, Perkinses, and Adamses were serving their country during the Revolution in the Continental Army or in Congress for modest salaries, the Crowninshields were doing so at sea—for the capture or destruction of British shipping certainly served the American cause—and making a great deal of money at it. Lest we sneer at the legalized piracy that was privateering, remember that it entailed great risks: a privateers-man stood in greater danger of death by gunshot or drowning than did the ordinary soldier of the Continental Army.

George Crowninshield married his boss's sister; his own sister married the boss himself. No sooner had he thus allied himself with the Derbys than he fought with them. He came to hate his brother-in-law, and he was a good hater. An historian of the family says of him: "George Crowninshield was like the badger of proverb: he never bit but what he made his teeth meet."[6] Their fellow townsmen spoke of the Crowninshields as possessing "fair faces but black hearts." Perhaps

George hated the Derbys because he would be second to none. At any rate, he and his sons set up on their own as the firm of George Crowninshield and Sons.

The company's first coup was to come close to cornering the pepper trade to the United States and Europe from the wild west coast of Sumatra. The Dutch in theory, the native rajahs in fact, controlled the island, and the Crowninshields dealt with the rajahs. The difficulty was that the rajahs would not sell pepper except for coin, and coin was always in short supply in the young United States. Therefore the Crowninshield ships had to make a series of preliminary voyages and trades before they could accumulate enough coin to pay for the pepper. Then they had to get it back to Europe or Salem. It was a trade that took seamanship, diplomacy, hard but fair bargaining, guts, and luck. The company also did well in Arabian (mocha) coffee. For a time the Indian Ocean was its pond.

Pepper and coffee founded the fortune of George Crowninshield and Sons. Privateering in the next war against Great Britain, the War of 1812, consolidated it. The Crowninshields sent to sea the largest single fleet of American privateers to prey on British shipping. Not only was theirs the largest fleet but also—which does not necessarily follow—the most successful. The company made some twenty million dollars in today's money out of British prizes. That may not seem a huge sum now, but it was proportionately greater then. The Crowninshields owned more ships and employed more seamen than the United States Navy itself.

As soon as they could afford to do so, the Crowninshields took political as well as economic supremacy away from the old families of Salem, particularly the Derbys. The merchants of the New England ports were Federalists almost to a man, and Federalists who followed the policies of Hamilton rather than those of President John Adams. Accordingly the Crowninshields practically had to be anti-Federalist, which made them Jeffersonian Democrats in fact if not in name. After several defeats, Jacob, George's second son, finally crushed the Federalists by beating their candidate in the congressional elections of 1803. The contenders on both sides fought dirtily and savagely, but the Crowninshield savagery was the stronger. In 1814 President Madison appointed another son, Benjamin William, as secretary (naturally) of the Navy. Ben later represented Essex County in Congress. I am a descendant of Ben's.

When the War of 1812 ended, George Crowninshield, Jr., the eldest of the brothers, had built for himself an hermaphrodite brig, elegantly fitted out and painted in herringbone pattern on one side of the hull, in stripes on the other. He christened her *Cleopatra's Barge,* and she is famous as "the first American yacht." Since one hates someone one has injured, George hated the British, and therefore admired Napoleon. He sailed in the *Barge* on a voyage to the Mediterranean in a feckless search for Napoleonic relics. Shortly after returning to Salem he died, leaving no legitimate children, and the *Barge* was later lost while serving as the Hawaiian royal yacht.

The Crowninshields were sometimes just plain wicked. If Johannes Kaspar may perhaps have been a murderer, a descendant of his, Richard Crowninshield, Jr., certainly murdered, and not for the relative honest motive of passion but for just plain pay. His father had been one of the famous group of brothers, but they did not take him into the company, apparently because, though like the others he was a sea captain, he was not a successful one. There lived in Salem a certain Joseph White, eighty-two years old, who had made money, like the Crowninshields themselves, as a master mariner and a merchant. His favorite niece had vowed to marry a man named Knapp, of whom White disapproved so much that he prepared to disinherit her. By 6 April 1830, it looked as if the contending parties might be reconciled. All the same, on the next morning Captain White was found dead in his bed, his skull broken by the proverbial blunt instrument and no less than thirteen stab wounds near his heart—a case of overkill. Within a few days an informer for the police declared George Crowninshield had told him that two Knapp brothers had offered George and his brother, Richard, Jr., one thousand dollars to kill White, perhaps to forestall his changing his will. The Knapps and the Crowninshields were thrown into jail, where on 5 June 1830 Richard managed to hang himself, thus in effect confessing that he had a part in committing the crime. No less a man than Daniel Webster prosecuted the remaining prisoners as accomplices. Generations of American schoolchildren had to read and even memorize his eloquent speech describing the midnight murder. The Knapp brothers were convicted and hanged. No one doubted that George Crowninshield was one of the gang, but the evidence against him was weak, and his case was dropped. He lived to an advanced age, childless, and still protesting his innocence.

When in my youth a number of Crowninshield descendants gathered together at some festive occasion like a wedding, we would take a perverse pleasure in raising the cry "Crowninshields this way!" and then drinking two toasts, first, "To the hired murderer!" and then, "To the worst blood in New England!" We were giving ourselves too much credit, for the hired murderer was only a collateral ancestor of ours.

By 1830 the great days of Salem and the seafaring Crowninshields were over. In the opening of *The Scarlet Letter,* Nathaniel Hawthorne, himself a Salem man, describes the stagnation at the old Customs House. My great-grandfather George Caspar Crowninshield left Salem for the Boston suburb of Longwood. He did not go to sea but stayed at home and managed his not inconsiderable capital. Indeed he increased it by marriage. Just as Charles Francis Adams the first married the daughter of Peter Chardon Brooks, reputed the richest man in New England in his time, so George Caspar married the daughter of David Sears, the richest in *his*. The Searses set themselves up to be, as we used to say, "some punkins," being descended from a prominent Pilgrim Father. My own father would scornfully allege that David Sears came from a livery stable on Cape Cod. That is, he was a *nouveau riche* in the Boston of the mid-nineteenth century. These concentrations of wealth, though large for the time, did not last many generations. The families were prolific, and though I believe fathers might legally leave all their money by will to their eldest sons, they usually in fact divided it equally among their children.

One of the offspring of the Crowninshield-Sears marriage was my grandmother, Fanny Cadwallader Crowninshield, named after a Philadelphia friend of her mother's. As a young woman she must have been exceptionally beautiful, for she was chosen as one of the local belles to dance with the Prince of Wales at a ball given for him when he visited Boston in 1860. She married my grandfather Adams in 1861. Otherwise Fanny sounds a bit stuffy, and whatever else may be said of the Crowninshields, stuffiness was not one of their usual traits. My mother claimed, for instance, that Fanny refused to recognize the social existence of Mrs. "Jack" Gardner, because she held that Mrs. Jack was "no better than she should be," that is, a good deal worse morally than she ought to be. No one but my grandmother was the loser by taking this line of high respectability. She did no harm to Mrs. Jack, who was a woman of the greatest charm and distinction, a friend of all the ablest artists, writers, and musicians of her time, and the creator of the famous Isabella Stewart Gardner Museum ("Fenway Court") in Boston.

Of my four grandparental families, I leave the Adamses to the last, for far too much has already been written about them. My grandfather, John Quincy Adams II, was the eldest of the four sons of Charles Francis Adams, minister to the Court of St. James during the Civil War, and the only one of the four who was not a writer. Charles II (who was also a railroad magnate), Henry, and Brooks all wrote like mad, but my grandfather not a word more than he could help. But if the others were famous, my grandfather was more charming. My mother adored him, and my father declared that he was the most popular man in Massachusetts, in spite of his adopting the then unpopular side in politics. As an abolitionist his own father had been a founder of the Republican party, and his son might have been expected to remain one. Instead, after the end of the Civil War, he became a Democrat, an outspoken supporter of reconciliation between North and South—not the South of the carpetbagger state governments but of the Old South, now prostrate. He ran four times as a Democrat for governor of Massachusetts but never won. My father used to say, on what evidence I know not, that the only time he had a chance of winning he refused to run. Unlike his brothers, he may have had a lazy streak. Because he was a prominent and able northern Democrat, President Cleveland sounded him out in succession for the secretaryship of the Navy and the ambassadorship to Russia. Think what it would have meant to have been ambassador to the court of the czar during the last days of its glory! Perhaps encouraged by his wife, he turned the offers down. Both enjoyed the pleasures of home. John Quincy II may also have lacked, as his namesake and grandfather, John Quincy Adams, conspicuously did not, a certain toughness. At any rate he died at a relatively early age from the shock brought on by the threat that the value of the family investments would collapse during the financial panic of 1893.

Now let me look at how much these ancestors of mine had in common. In the male lines, all were of English origin, except for the Crowninshields, who soon assimilated. If I were to look for roots—and in time I did—I should have to look to England. They all came from Massachusetts Bay—not just from the state but from the coast of the bay itself, from Salem on the North Shore around to Quincy on the South. Not all of their forebears had come over in the *Mayflower* or in Winthrop's fleet, but all had been settled on the bay before the American Revolution. That is, they were all what would have been called in my youth Yankees, in the special local sense of families who had come to New England in colonial times, as distinguished from the "newer races" like the Irish. Today we should call them WASPs—white Anglo-Saxon Protestants. Though many of the Yankees were not Anglo-Saxon but Scotch, French, even Irish in origin, few of them and none in the early generations were Catholic.

All of my grandparental families had some connection with seafaring, even the Homanses, who had been founded by a master mariner, and even the Adamses, though that came later through my Uncle Charlie and in the special form of seafaring that is yacht racing. I was to become a sea captain myself and an historian of Massachusetts sailing shipping.

Whatever their ultimate social origins, which like those of all families must have been low, they had become members of an upper class. Sociologists are preoccupied with class but will not often speak of a higher class in American society than an upper-middle one. Make no mistake about it: my grandparents were of the upper class. Not that they were aristocrats; I cannot bring myself to call any upper class an aristocracy unless its wealth and power are based on land. No one could have written of them as Goldsmith did of the British aristocracy of the eighteenth century:

Pride in their port, defiance in their eye,
I see the lords of humankind pass by.[7]

They were not aristocrats but merchants and professional men: Marxists would call them bourgeois. What New Englanders often called them was Brahmins. Oliver Wendell Holmes, Sr., in his novel *Elsie Venner* had originally applied this name to the New England intellectuals, as resembling the Brahmin caste of India. But people soon extended the word beyond the intellectuals to mean the upper class generally and specifically a Bostonian upper class.

No one would have mistaken a Brahmin for a "lord of humankind"; he was much too mild. Specifically, though some Brahmins were certainly very rich for their time, it did not take much money to become and remain a Brahmin, and, more important, to pass the status on to one's children. The Homanses certainly commanded over several generations good professional incomes but never accumulated large fortunes to leave to their heirs. What it took, rather, to become and remain a Brahmin was what we should now call a certain style of life and a certain, often rather low, level of intellectual cultivation, usually produced by attending a good grammar school and a good, but still highly provincial, Harvard College. To use words that now provoke scorn, the Brahmins were gentlemen and ladies. Other people were not. The distinction is now fast fading. We were not able to muster up "pride in our port, defiance in our eye"—whom were we going to defy?—and seldom talked about class. Nonetheless we were class conscious. By profession all sociologists are class conscious but usually about other persons' classes, not their own.

What the Brahmins of my generation escaped, unlike some of their descendants today, was a feeling of guilt about belonging to an upper class. I myself was not conscious that my ancestors had exploited anyone. Instead they were, with the possible exception of the Crowninshields, morally *good*: they had deserved well of their communities, their states, their nation. Even the Crowninshields had paid their seamen good wages and good prize-shares. Had they not, they would not have been so successful.

What is more, my grandparental families were, with the exception of the William Perkinses, famous to one degree or another: the Homanses famous in the annals of Boston medicine, the Crowninshields in the annals of American seafaring and even of American crime, and of course the Adamses famous nationally and even internationally in statesman-ship and literature.

To possess famous ancestors has long been recognized as a mixed blessing. The obvious danger is snobbery, not the generalized snobbery that goes with belonging to an upper class but the individual snobbery that goes with being, as the Spanish would say, an *hidalgo*, a "son of someone," and above all the danger of talking too much about it. I have been guilty of talking too much about my ancestors. I may be doing so now. Still, I think I am improving as I grow older. At least some of my Adams kin are more guilty in this respect than I. Indeed I am heartily sick of hearing about the Adamses.

Prominent ancestors present to their descendants a danger far more insidious than snobbery. If ancestors are both famous and morally noble—the two need not go together—if, that is, the ancestors are good models, they may challenge their descendants to a noble emulation, inspiring them to achievements they would not otherwise have under-taken. Unhappily descendants may also try too hard to emulate their ancestors and thus fail to "stay loose." I am a great admirer of Samuel Butler's *The Way of All Flesh* and, among the good things in it, the advice Miss Pontifex gives Ernest's trustee about how he should treat Ernest: "Above all, do not let him work up to his full strength, except once or twice in his lifetime: nothing is well done or worth doing unless, take it all around, it has come pretty easily."[8] (Of course what comes easily to one person may not do so to another.) Not only may a descendant try too hard to emulate an ancestor, he may try to *be* the ancestor. He may adopt a role model he would not otherwise have chosen and one at odds with his own real abilities. He will try to be the ancestor, not himself.

Still worse, if one has famous ancestors, one has nowhere to go but down. Even if one tries to emulate them, one can usually at best equal their achievements, not better them. If one tries and fails or, knowing one's insufficiency from the beginning, does not even try, guilt sets in. It is a nobler guilt than what some persons feel from simply belonging to an upper class, but it is still guilt. Guilt, like trying too hard, gets in the way of a person's easy and effective action, because it motivates him in ways irrelevant to his dealing with the problem at hand. I attribute the tendency to drink, suicide, or both, which has afflicted members of several generations of the Adams family, to their feelings of guilt about not being able to live up to their ancestors' achievements, especially when that guilt has been exacerbated by unsuccessful sibling rivalry: at least one other member of their generation has been able to excel.

I am lucky to have among my ancestors several different models to choose from. I can be an Adams in writing if not in politics without bearing the name and so being required to live up to it. And if the pious achievements of the Adamses get me down, I can always identify with the Crowninshields, those selfish, mercenary, quarrelsome, but bold, intelligent, fighting seamen. Be not righteous overmuch! After all, I bear a Crowninshield name.

But if I had my choice, I should prefer to be an ancestor, not a descendant. The founder of a famous lineage, unlike his descendants, has nowhere to go but up, and up is a good place to be. Damn Emerson and his sneer at "the bitch-goddess success"! After all was not that hypocrite a success himself?

NOTES

1. Henry Adams, *Mont-Saint-Michel and Chartes* (Boston: Massachusetts Historical Society, 1919), p. xiii.
2. Printed from the original ms.
3. Carl C. Cutler, *Greyhounds of the Sea* (Annapolis: U. S. Naval Institute, 1930), p. 333.
4. Walter M. Whitehill, *The Provident Institution for Savings in the Town of Boston: 1816-1966* (Boston: The Provident Institution, 1966), p. 99.
5. For the Crowninshields, see David L. Ferguson, *Cleopatra's Barge: The Crowninshield Story* (Boston: Little, Brown, 1976).
6. Ibid., p. 21.
7. Oliver Goldsmith, "The Traveller" (many editions), lines 326-27.
8. Samuel Butler, *The Way of All Flesh* (many editions), ch. 35.

2

THE BACK BAY

Sociologists are preoccupied not only with class but with ethnic differences. I was preoccupied with both long before I became a sociologist. Perhaps more than any other American city, Boston had from the beginning been divided by the irregularities of its hills and waterfront into distinct neighborhoods or "urban villages." As the city expanded with the great immigration of the nineteenth century, new people took over the neighborhoods from those who had occupied them before, but the neighborhoods themselves remained and even increased in number: Beacon Hill, the Back Bay, the North, South, and West Ends, East and South Boston, Charlestown, etc. Moreover ethnic differences had come in to reinforce what I suspect had once chiefly been class differences between the districts. The Irish Catholics had come to dominate Boston politics, but they were by no means the only immigrants. I was born just at the time the tide of immigration flowed strongest, and now it flowed less from Ireland than from Italy and Russian Jewry. The sour smell of Italian laborers filled the subways. The recent newcomers could speak hardly any English, and they tended to settle near compatriots who arrived earlier, protected by ward bosses for a price in votes. In short, the "urban villages" tended also to become "ethnic islands."

The concentrations of the immigrants tended indirectly to encourage the concentration of the descendants of the earlier arrivals. Thus the Homanses lived in winter on an ethnic island, largely Yankee, which was also a class island, largely Brahmin. This island consisted of two linked parts: the "Hill," really the western slope of Beacon Hill leading up to the State House, and the "Back Bay," the flatland to the westward.

The Hill had and still has great charm, with small, steep streets lined with houses often of great distinction, since they were pre-Victorian. Because we did not live on the Hill until late in my teens, my experience of living on a class and ethnic island came first and most strongly from my earlier life in various parts of the Back Bay. The Back Bay was so-called because for the first two centuries of Boston's history it was "back," that is, westward, of the main part of the city, and a "bay" because it consisted of salt marsh flooded at high tide.

As the city expanded in the middle of the nineteenth century, speculators filled in the Back Bay and began to cover it with houses built on piles driven through the fill and mud. In my youth there were still a few vacant lots, on which we played. Socially, the Back Bay was a rectangle, bounded on the north by the Charles River Basin, on the south by Boylston Street and the yards of the Boston and Albany Railroad, on the east by the Public Garden, and on the west by the Fenway, originally called the Muddy River. It was laid out in the conventional grid. The cross streets were alphabetized by naming them after British peerages—and this was characteristic of the tone of upper-class Boston: Arlington, Berkeley, Clarendon, etc. The great lengthwise street was Common-wealth Avenue, which had a dual carriageway with a grass mall in between, shaded with great elms and studded with statues of American worthies, from George Washington on horseback looking down the mall from the Public Garden in the east to a highly improbable Leif Ericsson at the other end shading his eyes at the dazzling prospect of Vinland the Good—in fact the Muddy River and the squalor of Kenmore Square.

Most of the houses of the Back Bay were built in the period 1850-1900, which, in spite of a number of interesting, indeed fantastic, variations, gave them a certain consistency. Commonwealth Avenue might even be called distinguished. But in its cities New England never felt it ought to show off, as New York or Washington did. None of the houses on Commonwealth Avenue, not even my Uncle Charlie Adams's, with its double staircase leading up to a *piano nobile*, ever seemed to me to count as a really great house, and most of the other houses in the Back Bay seem today to have been positively mean or shoddy.[1]

Such was the house in which my family lived longest, at 289 Marlborough Street. It was very narrow and dark but still five-stories high, looking out in the rear over a squalid backyard and alley. On the lower floors it was only one smallish room wide; on the upper ones two even smaller bedrooms could barely be cramped in. Narrow steep stairs led from one floor to the next. Characteristically the kitchen lay below the ground level. If one went down there at night and turned the light on, swarms of cockroaches scuttled for safety. Here our long series of cooks sweated over the black coal-range. From this hellhole our food was sent up by a dumbwaiter, and supposed to stay warm, to the pantry next to the dining room on the floor above. At the very top floor of the house, crammed into their tiny cells, with no hot water, lived—if that is the right word for their existence—our uniformly Irish maids. I can only hope that their conditions were at least better than those they had known in Ireland. Including our cook, I think there were three of them. It is in the matter of servants that the life I lived then differed most from the one I live now; though we children loved some of our maids, I am not sure that the change has been for the worse.

When we lived in the Back Bay, single families occupied almost all the houses. Many of the families, but not ours, also owned houses in the country, which they used in spring and fall, and all who possibly could got away to the mountains or the sea for the summer. But they still spent the winter in Boston. The men walked downtown to work. The great ladies—not my mother but, say, my Aunt Fanny Adams—were still driven to Tremont and Washington Streets in their Packards, Pierce-Arrows, or Cadillacs by liveried chauffeurs, who waited while they did their shopping.

The Back Bay was also what is now called an urban village. Not only did single families occupy most of the houses but we knew many of them, not all of course but some in nearly every block. What is more, many of the families had known one another for generations. The surest sign of it was that, when I met some lady or gentleman hitherto unknown to me, she or he would be sure to say: "George Homans? Oh, yes, of course, you must be Abigail's [or Robert's] son," and then go on to climb down the family trees until the branches met in some common ancestor. Like class and ethnicity, I learned about extended kinship early. I never knew a time when I felt I was a social isolate, when I was not an insider, when I had no social identity. My ethnic identity remained more precarious.

Thanks largely to zoning laws, the exterior appearance of the Back Bay today remains recognizably much as it was then. Physical decay has gone only a little further. But otherwise it is a whited sepulcher; its social interior has been gutted. The automobile has done its worst. Most of the kind of families that then lived in the Back Bay have moved permanently to the country, and their members drive or commute to work. The houses have been divided into rented flats or condominiums, often occupied by the most transient of residents, such as students. My only hope is that the better sections of old Boston may be partly restored by the price of gasoline, which may bring some of the old types of resident back. This is the process now called by the nasty name of "gentrification."

Since we knew many other families, our mothers dragged us to many parties, usually birthday parties, of our contemporaries, the boys in blue serge suits topped by those choking, stiff, Eton collars that flared on top of one's jacket, the girls, only a little less shy than ourselves, in black velvet dresses with blue sashes and lace collars. We played blindman's buff, pinned the tail on the donkey, fished for presents—when much to my mother's embarrassment I complained loudly if I did not get what I wanted. We slurped ice cream, always covered with spun sugar, snapped our crackers, and put on our paper caps.

But just as in Harlem today, we children played mostly in the streets. In spring, when the ground dried, we played marbles on the miserable grass plots in front of our houses. Our own became so much a center of congregation for the children of our block that all our grass, whose attachment to life was feeble at best, was killed. Later we played baseball in the middle of the street, cars still being few enough to make that possible. In winter the snow was not plowed but packed down, and we amused ourselves by catching rides on the runners of the big horse-drawn sledges called pungs. At Halloween there was no damned nonsense about "trick or treat," nor did our parents nervously shepherd us from door to door "trick-or-treating." Boys were expected to be mischievous, though not vicious, and all we did was play tricks. There was a method of folding a sheet of paper so that it would briefly hold water. From the roof of our house we would launch these "water-bombs" at passersby on the sidewalk below. In those days some men still wore, not for ceremonial occasions but for everyday use, tall silk hats, irreverently called "plug" or "stovepipe" hats. One obviously scored 100 if one hit one of these with a waterbomb. I never succeeded.

Like children and adolescents everywhere, we formed gangs, in theory hostile to one another. We climbed along the rickety wooden fences separating the backyards from the back alleys that ran parallel to, and between, the longitudinal streets of the Back Bay. We committed minor delinquencies and talked big about committing major ones. But we did no damage to persons and little to property. We never got into trouble with the police, who were big, genial Irishmen, pounding their beats under tall grey helmets modeled on those of London bobbies. My own gang was the smallest in the neighborhood, and we crept about by stealth, as if we should be in danger when we ran into others. Thus we manufactured our own excitement, for if there had been a confrontation I doubt that we should have had to take much more than verbal abuse. The boys and girls of the Back Bay were really very "nice" kids compared to some upper-class WASP youngsters I met later. I do not mean that they were sissies, but only that they were for the most part reasonably honest, fair, and generous. I cannot remember a single bully or son-of-a-bitch among them. My experience of such people was not to come from the Back Bay.

From the Back Bay we sallied forth occasionally to go to church. Neither of my parents was deeply religious, so our churchgoing was far from regular. My father went for largely sentimental reasons, for his church was the one his family had attended in his youth. I myself was christened there. This was King's Chapel in downtown Boston, just a short walk over Beacon Hill from the Back Bay. The only service we always went to was the so-called Children's Service on Easter afternoon, when the chancel was surrounded by flowers in pots, and at the end of the service each youngster got one to take home. For Easter we would all of course wear our best clothes. I had to wear my strangulating Eton collar. Father was very grand in a "cutaway" and a tall silk hat, carrying a gold-headed cane.

Outwardly King's Chapel is forbidding: square in body, with a squat, square tower, built of big square blocks of stone almost black with the grime of centuries. But its interior is ravishing in its Georgian elegance. Many churches in London are graced with the same elegance, and King's Chapel was modeled on them. It got its name because it was originally the church of the royal governor and garrison of the Province of Massachusetts Bay. Hence, unlike the other churches of colonial Boston, which were of Puritan origin and thus what we should now call Congregational, King's Chapel belonged to the Church of England. After General Washington drove the royal government and garrison out of Boston, the church, while keeping its name, was taken over by one of the earliest Unitarian congregations in New England, so that it rejected both Episcopalianism and Congregationalism. King's Chapel was in my time and still is Unitarian.

Our minister dressed in a black gown with white bands at the neck, so that he looked in the pulpit—I always hoped he would be crushed by the great sounding board precariously suspended above it—as New England clergymen must have looked for many generations. But what he preached was certainly not Calvinism. Many jokes have been made about Unitarianism: that it believes in the Fatherhood of God and the Brother-hood of Man in the Neighborhood of Boston, and that it addresses its prayers neither to God nor our Lord Jesus Christ (and certainly not to the Blessed Virgin Mary) but rather "to whom it may concern."

To speak more seriously, I came in time to recognize that what our minister preached was the gospel according to Ralph Waldo Emerson. This gospel, if too optimistic, is at least concerned with the saving of souls. Should you doubt it, read the essay on self-reliance. Since then Unitarianism has become utterly sentimental, concerned not with the salvation of individuals but with the material needs of groups of one kind or another, as these needs are defined by well-meaning "liberal" out-siders. Of all types of religious belief—if indeed it be religious belief—this is the one, the religion of sentimental humanitarianism, that I now hold in the greatest contempt. For me Jesus Christ came into the world to save sinners not society. The only advantage of sentimental humanitarianism is that any church adopting it as a doctrine is pretty sure to destroy itself.

For me, without yet knowing why, the service, the ritual, of the church was much more important than the formal doctrine. A Unitarian congregation is free to adopt any kind of service it likes. In practice, Sunday morning service in King's Chapel was the old Morning Prayer of the Church of England, which derives from Cranmer's Prayer Book. The Unitarians made only a few changes, but these my father delighted in pointing out. "George," he would say, "it is just the Book of Common Prayer with all references to the Trinity and to miserable sinners taken out. We Unitarians just cannot bring ourselves to admit we are miserable sinners." I have since come to believe that some doctrine of original sin is crucial to the survival of any religion, and that it would be well for everyone, everywhere, to recite once a day the General Confession of the Church of England, which puts the matter succinctly: "We have left undone those things which we ought to have done; and we have done those things which we ought not to have done; and there is no health in us." At King's Chapel we were at least not denied the glories of the Book of Common Prayer and the King James Bible. They have abided with me.

From Boston's beginning the youths of the neighborhoods had fought with one another whenever they found any ghost of a pretext. So it was with us. Though the neighborhoods had distinct and recognized borders, there were places where the youngsters of the different groups came into contact. When we Yankees coasted on the Common or skated on the Basin or the pond of the Public Garden, we became conscious of other youngsters of a decidedly rougher and, to us, nastier cast than our own, youngsters who found little trouble and much pleasure in pushing us around—though they never used knives as their successors might today. They did not come from the Back Bay or the Hill, and we referred to them collectively as "muckers."

The muckers we came into closest contact with were not Irish but Italians from the neighborhood closest to us, that is, the West End—west in relation to old Boston but actually east of the Back Bay. Sometimes groups of them invaded the Back Bay looking for trouble. One such group, three in number, caught me alone in the dead end of a back alley and beat me up to the extent of a couple of black eyes. Naturally I had offered them no provocation, especially because I was both small and weak for my age. To them my appearance alone must have constituted sufficient provocation. I expect they judged I was a sissy, whose relatively fancy clothes positively yearned for a fist. The West End as a well-integrated Italian community has since been destroyed by one of the earliest and worst examples of "urban renewal."

Though there were a few blacks in Boston, largely in the South End—our much admired laundress was a black—they had been there for a long time and, though certainly not integrated, they had become an accepted part of the community. The great immigration from the South had not yet begun, and I never came into contact with a black youth.

We youngsters did not articulate the social ideas we learned in the Back Bay. Had we done so, they might have sounded something like this: "We are a group, the Yankees, and we are different from other ethnic groups. Not only are we different, we are better than the others, especially in a lingering respect for intellectual attainments even on the part of those of us who have not acquired them. We are perhaps worse than other groups in our reluctance to fight. Yet is our betterness really betterness when it has done us so little good? We have lost political power in Boston and even our control of the State House is in jeopardy. It is only a question of time before we lose our other superiorities. Our financial power may be the last to go. Nor is it merely a question of our superiority: our very identity is at stake. We are a great group with a great history, but we are bound to disappear as surely as Cooper's Mohicans." We had also learned not to be quite so sentimental about the proletariat as some of our later, Marxist, friends affected to be. After all we had suffered at its hands.

My later experience has reversed some of these inarticulate judgments. How could we have been so worried? In a strange way we Yankees have won, not lost, and won in a way I never conceived in my youth. Who would have believed then that parochial schools would be closing, not opening, that the once-conquering Catholic Church would be hard put to fill her seminaries, that her newer churches would look for all the world like colonial meetinghouses, and that in them the priest would repeat the Mass—which I bet will soon be called Holy Communion—in English and facing the congregation? Of course it is our culture not our numbers that has won. It is not the old Yankee culture, but then that too had been changing and was bound in any event to change further. Still, it is a descendant whose cultural genes have more Yankee in them than anything else. In the process much has been lost. For instance, the Irish have given up their lovely brogue for the most nasal of Yankee dialects. Perhaps all I am saying is that I should never have believed that we would all become so American, though our convergence still has far to go.

Perhaps we were even then more American than we thought. The Boston Brahmins believed they were different, especially in their intellectual cultivation, and other Americans, while making fun of Brahmin pretensions, believed so too. Yet when I compare my childhood with what I have read or been told about the childhoods of my contemporaries from other parts of the country, I am more struck by the similarities than the differences and above all by how American we all were.

In only one way my childhood experiences may have differed from those of most Americans. My Uncle Arthur Adams was then still a bachelor and especially devoted to my mother and her children. He gave her her first car and me, at the age of ten, my first sailboat, *Sheldrake*. But then I believe Uncle Arthur was devoted to all children. He was that rare thing, an outwardly warmhearted Adams. On Sunday mornings in winter my sister Fanny and I would walk around to his flat, and he would take us to see the sights, either by way of the then splendid subway and trolley system of Boston or, even more exciting, in his open, red Stutz Bearcat. Had it not been for him, I doubt whether we should ever have seen the Old Aquarium at the outer end of South Boston, or the Old North Church, or the frigate *Constitution* ("Old Ironsides") and the Navy Yard, or Bunker Hill, or Concord Bridge. Most Bostonian children do not see these things. Their parents assume that the sights will always be there; accordingly there is no hurry to see them on any particular day, and the kids wind up never seeing them at all.

More important for my future, Uncle Arthur haunted the waterfront. He taught me to watch the harbor and shipping, and later I continued to do so on my own hook. What fun it was to cross the harbor to East Boston on the old walking-beam ferryboats, fare one cent. In East Boston in World War I, I saw the huge interned German liner *Kronprinzessin Cecilie*. At the foot of State Street there always seemed to lie one of the little white banana ships of the United Fruit Company.

We were especially interested in the sailing ships, though after World War I they were disappearing fast. The fishing schooners still berthed in tiers at T-Wharf and the new Fish Pier. Uncle Arthur took me to see the famous schooner *Columbia* fitting out for her maiden voyage to the Banks. She had been designed by W. Starling Burgess to be a working fisherman but also fast enough under sail to beat the even more famous Nova Scotian schooner *Bluenose* in the Fishermen's Races. Like that of many beautiful vessels, the life of *Columbia* was short. She was lost with all hands on Sable Island.

There were also the big, Down-East-built, four-masted wooden coasting schooners of the coal, lumber, and salt (from Turks Islands) trades. I even saw and went on board what I believe was the last square-rigged commercial sailing ship owned in Boston, the beautiful, Clyde-built, steel bark *Belmont*.

Sailing and the sailing ship meant romance for me and many coastal New Englanders of my time. Probably the sailing ships meant romance because they were disappearing so fast. I doubt—but I am not sure—that they meant romance when they were the only ships there were. At any rate in winter I became a harbor watcher and in summer I spent most of my time sailing in *Sheldrake* out of Marblehead and later The Glades, North Scituate. When I could, I photographed the little two- or three-masted schooners that crept down the coast from Maine or the Bay of Fundy with deck-loads of lumber over which their booms could barely swing. I also became addicted to reading about the history of New England shipping.[2]

I sound here again the theme of seafaring, which came down to me from my ancestors and in which I was to take part myself.

NOTES

1. See Bainbridge Bunting, *Houses of Boston's Back Bay* (Cambridge: Harvard University Press, Belknap Press, 1967).
2. Beginning with Samuel E. Morison, *The Maritime History of Massachusetts: 1783-1860* (Boston: Houghton Mifflin, 1921).

3

PARENTS

My remoter ancestors surveyed and myself placed in my environment, I turn next to my immediate or, as we should now say, my nuclear family. My father, Robert Homans, the eldest of six children, three boys and three girls, was, like me, born in Boston and brought up on Beacon Hill and the Back Bay. He attended a good private school in Boston and then went on to Harvard, as his ancestors had done for three generations, graduating in 1894 as chief marshal of his class. Election as chief marshal was a measure of a man's popularity and the respect in which he was held, not of his academic record. My father's academic record was good, but not as good as it might have been, had he spent less time in social and athletic activities.

Since his family had already designated his brother John as the surgeon of his generation, my father attended the Harvard Law School. There for the first time he put all his energy behind his first-class intellect. He made a great record and was elected president of the *Harvard Law Review,* the highest academic honor a student could receive. On the strength of that performance, Mr. Justice Horace Gray of the United States Supreme Court chose him to spend a year in Washington as his law clerk. On returning to Boston he joined his acquaintance Arthur Dehon Hill and his close friend Robert Shaw Barlow to form the firm of Hill, Barlow, and Homans. In the trend towards shortening the names of law firms, it is now simply Hill and Barlow. I became familiar with its offices in 53 State Street by stopping in there before or after my gritty trips on the railroad in summer from Marblehead up to Boston for appointments with the dentist who was vainly trying to straighten my teeth. (My father claimed that the New England jaw had been narrowing for three hundred years.) The office was drier and dustier than the train or the August weather, the rooms trimmed in golden oak with steel engravings of famous judges hanging on the walls.

The firm was successful, though looked on a little askance by the more conservative moneyed men in Boston for its reputation of taking what we should now call the "liberal" side in a number of cases. Father liked to say that the firm enjoyed "a small but active practice." In contrast to the specialization of many lawyers today, Father practiced all kinds of law: corporation, medical, admiralty, whatever came along. He served as the highly responsible trustee of a number of estates. Unlike, again, many lawyers today he also argued all of his own cases that went to court. I used to go down to the Suffolk County Court House to hear him and swelled with pride when I overheard other spectators comment on how well he had argued. Criminal law he did not usually practice, though he undertook for a time as a public service the job of assistant district attorney of Suffolk County. I also suspect that he left most of the cases, such as divorce, that hinged on personal relations to Barlow, who was, so to speak, the sex specialist of the firm.

He became one of the leaders of the Boston bar. Yet he seemed hardly to realize it. He would take, as if it were a duty, a vacation every summer, complaining all the while that the firm's business would be gone by the time he got back. It never was. And in spite of the judgment by the business community that the firm was a bit too "liberal," the Brahmins bestowed on him the highest honor at their disposal. That is, he was elected a member of *the* Corporation—as if there were no others—the seven-member body entitled "The President and Fellows of Harvard College," the supreme governing body of the university. The Corporation has been self-perpetuating, filling its own vacancies, ever since Harvard was founded in 1636. Several of my Adams ancestors had been members, one even remarking scornfully: "What can you expect of a body of men half of whom believe that keeping a horse chestnut in your pocket will ward off the common cold." My uncle Charlie Adams had been a member and very successful treasurer for many years before resigning to become secretary of the Navy in 1933. As a member of the Corporation Father played a leading hand in choosing a new president when A. Lawrence Lowell resigned in the same year. Though for decades the Corporation had acted on the policy that no one but an academic should be president, this time two other members thought they would make excellent candidates for the job. Father first persuaded them to withdraw and then went on to be the first member to support James Bryant Conant, professor of chemistry, who finally was elected president.[1] Father came home to dinner just after his first interview with Conant and exclaimed, "George, I think we've got the man!"

In his career in the law, particularly in early middle life, before it was too late, Father suffered what I suspect was the greatest disappointment of his life. Though it would have meant a financial sacrifice, he would have dearly loved to be appointed a judge and get a shot at becoming chief justice of Massachusetts or even associate justice of the United

States Supreme Court. But politicians make judicial appointments. As was natural for Yankees in those days—my grandfather Adams was the exception—Father was a Republican. However, he came increasingly to represent the wing of the party that was not dominant in Massachusetts. He did not belong to the machine led by Senator W. Murray Crane, of the paper-making family of Dalton, whose finest product was Calvin Coolidge. Indeed he followed Theodore Roosevelt as a Progressive, when Roosevelt split the party in the Bull Moose campaign of 1912. This was not the kind of behavior likely to persuade governors like Coolidge that he was a deserving candidate for a judgeship. Rewards should go to the loyal.

Father would have made an excellent judge. He had just the right temperament. If anyone can ever be scrupulously impartial, he could have been. He would also have been utterly conscientious in carrying out the mere drudgery that goes with any job, however exalted. He was highly intelligent and, what does not always go with intelligence, shrewd in his practical judgments of the world. What he would not have been was a legal theorist and innovator like a man he greatly admired, Mr. Justice Holmes. He was intelligent but not intellectual. Yet he would not have made a less effective judge for that. It takes all kinds to make a judiciary—except the corrupt.

One of Father's strongest traits was a sense of *noblesse oblige*. Persons like him had enjoyed all the advantages of American society. Therefore they should be the first to undertake the burdens of responsibility when the society was in danger. I suspect it was this trait that led junior members of his firm to refer to him as "the old Roman." He foresaw, as of course many others did too, the entry of the United States into World War I, and despised President Wilson for not getting us into it sooner. He dreaded the possibility that Germany might defeat Great Britain and France. In any event, he was determined to do what he could himself, and that, for him, meant entering the Army. I am sure that his membership in the Society of the Cincinnati and the fact that his ancestors had served in all the major wars of the Republic also supported his decision. Though he was already over forty, married and with three children, so that he could easily have escaped the later draft, and though he would have had to give up a lucrative law practice, he volunteered before our entry into the war to attend the first Officers' Training Camp at Plattsburgh, New York, was commissioned major, and finally sent to France with the 76th Division in July 1918. Not only he but his two brothers served in the Army in various capacities in France, and my aunt Helen died there as a nurse in a French army hospital during the great influenza epidemic of 1918. In private, Father was scornful of those

Bostonians of his age and class who continued to pig it at the Somerset Club or make money at Lee Hig (as the now defunct brokerage house of Lee, Higginson & Company was then called) instead of volunteering to serve their country.

Noblesse oblige was exigent. It demanded that he should share in the real dangers of war. Accordingly Father yearned to command troops in action, but in this ambition he was disappointed as in that of becoming a judge. In France he wound up at the Command and General Staff School at Langres to be trained as a staff officer and was there when the war ended. I think the Army was correct in its decision about him. He was really too old for trench warfare, but he would have made an admirable staff officer, that is, a planner. We watched him with pride as he rode on horseback up Beacon Street in the parade of the 72nd ("Yankee") Division upon its return from France in 1919.

My father was the best man I have ever known: he not only had an excellent mind but was morally *good*. I never knew him to take a mean action. Yet I do not want to make him out too good to be true. He was very popular with his contemporaries—except for the very few who did indeed find him too good—and very convivial in his social instincts. He loved and was skillful at all kinds of games of cards, especially bridge. He had a sturdy sense of humor and could be both gay and witty. He especially delighted in occasions that combined drinking with singing. From his father he had inherited both his conviviality and his excellent voice. He loved singing all sorts of traditional songs, including hymns. I learned the words of the songs from him, but, alas! I did not inherit his voice. I am like my mother and cannot even keep a tune. His convivial instincts were all that ever got into the way of his abiding by the spirit of the law and not just its letter. The Prohibition Amendment to the Constitution made illegal the sale of liquor but not its purchase. When the law first went into effect, my father swore roundly that he would buy no more liquor. Long before the amendment was repealed, Father had rather sheepishly retreated from this austere position and, just like the other scofflaws, patronized a bootlegger.

There was only one subject on which, in my view, his sense of humor failed him. That was the Porcellian Club, the oldest and most prestigious of the final clubs at Harvard. A final club is a club election to which precludes election to other final clubs. For Father no human institution seemed to have equaled the Porcellian Club in excellence. It was sacred: one referred to it, if at all, only with bated breath. Not only was Father a member, but also his own father and his brother Jack. One of his great disappointments was that I, though what was called a "legacy," was not considered worthy to become a member. My brother Bob *was* elected, but that was after Father's death—alas! for it would have delighted him. There were plenty of others who took the Porcellian just as seriously as Father did. The whole mystique of the P.C. and other final clubs has faded since my youth. Then it was so powerful as to be incredible to someone not directly exposed to it. There were men who felt life held no further meaning if they failed to "make" the right club.

My father had a number of maxims he was fond of pronouncing. The most frequent was "Never help out!" It was supposed to have been handed down in the Homans family as the result of an accident suffered by one of its women. She was upstairs in her house and heard someone cry out as if in trouble. She rushed to help, slipped on the stairs, and broke her neck. I doubt that the story was true, but if it was not, it would not have been the first time a myth has grown up to rationalize a maxim. The maxim did not, of course, mean that one should never help another person out, only that one should not do so unless asked. People may not appreciate unsolicited help, since it symbolically lowers their status relative to the helper. Indeed they may not be properly grateful for help even if they have asked for it. (At an early age I was beginning to learn some generalizations about social behavior.) Like other maxims I suspect this one grew up to meet a real need. It was very difficult for the Homanses I knew—my own guess is that the trait was more Perkins than Homans—not to volunteer to help others. It certainly was not difficult for the Crowninshields, nor for the Adamses, except in their case for the more impersonal kind of help that may come from political action. I myself have encountered no pangs in living up to the maxim. But my father was not always able to practice what he preached, and among the few persons who did not like him there may have been some he tried to help out.

Another maxim he tried to instill in me had less effect. Just before I left home for the first time to go to boarding school, Father took me aside to give me paternal advice upon my entry into the great world. His heart was not in it, but he felt it to be his duty. After some veiled warnings about masturbation, which reflected the conventional wisdom of the time, he did say one thing that really interested me. "George," he said, "never try to be funny. All the Homanses think that they are funny, but most of the people they try to be funny about are not amused." Both he and his brother Jack, and no doubt their father too, were naturally witty and amusing, but people who took themselves seriously may not have appreciated being the objects of their wit. I myself have not been able to forbear trying to be amusing, though I am sure I have often gotten just those results Father predicted.

Though Father was very busy, he was a good family man. He spent all the time he could with his children and even seemed to enjoy it. He played all sorts of games with us, from baseball and tennis to poker, bridge, and chess. He helped teach me to swim. He was an excellent horseman, as my mother was a horsewoman, and he taught me to ride. He went so far as not to believe the horseless carriage was here to stay— he may be right: it may not be—and never took the trouble to learn to drive a car; my mother did all the driving in the family. Alas! his teaching of riding never took with me; horses and I have always inspired mutual distrust. I have come to hate the stupid beasts. What did take with me was his delight in working in the woods. Though he enjoyed sailing, it was not he who taught me that. Instead he hired a retired Marblehead yachtmaster to do so, and a very good job he did.

Father had been a good athlete in his youth, particularly in baseball. Although I was healthy enough, I was small and weak. What I clearly was not going to be was an athlete. That made my father's nonathletic influence all the more important. He encouraged me to read—not that I needed much encouraging—the classic novels he had loved in his youth: Cooper, Scott, Dickens, Thackeray, Marryat, Dumas. (My mother introduced me to Jane Austen.) I have never lost my taste for novels of almost any kind. As for my schooling, he was not one of those who believed then as now that good grades really did not correlate with success in later life. He urged me to work hard in school and get good grades. I got them and he praised me. Himself an achiever, he wanted me to be one. More important, he began, when I was hardly out of childhood, to urge me to think about what I was going to do in life. Without trying to impose any plans of his own—though he did keep reminding me that I would sooner or later discover that a good income was not something to be sneezed at—he was always ready to support me in the plans I made for myself, even when they changed from naval officer to newspaperman and finally to scholar.

Only once do I remember his spanking me and then only half-heartedly for some misdemeanor the nature of which escapes me. As I grew into a young intellectual I must have maddened him at times. In the first rapture of my reading Pareto I went out of my way to stress that the values Father held dearest, such as the duty of every citizen to serve his country, were but "non-logical residues." Yet his strong self-control kept his mouth shut. And of course the values he held then are my own today. Only once did I drive him beyond endurance and I did so as an aesthete and not a sociologist. One day at luncheon I was holding forth about some poet or other literary figure. Father turned to my mother in exasperation and cried, "My God! We have produced a *precieux*!" I knew that a *precieux* was *ridicule,* and I hope that since then my manner when talking about literature has become less affected.

I could not have been blessed with a better father. I enjoyed being with him; I greatly admired and respected him. Yet I never felt emotionally close or intimate with him. Later I came to wonder whether this was not generally true of the relations between even the best of fathers and his sons. According to Freud a son comes to identify with his father by working through the Oedipus complex. I do not believe in the Oedipus complex. Not even later, when I was writing down my dreams, could I find in them a sign however tenuous that I desired my mother sexually and resented my father as my successful rival. As I grew older I recognized that I identified with my father in that I had acquired many of his values. But that was something far short of complete identification; in many ways I was going to be quite different from him. Though I never underrated my father's intelligence, I knew that he was not an intellectual and that I was one. He was very popular with many different men and women; I knew that I was going to be popular, if popular at all, with only a very special coterie. Worst of all, I knew that I was never going to be good in the sense in which he was good. Positively wicked I might not be, but I would at times be bitchy. (There ought to be a masculine word for this vice, which is just as rife among men as among women.) I would never have my passions fully under control.

My father died of cancer in 1934 at the relatively early age of sixty-one, when I was twenty-four. At least I was able to tell him before he died that I had been elected to the Society of Fellows at Harvard and so had gotten as a scholar a start in life.

So far I have written as if I were an only child. I was the eldest, but was followed by two girls, my sisters Fanny and Helen, one year and three years younger than I respectively. We were near enough both in age and temper so that we could and did continually "bicker," as my father called it, at meals and other times. That is, my two sisters on one side, and I on the other—which made the two sides about equal—continually exchanged streams of verbal abuse, designed to bring out our respective shortcomings. (My brother Bobby was too much younger to be able to get into the act.) Our parents must have found our bickering tiresome, but they did little to stop it; they "bore it bravely." And it had its useful side. Since both my sisters were and are highly intelligent, bickering served to sharpen our wits and tongues and toughen our emotional hides. Today I am pretty well impervious to insults and one-upmanship coming, for instance, from other sociologists, because in the past I was inured to such assaults from those far greater experts in the business, my sisters. Our fighting was almost always verbal rather than physical, though once my sister Fanny, goaded beyond endurance, picked up a lemon meringue pie and landed it full on my face, the only time I have ever seen this feat accomplished—though naturally I could not see *much*—outside the old slapstick comedies. My mother simply left the table in disgust.

I must not imply that our conversation ran only to bickering. Both my parents were interested in politics, and much of our talk was political. Before his legal practice became too demanding, my father had been elected from the Back Bay to the old Boston Common Council and later to the House of Representatives of the Great and General Court, which is the official title of the Massachusetts legislature. Even after he had left electoral politics, my father served as campaign treasurer for several politicians.

As for my mother, she served for a number of years as president of the Good Government Association—popularly called the "Goo-Goos"—designed to support what it considered worthy candidates for political office in Boston.

Both of my parents were Republicans of the liberal wing. But in Boston the distinction between Republicans and Democrats was hardly ideological at all; it was ethnic. If one was a Yankee one was almost certain to be a Republican; if one was an Irishman, a Democrat. (The "other races" did not seem to count as much then as they do now.) For a couple of decades the Irish had taken political control of Boston away from the Yankees. In the legislature Father got to know several Irish politicians well and liked them personally. He used to say: "I had a much better time with the Irish, but you could not trust them, as you usually could a Yankee." In fact, the Republican machine in Boston became in time somewhat less clean than the proverbial hound's tooth.

My parents' target in Boston politics was precisely corruption. From Lincoln Steffens to Robert Merton, writers have lauded the help in adjusting to the laws and other complexities of American life that ward bosses provided for immigrants. No doubt they did so, but at a price. In return for help the boss expected his people to vote for the political candidate of his choosing, who was often himself. His ability to deliver the vote made the "interests," which wanted franchises favorable to their enterprises granted by the holders of political office, willing to give him money for his support, and the money in turn allowed him to help the people of his ward. Thus the circle was closed, and the system perpetuated itself. But no system can get away with that for long. In his novel *The Last Hurrah*, Edwin O'Connor showed how the New Deal, by vastly increasing federal assistance to the poor, destroyed the foundations of the boss's power.[2] Also the children of the immigrants were growing up and learning to find their own way around in American life.

Unfortunately, once corruption has become a way of life, it is not easy to eradicate. Should its original base erode, it will soon find another. The very increase in the amount of humanitarian legislation gives the citizens who are its beneficiaries and the bureaucrats who administer it further incentives to bribe and be bribed respectively. In the long run nothing does more than corruption to undermine the people's confidence in their government. Massachusetts, I believe, perhaps just because of its record of "liberal" voting, is now one of the most corrupt states in the Union. The fact that the corruption is usually petty does not make it any less sickening. There is something magnificent about a really huge bribe.

The chief target of my parents in the fight against corruption was usually James M. Curley, the greatest politician of Boston in their time and the subject of Ed O'Connor's novel. He was several times mayor, once governor, and once congressman, though he carried out the duties of this last office from a jail cell. Jim Curley was a great man, worthy of better actions and perhaps better times than his own. He was a marvelous speaker, one of the two or three greatest I have heard, and that in the days when orators had to speak in the open and not to a microphone. Jim could be both sincerely and hypocritically eloquent and, when he chose to be, enchantingly witty. Whenever Jim Curley ran for office, the Goo-Goos under my mother's leadership automatically opposed him. For though he did much to help the city, or so at least the humanitarian liberals claimed, and though little money stuck to his own hands but went towards campaign expenses and gifts to his supporters, Jim Curley was undoubtedly corrupt. Unfortunately he was just as undoubtedly witty. In one campaign he asked, "Who's Abigail Homans?" and answered his own question, "Why, she's just another social climber." This crack gave Curley himself and many others, including the Homanses, a great deal of pleasure. Knowing that a Yankee could no longer be elected mayor of Boston, Father's policy always was: "Support a *good* Irishman." Curley was not a good Irishman, but there were plenty of Irish who were, and Curley did not always win. Still, election night after election night my parents would walk down to old "Newspaper Row" on Washington Street to watch the returns being chalked up outside the offices. Hope sprang eternal, but my parents usually returned disgusted with the results.

As persons concerned with politics, my parents were in touch with many Republicans in state office. But like many others, my mother got nowhere with Calvin Coolidge. Placed next to him at some ceremonial dinner, she felt she must "make an effort" and try to talk to him. She tried all her conversational gambits. Finally she was reduced to that feeblest of openings: "Tell me, Mr. Coolidge, what is your hobby?" Said Calvin: "Holdin' office." End of conversation. Cal was no fool and enjoyed his brand of humor just as much as Jim Curley did his.

My parents—though at this time my father was nearing his death— were much closer to the great trio of liberal Republicans who were beginning to take power in the Commonwealth during the thirties. There was Henry Cabot Lodge, Jr., representative in the legislature, U.S. senator, soldier, and later envoy to Viet Nam. He was the person who persuaded General Eisenhower to run for president as a Republican. There was Christian A. Herter, congressman, governor, and later U.S. secretary of state. He persuaded president-elect Hoover to appoint my uncle Charlie secretary of the Navy. He was reluctant to accept, until my mother convinced him it was his duty as an Adams. Finally, there was Leverett Saltonstall, speaker of the Massachusetts House, governor, and U.S. senator for many years until he retired.

As governor, Leverett appointed my mother head of the women's side of Civil Defense in the Commonwealth during World War II, and later— which he had the right to do as governor—a trustee of the Massachusetts General Hospital, a job she greatly enjoyed. (My father had been a trustee earlier.) Still later, Governor Hurley, though a Democrat, kept her in this office. At some political ceremony, still another Governor, Dever, patted her hand—which she thought was taking a bit of a liberty—and assured her, "Abigail"—another liberty—"so long as I'm governor you'll always have that job." She remained active in the Ward Five (Back Bay) Republican Committee and in raising money for the better candidates of her party.

Another event in Massachusetts history made more difference to my future thinking than the corruption of Boston politics. That was the trial, while I was still a teenager, and execution in 1927 of Nicola Sacco and Bartolomeo Vanzetti. The paymaster of a shoe factory and his guard had been shot and killed, and the killers had made off with the money the victims were carrying to meet the payroll. Sacco and Vanzetti were arrested and charged, the former with doing the actual shooting and the latter with being his accomplice. They were found guilty by a Norfolk County jury. Both men were anarchists in their political views, and it was believed they wanted the money to finance their terrorist activities. Judge Webster Thayer, before whom they were tried, was said to have remarked to some golfing companion that "he would get those reds." The minds of the jury were said to have been affected by the "Red Scare" that followed the Bolshevik Revolution. And anarchism threatened the upper class in

Massachusetts, who—though this does not follow—in turn controlled the institutions of the Commonwealth. For all these alleged reasons, a number of radicals—I will not call them liberals, for that word has acquired so many different meanings—set up a cry that Sacco and Vanzetti had not received a fair trial, indeed that they were innocent.

Contrary to the myth of an upper class united in defense of its interests, no issue was more often or more heatedly argued among Brahmins during the mid-twenties, and, as far as I could tell, there were as many on the side of Sacco and Vanzetti as on the other. Professor Felix Frankfurter of the Harvard Law School wrote an eloquent and controversial book arguing that the evidence was inadequate to convict. On appeal, the Supreme Judicial Court of Massachusetts confirmed the conviction. Yet the agitation remained so great that Alvin T. Fuller, the governor, took the unprecedented step of appointing a special committee to review the evidence and the conduct of the trial. The chairman of the committee was President A. Lawrence Lowell of Harvard, the other two members, Samuel Stratton, president of the Massachusetts Institute of Technology, and Robert Grant, probate judge and a distinguished novelist. They examined the evidence, concluded that the trial was fair and the evidence sufficient to convict. Governor Fuller then let the execution of Sacco and Vanzetti go forward.

I did not know Lowell at the time but did so later, first as a friend of a friend of mine, Mrs. Frederick Winslow, and then as a Senior Fellow of the Society of Fellows at Harvard, of which I was a Junior Fellow. (I also came to know Judge Grant.) Lowell used occasionally to talk about the case and especially about "circumstantial evidence." Most evidence in cases of murder must be circumstantial, as the murderers are seldom caught in the very act of doing the deed. Lowell had his prejudices, as we all do, but I am sure, after coming to know him as intimately as I did, that he was a man of integrity and would have assessed the record of the case fairly.

I became especially interested in the case when my father's law firm was drawn into it. His partner Arthur Dehon Hill had not been counsel for the defense in the original trial of Sacco and Vanzetti but he became counsel later and, at the very end, as a last resort, just before the execution, Hill went to Mr. Justice Holmes of the U.S. Supreme Court, then on vacation on the North Shore, and asked him to grant a writ of *certiorari*, which would if granted have taken the case into the Supreme Court for review. Holmes refused to issue the writ.

In the family, Father often talked about the case. He defended Hill's right to do what he had done, but was afraid that it might hurt the firm's business. That was always one of his worries. But neither in this case nor in others did the firm, if it suffered at all, suffer long. Father also felt that Judge Thayer's remarks, if truly reported, were wholly out of order. Yet he also felt that the judge's actual conduct of the trial was fair and that the evidence warranted conviction. I agreed with my father and still do. When arrested, both Sacco and Vanzetti possessed arms and ammunition. The ballistic evidence at the trial, which has been strengthened by later evidence, showed that at least one of the killing shots had come from Sacco's gun. Both men were identified as being present at the scene of the shooting, Vanzetti in the getaway car.

Perhaps Mr. Justice Holmes made the best comment on the case later in a personal letter to his friend and long-time correspondent Harold Laski. He is writing in 1930 about Trotsky's *History of the Russian Revolution*:

> I feel the tone that I became familiar with in my youth among the abolitionists. He [Trotsky] to be sure takes his principles for granted. I should like to see them stated. If he still believes in Marx I thought that *Capital* showed chasms of unconscious errors and sophistries that might be conscious. I think that the wisest men from Confucius and Aristotle to Lincoln (if he is entitled to the superlative) have believed in the *via media*. Of course that is unpopular in times of excitement and once in a thousand times it is the extremists who get there. But I have not had a very high opinion of the intellectual powers of such extremists as I have known or known about. All of which is painfully near rudimentary twaddle—but I say it because little things once in a while make me wonder if your sympathies are taking a more extreme turn as time goes on. I am always uncertain how far Frankfurter goes. But I notice that he and you are a good deal more stirred by Sacco and Vanzetti, who were turned into a text by the reds, than by a thousand worse things among the blacks. Indeed, so far as I can judge without having read the trial I doubt if those two suffered anything more from the conduct of the judge than would be a matter of course in England. It was their misfortune to be tried in a community that was stirred up, if not frightened by manifestations the import of which was exaggerated, and, without knowing anything about it, I presume that the jury felt like the community.[3]

My opinion that Sacco and Vanzetti were guilty put me at odds with some of my closest friends, such as my tutor, Benny DeVoto at Harvard. But they soon got over it. What I think I learned from the case is much more important, because it has remained with me for the rest of my life. First, idealists, especially those who want to bring into being the perfect society—and anarchists are certainly idealists of this sort—are not to be presumed, just because they are idealists, to be also morally good. On the contrary, the stronger their idealism, the more ready they are to use any means to reach their ends. And any means certainly includes killing. President Lowell coined the best name for such people: he called them "unscrupulous idealists." These observations are not original. I should have learned them earlier, but in fact they were brought home to me by Sacco and Vanzetti, and later experience has certainly not taught me to abandon them.

Second, those who sympathize with the idealists are idealists themselves, though they will not go as far as the extreme idealists to use evil means to achieve ends presumed to be lofty. But they will go some distance; they are certainly prepared to lie in what they consider a good cause, not always to lie consciously but to lie nonetheless. I am not of course saying that they are the only liars. But their idealism ought to put a heavier burden on them than on the ordinary liar to be scrupulous in what they say. They do not stand up to the burden. The pattern of behavior they revealed in the case of Sacco and Vanzetti I have seen repeated in my own country in the cases, among others, of the Rosenbergs and of Alger Hiss, though the latter could not claim the sympathy due an underdog as Sacco and Vanzetti could. The unscrupulous idealists and their humanitarian sympathizers have been, to my mind, the curse of this century as of earlier ones.

I have talked about my mother's public life: I turn now to her life at home. My feelings towards her were more mixed than those towards my father. She had great qualities, but was not good all the way through as my father was. Though she had had many suitors, I suspect that for many years she was not much interested in getting married, and by the standards of upper-class women of her time, she married rather late in life. Yet afterwards she would assure my sisters and any other young women who would listen: "If you feel the slightest inclination to marry someone, you had better do it!"—which was certainly not the way she herself had behaved. My father's courtship of her was prolonged, and he did not marry until he was over thirty. His comment was: "Homans men marry late in life, and Homans women never marry." He had three sisters who never did. Still, his prophecy was hard on my own sisters, both of whom married, one of them twice, as if to spite him.

The marriage of my parents was happy. They shared many interests: horsemanship, charities, politics, playing games of all kinds, especially bridge, and working on their country place, which I have inherited, in Medfield, Massachusetts. Socially they were a popular couple. None of this meant that they always agreed. Their children remember hearing them argue for hours behind closed doors, earnestly but never acrimoniously. Yet my mother had a mulish streak in her, or perhaps she simply could not help getting bored with some kinds of tasks. At any rate, there were some surprising things she just would not do, even for her husband and her children.

We had a normal interest in food. But she did not care what she ate, with only one kind of exception. As a "lady" she had not been taught in childhood how to cook. Ladies employed cooks and did not cook themselves. What she had been taught to do was fine needlework, a skill considered since the Middle Ages to be suitable for a lady. She never did an hour's work in her life for which she was paid—which did not prevent her from often working hard. But not at anything to do with cooking. Throughout my childhood we employed a series of cooks. None of them lasted long. It was not that my mother was hard on her servants—on the contrary. For the cooks the very opposite was true; she never presented them with any challenge. She took little trouble about ordering food. She had her cooks prepare the same old standard, if wholesome, dishes day after day, and sooner or later they got bored. Her children complained, but we got nowhere. I have always adjusted easily to "institutional food," for our fare at home could not have been more institutional.

There was one exception to her lack of interest in food, but that goes far to prove the rule. She was especially fond of certain fresh fruits and vegetables in season, such as asparagus, strawberries, cherries, and melons. Yet even this exception did us little good, for once the season for the staple began, she served it day after day as long as it lasted, and we were ready to scream long before then. Plain cherries are all very well, indeed a treat once in a while, but not as an utterly steady diet. Her children would not have grudged Ma her cherries. What galled us was her forcing them on us for weeks on end.

Away from home she behaved in just the same way. When lunching at the most distinguished kind of restaurant in Paris, she would scan the menu meticulously and finally tell the waiter: "Just bring me a chicken sandwich." Her children would blush for shame. She ought to have gone for the pressed duck or some other expensive *specialité de la maison*. Not until later did we realize that her behavior was to the highest degree aristocratic; she was indulging her real tastes instead of those she was expected to have.

Her lack of interest in food was matched by her lack of interest in clothes. The former, from what I have heard, she inherited from her mother; the latter she certainly did not. My grandmother Adams was notoriously avid for clothes designed by the best *couturier* in Paris and for the most opulent jewelry. Throughout her life my mother held neither of these tastes, which were characteristic of upper-class women of her time. When *her* mother died, she sold all her jewelry except for a small pearl necklace. Nor did she worry about what dresses she wore. Not that she ever looked untidy; it was just that when it came to buying a new dress, she did not shop around but took the first at all suitable one the saleswoman showed her. She even allowed my aunt Fanny to hand down to her my aunt's secondhand dresses. As an Adams, I suspect she felt that nothing of this sort could demean her and that it gave Aunt Fanny pleasure. Perhaps I should not speak of this trait of my mother's as asceticism. It really was boredom with food and clothes and occasionally some more important things, and when she was bored she could be mulish.

Her children sometimes suffered from her mulish moods. In my first year at boarding school I caught pneumonia and was kept in the school infirmary until after the other boys had left for the Christmas vacation. The doctor soon certified me as cured and discharged me. I was passionately looking forward to enjoying the Christmas vacation at home. Instead when I got to Boston Ma insisted in quarantining me, all alone in an upstairs room in my uncle Charlie's house. She was convinced that I was still infectious, and how boring would it be for her to undergo the rigors of Christmas with not only me but her other children down with pneumonia! I raised hell; my mother relented, and my exile lasted only one day.

When suffering from another infectious disease, whooping cough, I was exiled for some weeks from taking my meals with the rest of the family and sent to eat with the help in the kitchen. Ma did not seem to worry whether the help got whooping cough, or perhaps she assumed they had all had it already. This time my exile was also my gain. Our maids were all Irish, and at this time some of them were fresh from the Old Country. They told me lurid tales of the recent Irish Rebellion—"the troubles"—especially of the atrocities committed by "the Bloody Black and Tans," that is, the British troops. I did not believe much of the latter, or rather I believed that the Irish were just as capable of atrocities as the English. But I did get an idea of what it was like for ordinary people to go through a revolution. The maids also taught me to eat a small sea snail called a periwinkle that swarms in millions on the New England as on the Irish coast. Except in famine a periwinkle is not worth eating.

To end my account of my mother's asceticism I must report that neither she nor her brother Charlie could be brought to go further than just barely tasting any form of alcohol. The tragic alcoholism of their brother George must have had something to do with that. But she did nothing to prevent my father from enjoying his cocktail.

My sisters and I never doubted that our mother loved us. But when we were out of her sight, we were often out of her mind too; she did not worry about us. Her apparent lack of interest may have just been the other side of her greater interest in my father. More likely, it may have reflected the way her own mother had brought her up. Still, one likes to think that one's mother worries about one a little.

Her failure to worry may have had a good, though unintended, and certainly long unappreciated, effect on me. It allowed me a lot of independence early in life, and psychologists affirm that "independence training" is good for the personality. When my uncle Arthur gave me my boat *Sheldrake*, and I was allowed to sail her in the waters around Marblehead, my mother never seemed to worry—and I do not believe she did worry—about how far out to sea I ventured, or in what stormy seas, or how late I got home. I was expected to look out for myself, and I did so successfully, with the help of some natural timidity and of *Sheldrake* herself, who could keep the sea in anything short of a full gale. I should have been much more timid had Ma shown any signs of worry. She had been treated in the same way in her own childhood, sailing in Quincy Bay in an earlier *Sheldrake*.

In the same way she never tried to supervise my sisters, me, and our friends when we played together in the house or out of doors. Only if she heard terminal screams of pain or anger or the crash of broken glass did she appear on the scene and, as she put it, "read us the riot act," not because she was particularly worried about us but because we were interfering with something like reading a novel that was amusing her. I have since read much and been told more about the stereotypical Jewish mother. One way of describing my own mother is that nothing less like the Jewish mother could well be imagined.

Her failure to worry about her children had its embarrassing sides. She never concerned herself greatly to see that I looked clean, particularly in minor matters such as hands, fingernails, and ears. Only some unsubtle birthday presents, such as a nail file, from my aunts or the mothers of my friends finally brought home to me that I was deficient in these respects. Nor did she worry about our health, unless a high fever actually kept us in bed, when she became indefatigable in trying to keep us amused, especially by reading to us. There was one exception to her lack of hypochondria about her children. She herself had poor teeth, and she took us to the dentist more often than I suspect was strictly necessary.

In the same way she did little to teach me manners at table or elsewhere. What few manners I learned, I learned from my father or, later, from observing the families of my friends. Thus I should never have learned at home that I ought to remain standing at table until the lady of the house was seated, much less to push in her chair. Good manners still do not come naturally to me. I have to think about them, and often I do not think quickly enough. My having to observe the manners of others and to think consciously about my own if they were to fall within the bounds of acceptability may have helped me to become an observer of social behavior.

Yet my picture of my mother so far is biased. When she was with us, when we were actually in sight, she always gave us a good time. Like Father, she loved to play parlor games with us. She loved reading to us at any time, even when we were not in bed sick, her taste running to novels and rather sentimental verse, such as Oliver Wendell Holmes's "Grandmother's Story of Bunker Hill Battle," which moved her to sobs. She was avid also in reading novels to herself. Not for her were the works of the avant-garde. She read French easily; she had spent an adolescent year as a student in a convent in Paris. She tried to read Proust, because someone had told her she must, but she could not get very far into his great book. She never even started to read those other classics of her time, Joyce and Mann, and I never could get her to read my favorite, *Moby Dick*. Among the moderns, Galsworthy was just her speed; among the classics, Jane Austen, whose delicious ironies she taught me to appreciate. I too became a great reader of novels, though my taste in those days ran more to Dickens, whom my father loved and she could not stand. The humor was too masculine for her: "All that drinking!" There were hours after lunch when one could have seen both of us stretched out on sofas reading, I chewing one of those white cotton ties we wore in those days and twisting my hair, which I still had, until we both went to sleep.

She gave me, and I think herself, much pleasure in another way. As a rather lonely little boy back on vacations from boarding school, I was taken by her to museums, particularly art museums. Her Adams uncles had done the same for her when she was young. She was in no sense trained as a historian or critic of art, but she knew her way around in a general way in the field of painting, at least through the impressionists, and I am sure I owe to her my own interest in almost any kind of *objet d'art*. She also attended regularly the Friday afternoon concerts of the Boston Symphony Orchestra. But she never had the intuitive understanding, as distinguished from the mere enjoyment, of music that she had for paintings and porcelain. She never required her children to get any musical training whatsoever. No piano lessons! In this she was wholly unlike her sisters-in-law, my aunts Katharine and Marian. I remain musically illiterate.

Ma also gave us a good time in a very special way when we were absent from home. She was an indefatigable letter writer and a very good one. Her delightful autobiography, *Education by Uncles*,[4] is just in the style of her letters. One of the characteristic poses in which I see her is sitting at her desk, writing letters or catching up on her line-a-day diary, which she kept for most of her life.

Later, after my father's death—she outlived him by forty years—and with the confidence born of many years of public service, she became, with the series of pug dogs she always took around with her, a bit of a recognized "character" on the Boston scene, the kind of person others speak of as "wonderful." She played up to the character she had become, thus stereotyping it still more. Stories began to be told about her, but she told the best about herself. As she walked down a Boston street at some time during her sixties, a man tried to snatch her handbag. She clutched it all the more firmly and shouted, "God damn your soul!" This startled the thief so much that he took to his heels. Had he known her, he need not have been so startled. Her language could be far from ladylike.

"Characters" can get away with behavior that ordinary mortals cannot, and Ma as a licensed "character" said and did in later life some outrageous things. But from a taxi driver whom she often employed she got her comeuppance at least once. She was in the back seat giving him directions, and as she was wont to do, emphasizing her points by poking him with her cane. Finally he said, "Mrs. Homans, if you do that once more, you'll be out on the street." She was honest enough to tell this story on herself.

She supported her reputation as a "character" with her real ability as a wit. Of her many cracks, I like the following best. She was always fascinated by the weather, which is natural enough in a New Englander who has so much weather to be fascinated by, and she taught me many folk generalizations about its behavior. She loved the seasons in New England and especially, as well she might, the fall. Someone once drew her attention to the soft air and bright leaves of an October day. "Remember," said she, "Hell would be fine in October."

She died in 1974 in her ninety-fifth year.

About the two "sides" of my family, the Adamses and the Homanses, I felt emotions as different as those Proust felt for Swann's Way and the Guermantes' Way, and both emotions were mixed. The Adams side meant largely my uncle Charlie, his wife, Aunt Fanny, and their son, my friend and contemporary, Charles, Jr., or "Chas." My uncle Charles Francis Adams was treasurer of Harvard University, later secretary of the Navy, a great trustee, a leading citizen of Boston and, what was more important in my eyes, a great seaman. The Adams side included in theory my mother's other brother, Arthur, of whom I was very fond but who never felt to me like an Adams at all.

I saw a great deal of Uncle Charlie and his family throughout my early life, in the Back Bay, in their country place above the Sudbury River in Concord, in the summer in The Glades, North Scituate, and serving as crew for Uncle Charlie in yacht racing at Marblehead. Aunt Fanny was one of the great women executives I have known. When she took me off my mother's hands, which was often, she did much to organize my life and she did it both well and kindly.

Above all, to the Homans children the Adamses meant money. Perceptions like this a child picks up very early. Uncle Charlie did not mean really big money, like J. P. Morgan—though my cousin Catherine Adams married J. P. Morgan, Jr.'s son—but he meant more money than we did, and we were well-off. Uncle Charlie lived in what was by Boston standards a grand mansion on the sunny side of Commonwealth Avenue, we in a mean house on Marlborough Street. He had a car, a Packard or a Pierce Arrow, and a chauffeur, the genial Barr. We too had a car, but it was a mere Nash and my mother drove it. Uncle Charlie gave me my first car; my father never would have done so. If he so wished, Uncle Charlie could also afford to order every year—at least in the glorious years before the Depression—a new racing yacht from the drawing board of one of the best yacht designers. True, my parents spent money on horses, but horses are not in a class with yachts as an extravagance.

Uncle Charlie's house meant money in the most tangible sense of the word. I often played there with my cousin Chas, and one of my earliest memories is that of playing with real twenty-dollar gold pieces, which Uncle Charlie received for attending meetings of the directors of the many boards he served on, notably that of the American Telephone and Telegraph Company.

Uncle Charlie meant money, yet we children soon came to understand that money was not everything. For all Aunt Fanny's Packard and liveried chauffeur, Ma was a much more popular and important woman in Boston than she was. Though she accepted Aunt Fanny's hand-me-downs, she herself did not lack a sense of the importance of money. She did not spend it freely, except on horses and charities, yet she thought it a very good thing to have. Whenever anyone of her acquaintance became engaged to be married, the first question she always asked about the prospective spouse was: "Does he [or she] have any money?" I am sure she thought I was mad when I married a woman altogether without money. But then she herself had married a man with no inherited money, though a good professional income.

With the money, I felt in Uncle Charlie's household a certain emotional coldness, such as I never felt with any of the Homanses or indeed with my mother and her brother Arthur. Indeed "coldness" is not the right word, though I am at a loss to find a better. Uncle Charlie never failed in his kindness to me, even under trying circumstances. He was very fond of my mother, and she of him. He could be moved to tears by the thoughts of old friendships or indeed by the sight of an American flag flying from the masthead of a man-of-war. Such moments aside, realism and good judgment were what reigned in Uncle Charlie's presence and conversation, and these, though both rare and vital, are not inherently warming. To be whole a man or woman needs a little gaiety, even foolishness, just as Robert Frost insisted that, in order to enjoy life, a man needs to be just a bit coarse. For me the Adamses came to represent the coldness of realism, the Homanses the warmth of gaiety and even slight foolishness. I believe myself to be both cold and just a bit silly.

Let me now look at the Homans side, and particularly at my then surviving two maiden aunts, Katharine and Marian. Both of them possessed in the highest degree the dangerous passion of the Homanses for "helping out." It may have been for their benefit that the maxim against it was promulgated. They wore themselves out to the point of nervous exhaustion working for the Boston charities they supported. When she was tired or agitated, as she often was, Aunt Katta's voice would rise to a high, thin scream, a danger signal her nieces and nephews soon came to recognize. Even within the family the aunts helped out a little too much. They were more concerned than even the Adamses with family heirlooms. Indeed some of the things they considered heirlooms, the Adamses would have scorned to treat as such. When she was a young bride, they may have been disturbed by the cavalier way my mother treated various pieces of furniture she had received from the Homanses. She worried no more about such things than she did about food and clothes, but what did not the aunts consider sacred? I am afraid they could not bring themselves to forgo pointing out to Ma her shortcomings: "Oh! Abigail, why did you stick Aunt Lizzie's chair away in that corner?" They may also have been disturbed by the lack of thought she took for her children. I am afraid that Ma resented their well-intentioned criticism, and that we picked up some of her attitudes towards them. At least my father once had to warn me, though not at all roughly: "You must not make fun of my sisters." Later the whole relationship between my mother and her sisters-in-law calmed down. She no longer felt that she must keep them at arm's length, at least not Aunt Marian. They also had many friends in common.

The fact was that the aunts did help out and to very good purpose. They were endlessly kind to my sisters and me, having us to stay, playing games with us, and taking us to shows. Aunt Marian was a bit stagestruck. I believe it was she who took me to my first performance of a play by Shakespeare. On the Homans side they represented the same kind of personal, individual interest that Uncle Arthur did on the Adams side, at least until he married and had children of his own. They took the same interest in all their other nieces and nephews that they did in us and extended it to the next generation, including my own children.

And yet! And yet! Our feelings towards the Homans aunts remained ambivalent. Aunt Katharine's efforts to help out proved sometimes embarrassing. Once when she visited me at boarding school, she insisted, rather publicly, in brushing my blue serge suit, which each of us scholars had to wear with a stiff collar to chapel on Sundays. I had never done so myself; our disenchanted masters never tried to make me; my family had given up without a struggle. The task would have been impossible. But Aunt Katta tried to accomplish it. Early I learned from her something about the seamy side of altruism. There is no doubt that Aunt Katta was a great American altruist, no possible doubt whatever. For her, man's and especially woman's chief duty was to do good to others. It was a disaster that she never married and had children of her own, who would have been an even more appropriate target for her altruism than we, and who might—though I doubt it—have exhausted her whole supply. In the meantime she had us, and she *would* do us good, willy-nilly. We often appreciated and enjoyed it, but some of our interests differed from hers, and there were times when we wanted to escape from Aunt Katta's altruistic importunities. Then we did not propose to let her do good to us, and we showed it. Unfortunately doing good to others also did good to Aunt Katta, and when she was denied her chance there might be trouble. Though she tried to keep them under control, she could not quite manage to prevent letting her vexation and frustration show. She was up against some young but keen observers. In some inchoate and unconscious way, I concluded that there is no such thing as pure altruism, that every altruist is to some degree on an ego trip. Perhaps this was an unclean thing for a nice little boy to learn, and some grown-ups never learn it. For me, as Kipling would say, "God help us, for we knew the worst too young!"[5] Perhaps in reaction to Aunt Katta, there is little of the altruist in me, and that is part of my conservatism.

I felt the contrast between the Homanses and the Adamses most at Christmas. The Adams kin met at Uncle Charlie's house for dinner on Christmas Eve, the Homanses on Christmas Day at Grandmother's house, where I was born. I believe the Adamses were among the last of the Brahmin families to keep the Puritan rule against celebrating Christmas at all. True or not, I sometimes felt that their hearts were not in it. We went up the grand staircase past Uncle Charlie's yachting trophies and the marble busts of baldheaded ancestors. I do not remember whether there was even a Christmas tree. If there was, little was made of it. We were given our presents and it was all very nice. But there was mighty little of what Ma would call "delicious gaiety." If I should try to describe now what I felt then, I should say that the conversation was too damned judicious. Christmas is one of the times when the judicious should be in abeyance, and people should be both gay and silly.

At the Homans Christmas dinner, the men all came in white tie and "tails," the women in their best evening dresses, the children in their best frocks or suits, including those damned Eton collars. Before dinner we gathered around the Christmas tree, and much was made of it. It was decked out in German glass ornaments, including a marvelous glass peacock, which seemed to have come down through so many generations as to count as an heirloom. The tree was lighted with real candles, making conflagration an imminent hazard. Oh! the pungent smell of hot wax dripping upon balsam needles! While we gathered around the tree we all sang "Oh! That wonderful tree," "Oh! Little town of Bethlehem," and other carols. Unlike the Adamses some of the Homanses could sing. Then we went down to dinner past the Piranesi prints. Besides the traditional Christmas dishes, such as plum pudding, we were served special ones believed to be cooked from recipes unique to the Homans family. Such was something called Marlborough Pie, which appeared only at Christmas. Much was the fussing over whether it had come out right! At table the talk was apt to turn to hoary, supposedly funny, and sometimes ghoulish Homans conversation-pieces, such as: "Does anyone know the whereabouts of the key to the Homans tomb in Dorchester?" In my time, no one ever did. After dinner we opened presents, each coming with some little message or verse. (No Adams would have accompanied presents with doggerel.) I shall not deny that a certain amount of one-upmanship went into the giving of presents. Or perhaps I should say upwomanship, since it was especially endemic among the women of the family, both those born and those married into it. My mother, I regret to say, was rather good at this game; no one could snow her under. But the whole tone of Christmas was one of openness, warmth, and gaiety—and if you cannot have these things without some silliness too, then let us by all means be silly. In short, the Homanses celebrated Christmas as a human festival. "When at home," we were justified in saying, "do as the Homans do!"

NOTES

1. James B. Conant, *My Several Lives: Memoirs of a Social Inventor* (New York: Harper & Row, 1970), pp. 81-84.
2. Edwin O'Connor, *The Last Hurrah* (Boston: Little, Brown, 1956).
3. *Holmes-Laski Letters: The Correspondence of Mr. Justice Holmes and Harold J. Laski, 1916-1935* ed. Mark DeWolfe Howe, 2 vols. (Cambridge: Harvard University Press, 1953), 2:1265-66.
4. Abigail Adams Homans, *Education by Uncles* (Boston: Houghton Mifflin, 1966).
5. Rudyard Kipling, "Gentlemen-Rankers." (many editions).

4

SCHOOL

My subject now is the making of an intellectual. An intellectual person need not be an intelligent one, so I shall make no claims for my intelligence, but I certainly became an intellectual, whom I shall simply define as someone with a special interest in general ideas.

Some of the influences that made me an intellectual were genetic, that is, physically inherited. Until I reached college I was always small for my age and slow in development. The onset of puberty, for instance, came late for me. Year after year as an adolescent I was decidedly the smallest boy in my school class. (Nobody who looks at me now can believe how small I was then.) My size meant that I could not compete as an equal in many of the games, such as football, most highly valued by my contemporaries. I was also unreasonably—as it seems now—ashamed of being small. But genetic characteristics, such as physical size, do not usually act alone to determine behavior: they interact with learning. By way of differential reward, a small boy is apt to learn different actions from those a big one does; and my small size may have helped make me physically timid. In her frank way, my sister Fanny once declared that I was timid, except in sailing a boat.

Naturally—and here again differential learning comes in—I tried to compensate for my small size. A few sports do not require the kind of strength that goes with weight: when young I was not at all bad at cross-country running. And there is one sport in which light weight is a positive advantage. I do not mean being a jockey but being coxswain of a rowing crew. Luckily both my secondary schools made rowing a major sport. The job also requires a loud voice, and that I had both then and now. It requires skill and judgment in handling a boat, and from my early upbringing I had that too. Finally the coxswain's role is one that inhibits the inferiority complex said to be brought on by physical smallness. He gives orders to, criticizes, and sometimes even encourages as many as eight other men, who are bigger and usually older than he, and who under other conditions could easily put him in his place. But while rowing they cannot talk back to him; they must save their breath for more important work. In my last year of boarding school I finally got too heavy to remain a coxswain, but by then the damage had been done: I have never been reluctant to boss others around or to speak up before persons theoretically my betters.

I also compensated intellectually for physical inferiority. Here again genetics interacted with learning, for whatever else may be said of the Adamses, many of them were avid readers, writers, and scholars. Yet if to compensate meant to make an extra effort, I am not sure it is the correct word to use. For I always enjoyed my school work and book learning, and it always came easily to me. For instance, I always read much further ahead in my textbooks, particularly history, than the point the class had reached at the moment. The sign that book learning came easily was that I did not have to work hard to get good grades—not that my grades were all *that* good; they were seldom the best in the class. This is an excellent strategic position to occupy; one is intellectually respected but one does not have to struggle to remain at the very top of the greased pole.

Much of what I learned from books I learned not at school but at home, from our excellent library. I have spoken of my avid reading in the English and American classical novelists—not yet George Eliot or Henry James, which our library did not contain and which I came to love only later. The novelists taught me, sometimes by counterexamples such as Uriah Heep and seldom by direct preaching, what a gentleman or gentlewoman ought to be. Not necessarily a gentleman in the class sense, though they certainly taught that too, but a gentleman as an ideal model of behavior. Thus Natty Bumppo, Cooper's heroic backwoodsman, was surely a gentleman. Of course so long as I had my father's example before me I did not have to learn from books what a gentleman was. Nor does one learn wholly either from books or from live models. One finally learns from one's own experience. As Justice Holmes said, "Life, not the parson, teaches conduct."[1] My own experience was never enough to make me a gentleman, and I have no right to claim to be one. But I have always held it before me as the noblest ideal of human behavior that one might actually and occasionally attain. The gentleman overlaps with the Christian but makes fewer contradictory demands.

One book in our library set in motion a special and enduring current in me. I came on it myself; my parents did not urge me to read it. It was entitled (I still have it) *Popular Romances of the Middle Ages*.[2] It contained excellent short versions of several medieval epics and romances. What I enjoyed most were not the stories of King Arthur and his knights nor the various French *chansons de geste* but a version of *Beowulf* and of three of the Icelandic sagas: *Burnt Njal, Grettir the Strong,* and *Gunnlaug of the Worm's Tongue*—that is, stories in the Germanic heroic tradition. Our library also contained a set of Carlyle, in which I read his adaptation, entitled *The Early Kings of Norway*, of the greatest of all the sagas, Snorri Sturluson's *Heimskringla*. Finally at the second of my schools, I was required to read—not that I did not love it—Longfellow's verse rendition of *The Saga of King Olaf* [3] (Trygvason) from the *Heimskringla*. It still holds for me moments of great drama. Take the sea fight off Svold between the Danes and the Norse in which King Olaf met his death. The king and his men are defending themselves near the poop of his great ship, *The Long Serpent*, among them Einar Tambarskelver, who was a skilled archer. An enemy arrow strikes Einar's bow and breaks it. Following Snorri's original account, Longfellow wrote:

> *"What was that?" said Olaf standing*
> *On the quarter-deck.*
> *"Something heard I like the stranding*
> *Of a shattered wreck."*
>
> *Einar then, the arrow taking*
> *From the loosened string,*
> *Answered, "That was Norway breaking*
> *From thy hand, O King."*

I have since read and reread many of the sagas, in translation, but in full translation, no longer in shortened versions. Why do I get more pleasure and indeed more emotional nourishment from reading them than from, say, the Arthurian romances or the modern romances of Tolkien? I do so in part for the same reason I enjoy classical English novels. The sagas are themselves semihistorical novels. The uninformed sometimes believe they are epic poems, but in fact thay are in prose. In them, unlike the romances, the story takes place within the institutions of a thoroughly real and believable society. No doubt the sagas contain unbelievable creatures, such as trolls, but the society is real and described consistently across the whole corpus of literature the Icelanders themselves considered to refer to their own country. But why this demand of mine for a literature whose drama occurs within a real society? I have no explanation. Yet a sociological interest in literature has been so strong in me that I have often taught seminars on the society of classical Iceland, requiring my students to use the sagas themselves as their sources, much as I might ask them to work out the institutions of Victorian England from reading Trollope's novels.

The sagas also provided at a more violent and primitive but perhaps deeper emotional level than the English novels an ethic of stoicism and deliberately understated endurance, which is one of the attitudes that sustains life, though I cannot always summon it up for myself at need.

One of the recurring characters in the sagas is a rather unlovable and unscrupulous but shrewd political operator. Yet the gentleman is not absent, though he is somewhat quicker on the draw than his English counterpart. An example is Gunnar of Hlitharendi in *Njal's Saga*.

There was one last reason for my fascination not only with the sagas but with the whole literature of the Germanic heroic age. I have already mentioned it in my chapter on ancestors: a search for personal through ethnic identity. My roots were in England, and whatever evil connotations two world wars have attached to the word "German," the English are ultimately of Germanic origin, as are the Flemish, Dutch, Frisians, Danes, Swedes, Norwegians, and Icelanders, to whom no such taint of evil attaches. For us *Beowulf,* the *Eddas,* and the sagas are what the *Iliad* and the *Odyssey* were to the Greeks or the Old Testament was and is to the Jews: they define our profoundest values in their earliest manifestations.

As for formal schooling, my parents sent me first to Miss Woodward's, a good private elementary school in the same block as our own house on Marlborough Street. Many of my schoolmates are still among my friends. Then at age nine I went to the Browne and Nichols School, at that time located on Garden Street in Cambridge. I traveled out from Boston and back on the subway and trolley cars. Browne and Nichols was—and still is—a really excellent private school that maintained the old New England standards of scholarship. Overall, in its academic standards and its teaching, it was the best school I ever attended. Father had chosen well. But though Browne and Nichols took students as far as entrance to college, Father did not leave me there but sent me at thirteen to St. Paul's School, Concord, New Hampshire, an Episcopalian boarding school. Of that later.

Browne and Nichols taught all academic subjects well. There I plunged at once into learning both French and Latin. But I was especially influenced by a man who introduced a different kind of note into my education. Horace Taylor taught what was then called natural history. At Browne and Nichols it had not yet achieved the status of a full-fledged academic subject but stood somewhere above carpentry. Accordingly Horace Taylor was not under pressure to make sure we learned anything specific. He was free to do anything with us that interested him, and he was an interesting and original man. He took us on the usual nature walks and taught us to identify the chief wild species of New England flora and fauna.

But Horace Taylor did a great deal more than that. He developed a set of cards with slots in them, each card devoted to some physical characteristic, such as a hooked bill, and the slots representing the various wild species, in this case birds, that possessed it. If we laid the relevant cards on top of a bottom card containing the names of the various species, the one name that showed through all the slots would be the species we wished to identify. By this process Taylor taught us the uses of careful observation and, above all, the principles of taxonomy, or classification. This method may be commonplace now. It was not then, and I was immensely entertained and intrigued.

More important still, Taylor gave us a good account, with charts showing how the principal branches of the animal kingdom are related to one another, of the Darwinian theory of evolution. As far as I know he told us nothing—he may have known nothing, since he was largely self-taught—about the Mendelian genetics that provides the underpinning of Darwinian evolution. But Darwin's theory even without Mendel is still a good theory, and Taylor did show how competition between and within species might lead to the differentiation of species. Without planning to do so, he showed us how careful observation and a good taxonomy, as represented by his cards, might lead to a truly explanatory theory.

My father had turned over to me a cabinet containing miscellaneous specimens of natural history ranging all the way from minerals to birds' eggs, which had been his as a boy and which was a common feature of Victorian households. Among the specimens, the cabinet held various exotic and beautiful seashells as well as the always less spectacular native ones. My family went to the seashore every summer, first to Quincy, where I met the famous horseshoe crabs that Henry Adams had brought into his own discussion of evolution in the *Education*,[4] then to Gloucester, to Marblehead, and finally to The Glades, North Scituate, where my mother spent summers in her childhood. If a boy lives by the seashore it is difficult for him not to become a beachcomber on the sands or in the tidal pools. Under the stimulus of Horace Taylor I determined to become more than a casual beachcomber but rather a systematic collector of native shells. Taylor's teaching and practice made it clear that to be a natural historian of shells, a conchologist, it was not enough to pick up the highly visible and clean ones. He must also search for obscure, homely, and dirty ones, and remember that there are land snails and freshwater clams as well as the whelks and limpets of the clean salt sea. So I faithfully spent a good deal of time at the bottom of dank ditches in search of land snails. The result of my efforts was not only a good collection of local molluscs but also a manuscript written when I was thirteen entitled *The Shells of Marblehead*. It was my first scientific work, but the manuscript has disappeared.

From the fact that I wrote something of this sort I infer that a strong didactic, even pedantic, bent was strong in me from an early age. It manifested itself in other ways. From time to time during the winters I insisted on giving lectures on shells to that captive audience, my family. I would stand behind a table with a few specimens displayed on it, my father, mother, and two sisters seated in front. Then I would hold forth on the points of interest of each specimen and the presumed habits of the animal that had once inhabited it, showing off my knowledge of a splendid mass of technical, usually Latin, words. After one of my lectures, when I had gone upstairs to bed, my father came into my room and asked me whether I knew the meaning of the word *anus*, which I had used freely in my lecture. He tried to keep a straight face but was obviously amused. Of course I knew what an *anus* in a mollusc was, but I did not identify it closely enough with my own to feel embarrassed by using the word. Note: my father definitely did not forbid my using it again. How could my family have endured the presumption, the pedantry of my lectures? The fact that I gave them I take to be evidence that I was a born teacher, though not necessarily a born *good* teacher. I did not then dream that I was to become a professor. My thoughts about a future career lay elsewhere.

Finally, the study of evolution combined with actual collecting gave me an idea, the sort of thing I would later learn to call a testable hypothesis. Taylor had told us about the Galapagos Islands and Darwin's finches: how Darwin had hypothesized that what had probably been a single species of finch had managed to reach the Galapagos from the South American continent and had there differentiated into a number of different species, each adapted to occupy some hitherto empty ecological niche. At least Taylor had taught us that isolated populations, isolated for instance on islands, might for various reasons, including what we should now call sheer genetic drift, develop characteristics somewhat different from those of the main body of a species.

Now it happened that I had islands at my disposal. In summer I was a rather solitary boy spending long hours sailing in my boat *Sheldrake*. We were then living at Peach's Point, Marblehead, which sticks out into Salem Bay. The bay is full of islands and of island-like reefs. Many were uninhabited and, with the help of *Sheldrake*, I had been able to explore them. They were no match for the Galapagos, since at most they lay only a mile or so away from the mainland. But if they were not isolated enough to evolve distinct species of birds, they might have been able to evolve distinct species of land snails—sea snails obviously would not do. So I returned to the islands, this time to explore them for land snails. And at least on Eagle Island I found some specimens of a species related to the common European edible *escargot*, though not as large.

I took my specimens to the curator of molluscs at the Boston Museum of Natural History, with whom I had struck up a friendship. The museum, then in a big brownstone building on Boylston Street, was one of my favorite haunts. I can still see the huge skeleton of a whale that hung precariously over my head as I went up the main staircase. The curator showed interest in my specimens and asked me to give them to the museum in return for duplicates of other species. As far as I know, my specimens are in the current museum, though certainly not on display, for they were homely things. I do not know what interested the curator in them. Were they really somewhat different from the mainland forms of the species, even if only in some superficial respect such as the pattern of striping on the shells? Or did he just want to get specimens from such unlikely places as Eagle Island in order to add to our knowledge of the distribution of the species? But the meaning of his action was clear to me: I had independently tested an hypothesis from evolutionary theory, and the test had been in some way successful.

My interest in conchology disappeared, together with such things as stamp collecting, toy trains, and lead soldiers, at about the onset of puberty. One day these things engaged my imagination; on the next they bored me. I doubt that the developmental psychologists have yet explained these sudden transformations. Yet I am sure that my intense interest in natural history left deep traces. I claim that I am still a natural historian, though now a people-watcher rather than a shell-watcher. For the moment my interests turned more decidedly than ever towards literature.

In the fall of 1923 I entered the second form at St. Paul's School, Concord, New Hampshire, from which I graduated in 1928. St. Paul's is one of the famous "church" (Episcopal) boarding schools in New England, originally modeled, though in my time the resemblance was not great, on the English "public" schools. Other examples of the class were St. Mark's, Groton, and Middlesex. Accordingly the Harvard Admissions Office began to refer to them as St. Grottlesex schools. Other New England schools, at least as famous, just as good or better scholastically, older and larger, such as Andover and Exeter are *not* St. Grottlesex schools.

I often asked myself why my father decided to send me to one of these schools and specifically to S.P.S. (as its "old boys" usually call it). Though my parents reached many decisions jointly, I am sure this one was chiefly his. It was a new departure for the Homanses. He himself, like my mother, had attended a good Boston day school. Of course when he was growing up the St. Grottlesex schools were not nearly as well established as they became later. In my time these schools admitted only boys, but they had their feminine counterparts, such as Westover, which my sisters attended. The only reason Father ever gave me for sending me to S.P.S. was that it would "broaden" me, since unlike Groton, for instance, few of its scholars came from the Boston area, and indeed only two other Bostonians were in my form.

"Broaden" me it did, though not quite in the way Pa expected. Getting a young man away from home, especially as solitary a one as I, is probably good in itself. If one survives boarding school at all—and I certainly did not enjoy my first year—one learns to get along after a fashion with a varied body of one's contemporaries for twenty-four hours a day and for months on end. On the other hand, boarding schools—and this was very true of St. Paul's—tend to be located in isolated places, perhaps to shield their scholars from facts of life that students at a big-city high school cannot escape. In my time, they also isolated their scholars from girls, except for a couple of big weekends, when one was allowed to invite a girl, properly chaperoned, to the school.

But for Pa "broadening" meant meeting new kinds of people. Within ten minutes of my arrival at school, my new companions with delighted ridicule taught me that I had an accent. They found my flat *a*'s and nonexistent *r*'s, as in "Haavd" (Harvard) endlessly amusing. I had never before realized that I spoke with an accent, and I am proud that I never, consciously or unconsciously, gave in to the pressure of alien speech. I still talk like a Yankee Bostonian, that is, like a Yankee Bostonian of my time, for the old speech is itself changing.

In other ways than accent the "broadening" process failed because, except that they did not come from Boston but from New York, Philadelphia, Baltimore, Pittsburgh, and Chicago, many of the boys were very much like myself. Most of us came from what is now called the "Eastern Establishment" and were members of "old families," which in turn meant "old money." In the Homans case that did not mean much money: I suspect that our family income was below the median for S.P.S.

But not all of my fellows represented "old families." What did "broaden" me was meeting a few examples of boys from families that were *nouveaux riches*, purse-proud, and, to my mind, coarse. None of them ever displayed—in contrast to the Rockefellers—the slightest recognition that great wealth entailed public service. None of them showed the slightest awareness of *noblesse oblige*. Money was to be spent as blatantly as possible on cars, race horses, polo ponies, and mansions at Aiken or Palm Beach: Newport was already becoming a bit *passé*. (I myself did not consider money spent on a sailing yacht ostentatious.) What is more I never found any of these boys, with one possible exception, whom I hated for other reasons, particularly talented, intelligent, or interesting to talk to. Their fathers must have been intelligent,

cularly to S.P.S. As I have said, he thought that one of the greatest
leges he had enjoyed in life was membership in the Porcellian Club
arvard. Though the P.C., like all human institutions, sometimes made
akes, he believed its members included the finest gentlemen in the
d. He meant *gentleman* in no stuffy sense: a gentleman was gay,
ivial, generous, brave, truthful, high-minded and public-spirited, not
rich. Father—and there is something of great importance in his
—did not define class by money but by character and style of life.
e money was necessary to produce these things, but not necessarily
n. Pa yearned, for my sake, that I be elected a member of the
ellian. And no doubt he had noticed that, in those days, graduates
, say, Exeter and Andover, while no doubt the salt of the earth, were
h less likely to be elected to the P.C. than the graduates of the St.
tlesex schools. Therefore Pa thought, quite logically, that I should be
n the opportunity to make friends among the latter. As for S.P.S.
ifically, I believe that as graduate grand marshal of the Porcellian he
been especially impressed by some of the S.P.S. graduates who were
ergraduate members during his term of office. Alas for his hopes! At
aul's I did not become specially friendly with my form-mates who
become members of the P.C., and I was not elected myself.

hough St. Paul's was not overall as distinguished academically as
vne and Nichols, it was still a very good school. I continued my study
atin and French and began German. By the time I graduated I could
all of them easily. Yet the very method that taught me these skills
ed me of confidence that I really commanded them. In spite of good
es, all those blue pencil marks on exercises kept persuading me of my
rance, because they picked up errors of detail but failed to convey
good grasp of the whole. It took later experience to convince me that I
y could read these languages. We also studied mathematics and a
in amount of physical science, together of course with English, both
mar and literature. There was an especially good course on English
titutional history, which taught me many elementary facts and ideas
uld otherwise have had to pick up later. Courses on this subject are
ly given now, though they describe the origins of our liberties.
ead, let us eschew racism and learn about the bureaucracy of Han
a! Music and drawing were treated as extracurricular subjects, and
te was unheard of.

hose of us who possessed any scholarly bent learned more than do
arly endowed graduates of good secondary schools today. Mathema-
nay be the exception. Besides algebra and trigonometry, our teachers
d easily have introduced the best of us to calculus, and I wasted much
later getting command of this essential intellectual tool. On the other

for I am not such a fool as to believe it does not tak
with other qualities, to make a great deal of mone

These were the boys who could not believe the
me draw up in front of the North Station in Bost
took the train to Concord, in a beat-up, horse-draw
packed in an old, black, horsehair trunk labell
grandfather). None of them would have conceive
Central Station in New York in anything less than
chauffeur in livery, with a trunk of the latest m
one's own initials. Most of those boys seemed to c
Palm Beach and often both, though there were
places that displayed none of these characteristic
ened" me was that I had not run into the like of t
their extenuation, remember that this was the deca
of F. Scott Fitzgerald, just before the crash of 1929
in which the rich could afford—in many senses of
ostentatious.

Of course, many of the boys fitted into neither
of refined old families or coarse new ones, includ
the school on scholarships. Much to the credit of
who the scholarship boys were.

At St. Paul's I suffered a little mild hazing. A
both more motives and more incentives for ha
school, since the boys live together more closely a
was a natural target for hazing: very small, and th
somewhat "different" from other boys, and, wors
showed himself, when not under immediate atta
stuck on himself. Some of the hazing I received at t
nouveau riche crowd. Since I had never suffer
decided that on the average the members of the E
Brahmins, were greater, because "gentler," gentlem
cities. I say "on the average" because most of the b
fine fellows as one could meet anywhere. The
minority—and usually went to Yale.

My "broadening" had re-created in me, the
different way, my father's ambivalence towards tl
tolerate, even encourage, the wealthy, because I be
produces them and that they help produce. Tl
capitalism is some of the capitalists. But that is
system.

Besides "broadening," I have come to believe t
undisclosed purpose in sending me to a St. C

part
priv
at H
mis
wor
con
just
view
Som
muc
Por
fron
muc
Gro
give
spe
had
und
St.
late

T
Bro
of L
read
robl
grad
ign
my
real
cert
gra
con
I sh
har
Inst
Chi
dan

T
sim
tics
cou
tim

hand, we learned much more in the way of languages, both in their number and in the thoroughness of our knowledge of them. I know this by comparison with my son who followed me to S.P.S.

The reason we learned more was certainly not that our teachers had greater natural abilities than those of today. Even less was it that they knew better methods of teaching. If anything the modern methods of teaching languages are better than those of my time. What then made the difference? I had to face this question when I was associated briefly in the 1960s with an organization called Educational Services, Inc. in trying to improve the teaching of social science, especially history, in secondary schools. I concluded that the superiority of my teachers in my youth lay in nothing more than their conviction that, if they could teach a subject, it was their duty to do so, a conviction not yet undermined by the sentimentalities of the schools of education, whose graduates infuriated me with their slogan: "I don't teach English [or whatever]; I teach children." A body of teachers can teach, not children, but any number of languages *to* children, if only they possess the faith that they can and must do so. That is the only secret of good teaching.

Nor had our teachers yet been corrupted by the notion that high scholarship, when the excellent scholars must needs be few in number, was undemocratic or even elitist. Competition is a fact, though not the only fact, of social life in all societies, and youngsters should get used to living with it, to learn to win without guilt and lose without loss of self-respect.

In fact, though the system supported good scholarship, it did not unnerve the nonscholar with a conviction of hopeless inferiority. The reason was that scholarship made much less difference than it does today. It was important that graduates should be admitted to the Ivy League colleges, particularly Yale, Princeton, and Harvard, but largely for social reasons. Moreover, practically any damn fool could gain admission, so long as his parents could pay the fees, which was no problem for parents of S.P.S. boys. The result was that, though the inferior scholars did not learn much, the school put little pressure on them to learn more. They certainly were not stigmatized for their academic weaknesses. On the contrary, the body of the students and even some of the masters looked on academic ability somewhat askance. Real fame was acquired by athletic ability. At the time, being a good scholar but a lousy athlete, I was inclined to resent this fact of school life. I have since come to wonder whether I was wise to do so. Some people condemn what they call the overemphasis on athletics at schools. I am not sure it is so bad. In a good society everyone ought to enjoy sometime in his life at least one moment of glory. Most athletes will not achieve any further glory after their school days are over, so let not us scholars begrudge it them while they still have it; our time will come later. Of course, there are a few, terribly irritating, exceptions, who are both great athletes and great scholars. Their very existence leads one to lose faith in the justice of things.

I was a good scholar in all of my subjects, though happily never first (*primus*) or second (*secundus*) in my form, so I had no outstanding reputation to maintain. I even did perfectly well in mathematics and physics, though natural history had lost its charms for me. Instead my interests, both intra- and extracurricular became overwhelmingly literary, and fortunately so, for the only subject in which the teaching at St. Paul's was clearly superior to that at Browne and Nichols was English literature. It was mostly carried out by four remarkable men: Francis Beach ("Bitch") White, Gerald ("Jerry") Chittenden, Willard ("Chappy") Scudder, and John Richards. Besides being excellent teachers, each in his own way, they were also men of the world, again each in his own way.

All youngsters that have any taste for writing at all set up at some time, usually earlier than later, as poets. I did. Some seem to have naturally good taste in poetry. I did not. Though I had read much classic English poetry from Shakespeare through Swinburne before I went to St. Paul's, my taste in it was, like my mother's, pretty sentimental. Moreover, though the masters at St. Paul's were excellent in dealing with the English classics, they did not venture far into what had not yet become classic, that is, modern poetry and prose. Perhaps they did not consider it their job to teach the moderns. Of poets still alive they admitted Kipling to the canon—and let us not be snobbish: Kipling is sometimes a great poet. They also admitted Masefield, whom I do not now consider to be great but who captured me then as the poet of the sailing ships. On my own hook I discovered "The Ballad of the White Horse," by G. K. Chesterton, again a second-class poet who appealed to me for an extraneous reason, in this case my identification with the heroic age of the Germanic peoples. The poem is concerned with the struggle between King Alfred and the Danes.

The only great contemporary poets that our teachers asked us to read were Robert Frost and Edwin Arlington Robinson, and both were native New Englanders. Yet they did not ask us to read Emily Dickinson, not a contemporary poet, but still the quintessence of New England. It took my form-mate Brad Trafford to introduce me to Housman. Of Yeats I remember only that we read the feeble "Innisfree." We had heard of Pound but had not read him; we had not even heard of T. S. Eliot. Thus though I was living in an age of great poetry, my knowledge of it was scant and my taste often vulgar. I was only just beginning to free myself from the notion that the test of great poetry is whether it brings tears to one's eyes. Not until I reached Harvard did my knowledge of, and taste in, poetry begin to improve.

I published my first verse and prose in my first year at St. Paul's in the school magazine, called *Horae Scholasticae,* which combined local news with literary efforts. My verse, heavily modeled on Masefield, concerned the coasting schooners. At least I wrote on a subject I knew something about. Later I published both prose and verse on other subjects, but I became for my age something of a self-taught expert on sailing-shipping, which replaced my former interest in shells. What is more, the editors of the *Horae* accepted the very first manuscripts I submitted. Had they not, I do not know that I should have continued. My friend Fred Skinner insists that immediate reinforcement is the surest guarantee of a person's repeating an action. Immediate reinforcement I got, and I have remained a writer, though not always a "literary" writer, ever since. Always the great little competitor, the great little chaser after what the English would call "gongs," I tried for every academic-literary prize, and there were many. If I was never quite at the top in purely academic competition, I did quite well in the literary one, winding up as one of the two head editors of *Horae Scholasticae.*

What now interests me more are the social results of these, after all, pretty commonplace literary concerns. In my second-form year I had been a lonely little boy. As time went on I began to make friends, especially among those who shared my literary interests, and my later years at St. Paul's were quite enjoyable. I am certainly not going to boast of having suffered a blighted childhood or adolescence. In time too, the friends became mutual friends, and the other boys began to recognize us as a clique. They even gave us a name: we were the "fairies," and they exploited with delight every variation on this theme. They called us "fairies" because of our literary interests. I am not sure that most of the boys that bandied the word about had any clear idea what it connoted among adults. Indeed I never encountered any evidence at all in my time that S.P.S. boys practiced homosexuality. In this respect the school differed sharply from the English public schools on which it was supposed to be modeled. And none of my friends called "fairies" turned out to be homosexuals in later life. How innocent we were! We took our title simply as recognition that our interests were, because literary, disapproved, and we rather gloried in it.

The "fairies" were not distinguished by their literary interests alone. Some of the masters diagnosed us as suffering from an ill-defined, but virulent and possibly lethal, disease called "bad attitude." The "fairies" were highly articulate and fond of discussing, freely and in public, the institutions of the school, from the rector on down, with something less than becoming reverence. This was "bad attitude." My friend Budd Pollak, one of the few ethnic Jews in school—there was no prejudice against the admission of ethnic Jews as there would have been against religious ones—was deeply infected. He had founded and publicized the Radiator Athletic Club; no one qualified as a member who was discovered during the long, cold winter at Concord more than a few feet away from a radiator. Any joke of this sort was sacrilege in what was then the most famous school for ice-hockey in the United States. The bad-attitude boys were not rebels; they were loyal sons of old St. Paul's. But they loved to talk; they were witty; they thought it was fun to make fun of what the rest of the school held sacred. And it *was* fun, especially as none of our amiable schoolmates took physical reprisals against members of the Radiator Athletic Club.

Though certainly recognized as a "fairy," nobody ever accused me of "bad attitude." I should have dearly liked to have been, but I did not possess the first qualification: I was just not a witty enough talker. My father had warned me against trying to be funny. I had disregarded his warning but was still not funny enough. Others may charge that I was displaying early in life a tendency not to get too far on the wrong side of the Establishment. Yet there is more than one establishment, and I am now on the wrong side of the Eastern Establishment, which has become "liberal" and not, like me, conservative. Had he felt I had been infected with "bad attitude," the rector of the school would never have appointed me a member of the Student Council in my sixth-form year. My fellows would never have elected me.

St. Paul's School was a "snob" school. It was known to bestow social *cachet* on its scholars and itself to receive social *cachet* from the families of those who attended it. But it was far more than just a "snob" school, though it is a little difficult to weigh the imponderables that made it more. As I have said, among them was not, with some exceptions, the teaching it provided. The best I can do in retrospect is to say that we carried on, or thought we carried on, our affairs with a certain style, all the way from the rituals connected with our rowing, through our debating clubs, and the *Horae Scholasticae*. Even the rector. Dr. Samuel Smith Drury, had undoubted style, though it was not of a kind I particularly admired. He tried to be at ease with the boys, but only succeeded, at least in my case, in making me uneasy with him. He certainly had style as a preacher, and though there were plenty, even among his own staff, who criticized him, he was a great headmaster, and under him the school enjoyed high morale. I confess I do not understand how he did it. The school had not always enjoyed high morale before and was to suffer from low morale later. Above all, we were taught by men most of whom were both gentlemen and men of the world, so far as schoolmasters can ever be both. I know I have used the word *gentlemen* too often, but I still must insist that they helped us by their example to try to be gentlemen too. Aware that we had style, I think we tried in later life to act with style whether it was in business, or law, or in writing, or even on the polo field. To try to act with style is one motive towards achievement. Most of us were better, and certainly not just intellectually, for going to St. Paul's.

Part of our style, though few would admit it today, we owed to the fact that St. Paul's was a "church" school. Its leaders, though not all its masters, took seriously its purpose of inculcating in its scholars the ritual and doctrine of the Protestant Episcopal Church or, to call it by its original name, the Church of England. All students were required to attend services in the really beautiful neo-Gothic chapel, every morning before classes and twice on Sundays, for morning prayer and evensong. My parents did not send me to St. Paul's for religious reasons. Yet exposure to the Church of England did me good, in a very mixed way.

Let me state straightaway that I never remember a time when I even half-believed the doctrines of any Christian church, not one single doctrine over the whole range from the existence of God through the immortality of the soul and on to the Redemption. I never believed a word of doctrine even when very young and not yet exposed to the writings of skeptics; and I cannot explain why. I was sensible enough not to parade my agnosticism, nor to scoff at true believers. I came to feel that it was natural to believe, and that it was I who was the unnatural man. The doctrines of Christianity have provided me neither with a source of guilt nor a solace for pain. Nor have I ever undergone the emotional agonies of a loss of faith, for I never had any faith to lose. So little was I a believer that it never cost me a pang to recite in chapel either of the two forms of the Creed. The Creed did not make any difference to me intellectually, and I liked the language. If the reader condemns me as a hypocrite, he will discover that I was not a hypocrite in quite the way he doubtless thinks.

Perhaps I was not so unnatural in my unbelief as I thought I was. There may have been many agnostics, but if we all kept our mouths shut, we should, to use the sociologists' phrase, suffer from collective ignorance and never realize our numbers. "Sensible men," says Waldershare in Disraeli's novel *Endymion,* "are all of the same religion." And when he is asked, "And, pray, what is that?" he replies, "Sensible men never tell." Perhaps it is not sensible for me to reveal my agnosticism even now, in an age that has lost the force of "religious" religions only to compensate by abounding in "secular" ones. The will to believe, it seems, is a constant.

Besides attendance at chapel, the school also required us to attend regular academic classes called sacred studies. Some of these taught me a good deal of church history, which was interesting in itself and useful to me later. They also taught me apologetics, whose value is much more questionable. I regret to say that a few of my friends and I, in the discussions that took place in sacred studies, enjoyed much quiet fun at the expense, as we thought, of the parsons who laid before us the various proofs of the existence of God, such as Paley's Watch. We enjoyed a double advantage over the parsons. On the average we were more intelligent than they; and there is no proof of the existence of God: the best is *credo quia absurdum*. Quiet our fun had to be; the authorities would at once have taken in hand any really ranting, public atheist. These exercises in attacking and defending a doctrine had a carryover for me in a skeptical stance towards all religious doctrines, including the doctrines of a religion much less valuable to mankind than Christianity, namely, Marxism in all its many sects. Scientific doctrine is something else, but neither Christianity nor Marxism falls into that class.

An agnostic in doctrine, I still was not a wholly lost soul. I came later to make a sharp distinction, which was inchoate in my thinking before I left St. Paul's, between the doctrines of Christianity, on the one hand, and, on the other, its rituals and what we should now call its values. Whatever I thought of the doctrines and of the oceans of blood that had been shed over them, I held that the values of Christianity, charity and humility foremost among them, were good for me and mankind. I was beginning to make the distinction the great sociologist Pareto was to make between what he called the *residues* of men and the *derivations* by which men rationalized them. At the extremes the values of Christianity come into conflict with one another, as all values must, but when not driven to extremes they at once helped people to live together and were the product of that life. This was not true of the values of Marxism, which seemed to me in practice, if not in theory, to support envy, hatred, malice, and all uncharitableness. I was a Christian in that I heartily accepted the values of Christianity, even though, like all sinners, I did not live up to them.

Like the Unitarian King's Chapel in Boston, the Church of England possessed the special advantage, which it is now eagerly throwing away, that its values—and of course its doctrines too—were expressed in some of the most beautiful English ever written, that is, in the King James version of the Bible and in the Book of Common Prayer, formed by Bishop Cranmer. The values of Christianity and the glory of the English language came together for me in the chapel service, and I forgot about the doctrines.

Indeed I committed myself to the Church of England by going through the sacrament of confirmation and becoming a communicant. In my cynical moments I argue that St. Paul's bribed me to do so. A communicant might partake of Holy Communion before breakfast on Sunday and then be exempted from attending morning prayer, which was longer than Communion and often duller, because it included a sermon. But if I was bribed, I was ready to be bribed. No doubt at confirmation I assented to a lot of doctrine that I did not believe a word of. I was a hypocrite but I belonged to a true church.

In the end I came to think a little differently even about doctrine. It was not that I came to believe literally in the existence of God and in a life after death but rather to understand that these and other doctrines are projections of the deepest hopes and fears of mankind. Thus the doctrine of the Redemption, though a myth, is a magnificent one. The words of the atheist Robert Ingersoll, "An honest God's the noblest work of man," are not silly. I began also to understand that the absence of a firm doctrine justifying them might help weaken the values themselves. True, values have a way of growing new justifications when the old ones wither. Yet it is well to keep doctrine as unchanging as possible, if religion is to provide mankind with the emotional security it needs so badly. Unitarianism had undertaken to abandon not only an unchanging doctrine but any doctrine at all, and as a result was sinking into a swamp of drooling sentimentality about social justice. Christ came into the world to save sinners, not society. Today the Episcopal Church seems to be going the same way, and the disease may even have infected the Church of Rome. A sentimental church is a dead one.

Here am I, an unbeliever, who nevertheless believes that religious belief is natural and necessary to human social life. I have never resolved this contradiction, if it be one, and there are even times when I am skeptical about this last belief itself. Writers like Dostoevsky claim that, without a belief in God, a man can find no meaning in life and morality. I am not so sure that a man who enjoys a good digestion needs to have a God too. But then he will not keep his good digestion forever.

NOTES

1. *Holmes-Pollock Letters: The Correspondence of Mr. Justice Holmes and Sir Frederick Pollock,* ed. Mark A. DeWolfe Howe, 2d ed., two vols. in one (Cambridge: Harvard University Press, Belknap Press, 1961), 2:178.
2. George W. Cox and Eustace H. Jones, *Popular Romances of the Middle Ages,* 2d ed. (London: Kegan Paul, 1880).
3. Henry W. Longfellow, "The Saga of King Olaf," in *Tales of a Wayside Inn* (many editions).
4. Henry Adams, *The Education of Henry Adams: An Autobiography* (Boston: Massachusetts Historical Society, 1918), p. 230.

5

HARVARD COLLEGE

In September 1928 I entered the freshman class at Harvard College, as all my Homans ancestors had been doing since 1768 and all my Adams ones from earlier still. It had not been obvious from the first that I should do so. My father felt it his duty to keep the question what career I should embark on steadily before my mind. It was my decision, not his. He was prepared to support what I had decided, so long as it was not outrageous, but he would not let me escape the issue. My mother was more inclined to believe that it made little difference what I did, so long, of course, as I did something: there was never any question of my living in idleness. She once asked me, "Why don't you go into the Church, George? You would be sure to become a bishop." (By "the church," she meant the Episcopal Church.) Her faith in my lack of scruples was touching. Moreover, though none of my kinswomen had ever gone to college, my parents insisted that both my sisters should do so, in order that they could support themselves in white-collar jobs in case they never married, which Father assumed they would not.

In early adolescence my romantic view of seafaring led to my deciding to become a naval officer by graduating from the Naval Academy at Annapolis. My father duly got his friend, classmate, and our congressman, George Holden Tinkham, to promise me an appointment. But towards the end of my years at St. Paul's I confessed, first to myself and then to my father, that my naval ambitions had evaporated and literary ones taken their place. If that eliminated Annapolis, the only alternative was Harvard. Pa was prepared to "broaden" me by sending me to a non-Bostonian boarding school, but "broadening" did not extend to a non-Bostonian college of liberal arts. Then tradition must take over. Eventually I became a naval officer by a different route.

While an undergraduate I studied no sociology. It never so much as occurred to me, although President Lowell had brought Professor Pitirim Sorokin to Harvard to found the Sociology Department in the very year I entered as a freshman. Yet if I learned no theoretical, I learned much practical sociology. One of the routes by which a person gets interested in this subject is by living in an environment in which people are highly conscious of social relations. This rule holds good more often of micro-sociologists like me, who are concerned with the face-to-face interactions of persons, than of macrosociologists, concerned with the characteristics of whole societies. For us microsociologists the laws of sociology are the laws of snobbery, and an undergraduate of my background found Harvard to a high degree "socially conscious"—in the bad sense of the phrase.

For students like me—there were plenty of others who took no part and could not care less—the guts of the Harvard social system were the so-called final clubs, which one might be invited to join no earlier than one's sophomore year.[1] As I have said, they were "final" in the sense that, unlike other clubs, once a man had joined one of them, he might not join another. Though it is now difficult to believe, there were also "waiting" clubs, which one might join while waiting, sometimes in vain, for election to a final club. Some "waiting" clubs managed to turn themselves into "final" ones and make it stick.

The final clubs were not fraternities in the pattern common in American universities. That is, their clubhouses provided no sleeping quarters but only meals, drinks, and other amenities. Some of them had indeed begun as fraternities but, as a result of troubles the nature of which I have forgotten, the Harvard authorities abolished fraternities as such. They promptly reestablished themselves as clubs, their new names thinly disguising their fraternal origins. Unlike the secret societies at Yale, the final clubs were not dedicated to esoteric good works and uplifting exercises. They were purely social. The system, as a system, had become fully elaborated by the beginning of the present century but flourished only until the Great Depression. It is still in existence today, though in a weaker and more utilitarian form. It has lost its mystique.

In my time there were, I think, nine clubs that undergraduates in my position recognized as final. There may well have been others at the bottom of the heap, but we were hardly aware of them; the socially conscious tend to look upward. As in a caste system, when one had once become a member of a final club, one always remained a member. The clubs were ranked, with the Porcellian, my father's and also the oldest, at the top, followed by the A.D. (once the Alpha Delta Phi fraternity). When I say they were ranked, I mean that those who belonged agreed that a ranking existed, without necessarily agreeing that it was fair. One might sincerely believe that one's own club was the best, while recognizing as a social fact that an ill-informed and corrupt undergraduate body placed it only fifth in the pecking order. Again, as in a caste system, there was a greater consensus about the ranking of clubs at the top and the bottom than about those in the middle. A club could change its place in the ranking only by collective action, as by declaring itself a final, not a waiting, club. The system presented an excruciating dilemma to those seeking entrance into it: "Shall I accept an invitation to join Club Y now, when it is possible, though not certain, that I shall be invited to join Club X, of higher rank, later? And think of my despair if I turn down Y, wait for X, the invitation from X never materializes, and I join no club at all? What will life have to offer me then?"

As my father recognized and was indeed obvious, the persons who became members of final clubs were apt to be "preppies" and especially preppies from one of the St. Grottlesex group of schools. They were also apt—the criteria overlapped—to have come from "old" families, particularly "old" families from the eastern seaboard. They were also apt to come from wealthy families, whether the wealth was new or old.

Meeting these criteria was not sufficient for election. Clubs elected some undergraduates who met none of them and failed to elect others who met all. To give the system its due, a club usually elected a man because its members found him attractive, perhaps not as attractive as others who had joined clubs of higher rank, but still attractive. To be sure, why some persons found certain others attractive remained, and still remains, a profound mystery. A background of money could help one acquire the style of life that helped to make one attractive, but money did not do its work directly, nor was much money required. A man could also be attractive for reasons politically internal to the system. Like castes, clubs were always jockeying for status, and if one could induce to join one's club a man whom a club of higher rank was known to be after, one had brought off a great coup.

Only a few criteria were positive bars to election. In my time—not now—no blacks were members of final clubs. But then no blacks attended prep schools or came from "old" families with money. Nor until my time were Jews accepted, though there were plenty of Jews who attended prep schools, came from old families, and possessed plenty of money. But it was already clear that the latter ban was on the way out. My Jewish roommate, Budd Pollak, was elected to my own final club. The ban against certain ethnic groups, such as the Catholic Irish, had broken down even earlier. John Fitzgerald Kennedy, later president of the United States, was also elected to my final club. Indeed there was no prohibition on grounds of religion alone. The former Irish and Jewish taboos were social, not religious.

In the fall term of one's sophomore year, the clubs gave a number of cocktail, punch, and dinner parties, usually not at the clubhouses themselves. To these parties, the members of a club would invite those undergraduates whom they had decided they would like to induce to be members, or at least to consider, and whom they thought they had some chance of persuading. They also invited a few sophomores about whose social charms they were doubtful but who were "legacies," that is, men whose fathers or brothers had been members. The "brothers immediate" always carried out the actual elections, but graduate members, though no longer "brothers immediate," were apt to ask embarrassing questions if certain legacies were not even considered. These parties were among the most alcoholic one ever attended, partly because Prohibition was in effect, and it was one's patriotic duty to "strike a blow for freedom," partly because one was, as a sophomore, far less inured to hard drinking than one was to become later, and partly because, knowing one was being "looked over," one was under tension and sought surcease from it in alcohol.

I was most definitely a Porcellian legacy and invited for a time to its parties. Naturally my father felt he ought not to do anything to urge my election. His place was taken by his law partner, Robert Shaw Barlow ("Ba"), who was later to become my closest friend of the older generation. Ba had "waited" for the P.C. for all of his undergraduate life and had only been elected at the last possible moment, the spring of his senior year. Clearly he considered his "waiting" as time well spent and remained always fiercely loyal to the P.C. He was indefatigable in dining and wining me in the company of influential members of the club. But it just did not work. Later the story got back to me that one of the members had said: "How can I vote for someone who insults me every time he meets me?" I can well believe I did just that—not that I intended it, but being shy, ill at ease, and somewhat drunk, the pressure I felt to say something, anything, led me to let fly with what could be taken as insults.

The syndrome has often been described. I have never found it easy to make small talk, the precious petty cash of social intercourse. Still worse, whenever people have brought up topics I thought I knew something about—and such topics have been many—I have never hesitated to correct their mistakes promptly and decisively, a trait not calculated to endear me to my interlocutors. Some of my Homans aunts and uncles wondered whether the word "intemperate" both in speech and writing should not be applied to me. My uncle Bill Homans conceded that when I was intemperate, I was usually in the right intellectually; but that only made my intemperance still less endearing. Before I left St. Paul's I was well aware that I was not generally popular. I accepted the judgment as right and fair. I never rebelled against it, but neither did it unnerve me, and I made no sustained effort to reform. I was not a social pariah; it was just that I was not to everyone's taste. Unfortunately the "everyone" in question was just the kind of person who was apt to be a member of the P.C.

Being "looked over" by the P.C. did not lack its moments of delightful bathos. Ba was a highly realistic, even cynical, man, yet even he once managed to state with conviction: "George, if you do not join the P.C. you will never meet an attractive woman!" Of course when he produced this masterpiece he was trying to persuade me to "wait" for the P.C. as he had done himself. But when I decided not to wait, he did not hold it against me; in the later years our relationship became closer than ever. Then there was one eccentric and ignorant socialite and sportswoman, a cousin of mine, who, hearing the name Hitler for the first time, exclaimed, "Who's Hitler? Is he the man they've just taken into the P. C.?"

For the reasons given, the P. C. did not elect me to membership during my sophomore year. Both my father and Ba thought I ought to wait. Even if I were not elected until the eve of commencement in my senior year, I should still have gained one of life's great prizes. I was more skeptical about my ultimate election than they were. I judged that the "brothers immediate" would vote for me only because they admired my father, and I foolishly wanted to be loved for myself alone. Moreover, I did not propose, in exchange for the frail hope of finally being elected to the P.C., to forgo for the duration of my college years the fun of being a member of some club. So I decided not to wait. Of course I might have to wait willy-nilly, unless some other club was willing to take me, and that was far from certain.

In fact I was turned down by one other final club. Then in my junior year the Spee Club (*ex* Zeta Psi) invited me to join and I accepted. When I broke the news to my father, he was obviously disappointed but never, good man that he was, upbraided me. I do not think my mother cared much, one way or the other. The Spee stood somewhere in the middle of the ranking of final clubs. It was a bit of an upstart and a bit on the "liberal" side in its standards for membership. When Father and Ba were undergraduates, it had not yet set itself up as a final club, and both had been members. I cannot say that our activities at the Spee were elevating: drink, cards, and gossip were our staples. But its members included some very good and intelligent fellows and old friends of mine. I thoroughly enjoyed myself and never regretted not waiting for the P.C.

The best club of all, in my opinion, was the Signet Society. Though it had its own clubhouse, it was otherwise outside the club system. It might elect men who already belonged to final clubs as well as those who belonged to none. Its members were supposed to be undergraduates who had pretensions to intellectual or artistic distinction: editors of college publications, especially of the daily newspaper, the *Crimson,* persons of note in the fields of music, the fine arts, or drama, scholars of parts, and men who liked to talk on intellectual subjects, even if they had achieved nothing in them. I was elected as a would-be poet and an editor of the literary magazine, the *Advocate*.

The Signet was not large but included undergraduates and graduates from all the social strata of the college without discrimination, at least not social discrimination. Perhaps it included proportionately more of the middle stratum than of the others, men, that is, who were not members of final clubs but who had attended good prep schools or the equivalent. We certainly tried hard to attract "black men" of distinction. ("Black" was a class and not a racial term.) The chief feature of life at the Signet was its daily luncheon, where the members made and met more lively arguments on a greater variety of subjects than at any other place at Harvard. There, more than in the classrooms, we had to sharpen our wits, or at least our verbal skills. There, for instance, I was driven to fury by the intellectual arrogance of Lincoln Kirstein, later the great patron of American ballet. My fury became doubly furious when I discovered that his arrogance was usually justified by his real expertise. Unwittingly he taught me much about modernism in the arts. At the Signet I also encountered the "liberal" views of the bright young lawyers who were soon to leave for Washington to form the junior staff of the New Deal. It is a group that has increased in power steadily ever since.

To turn to another area of social organization, my undergraduate years were a period of transition in housing and its concomitants at Harvard. When I entered, freshmen roomed in the freshman dormitories built since about 1910 in Georgian style down by the Charles River, whose banks were only then ceasing to be wild salt marsh. If they wished, seniors roomed in the Yard, the original center of the college. These housing arrangements gave members, at least of the youngest and oldest classes, some sense of unity.

For the two intermediate classes Harvard made no systematic efforts to provide housing. Some undergraduates, including my three roommates, rented flats in one of the "Gold Coast" dormitories along Mount Auburn Street. They were so called because private real-estate speculators had originally built them around the turn of the century to cater to the tastes of wealthy undergraduates. Harvard University had gradually bought them up, but continued to operate them as if it too were simply a real-estate agent. For instance, it provided no common dining rooms as it did in the freshman dormitories. Other undergraduates banded together in groups, each group renting one of the squalid, wooden, and privately owned "rat houses" that studded the area between Massachusetts Avenue and the river. Still others picked up rooms in Cambridge where they

could, as their predecessors had done for a century; or, if they were poor
and came from Greater Boston, lived at home and commuted to Harvard.
This social chaos provided one weak justification for the clubs, which
served meals. But undergraduates who were not members of clubs or
other extracurricular organizations could simply sink without a trace,
isolated from Harvard and their classmates except for the weak link of
attendance at lectures.

On top of his ending President Eliot's wide-open "elective system,"
which had allowed a student to take any courses he pleased, President
Lowell had long been determined for both educational and social reasons
to put an end to this unhealthy situation in housing. While I was in
college, Edward Harkness, immensely wealthy because his father had
been a partner of John D. Rockefeller the first, gave Lowell a huge sum of
money to put into effect the so-called House Plan, modeled in part on the
colleges of Oxford and Cambridge but not identical with them, if only
because the English colleges, but not the houses, were semi-independent
corporations administering their own endowments.

Under the plan, seven houses were originally set up, consisting
physically in part of wholly new construction and in part of adaptations
of the existing freshman and Gold Coast dormitories. Until they became
and remained overcrowded after World War II, the houses provided
students with a fairly opulent standard of living. According to one theory,
President Lowell wanted every undergraduate to learn to live like a
gentleman. Then after he graduated he would try to earn the money that
would let him continue to live in the manner to which he had become
accustomed and would eventually give some of his winnings to Harvard
to help swell its endowment. According to this theory, living like a
gentleman included enjoying an open fire in winter, and therefore all the
suites in the first houses were provided at vast expense with fireplaces
and chimneys. Though the university could not reproduce them now
without going bankrupt, the cost was relatively not so great then. The
Great Depression was beginning, and in those days prices, including the
costs of construction, actually went down in a depression, just as classical
economics said they should. They went down, so to speak, for the last
time.

Each house was now occupied by members of the three upper classes.
Every upperclassman, except for certified commuters, was required to
live in a house. The freshmen were transferred to the Yard. Each house
was provided with a common room and dining hall, and all members
were required to take, or at least pay for, a certain number of meals there
every week. This requirement helped undermine the clubs, which had
provided three meals a day for their members. I suspect that President

Lowell was not unhappy with this result. In those days our meals in a house dining hall were served by waitresses, and our rooms cleaned and our beds made not by ourselves but by cleaning women referred to in Harvard tradition as "goodies," like Goodie Two-Shoes in the nursery story. By the end of World War II these amenities had disappeared forever. Let no one say that the standard of living of the upper class has not gone down since my youth, and in no respect more markedly than in the ability to afford domestic service.

Every house had its master's lodge, where lived a resident master and his wife. Suites in the house were provided for resident tutors and offices for nonresident ones. Mr. Lowell believed that, as in Oxford and Cambridge, a tutor attached to a student's own house should supervise the assigned reading and written papers necessary to prepare him for the general examinations in his field of concentration. (More later on these institutions.) Every house possessed a small library to hold the books required for tutorial reading. Students would also have the privilege of taking meals with tutors, if they so wished. Few did. According to the theory of the House Plan, the new potential for social ties both among undergraduates and between undergraduates and the teaching staff would help support their intellectual ties and put an end to the current social chaos. The houses would become communities to which all members of Harvard society would naturally belong. Harvard had not been a community of this sort for a century.

In my senior year I joined one of the houses, indeed the one to which, though now a nonresident, I still belong. The house was Kirkland, named after a distinguished president of Harvard in the early part of the nineteenth century. Physically it combined a former freshman dormitory, an eighteenth-century wooden building that served as a library, a new master's lodge, and a new annex for additional students' suites. I joined Kirkland in what I now consider to be a mildly corrupt manner, though I was then quite ready to corrupt or be corrupted or both.

Kirkland was one of the last of the original group of houses to be completed. The newly appointed master, Professor Edward A. Whitney, was afraid, perhaps unduly afraid, that the house would not attract enough students, or perhaps not enough of the kind he preferred. Students were much freer than they are now to choose which houses they wanted to live in, and masters freer to choose students. I had taken an excellent course on English intellectual history with Professor Whitney, knew him a little, and liked both Mrs. Whitney and him very much. At the same time my three roommates and I were about to be thrown out of our suite in Westmorly Hall in the Gold Coast; Westmorly was to be remodeled to become part of Adams House. We had other friends who would have to join houses. We were all members of clubs, though not of the most distinguished ones, and we were not particularly "fast" or debauched. Whitney may have thought that if he could attract us to Kirkland House, we might in turn attract other suitable undergraduates. Today such a notion would be greeted with derision. I do not know which of us, Professor Whitney or I as spokesman for our group of eight, first approached the other, but we did get together and made a deal. I undertook to deliver our group to Kirkland, provided that Professor Whitney would assign us a group of contiguous suites in the new part of the house, the annex. I speak of this deal as mildly corrupt, for I suspect that the Harvard administration would have frowned on such bargaining, had it known of it, and it certainly would violate the present regulations. We much enjoyed ourselves for one year, our senior year, in Kirkland, working with Professor and Mrs. Whitney and doing, I believe, more than our share in getting the house off to a good start.

In my articles in *The Harvard Graduates' Magazine,* of which I shall speak later, I had poked a little mild fun, with a studied affectation of world-weary superciliousness, at the developing House Plan. I believe I should have taken that stance towards any new institution. Such a thing filled me then and fills me still with anxiety, which all too often has turned out to be warranted. In the case of the houses my fears were groundless. True, they have not fulfilled all the hopes, social or intellectual, that President Lowell entertained for them. The reason has been partly that inflation since World War II has not allowed all the facilities originally planned for the houses to be maintained. They have become overcrowded, and the amount and quality of tutorial supervision provided has declined. Yet as human institutions go, I think the houses have succeeded pretty well, not only in doing some good but, what is rarer, in doing the kind of good they were meant to do. Harvard today would be a far worse place if we abandoned them and returned to something like the old regime.[2] Lowell, with Eliot but in a very different way, was one of the two great modern presidents of Harvard.

In surveying Harvard society, I have made no mention of girls, though I certainly lacked no interest in them. To avoid being classed as sexist I must call them women now. Harvard College was still exclusively masculine. To be sure, Radcliffe College for women had been in existence for some time, and Harvard professors lectured to its students. But its classes were separate from those of Harvard. Even I, in the early years of my associate professorship after World War II, gave a lecture one hour to a Harvard audience and then walked across the Cambridge Common to Radcliffe to give the same lecture to its undergraduates; a silly arrangement, except that the second lecture was usually better than the first.

While I was an undergraduate, no Harvard undergraduate, at least no one in my group, ever admitted to knowing a Radcliffe girl. If we knew none, why did we make stupid jokes about how unattractive they were? For myself it was a fact that I never dated a Radcliffe girl. This situation changed when women like my sisters began to attend Radcliffe, and today, of course, the two institutions are socially and educationally one.

For girls, men of the club type looked to Boston society. In our freshman year we attended the Friday evening dances, but these were little more than extensions of the dancing schools I had been taken to since I was a boy. From our sophomore year onward we were regularly invited to debutante balls, where girls were supposed to be presented to "society," and often invited to dinners before them. The debutante system was then at its height, not only the balls themselves but all their attendant institutions, such as the stag line, "cutting in," and ushers' dinners. To be invited by a girl to serve as usher at her "coming out" party was to score a bull's eye. It seems to me that in my sophomore year I went out to a party nearly every evening until Christmas. Bear in mind that I, like the rest of us, was clad in a boiled shirt and collar, white bow tie, and a tailcoat. Outdoors I wore a bowler hat and a black overcoat with a velvet collar, called a chesterfield. If one were taking a girl to a dance, one was bound to send her a corsage, orchid or gardenia, and take her out to supper in the intermission of the dance. Taking a popular girl out to supper often gave one the only chance one was likely to have to talk with her for more than a minute, and again one scored a bull's eye. After Christmas the number of parties petered out; and after sophomore year, sated and sophisticated, one attended fewer big parties and more smaller, intimate ones, especially if one had established a close tie with one particular girl, now a postdebutante.

For the very popular girls, the belles of the ball, "coming out" was a heady experience. Think of being cut in on by a different man every few steps of a dance! It was so heady that many of them never got over it. For many other girls it was a cruel system, not just because it was competitive, for many social systems are, and must be, but because it was so visibly competitive. Think of sitting on a chair beside the dance floor for an hour without a man's coming up to ask one to dance! In these circumstances a girl usually sought refuge in the ladies' room. And think of getting, as the phrase went, "stuck" with someone! The code required that if a man were dancing with a girl, he must continue to do so until some other man cut in. But if any other saw you were "stuck," he was less likely to cut in. Think of a man's horror at finding himself with no one to relieve him of this female albatross hanging around his neck, the exchange of conversation getting shorter and shorter, more and more self-conscious and forced. If one went to dances with one's sister, one was responsible for her, and my two sisters, though spirited and intelligent, were not belles. I once made a deal with a friend of mine: "I'll dance with your sister, if you'll dance with mine." Those of us who survived the system will always be a bit "hard" socially.

The system was competitive for men as well. The most attractive girls discovered with uncanny speed what one's social standing at Harvard was. (The other universities in the Boston area did not count.) If one cut in on one of them, she could, if she wished, make it clear that one's assiduity was unwelcome unless one were a member of, say, the Porcellian or A.D. club. Her real reason may well have been that one was not in fact attractive, which one was certainly not going to accept. Instead one would, in this as in greater matters, blame the "system" not oneself. The result was a sorting-out process, which ended in men of a given social status in this miniature society dancing and dating with girls of a status roughly equal with their own. Someone referred to this process as the strategy of finding an "attractive pill." Since a "pill" was by strict definition an unattractive girl, the expression may seem self-contradictory. But the true meaning was different, and the strategy made perfectly good sense. If one were of middle to low status, it was a waste of time pursuing the belles. Look instead for other girls whom, on closer acquaintance, one would find to possess less spectacular, but nonetheless real, graces of body, mind, and spirit. There were plenty of "attractive pills" to be found, and, unlike the really popular girls, they would be grateful for one's attention. They even took the curse out of being "stuck."

This other social life of Boston and its more fashionable suburbs formed the background of our masculine social life at Cambridge. I have acknowledged that it was a cruel system. It was often also a coarse one, made so by the fact that Prohibition was in effect and challenged many to exhibit the most visible and vulgar effects of drunkenness. Today the young, with some help from the economy, have gotten rid of the system, and it is probably good that they have done so. Yet the young have never lost their native skill for being cruel to one another, and they can be just as cruel in a commune as in a cotillion. Still, I am glad to have taken part in the system. Even if it put one in one's place, at least the place was there. It had a structure. It often displayed a visual and musical elegance that has been killed by jeans and rock. I am glad to have known the last of self-confident high society. Its Homer, the chronicler of its splendors and miseries, is F. Scott Fitzgerald.

The academic side of Harvard cannot easily be disengaged from the social. My great-uncle Henry Adams (like my Homans grandfather a member of the class of 1858) claimed in his *Education* that Harvard offered him no education and precious little else. But then no other experience ever educated him either. He blamed Harvard, for instance, for not having introduced him to *Capital*, which was unfair since Marx's and Engels's great book had not been published at the time he graduated.[3] Still, in the main he must have been correct. The university was a provincial New England college, and the intellectual fare it offered was sparse and dry. By the time I entered, it was my own fault if I did not get an education, for since 1869 President Eliot had turned Harvard into one of the world's great universities, which had much to offer if I both could and would find it.

By and large I did not. While my interest in the Navy had weakened, it was far from dead. My uncle Charlie was secretary of the Navy under the Hoover administration, which coincided with my undergraduate years. I enrolled in the Naval Reserve Officers' Training Course (NROTC), which thereafter filled one of the four courses I was required to take every term at Harvard. I got nothing of intellectual or practical value out of naval science, as it was called, except a command of celestial navigation. Even that was wasted, because by the time I was called to active duty in 1941, the methods of making the calculations had been changed, and though they were simplified, I still had to learn navigation all over again. On the other hand, naval science demanded little work, which left me with extra time for other pursuits. Upon my graduation in 1932 I was commissioned an ensign in the Naval Reserve.

My father, of the class of 1894, attended Harvard under the regime of President Eliot, who had introduced the "elective system." That left an undergraduate free to take any course in the catalogue he pleased, from Shakespeare to sanitary engineering. It had unshackled the students from the old required recitations. But like many good things it began in time to display the defects of its virtues. Free to choose any course, a student could create utter intellectual anarchy for himself. In reaction to the anarchy, A. Lawrence Lowell, Eliot's successor and president in my time, had introduced a still newer system, which in many variations is now standard in most American universities. A student was required to take a certain number of courses and pass a general examination in a single academic field, called his "field of concentration" at Harvard, his "major" elsewhere. A tutor was to guide him in his preparation for his general examination. The student then had to take a certain number of courses outside his field of concentration, distributed over certain broad academic areas: the natural sciences, the social sciences, and the humanities. This was the system of "concentration and distribution," designed to make a student a solid scholar in one main field, while still exposing him to the range of knowledge outside it.

To meet my distribution requirement in natural science I took a course in elementary astronomy, because I thought it would help me with celestial navigation. It was of no use for that purpose, but it did help me acquire a good intuitive understanding of Newtonian mechanics as applied to the solar system. I say "intuitive" because the course did not require, nor did I then possess, the training in the calculus that would have enabled me to use Newtonian mechanics rigorously. By the same token, though we knew that Einstein's theories of relativity existed, our professors made no effort to teach us anything about them. They presented the course to some extent as a history of astronomy. We learned what Ptolemy, Copernicus, Tycho Brahe, Galileo, and Kepler had done to lead up to the Newtonian climax. This course really did help educate me. It stood me in good stead, as a paradigm of scientific development and explanation, when much later I became interested in the philosophy of science as applied to sociology. Yet it is not a paradigm that social science shows many signs of adopting.

On the advice of my tutor, Benny DeVoto, I took a course on American social and economic history offered by Professor Arthur M. Schlesinger, Senior. Admirable as a man, Schlesinger was a dull lecturer. But his subject matter was far from dull. He jumped from the cotton gin and the introduction of textile mills into New England, to the development of machines with interchangeable parts, which made mass production possible, to the invention and effects of the McCormick reaper, and even the history of the two-pant suit, once a flourishing artifact of American culture, but now extinct. With all its lack of system, the course put before me a kind of history that was obviously important but to which no teacher of mine had given more than cursory attention before. It was a kind that, in the English medieval rather than the modern American field, I was later to practice myself. Social and economic history as a serious intellectual discipline had then hardly been invented, and Schlesinger was one of its inventors. This course, too, helped educate me.

The next one I mention was a curious failure. It was a course in philosophy with Alfred North Whitehead, who had come to Harvard from England rather late in life and who, unlike most professors, had been taken up by the socio-intellectual circle in Boston—very social, not really very intellectual—on whose fringes I was sometimes to be found. The circle treated Whitehead as a sage and expected him to be oracular. He did not always manage to resist the temptation.[4]

I remember Whitehead well: his chubby face, his turned-down hard collar with an Ascot tie, his hair curling over the back of his neck. But my memory of his course is dim. My clearest and quite bizarre impression is that of receiving a very good grade while not understanding a single word of what Whitehead, in his rather fluty voice, uttered. Later, when he was a Senior, and I a Junior, Fellow of the Harvard Society of Fellows, I had many talks with Whitehead and came to like him very much. Yet he never ceased to puzzle me. Within him were two different personalities, and there was no telling when one was going to turn into the other. One was a shrewd, penetrating, tough—but also high-minded—English man of affairs, who might have become a great merchant banker in the City of London, if he had not turned to mathematics and philosophy instead. The other personality was a kind of neo-Platonic mystic. I could feel at home with and benefit from the former but not the latter. Whitehead almost succeeded in killing in me any interest in his great love, Plato. Plato rigs his dialogues so that Socrates's opponents concede Socrates's position just when they ought to argue against it most fiercely.

I read most of Whitehead's books, some, like *Science and the Modern World*,[5] to my great profit. It was almost required reading among Harvard intellectuals in my time. But sometimes I was disconcerted to find him shifting from one of his personalities to the other right in the middle of a book. Thus the first part of *Adventures of Ideas* seems to me lucid and penetrating, when all of a sudden it slips into a language that seems superficially the same but whose meaning I simply cannot grasp. I cannot conceive how the same person could have written both parts. As for *Process and Reality*, it is beyond me that anyone can pretend to have penetrated it at all. Yet there are those like Professor Dorothy Emmet, a friend of mine whose sincerity I trust, who claim they have.

So much for my "distribution." Following my dominant interest, which had emerged at St. Paul's, I "concentrated" in English and American literature. This was probably a mistake, even though the Harvard English Department was then in its glory. I enjoyed the vast amount of reading required of me, and I have continued to enjoy it in later life. An education that helps give pleasure is not to be condemned. Yet I had read much of the literature already and I should have continued to read more without help from the English Department. For sheer utility in education I should have done better to have concentrated in mathematics, a natural science, history, or even a new language such as Greek.

But all was not lost. As a candidate for honors, the English Department required me to learn Old English, which again sounded the note of my identification with the heroic age of the Germanic peoples and stood me in good stead later when I became an historian of medieval England. And after Professor Kittredge had spent a whole year with us going over line by line just four of Shakespeare's plays, we understood, as well as we were ever going to do, just what Shakespeare meant by what he said. Once Kittredge had taught us that, he wisely left it to us to "appreciate"

Shakespeare as literature. Much the same was true of Fritz Robinson's course on Chaucer. Yet these courses, while providing much information, suggested few general ideas.

One course in my field of concentration did make a big difference, because it finally brought me into full contact with modernism in literature. This was a course on contemporary English, not American, literature given in the spring term of my junior year by Ivor Richards, then a visiting professor from the "other" Cambridge and later a regular professor at Harvard. Richards was a superb lecturer, especially in the detailed scrutiny of a text. In poetry, besides Housman, with whom I was already familiar but whom Richards helped me to understand more deeply, he led me to the poetry of Yeats, Eliot, Hardy, Bridges, Hopkins, de la Mare, and D. H. Lawrence. Of these I had read only the few and conventional poems that had appeared in the contemporary version of *The Oxford Book of English Verse,*[6] and some of them had not figured in it at all. Except for Hardy and Lawrence, all of these poets remain favorites of mine, especially the later Yeats, who with Eliot and, in the United States, Frost, formed the nucleus of what was the last great era of English poetry up to the present.

Richards was not the only man who brought Eliot to my attention. My older friend Charlie Curtis introduced me to *The Wasteland,*[7] and I myself reviewed *Ash Wednesday* for the *Harvard Advocate.*[8] Eliot puzzled me, as of course he did many others. I had never met poetry of this sort before. But I recognized at once the beauty of individual passages and finally the greatness of the whole. I felt quite differently about Eliot's pontifical essays and about Eliot the man. When he came to Harvard as Norton Visiting Professor, I took advantage of his inviting students to tea and found I could not talk to him at all. In this respect, Frost put me much more at my ease.

Richards did not deal with Ezra Pound, perhaps considering him an American and thus not within the scope of his course. But having acquired a taste for modern poetry I now read him. He too was great, but in a highly flawed way. I admired his translations—if they really were translations—which led me to read and indeed translate some of the Provençal originals. But, unlike Milton, Pound could not maintain the architecture of a long poem. A few rare passages of surpassing beauty apart, the *Cantos* are a swamp and a bore. The two other main modernists poets of my time, William Carlos Williams and Wallace Stevens, seem to me thoroughly secondary.

In dealing with prose, Richards was perhaps less successful, but not by much. I did not read *Ulysses* under his influence, for all of us who visited France at that time felt challenged to smuggle back through American customs—not that that presented the smallest difficulty—the old original blue paperback copy of that book, in those innocent days banned as obscene. Though with the help of a guidebook I studied *Ulysses* closely, I now find it, again a few passages apart, a largely unreadable *tour de force,* and I cannot read *Finnegan's Wake* at all. It was my friend Hans Zinsser as much as Richards who insisted on my reading some of Lawrence's so-called novels, which are really tracts. I cannot stand the cult of blood and sex in Lawrence. He is writing about doctrine and not about human behavior. But who am I to insist that a novel be concerned with human behavior? Finally, it was Benny DeVoto as much as Richards who made me see the virtues of some of Arnold Bennett's novels, particularly *The Old Wives' Tale* and the *Clayhanger* series.

Richards did most for me in unveiling a new understanding of Conrad. I had long been collecting and reading Conrad's books, but only as a novelist of the sea, a kind of superior Captain Maryatt. Richards asked us to read some of the novels, such as *Nostromo* and *The Secret Agent,* that do not have the sea as their background. They must stand on their own as novels of human predicaments. In many of Conrad's great stories that do take place at sea, the latter is often a convenience, one possible locale among others. Though *Typhoon* does indeed embody, as no other book does, the code of the sea, it also embodies something much more important and general: the unconscious strength that lies in the straightforward performance of one's duty.

I do not remember who started me reading Henry James and George Eliot, which I did at about this time. Hemingway never held much attraction for me, and I read no Faulkner until later. But while I was an undergraduate he had not yet written his greatest novels.

Richards also introduced me to the work of a man who, though often modernist in his style both as a painter and a writer of fiction, was also a great critic of modernism. This was Wyndham Lewis.[9] Richards certainly urged us to read his novel *Tarr*[10] and his best book of criticism, *Time and Western Man.*[11] My classmate Joseph Alsop, later a famous newspaper columnist, and his tutor in the English Department, Ted Spencer, later a close friend of mine, induced Lewis to come to Harvard in late November and early December of 1931, that is, in my senior year. Alsop, my friend Alex Williams, and I had formed a bit of a Lewis cult among the younger men. I first met him on 30 November 1931, when he gave a public reading in the Eliot House Common Room of the episode "Mrs. Bosun's Closet" from his recently published satire, *The Apes of God.*[12]

On 8 December, Alsop, Williams, and I entertained Lewis for dinner at Locke-Ober, the famous Boston restaurant. He insisted that he be seated at a table where he could keep his back to the wall, so that no one could get at him from behind. If we had any doubts after reading his books, we had none after that: Lewis was thoroughly paranoid. Though he had been a friend of both Eliot's and Pound's and of other modernists, he always saw himself as "The Enemy," as an outsider in a hostile world. Acting on this assumption made it come true: much of the intellectual world had good reason to view him as an enemy. That did not make him mistaken in his judgments about modernism: I have long ceased to believe that because a man is psychologically sick, his judgments must necessarily be sick too. Their truth must be tested by criteria exterior to the man.

After dinner we took Lewis for brandy at the apartment of our mutual friend Barlow, where he read to us about "Betty Bligh" in *The Apes*, and later for a longer and more serious talk with him at his hotel in Cambridge.

My cult of Lewis has remained alive over the years. Above all, I have admired and enjoyed his novel *The Apes of God*. I believe it to be the greatest satire written in English in my time. Indeed it is the only book of its kind. I recognized his targets, for we in Boston had our own, less fully matured, versions of the Apes, that is, members of the Bloomsbury Group and other adepts in London of the cult of modernism. I enjoyed some of Lewis's other novels, though many of them were potboilers. After World War II, I was melted by the stoic pathos of his last novel, *Self-Condemned*,[13] which is highly autobiographical, showing him penniless, sick, and going blind in Toronto in midwinter—"eyeless in Gaza, at the mill, with slaves." On the other hand, I could never summon up much enthusiasm for Lewis's symbolic novel, *The Human Age*, which came out in two parts, one before and one after World War II,[14] though I suspect it was the one of his works he set most store by. In *The Human Age* he used some of the techniques of modernism to attack its ideas.

What was the critique of what I loosely call modernism that Lewis developed implicity in his fiction and explicitly in his other writings, notably *Time and Western Man*? Lewis attacked the exploitation of the unconscious and spontaneous in language in *Ulysses* (the "stream of consciousness") and in Gertrude Stein (the "Stein-stutter," as Lewis called it). He attacked the exploitation of the childlike, the primitive, the psychopathological, what might be summed up as the softness in much of modern art. All of these trends ran counter to what he and I valued in cultural activity: the controlled, the orderly, the organized, the objective, the clear, the analytical, the logical. He also excoriated the corruption of those Western intellectuals who failed to recognize Soviet Russia for the tyranny it was and were ready to praise the Soviets for actions they themselves would have been the first to condemn if they had been taken by their own governments—and all without any excuse except the bare assurance from the executioners that what they did was for the benefit of the "workers."[15] Lewis was one of the first to describe the syndrome we should now call "radical chic." His anticommunism trapped him, as it did me, into a sneaking but brief admiration for Hitler, on the theory perhaps that "the enemies of our enemies are our friends." He and I abandoned Hitler when it became clear that he was going to try to do just what he said he would do, and might be successful.

On the other hand, I was less impressed by the dangers Lewis saw in the theme of time as represented in the works of Proust and Joyce. He thought it threatened the timeless objectivity of the greatest art, and he mistakenly associated it with the prominent place Einstein had necessarily given to time in the theory of relativity. Lewis came too early to analyze the association of sex with violence, which is so common a feature of modern literature and film. Yet on the whole I identified myself with Lewis because he had already become what I was only just beginning to be, an anti-intellectual intellectual. Or rather, persons like Lewis and me were the true intellectuals, while far too many of our peers had deserted intellectual standards. The majority, thank God! had not, or had not given a thought to the issues of modernism.

The one Harvard professor whom Lewis wished to talk seriously with—and I believe we arranged that he should do so—was Irving Babbitt, professor of comparative literature. Lewis's interest was natural, for Babbitt had traced back to a still earlier time some of the modernist themes Lewis had identified. I never took a course of Babbitt's, such as his famous course on French literary criticism. I was not then much interested in French literature. Several of my friends did take it, and some of them for the wrong reasons. Though his subject was French literature, Babbitt mispronounced the language in a most entertaining way. And he dropped the names of so many different authors that his students formed a pool before each of his lectures, the winner being the man whose guess came closest to the number of names Babbitt actually dropped.

Though I did not attend his lectures, I had been interested in some of Babbitt's books, particularly *Rousseau and Romanticism*.[16] Babbitt traced the themes of the Romantic Movement largely to the influence of Rousseau, and the themes of modernism in turn to the Romantic Movement. Rousseau had exalted the natural man, his sentiments and behavior untrammeled by conventional or intellectual control, by what the French would call *mesure*. The natural man was spontaneously good, and had only to be set free from artificial human institutions, when he would realize his full potential. If there was any trouble, the General Will of his community would force him to be free. The assumption of the natural goodness of man—the old Pelagian heresy—when once he has been set free of human institutions, which of course are themselves man-made, abandons by default the problem of personal and cultural morality, and has a way of winding up with institutions still more tyrannical than the traditional ones. Yet there is more than one Rousseau, a shrewd and hard-headed as well as a silly and sentimental one. I have travestied him—but not altogether.

There is much we can sympathize with in the ideas of modernism. Some of the writers and artists who expressed them have left us great works. And some who recognized the dangers of the ideas, including Babbitt himself and the group of New Humanists, of which he was one, often sounded too stuffy to be true. But there is more than one kind of boredom, and much of modern art has distilled boredom in its purest state. Under the pressure to remain in advance of the latest avant-garde, under the pressure always "to make it new," under the pressure, which continually increases, to *épater les bourgeois* before they have recovered from the latest outrage inflicted on their sensibilities, modernism, through the working out of its own logic, has moved steadily down a dead-end street. One of my friends, describing trends in Dutch painting in the seventeenth century, spoke of "the dead-end street that leads to Paul Potter's *Bull*." As a *cul-de-sac* the Bull has more to be said for him than for his analogues in modern art, such as William Burrough's *The Naked Lunch*[17] or the mere heap of bricks that, as I write this, adorns the yard of the Tate Gallery. What is more, these trends in modernism lead both to the deliquescence of culture and to political tyranny. I am afraid that our arts are too deep in the mud to be able still to pull themselves out.

Some modernists say that their cultural and political themes merely reflect the coarseness and violence of the capitalistic world. I shall not argue that the influence is all in the contrary direction but only that ideas as well as institutions have consequences, and that the modernists, the later-comers trying to out-shock their predecessors, and keeping up their striving decade after decade since the beginning of the Romantic Movement, have played no small part in making cultural corruption both real and respectable. Even the descendants of persons of high character, if they are exposed for generations to corrupt ideas, will in time become corrupted themselves. I do not exclude myself from their number. Lewis and Babbitt helped teach me these things.

I had come from St. Paul's to Harvard convinced I was a writer, and so as a freshman I went out for the *Harvard Advocate*, the undergraduate literary magazine, by submitting various writings of mine for publication. Published they were, and in due course I was elected to the editorial board. At my initiation I drank my first alcoholic drink, and since those were the days of Prohibition, a very bad one it was. It was not to be my last. To the *Advocate* I contributed verse, stories, and book reviews.

One of the unnerving experiences an undergraduate must go through when he moves from a preparatory school to a university like Harvard—or alternatively one of the experiences most apt to instill in him a wholesome humility—is to discover that he, who was top dog in some field at school, is no longer that at the university.

The person who put me through this experience was my classmate and fellow member of the *Advocate* board Jim Agee. Our contemporaries and younger members of the faculty who felt themselves competent to judge soon made it clear to me, though quite unintentionally, that Jim was a far better poet and indeed a far better writer of the literary sort than I was myself. They made it clear that Jim had a touch of genius about him, which he certainly did, while I, though competent enough, was not in his class. The editors of the *Advocate* reflected this judgment by electing Jim president, in effect editor-in-chief, for our senior year, while I took second place as secretary.

I was never close to Jim. He was from Tennessee and a devout Catholic. I was familiar with the Bostonian Irish Catholics, but not with his more ambiguous kind, at once more intense in devotion and more ridden by guilt, the very guilt making for the greater devotion. Jim helped me understand some of the characters in the novels of Graham Greene. For his part, I suppose he looked on me as a snob, and indeed the St. Grottlesex, clubby group would class him as a "black man." Yet we elected him to the Signet, where he seldom appeared for our luncheons; he was not one to talk much in a large group. I suspect he also looked on me as not quite a man: I certainly had not had the experience with drink, nor, as it was supposed, with women, that he had. For my part, I felt at times that he was a spoiled child, petulant if he could not have his toy just when he wanted it. I swear that some of the photographs of Jim make him look like one. He disappeared from the Harvard scene for weeks at a time on what the rest of us believed to be fearful orgies, even when he was responsible for getting out the next number of the *Advocate*. No doubt my views on Jim should be discounted, for I was jealous of him, while it would never have occurred to him to be jealous of me.

I was ready enough to accept the judgement of our peers and admit that Jim was the better poet. I am not so sure now as I was then. Some of the features of Jim's poetry do not seem to me now the embellishments we once admired.[18] In prose, on the other hand, Jim did turn out to be a great artist. Many good judges extol the commentary he wrote to go with Walker Evans's photographs of southern sharecroppers in their joint book

Let Us Now Praise Famous Men.[19] I found and still find it boring. But Jim's novel, *A Death in the Family,*[20] even I will accept as great writing. Jim was one of the early admirers at Harvard of Franz Kafka, and following up some hint by Jim, I myself tried Kafka. My first try was my last. Jim was also one of the first and probably the greatest critic of films.

The occupations differ greatly in the steepness with which eminence peaks within them. Thus there are many lawyers of the first class, and there is much to be said in favor of those of the second: they can do useful and important work and make much money. They can become big men in politics or business. In contrast, there are only two or three great concert pianists in any generation. The others must lead obscure lives as teachers and the like. The same is true of poets, and there is no honey in being a second-class poet. I knew enough about English literature to appreciate that. Who now reads William Mackworth Praed? I had come to believe that, compared with my most salient model, Jim Agee, I was a writer of the second class. Accordingly it would be well for me not to depend on literature as a means of earning a living, though writing of other kinds, such as journalism, might still be a possibility. I have continued to write verse, some of it published, off and on throughout my life, but I certainly have not set myself up as a man of letters. Note the wretched competitiveness of this young man! Note his worship of success! But note also, you smug liberals, who sneer at competition while practicing it avidly, that my silent competition with Jim Agee led me to reach a better decision about my future occupation than the one I might have reached without it. By competing I learned where *not* to compete.

Jim Agee died of hard work and hard living, while still in his forties, his greatest books still unwritten.

NOTES

1. Alexander W. Williams, *A Social History of the Greater Boston Clubs* (n.p.: Barre Publishers, 1970).
2. George C. Homans, *Report of the Committee on the Role of the Faculty in the Houses* (Cambridge: Faculty of Arts and Sciences, Harvard University, 1969).
3. Henry Adams, *The Education of Henry Adams* (Boston: Massachusetts Historical Society, 1918), p. 60.
4. Lucien Price, *Dialogues of Alfred North Whitehead* (Boston: Little, Brown, 1954).
5. Alfred N. Whitehead, *Science and the Modern World; Adventures of Ideas; Process and Reality* (New York: Macmillan, 1925, 1933, 1929, respectively).
6. Arthur Quiller-Couch, ed., *The Oxford Book of English Verse: 1250-1900* (Oxford: Clarendon Press, 1925).
7. Thomas S. Eliot, *The Wasteland* (New York: Liveright, 1922).
8. Thomas S. Eliot, *Ash Wednesday* (London: Faber & Faber, 1930). My review is in the *Harvard Advocate,* 117 (December 1930): 32-33.
9. For a life of Lewis, read Jeffrey Meyers, *The Enemy: A Biography of Wyndham*

Lewis (London: Routledge & Kegan Paul, 1980). For Lewis's visit to Harvard, see pp. 194-96.

10. Wyndham Lewis, *Tarr* (New York: Knopf, 1926).
11. Wyndham Lewis, *Time and Western Man* (New York: Harcourt, Brace, 1928).
12. Wyndham Lewis, *The Apes of God* (London: Nash & Grayson, n.d. [1931?]). I bought my copy in 1931. The dates of my meetings with Lewis come from my notes in this copy.
13. Wyndham Lewis, *Self Condemned* (Chicago: Regnery, 1955).
14. Wyndham Lewis, *The Human Age*: sec. 1, *The Childermass* (London: Chatto & Windus, 1928); bks. 2 and 3, *Monstre Gai* and *Malign Fiesta* (London: Methuen, 1955).
15. See Paul Hollander, *Political Pilgrims* (Oxford: Oxford University Press, 1981).
16. Irving Babbitt, *Rousseau and Romanticism* (Boston: Houghton Mifflin, 1919).
17. William Burroughs, *The Naked Lunch* (Paris: Olympia Press, 1959).
18. Robert Fitzgerald, ed., *The Collected Poems of James Agee* (Boston: Houghton Mifflin, 1968).
19. James Agee and Walker Evans, *Let Us Now Praise Famous Men* (Boston: Houghton Mifflin, 1941).
20. James Agee, *A Death in the Family* (New York: Avon, 1957).

6

DEVOTO, HENDERSON, ZINSSER

One of the standard complaints Harvard undergraduates make today is that they have no association with their professors outside the classroom, and if the class is large, mighty little inside. Whether they complain because something they paid for is being unfairly kept from them, or because they really pant for the association is not clear, for when they get the opportunity to meet professors, most of them do not avail themselves of it. Undergraduates in my time made no such complaint. We never expected to mix socially with our professors; most of us got what we expected, and we were, I suspect, none the worse for it. I myself never associated informally with any of the professors whose lectures I attended, with the exception of Professor Edward A. Whitney, who was the master of my "House" in my senior year. True, as a freshman, I was assigned as an advisor Professor Julian Lowell Coolidge, a Boston Brahmin and a distinguished mathematician. He did little to advise me, because both he and I knew that I, for good or ill, would study what I wanted to study, and my association with him was limited to his assigning me, from time to time, the duty of taking one or more of his many daughters out to the theater. He paid for the tickets. I was fond of him, and he became first master of Lowell House.

But I did come into close association with one junior member of the teaching staff, and he, partly by chance, became the person who made the biggest single difference to my intellectual life. This was Bernard DeVoto, whom I soon was to call Benny. I have already described how President Lowell, before setting up the "houses," had established fields of concentration ("majors") at Harvard and their attendant general examinations. He had also created tutorial: tutors were to guide students in their reading and the courses they took in preparation for their general examinations. Since the rule of "up or out"—be promoted after a given number of years or leave Harvard—had not yet been adopted, and since the Depression—this was the fall of 1929—was breaking over the country and academic jobs were few, Harvard was blessed with a large number of junior staff who remained tutors for some time and became skilled in the job. This feature of its education made the 1930s the Golden Age at Harvard, whatever it may have been elsewhere.

Benny was an instructor in English and a tutor. As a concentrator in English and American Literature, I was, beginning in my sophomore year, assigned to him as a tutee, and I saw him formally once a week, alone, for an hour, during the remaining three years of my college career. So expensive has tutorial become today and so rapid is the turnover of tutors, that a tutor and tutee cannot spend so much time alone together and with such continuity now as Benny and I did then. I do not believe there was any particular reason that the English Department assigned me to Benny rather than to some other one of the many good tutors in English. It was just the luck of the draw, and luck it was. Sheer chance has often served me well.

Benny, as he never failed to make clear, was a westerner from Utah, though not a Mormon. For reasons I shall not go into here, for they are analyzed by Wallace Stegner in his excellent life of Benny,[1] Benny came to Harvard as an undergraduate and never got over it. Though he was in the habit of making stereotyped jibes at the effete East and most of its inhabitants—what we should now call the Eastern Establishment—he in fact fell in love with the place if not the people. When I became his tutee he had just come back to Harvard from a spell of teaching and writing at Northwestern University, where he had married one of his students, the sharp-witted Avis MacVicar. He was to leave Harvard again, but eventually he returned to Cambridge and made it his home for the rest of his life.

When I first met Benny in one of the dreary, grubby, dusty, old tutorial offices in a Victorian building called Holyoke House, I met what I thought was the ugliest man I had ever seen: a squat body, a large, round, flat face into which a nose with huge nostrils had been pushed and broken, rather pop eyes, a mouth like a frog and ears stuck-out like the lugs of a jar. But Benny was one of those grotesques to whose grotesquery one soon ceased to give a thought.

In our first conversation it came out that I was an Adams descendant. I am afraid that in those days I was apt to encourage this fact to come out. Benny was interested, because he was a great admirer of *The Education of Henry Adams*, which was one of the touchstone books for intellectuals of his generation. It also came out, if not at our first meeting then soon after, that I neither drank nor smoked. At this point I got the first flick of Benny's "tough guy" stance—very characteristic of him and one of the standard poses of the 1920s. "What do you do," said Benny, "to smell like a man?" I had no answer. Not long afterwards I got off the wagon. Smoking took a little longer.

Under Benny's guidance I soon began reading a number of books in English and American literature that had not been assigned in my courses. He took his duties as a tutor rather casually. I do not remember that he assigned me any essays to write, as a tutor in an English university would certainly have done. To a great extent he let me choose the books that I was to read. Nor do I remember that his criticism of the books or of my comments on them was particularly penetrating. At least I do not remember any brilliant remark that he ever made about them. He was better at talking about prose works than about poetry. Indeed the only poets he insisted on my reading were Robert Frost, whom I had already read, and Francis Thompson. Though Benny was an unbeliever, he had a Catholic background, and some of Thompson's poems obviously made a deep emotional impact on him. He may not have emphasized poetry for the reason that he knew I considered myself a poet and had probably read more poetry than he had.

He was better on the subject of modern than of earlier literature, better on American than on English, and better on American literature that was not in the genteel tradition or, as he would call it, "beautiful letters." I doubt that he ever had me read a novel by Henry James, perhaps because he held the view that James had emasculated himself as a writer by becoming an expatriate and abandoning American themes. Benny himself, by the way, refused to visit Europe. His specialty and great admiration among the writers of the past was, naturally, Mark Twain,[2] a westerner who, like Benny, had come East, and among those of the present, George Bernard Shaw and H. L. Mencken. Though I read a great deal of Shaw and, of course, always enjoyed his wit, he could never become a god to me as he was to Benny: there is something finally inhuman about him. He does not speak to the human condition as Conrad does. Whether or not Benny was a particularly conscientious tutor, he was always good fun to talk to, and that was the main thing.

Of the books that Benny asked me to read, the two that made the most difference to my later thinking were not part of English literature. One was Bernard Mandeville's *The Fable of the Bees,* which appeared in 1724. Though in English, the English Department would not have considered it literature. Yet its message, "private vices, public benefits," remained in the back of my mind, and I am sure took a hand in shaping the kind of sociology I developed later. The other book was Vilfredo Pareto's *Sociologie générale* in the French translation,[3] which was ultimately to bring me into sociology. I shall have much more to say about Pareto later.

My own taste in literature was by no means identical with Benny's. I became an admirer of Mark Twain, but never a wholehearted one: his books always fell apart at some point and became for a time a little facile and cheap. On the other hand, I did become an enthusiastic admirer of Henry James and, above all, of Herman Melville—again the seafaring theme. I had read and absorbed *Moby Dick* long before I came to Harvard. Though Benny, I am sure, recognized in the abstract the greatness of Melville, I doubt that he shared my all-out worship. The vague but suggestive symbolism was not to Benny's taste. Yet he did nothing to discourage my decision to write my thesis, part of the requirement of the A.B. degree with honors, on a symbolic theme in three of Melville's novels: *Moby Dick, Pierre,* and *Mardi.* This subject was not then, at the beginning of the 1930s, as hackneyed as it was to become later. Melville had been rediscovered only recently. Neither of my parents, for instance, had in their youth read or even heard of him. In spite of my urging, neither succeeded in getting through *Moby Dick.* My thesis was judged worthy of highest honors in English and was printed in the *New England Quarterly,*[4] thus reinforcing with another gong my literary bent.

Benny was at odds with the dominant climate of opinion among the younger members of the English Department, men like F. L. Matthiessen and Ted Spencer. They were more apt to be admirers of James than of Twain, of Eliot in both criticism and poetry than of Frost. They may have looked on Benny as a bit of a coarse brute, and Benny by his manner did nothing to discourage them. They may have looked on themselves as purer spirits than he. And did not Benny, under the pen name of John August, write short stories, which I myself often found very amusing, and not only write them but sell them to the *Saturday Evening Post* and other popular magazines, thereby making for himself what was good money for those days? How could a Harvard scholar cheapen himself more? My identification with Benny confirmed me in the habit I had already established of looking askance at received, "liberal," avant-garde opinion, however advanced it purported to be.

Benny afforded me privileges that had no part in official tutorial. Early in our relationship, he took me to dine at the Ritz Hotel in Boston with his friends Alfred Knopf, the great publisher, and H. L. Mencken. We all had sense enough to shut up and let Mencken talk, which he did without pausing for breath for hours and without any lapse in the entertainment he offered us, though his themes varied little: his stories were scatalogical and concerned members of the Congress of the United States. Without doubt Mencken was the greatest talker I have ever heard. His talk was even better than his writing, and that was of the best. I regret that I never met him again.

Not only did Benny and I become tutor and tutee, we also became friends. I soon began to visit him and his wife, the tart and entertaining

Avis, at their first house on Mason Street. For years I spent at least a few days with them in one of the houses they rented in northern New England for the summer. I wonder how they managed to tolerate me. For years in winter, with a select group that included Emery Trott, Perry Miller of the English Department, and Fred Deknatel of the Fine Arts Department, I spent an evening every week or so at the DeVoto's later house in Lincoln, Massachusetts. Our main business was drinking, rationalized only by our singing what I suppose should be called American folk songs, while Avis played the piano. The gallons of whiskey that got spilled over that piano! I still fail to understand how I drove back to Cambridge and Boston after some of those parties and still remained alive. Later, after World War II, when the DeVotos, my wife Nancy, and I were all back in Cambridge, we became regulars at the DeVotos' Sunday afternoon cocktail parties. Benny served nothing but very dry Martinis, made with scrupulous respect for rules laid down by himself and other adepts of the great tradition. They came in large glasses; they were never "on the rocks" but "straight up," stirred not shaken, so as not "to bruise the gin," and Benny made a wholly fresh batch after each round. They were lethal. Benny's little book, *The Hour*,[5] is one of the classics of the literature on drinking.

The greatest service Benny did me was to introduce me to Professor Lawrence Joseph Henderson.[6] "L. J." had been brought up in Salem, the old home of the Crowninshields, the son of a ship chandler, that is, someone who sells provisions and other supplies to ships. The elder Henderson had business connections in the islands of St. Pierre and Miquelon at the entrance of the Gulf of St. Lawrence, islands that the British allowed to remain French after they had captured the rest of Canada in the Seven Years' War. The islands were to provide an overseas base for the French fishing fleet on the Grand Banks. (During Prohibition they also provided a splendid base for rumrunners.) His father sent Henderson to spend at least one summer of his adolescence at St. Pierre, where he learned to speak French and developed his admiration for French culture which remained with him for the rest of his life. A more unlikely place than St. Pierre in which to cultivate a taste for French civilization tasks the imagination.

Henderson attended Harvard College, where he was one of the few friends of the shy poet Edwin Arlington Robinson, and then the Harvard Medical School, where he earned the usual M.D. degree. Though he never ceased to admire the skills of the clinical physician, he never practiced medicine himself but turned to medical research. As a postgraduate he studied at the University of Strasbourg, while Alsace was still in German hands. The arrogance of the German officers reacted on

Henderson so as to increase his identification with France. Eventually he became professor of biological chemistry at Harvard, but in the Faculty of Arts and Sciences and later at the Business, not the Medical, School. His work on the chemical equilibrium of the blood made possible the development of blood plasma, which saved so many lives in World War II and later. He summed up his work in a book the force and succinctness of whose title I have always envied. The title is *Blood*.[7]

Even in research Henderson was never your standard laboratory scientist. For years he assiduously attended seminars offered in the Philosophy Department on what would now be called the philosophy of science, and he spared enough time from research to write two books in this field, *The Order of Nature*[8] and *The Fitness of the Environment*,[9] which still have much to teach us. Henderson also originated and taught for many years the first course at Harvard, and perhaps at any university, on the history of science. He was fond of saying, "All the undergraduates I most disapproved of took my course and liked it." He had in mind men like John Dos Passos, who began, but did not end, his intellectual life as a communist, while Henderson was always an extreme and outspoken conservative. When Benny, who certainly was not the kind of man Henderson disapproved of, was an undergraduate, he too took the course and made Henderson's acquaintance, and when he came back to Harvard became his friend. It was Henderson, the philosopher of science, who told DeVoto to read Pareto, with fateful consequences for me.

At some time in, I believe, my senior year, Benny decided it was time to present me to the great man. (Henderson's son, Larry, Jr., was a classmate of mine, but I hardly knew him then, so that he would not have been the person to introduce me.) Benny arranged that the two of us should dine with L. J. in his big, dark house on Willard Street, where he was living alone, since his wife had recently become a patient in a mental hospital. I saw a stout man of middle stature who, with his full beard, presented a striking resemblance to the late King Edward VII. In his younger years, his beard had been red, which earned him the nickname "Pink Whiskers." Henderson was not generally popular with his colleagues, and with good reason. As I have said elsewhere, his manner in conversation was feebly imitated by a piledriver. It was not that he was intentionally rude, but that he was passionate, and in passion he took no thought for what he said. He was at dinner once with Edward Pickman, sweetest of men. Pickman ventured some innocent remark. Henderson immediately retorted, "Stupid people may say that, Pickman!" I am not sure he was even aware of his unpopularity, which in any event did him no harm, for he stood well with the men who really counted in the university, President Lowell first among them. In almost the first words he addressed to me he was at the top of his form: "Homans, I have never yet served alcohol to an undergraduate, and I do not propose to start with you!"

Benny and he then proceeded to knock off several glasses of sherry before, and a whole bottle of Burgundy during, dinner. Plenty of water was made available to me. Though I record what I remember, my memory in this case may well have played me false. Henderson suffered from a duodenal ulcer, and at some time or another his physician forbade his drinking alcohol. Perhaps the ulcer had not yet been discovered, and perhaps Henderson was disobeying doctor's orders. With his French experience he certainly considered himself, and indeed was, a good judge of wine. Even as a physiologist he had no objection to alcohol. He once said to me in his paced-out, emphatic manner: "At the end—of any long, hard—piece of work—it is well to remain—pretty well alcoholized." This has justified me in considering many occasions as the ends of long, hard pieces of work.

Henderson's remark on meeting me was silly on two counts. It was far too late for him to corrupt me by letting me drink a glass of wine; I was already a hardened toper. Second, Benny and I may well have smuggled into the United States the very wine Henderson denied me. I deserved my reward.

I cannot emphasize too strongly that my undergraduate years were years of Prohibition, an era whose flavor it is now difficult to recapture. It combined the sordid with the romantic, the soak with the smuggler. At college we bought what was called "alky" from the bootleggers, whom we could spot by their derby hats and tattersall waistcoats. Under the Volstead Act, I think it was not illegal to possess liquor but only to sell it. If we were giving a big party, we mixed the alky with juniper drops in a bathtub, to produce what was called "bathtub gin," drunk in the form of "alky splits." The first drink produced a sensation that can only faintly be compared with having a garden rake scraped down one's backbone. We were lucky that the alky did not kill us; it did kill some people. Wisely, the college turned a blind eye to our activities, unless we did something under the influence of drink that was otherwise reprehensible.

When I stayed in New York with my roommate Budd Pollak, we would go out for an evening on the town, dressed in our uniform of derby hats and chesterfield coats, and stop in at a speakeasy, to which we were admitted only if someone first inspected us through a peephole. I am sure that this inspection was unnecessary. By the end of the 1920s Prohibition had been in effect for a decade, and the payments for police protection of speakeasies had long been institutionalized. But if the inspection was strictly an act, it gave a country boy like me a delicious *frisson*.

The even more romantic side of Prohibition was rum-running. After

1925, the Homans family spent its summers at a place we called The Glades, a point sticking out from the South Shore of Massachusetts Bay. (See chapter 12.) From time to time the rumble of trucks driving down our road to one of the beaches on the point would wake us in the middle of the night. They were picking up the liquor speedboats had brought ashore from the main supply ships lying outside what was then the three-mile limit of national sovereignty. I had read of the smuggling of brandy and silk from France to the southern coast of England during the eighteenth century. The literature made smuggling sound thoroughly romantic, which it cannot have been in fact. Here we were living through the same experience. When the trucks woke us, we wisely did not get up to see what was going on—we knew already—and we never reported anything to the police, though ours was a private road. Had we done anything, I am sure the police would not have taken any effective steps to stop the rum-running.

This was the romantic side of Prohibition. As I have said, it had a coarser side of vulgar debauchery, which I recognize as such more easily now than I did then. Under Prohibition to drink became a patriotic duty, to "strike a blow for freedom." Some of us took advantage of the sanction by drinking a great deal too much before we had learned to hold our liquor, by puking ("blowing a lunch"), and passing out. This did us little harm in Cambridge, where in our protected enclave we were licensed libertines. And undergraduates always helped one another out, turn and turn about, to get back to one's room and bed if one was drunk. Drunkenness was less attractive at Boston dances, where from time to time the cry would run along the stag line, "So-and-so has passed out!" In these circumstances, "society" began to become less distinguished and elegant.

This digression was necessary, for Henderson indirectly was responsible for getting Benny and me into rum-running. He owned a summer camp at Morgan Center, Vermont, near the Canadian border. I stayed there in the summer of 1931 when Henderson rented it to the DeVotos and several times later with Henderson himself. In the winter a local farmer, whose real name Benny changed to Eli Potter in some of his short stories, kept an eye on the Henderson property, and Eli himself owned a "sugar bush" (a maple-sugar plantation) that lay right on the border.

Benny got into the way of taking orders for wine and liquor from friends in Cambridge, especially Henderson, adding some orders for himself and sending them, with a suitable check, to Eli. Eli would fill the orders at one of the stores of the Québec Liquor Commission and then carry the stuff over the border through his sugar bush. He did the real smuggling and took the risk of arrest, which was small but not zero. Once

Eli had alerted him that the goods were ready for delivery, Benny and various companions such as Emery Trott and I would drive up north from Cambridge. We were not strictly needed for the operation, but we provided companionship for Benny, shared in the driving, and enjoyed the feeling that we were reckless adventurers. We spent the night at Rock Island, Québec, across the border from Morgan Center, in the Del Monty Hotel. (That was the way it was spelled: the proprietor's name was Monty. The hotel is still in existence.) There we would eat a big dinner accompanied by plenty to drink, and on the following morning, not a little hungover, would pick up the shipment from Eli, hide it as best we could in the car, and drive it back to Cambridge. We never ran into any trouble. The transportation of liquor was illegal, but by that time the officers of the law were not going out of their way to look for bootleggers. I make no claim to having been a hero of the underground.

Rock Island lies in that part of Québec called The Eastern Townships, presumably because they lay east of Montreal. Contrary to the assumption that all the settlers of Québec were French, the Townships were settled by English-speakers, often Yankees simply spilling over the border from northern New England, looking for more land to clear and farm. The French have gradually reclaimed the Townships, resulting in some lovely place-names, such as Notre-Dame de Crabtree Mills. I now spend most of my summers in North Hatley in the Townships. DeVoto, Henderson, and rum-running introduced me to this beautiful part of the world.

Benny also got me into a more socially responsible enterprise of his. As a part-time job he undertook to edit the *Harvard Graduates' Magazine*, a venerable, staid, and reasonably distinguished quarterly, which as a result of the Depression had fallen on hard times and was thought to need "new blood." Benny's own blood was new and he was supposed to infuse still more from others. He asked me to write for every issue a commentary on anything that interested me concerning undergraduate life. I wrote such columns for two years, that is, for eight issues.[10] They contained some of the best prose I wrote as an undergraduate, at least in style if not in matter. From an assumed stance of effortless superiority I exposed the trivial designs of lesser mortals, including President Lowell's "House Plan." My efforts were readable and irreverent enough to arouse much comment among the few graduates who still read the magazine. I enjoyed my supreme triumph when the story got back to me that President Lowell himself had said, "Young Homans is making too much noise!" I was, but the president never held it against me, and naturally I have come to believe that Lowell was quite correct in getting the houses founded. Unfortunately Benny and I between us did not make enough noise to save the magazine. In spite of our new blood, the Depression proved too strong for it, as it did for many other organizations.

Harvard treated Benny rather shabbily. He was due for promotion with the later possibility of a tenured position. He had strong supporters in the English Department, but most of the professors did not really consider him a scholar. When he was offered the editorship of the *Saturday Review of Literature,* Jim Conant, who had recently succeeded Lowell as president, wrote Benny urging him "to take the position which you said had been offered to you."[11] That "you said" infuriated Benny; he took the job and moved to New York. He proved to be an indifferent editor, perhaps because he assigned me so many books to review for his magazine. Harvard had made a bad mistake, for Benny proved to be a great writer and scholar, though not in English literature but in the history of the American West. He wrote three books on the exploration and settlement of the West: *1846: Year of Decision, Across the Wide Missouri,* and *The Course of Empire.*[12] These will keep his name alive.

He also became a great success as a columnist, writing an essay once a month for "The Editor's Easy Chair" in *Harper's Magazine.* Through his columns and his service on various federal advisory commissions he became an effective advocate for the conservationist movement, especially in restraining the efforts of lumber-, cattle-, and oil-men to pillage the national forests of the West.

When Benny resigned his editorship of the *Saturday Review,* he could have lived anywhere, since he was now a free-lance writer. He chose to return to Cambridge, which, with all his ambivalence towards it, had now become an addiction and his only possible home. When I too returned to Harvard after World War II, we resumed our friendship. Benny died in 1955 at the relatively early age of 58, his death brought on, I am sure, by many years of overwork in the effort to support his family and himself by his typewriter alone. By introducing me to Pareto, the book, and Henderson, the man, he had given a fateful turn to my life. But I miss him simply as a friend.

At some time during my later undergraduate years I met Dr. Hans Zinsser, who had recently come to the Harvard Medical School as professor of bacteriology. I do not remember how I met him, but it was inevitable that I should do so, for my older friends DeVoto, Henderson, and Curtis (of whom more later) were also friends of his. Moreover my great-uncle Brooks Adams, dying in 1927, left to my mother, his favorite niece, his house with all its contents at 33 Chestnut Street on Beacon Hill. We moved there, since both the house and the Hill were better than 289 Marlborough Street in the Back Bay, where we had lived for many years. The Zinsser house was only a little below ours on the other, the south, side of Chestnut Street.

After a few meetings with Zinsser in company with others, he urged me to phone him when I felt in the mood and find out whether he was free to pass an evening with me. I have no idea why he was willing to offer me so much of his time, since, as we shall see, we held only one main interest in common. But by this time I had learned that older men, when left to their own devices, were apt to do me good, so I asked no questions and took Hans at his word. We got into the habit of meeting at irregular intervals, usually just the two of us, either at Zinsser's town house or his country place in Dover, Massachusetts, to spend an evening knocking off the greater part of a bottle of whiskey—the liquor theme again—and talking. I was on my way to Dover for a session with Hans when the great hurricane of 1938 hit eastern Massachusetts. I found the further advance of my car blocked by fallen trees, and I expected to find my way back to Cambridge blocked too. But I was lucky on that terrible night and got back. Zinsser and I maintained our custom throughout the 1930s, until World War II separated us as it separated me from so many other friends.

Hans has told his own story in his autobiography—which pretends not to be one—entitled *As I Remember Him*.[13] He was a descendant of that highly cultivated group of liberal Germans who emigrated to the United States when the suppression of the Revolution of 1848 destroyed their hopes for German democracy. For at least a generation they kept themselves largely to themselves—Hans was brought up speaking German—partly, I am afraid, because they considered the rest of us Americans, even those supposedly educated, a little vulgar in culture compared with themselves. I suspect they were correct. But Hans did not wholly escape the Melting Pot. He had been brought up in New York City and always spoke English with a hint of a "toity-toid street" accent. Yet who am I, with my flat New England *a*'s, to criticize accents?

It would appear at first as if Zinsser and I had little in common, though I admired in him the qualities I had not. Like all cultivated Germans, he was a musician; I was musically illiterate. He was never happier than when he had a good horse between his thighs, while I hated the stupid beasts, which my parents had almost forced me to worship in my youth. Hans was a born adventurer, who delighted in taking off for strange and dangerous places, a tendency to which his subject, bacteriology and especially typhus and the other *rickettsiae*, lent itself. I am inveterately timid and anxious, except perhaps in a boat, and I dislike travel except by sea. That, as it turned out, I had to indulge in to satiation. But for me most travel is too much trouble: all that business of buying tickets, waiting in stations and airports, catching trains and planes. I might have felt differently if I could, like my nineteenth-century ancestors, have afforded to hire a *cicerone* to take care of all these sordid business arrangements.

As it is, I resemble Thoreau, who said, I believe, "I have travelled much in Concord." In my case, it has been in Medfield, Massachusetts.

Though not prone to adventures myself, I was entranced by Hans's accounts of his. Once he tried to get away from it all by shipping on a fishing trawler out of Boston, though he confessed that he had spent most of the trip lying on the forecastle drenched with spray and prostrated by seasickness. As a researcher on typhus fever, a disease that has killed whole armies and decimated peoples—he himself has told the story in his book *Rats, Lice, and History*[14]—Hans had accompanied the gallant but terrible retreat of the Serbian army to Salonika in Greece in World War I. He was fond of saying that he had seen in Albania the most beautiful women in the world. In 1923, in pursuit of cholera, he had gone to the Soviet Union and had learned at firsthand that the hopes many Western intellectuals held for the Bolshevik Revolution had nothing to do with reality; the regime was a bloody and cynical tyranny. John Reed, the Harvard man who was the first American historian of the revolution and one of the many idealistic enthusiasts for it, was lucky, Hans said, to have died of typhus before he was "purged," as he was bound to have been.[15] On the subject of the Soviet Union Hans confirmed me for good in views I had already tentatively reached for myself. Later Hans went on expeditions to Mexico, Tunis, and China.

We shared only one interest, but that was enough. We were both of us poets and writers in prose, and we spent a large part of our evenings together talking about, and reading, literature. Under the influence of copious draughts of whiskey, we read and recited much poetry to one another. He introduced me to the wit and wry humor of Heine, but my German was not advanced enough to let me understand and appreciate one of Hans's great enthusiasms among the German moderns, Rainer Maria Rilke. With the help of Charlie Curtis, he got me reading Dante, insisting that, knowing Latin and French, I need not first waste my time learning elementary Italian but should plunge right into *The Divine Comedy* in the Temple edition, which has the original Italian and an English translation on opposite pages. Dante has been one of my enduring delights, as how could he help being? We also read and discussed much modern poetry in English, particularly Eliot and Mac-Leish. In another interest of his among the moderns I could not follow him. In New York and later on a voyage by sea to Mexico he had fallen in with a continually drunken Hart Crane, who killed himself not long afterwards. Hans was not sure that "The Bridge" was a great poem, but at least it intrigued him. It never got as far as that with me. Though we both loved reading, quoting, and talking about poetry, and though as poets we ourselves were both traditionalists in technique, we did not particularly care for each other's verse. I thought him, at times, a bit on the sentimental side.[16] I may well be wrong. What strikes me now as curious is that our relationship survived without the slightest difficulty this disagreement about our own poetry.

Intellectually the main influence flowed from Hans to me rather than in the other direction, which was as it should be. Yet there were fields in which I succeeded in at least shaking him. I got him to take a fleeting interest in the Icelandic sagas and, in quite a different area, a serious interest in the critical works of Irving Babbitt, though some of Babbitt's views ran counter to Hans's unstated but indelible romanticism. It makes me happy to remember that Hans held some long talks with Babbitt when that old Roman was in the hospital on his deathbed. But I could not get Hans to accept Wyndham Lewis any more than he could get me to accept Hart Crane.

I have spoken of Hans the adventurer in the world and in science. I have spoken of Hans the rider and the poet. All of these descriptions are tame. I can best sum him up as a romantic, the person closest to being a pure romantic in feeling I have ever known. Remember that being a romantic in feeling does not imply that one is impractical in action. When I think of Hans I think at once of Yeats's lines:

> *When I was young,*
> *I had not given a penny for a song*
> *Did not the poet sing it with such airs*
> *That one believed he had a sword upstairs.*[17]

Hans was always young, and he *did* have a sword upstairs.

Of all the older men who began in those years the serious part of my education, that is, the part I should not have acquired as a matter of course, Hans was the one I loved, rather than enjoyed or admired, most. In order to break the automatic knee jerks of those modernists who assume that when one speaks of love between man and man one necessarily implies homosexuality, let me say forthrightly that my love for Hans implied nothing of the sort. As far as sex was concerned, love for each of us meant women only—and it was all too easy for each of us to fall in love with women.

Though I loved Hans, I could not express my love. I am sure I let him down emotionally. More than once he revealed to me in confidence some of the emotional involvements he had fallen into, and I am sure he was hoping for some enlarging or supporting response from me. I could never muster up any words at all, much less the right ones. I showed my inadequacy when I went out to see him at Dover just after he had returned from a voyage to China. He had felt extraordinarily weak on this expedition, he who had been so vigorous a rider, and when he got back to Boston his weakness was diagnosed as a symptom of leukemia. He told me he was dying, as indeed he was. All I could manage to say was, "Oh God!" I was unable to find further words to convey how much I should miss him. With men I have loved, I have been able to express that love only after they have died. But nothing less than moving speech to them during their lifetimes would have availed anything to them or to me. Emotionally I have failed them and myself.

I last saw Hans, very briefly, when I was home on leave from the Navy in World War II. He was dying tranquilly, without pain.

NOTES

1. Wallace Stegner, *The Uneasy Chair: A Biography of Bernard DeVoto* (Garden City, NY: Doubleday, 1974).
2. Bernard DeVoto, *Mark Twain's America* (Boston: Little, Brown, 1932).
3. Vilfredo Pareto, *Traité de sociologie générale*, 2 vols. (Paris: Payot, 1917).
4. George C. Homans, "The Dark Angel: The Tragedy of Herman Melville," *New England Quarterly* 5 (1932): 699-730.
5. Bernard DeVoto, *The Hour* (Boston: Houghton Mifflin, 1951).
6. On Henderson, see D. B. Dill, "L. J. Henderson, His Transition from Physical Chemist to Physiologist: His Qualities as a Man," *Physiologist* 20 (1977): 1-15 and *L. J. Henderson on the Social System: Selected Writings,* ed. Bernard Barber (Chicago: University of Chicago Press, 1970).
7. Lawrence J. Henderson, *Blood: A Study in General Physiology* (New Haven: Yale University Press, 1928).
8. Lawrence J. Henderson, *The Order of Nature: An Essay* (Cambridge: Harvard University Press, 1925).
9. Lawrence J. Henderson, *The Fitness of the Environment* (New York: Macmillan, 1913).
10. *Harvard Graduates' Magazine* 40, 41 (1930-31, 1931-32), columns entitled "Student Life."
11. Wallace Stegner, *The Uneasy Chair: A Biography of Bernard DeVoto* (Garden City, NY: Doubleday, 1974), p. 171.
12. Bernard DeVoto, *The Year of Decision: 1946, Across the Wide Missouri; The Course of Empire* (Boston: Houghton Mifflin, 1942, 1947, 1952, respectively).
13. Hans Zinsser, *As I Remember Him: The Biography of R.S.* (Boston: Little, Brown, 1940).
14. Hans Zinsser, *Rats, Lice and History* (Boston: Little, Brown, 1935).
15. Zinsser, *As I Remember Him,* p. 284.
16. Hans Zinsser, *Spring, Summer & Autumn* (New York: Knopf, 1942).
17. William Butler Yeats, "All Things Can Tempt Me" (1910), in *The Collected Poems of W. B. Yeats* (New York: Macmillan, 1933).

7

CURTIS AND PARETO

I was in the middle of my last year as an undergraduate and had no time to spare before deciding what I should do next. My parents were easily able to support me but not willing to do so except while I was preparing eventually to support myself. I had already decided that there was no honey in becoming a second-class poet or indeed any kind of "creative" writer. But so long as I did not try to be creative I could still write well. What were the openings for a writer of this sort? One obvious answer was to become a newspaperman and that was just what I decided to do, though only after a long talk with Zinsser, which he must have found thoroughly tiresome.

I now believe my reasoning was faulty. An ability to write well, especially to write both well and rapidly, may indeed be useful to a journalist, but it is not essential, and other qualities, which I never had a big supply of, are. I now believe that I should have made a perfectly good, even a very good lawyer. Because the law does not require any special gift for writing—though again it always helps—I ruled this career out. The one career for which I had already shown I was fully qualified, that is, scholarship, it did not even occur to me to consider. In those days, we men of the world were scornful of academics. The revolution in the standing of professors in America, which has inspired in some of them an arrogance to make one puke, had hardly yet begun.

My father never tried to force a choice on me, but once I had made my own, he would do his best to help me carry it out, and in this case he could do a good deal. As a leader of the Boston bar and a member of the Harvard Corporation, he had good contacts. Through, I suspect, his friend Grenville Clark, a leader of the New York bar and a fellow member of the Corporation, he set up for me an interview with Walter Lippmann, then and until his death the greatest of American newspaper columnists. If one aimed at becoming a newspaperman, this, in Pa's eyes, was the kind to aim at. My interview with Lippmann, while friendly, did not lead him to offer me a job. No doubt he needed a research assistant, and I certainly should have been a good one—for a while. What Lippmann did not want, and certainly was shrewd enough to see in me, was a research assistant who would in time try to become a columnist himself. I do not blame Lippmann in the least.

The other newspaperman my father put me in touch with was William Allen White, editor of the Emporia, Kansas, *Gazette*. Pa could not have found two more influential, or more dissimilar, newspapermen than Lippmann and White. Emporia is a small place, but White's editorials were read all over the Middle West and even the nation. White was going to Chicago to cover the Democratic Convention of June 1932. I was going there for other reasons. I made an appointment to meet him at the Blackstone Hotel.

One of the many organizations that flourished at that time for propagandizing against the Prohibition Amendment and the Volstead Act had recruited my friend Marshall ("Nig") Stearns and me to go to the convention as unpaid lobbyists to represent the views of "youth" on this subject, especially to try to persuade the state delegations to support a plank in the party platform calling for the repeal of Prohibition. Our efforts were wholly superfluous. Nig and I went around to a few of the headquarters of state delegations, only to be met everywhere with words to the effect: "Go away and don't bother us; we don't need any persuading." The convention did indeed adopt the repeal plank without a murmur, and when the Democrats came to power the next year, the Prohibition Amendment was promptly repealed.

Nig and I were left with nothing to do but attend the convention as spectators. But a political convention is not, in my opinion. a spectator sport. I was horribly bored, and I never attended another one. I was so bored that I went back to my hotel and went to sleep without waiting for the ballot by which the convention nominated Franklin Roosevelt for his first term as president of the United States. Thus I missed what I suppose must count as an historic occasion. Most of the speeches were interminable and atrocious, with one exception. That one was delivered by Huey P. Long, governor of Louisiana, on the far from earthshaking question whether his or a rival delegation should represent the state at the convention. In speaking, Long attempted no rhetorical flourishes at all. He was simple, sensuous, and passionate. Yet it was one of the few really powerful speeches I have ever heard. (I never heard Churchill speak in person.) I suppose Long was a local tyrant and deserved his later assassination. Still, he ranks with me as a speaker where Mencken does as a talker.

Thus the convention was not wholly a washout for me, especially because I did meet William Allen White. I liked him immensely, more than I did Lippmann, who seemed to me a little too much the "operator."

He was straightforward and kindly, without Lippmann's subtlety but surely just as wise, though not in the "intellectual" mode. I suspect that Lippmann had made up his mind in advance that I should not suit him, and saw me only as a matter of courtesy. White, on the contrary, actually offered me a job as an ordinary reporter in Emporia for the *Gazette*.

I have often wondered what would have happened if I had entered upon the job at once, but I did not. I felt that I had earned a vacation after working hard during my senior year at Harvard, so I took the summer off, planning to start working in Emporia in September. How should I have gotten along there, I a Yankee, a Harvard man, presumably a snob, speaking with an easily parodied accent—all characteristics that people told me would render me unfit to mix with the real Americans of the heartland? Yet these traits of mine did not seem to worry William Allen White.

My father saw a different kind of danger lying before me. At some time that summer he said to me, "When you get to Emporia, you are sure to fall in love and want to get married. Just remember that the girl will look differently out there from what she will in our parlor on Chestnut Street." This was the only overtly snobbish remark I ever heard him utter, and I am sure that he would have made much of any woman I did marry, but I did not marry until long after his death. In 1932 he did not have long to live; he died in 1934.

As it turned out I had to face neither danger. This was 1932, perhaps the worst year of the Depression. When at the end of the summer it became time for me to report to Emporia, I received a telegram and later a letter from White, saying that he had to go back on his offer to hire me. As I remember it, he said that the deepening Depression had hit Kansas so hard that he had no money to pay me: the *Gazette*'s staff car went around town with a chicken coop in the back seat so that subscriptions could be collected in kind.

Though White could not employ me full time in Emporia, it appeared that he could do so part time in Massachusetts. He was planning to write, and did write, a biography of Calvin Coolidge;[1] and he offered to pay me a small sum by the hour, plus expenses, to interview persons who had known Calvin during his political career in Massachusetts before he went to Washington. At that time a large number of such persons were still alive. From them I drew further insight into the operations of the Republican party in Massachusetts under Senator Winthrop Murray Crane, who held more real power within the state than did the other, more famous, senator, Henry Cabot Lodge, Senior. Crane ran a true political machine, by which I do not mean to imply that it was corrupt, for by the standards of the time it certainly was not. It was the Crane apparatus that started Coolidge up the ladder of state politics from the General Court to the governorship.

I developed a considerable respect for Calvin. Though he was certainly not a leader in the sense of an innovator, he was not the joke that some people made him out to be, and still do. He himself carefully cultivated the notion that he was a joke, in order to disarm his opponents. If you treated him as a joke, it was you, not he, who was apt to wind up as its butt. I have already described how Calvin discomfitted my mother. In the course of my work for White I picked up a number of Coolidge stories, of which, under iron self-discipline, I shall tell only one, which the painter Charles Hopkinson passed on to me. He went to Northampton to paint a portrait of Coolidge. Like many others, he found keeping up a conversation with Calvin heavy going. Some time after he had started painting, Calvin finally broke the silence by asking the question: "Are you sure you're using the best quality paint?" Hopkinson confessed he could not tell whether Calvin was asking the question to keep up his role as a fool or as that of a skinflint Yankee making sure he was getting full value for his money. Perhaps he was doing both at once.

Working for White as a research assistant was still far less than a full-time job. From the fall of 1932 until the fall of 1934 I was, like millions of my countrymen, technically unemployed. My sisters did not take my plight to be the result of the impersonal workings of the capitalist system but a sign of my personal worthlessness. They were sure I was going to be a deadbeat, supported by my family forever. Yet if I was unemployed I was far from idle. Encouraged by Bob Barlow and my friend Mrs. Frederick ("May") Winslow, I took an introductory course in Greek at Harvard. Reading Greek poetry from Homer to Theocritus, usually with a "trot" as I read Dante, has given me delight ever since.

These were the days before TV, before even radio was fully exploited. For the political campaigns of 1932 and 1936 I signed myself up as a volunteer with the Speakers' Bureau of the Republican party of Massachusetts. If, for instance, the bureau received a request to provide a speaker at a Methodist clambake at Leominster, the bureau might assign me the job. The bureau must have had few volunteers, for it never asked what were my qualifications for the job, nor what heresies I might be preaching, so long as I plugged the straight ticket, which I was quite ready to do. We never contributed anything to carrying the state; these were bad years for Republicans in Massachusetts as elsewhere. But I spoke to all sorts of people, in all parts of the state, using all sorts of arguments. I even invoked that mossy Republican idol, the protective tariff. I once took part in a triangular debate between a Democrat, a Socialist, and me. The Socialist quoted Marx at me; I quoted Pareto back at him. I knew some Marx; he knew no Pareto. In the course of these campaigns I lost all nervousness about speaking to an audience, which helps make a man a good teacher, though it is certainly not all he needs.

I was finally saved from unemployment and started in the discipline of sociology by the Italian economist and sociologist Vilfredo Pareto. Pareto came from an old and distinguished Genoese family. Indeed he was a marquis by rank, though he never used the title. His father had been a supporter of Mazzini's and of the Italian *risorgimento*. Upon Mazzini's failure, the elder Pareto fled to Paris, where Vilfredo was born in the famous year 1848. Later he returned to Italy and studied civil engineering at the Turin Polytechnic School, writing his thesis "The Equilibrium of Elastic Solids." Upon graduation, the Italian railway system employed him as a civil engineer. As a strong supporter of free trade, he became increasingly interested in the subject of economics and disgusted by what he believed to be the corrupt practices of the Italian parliamentary government in maintaining protectionism. His published articles on economics attracted the attention of Léon Walras, professor of economics at the University of Lausanne, Switzerland, who invited Pareto to join him there as a professor. He accepted in 1893 and spent the rest of his career at Lausanne. Walras and he founded the first great school of mathematical economics. Later Pareto became more and more interested in aspects of human behavior that did not fall within the field of economics as usually defined but still conditioned economic behavior. He wrote a book, *Les Systèmes socialistes*,[2] on socialist theories including that of Marx. He became steadily more sociological in his interests, his work culminating in the huge *Trattato di Sociologia Generale* (1916). It was translated into French as *Traité de sociologie générale*, and after the translation had been reviewed by the author, published in 1917.[3] The French translation was the one that persons like me read. It was translated into English, by Arthur Livingston and Andrew Bongiorno, in 1935 and then under the unfortunate title of *The Mind and Society*.[4] Pareto had died in 1923.

Pareto seems to have been a really strange man. One story has him inviting a number of friends to luncheon and deliberately drawing out his wife to make, for their amusement, thoroughly silly remarks. Not unnaturally she ran away with the coachman. Pareto took a mistress, to whom he dedicated the *Trattato* and whom he married just before he died. He adored Angora cats, kept a dozen or so at his Villa Angora in Céligny just outside Lausanne, and used to write with one of them draped across his shoulders. Let Freudians make what they can of this.

Some of his other traits were more important than these eccentricities. He suffered from insomnia, and spent his wakeful hours at night reading widely in Greek and Latin literature, quotations from which stud the *Traité*. Like the rest of us, he got down in the dumps from time to time and needed something to cheer him up. His cure was to open a volume of Hegel at random and start reading. This never failed to give him a belly laugh. Such is the proper irreverence with which to treat one of the alleged titans of Western thought.

William Morton Wheeler, a distinguished entomologist at Harvard, had run into Pareto's *Traité* and read it, as he read much sociology. His specialty was the social behavior of insects but he was interested in the social behavior of any species, including man. When Harvard awarded him an honorary degree, President Lowell composed a citation for him that read: "He has shown that insects, like men, can construct elaborate societies without the use of reason." Wheeler was a friend of Lawrence Henderson's and urged him to read the *Traité*. Henderson took to it from the very first chapter, which he thought was a sound statement of the philosophy of science. Later he claimed that the charm of the book consisted in its confirming him in all his prejudices. Soon he was more of an enthusiast for Pareto than Wheeler himself. There were years in the academic society of Cambridge and Boston when Henderson could not restrain himself from bringing Pareto into any conversation, and thus made a great bore of himself, without persuading many people to read the *Traité*, which is indeed formidable reading.

But Henderson did persuade a few, and they happened to be persons that made a difference to me. One was my family's friend and member of the Harvard Corporation, Charles Pelham Curtis, Jr. Another was my tutor and Henderson's former student, Benny DeVoto. I discovered later that Benny had started reading the *Traité* but never finished it. Still he urged it on me as a book that no one could claim to be an educated man unless he had read. I bought the *Traité* and read it through by July 1930, for that is the date I wrote on the flyleaves of my copies of the two volumes. At that time I probably knew more about Pareto's sociology than any other person at Harvard and perhaps the United States except Wheeler, Henderson, and possibly Charlie Curtis. Yet I had read no other sociology and had no suspicion that I was to become a sociologist.

The next step Henderson took decided my fate. Beginning in the fall term of 1932-33, he decided to hold an informal seminar on Pareto's sociology, the first such seminar, I believe, to be held anywhere and certainly the first in the United States. He wanted someone to serve as his legman and assistant in handling the arrangements for the seminar. He knew I was familiar with the *Traité*; he knew I was unemployed and he invited me to serve. I was delighted to accept. I had little else to do. The job carried no wages, but I soon discovered that my work would be light.

In effect, I was simply the junior member of the seminar. What I did not appreciate was that, as we used to say, from that moment I was a made man.

The seminar met for a couple of hours late in the afternoon for the better part of the academic year in, I think, the junior Common Room of Winthrop House. Henderson had rounded up a distinguished group of participants—already distinguished or to become so later. It included Joseph Schumpeter, professor of economics, author of one of the great books of this century, *Capitalism, Socialism, and Democracy*;[5] Crane Brinton, wise historian of revolutions;[6] Elton Mayo, a colleague of Henderson's at the so-called Fatigue Laboratory at the Harvard Business School, about whom I shall have much to say later; two of their junior colleagues: Fritz Roethlisberger and T. North Whitehead, son of the philosopher; Benny DeVoto, of course; Charlie Curtis; Hans Zinsser for at least occasional meetings; Talcott Parsons, then a faculty instructor (assistant professor) in sociology, who was to become the most prominent American sociologist; and Robert K. Merton, then a graduate student in sociology, a student of Parsons's, who was also to become a leading American sociologist. Many of the members were friends not only of Henderson but of one another. There was one exception. As a matter of courtesy, Henderson had invited Pitirim Aleksandrovich Sorokin, then chairman of the Sociology Department. The difficulty was that Henderson dominated the seminar intellectually; most of us tacitly understood that we challenged him only at our peril. But nobody, except perhaps Lenin, could dominate Sorokin, and after some argument with Henderson, he quit the seminar in a huff. Whether or not he was right on the issue in question I am not prepared to say, for I have forgotten what it was. Later Sorokin became an older friend of mine and did me a very good turn. I have had more of these than I deserve.

Indeed I remember almost nothing about the seminar and the discussions that must have taken place. Henderson worked slowly through the *Traité*, providing his exegesis of selected passages. After each of these, he would ask for questions. If there were none, he would go on. Except from Sorokin, I do not remember that there was much argument. On the rare occasions when even he could not defend what Pareto had written, Henderson would always remind us that "Pareto was old and tired when he wrote the *Traité*."

At the time the *Traité* had not been translated into English. Towards the end of the first year of the seminar Charlie Curtis approached me and suggested that we collaborate in writing an introduction to Pareto's sociology for American readers. I had learned that I was seldom the loser when I did what older men asked me to do, and I accepted. Why Charlie chose me as his partner I do not know, except that he knew I was a competent writer of expository prose and thoroughly at home with Pareto. He was a busy lawyer, while I, still technically unemployed, had time to spare.

Charlie was, so to speak, an hereditary friend of my family's. His tall, upright, noble sportsman of a father had long been a, usually unsuccessful, rival of my uncle Charlie's in yacht racing in Massachusetts Bay. Charlie, Jr., often served as a member of his crew, as I did of my uncle's. His beautiful and brilliant mother had been a very good friend, though not perhaps acknowledged as such, of Bob Barlow's. Charlie rode to hounds with my mother and father at meets of the Norfolk Hunt Club. All those horsy types, whose sympathies I could not share! Like my father and Barlow, Charlie was a devoted member of the Porcellian Club. For some time the Curtises were neighbors of ours on Marlborough Street, and the youngsters of the two families played together. Charlie's oldest son, Charlie 3rd, becoming one of my brother Bob's best friends.

Though much younger than my father, Charlie had preceded him in becoming a Fellow of the Corporation of Harvard College. From time to time the Brahmin community of Boston somehow agrees—or did in those days—that so-and-so is *the* coming young man and begins to load him with honors, such as a Fellowship of the Corporation, which it would take other men years to achieve. The community had so chosen my uncle Charlie, and he had served Harvard splendidly as treasurer for many years. Later it had chosen Charlie Curtis.

Charlie was a good lawyer. Socially he was an utter charmer, in spite of a stammer, about which, however, he never showed the slightest self-consciousness. Like his mother, he was widely interested in literature and ideas. With the help of Zinsser he made me read Dante and, under his sole power, Catullus. Nuts to Horace; Catullus is the greatest of Latin lyric poets and one of the greatest lyric poets of all time. Charlie's intellectual interests increased in strength after he became a Fellow and came into contact with some of the members of the Harvard faculty. Most Fellows pay little attention to the faculty as individuals; they have not the time. Charlie cultivated them. He became a friend of Whitehead's, of Henderson's, of Zinsser's, of DeVoto's. Charlie had read Pareto, as he seemed to have read everything else, and Henderson invited him to join the seminar.

I was much flattered by Charlie's asking me to work with him on the Pareto book, but I soon was surprised to discover that in one way—and one only—I was, though much younger and less experienced, the better man of the two. We would each write drafts of chapters and then meet to discuss them, usually at Charlie's dingy room in the office of Choate,

Hall, and Stewart—but then in those days all law offices were dingy. Eventually we would agree on the wording of one chapter and finally on most of the chapters in the book. Then I learned how a man can be trapped by even his greatest virtues. Just when I thought we had a chapter all put to bed, Charlie would have a new idea. Moreover, he was sure his idea was so good—and his ideas *were* often good—that we should scrap the chapter and rewrite it to embody the new illumination. So often did this happen that finally I was maddened into yelling to this much older and more distinguished man: "Come on, Charlie! If this goes on we shall never get the book finished." I am convinced that, without my protests, the book would indeed have never been finished nor so tightly organized as it is in fact. I came to wonder how a man could have a mind like Charlie's and still be a lawyer—that is, someone who, as I naively supposed, could construct in a fairly short time a coherent and logical argument. I also got into the dangerous habit of bossing around persons more important than I. Benny DeVoto was a good friend of the great publisher Alfred A. Knopf, and persuaded him to bring out the book, which he did, in colorful format, in 1934. Its title is *An Introduction to Pareto: His Sociology,*[7] and we dedicated it to Henderson. It was and still is a *good* introduction.

Charlie Curtis remained a friend of mine and of my family's for the rest of his life. He never ceased to charm and to bubble with ideas. Indeed he turned the unsystematic nature of his thinking into a positive advantage. His two best books are anthologies of ideas, short passages picked up from his enormous reading in the literature—artistic, philosophical, and scientific—of the West.[8] He does not try very hard to relate the ideas to one another, but each passage stands by itself, together in the second book with Charlie's commentary. They make the books a continuous treat, often amusing, often wise, and always stimulating, just to dip into.

Before I come to grips with the substance of Pareto's ideas, I must take a little time off. The *Introduction* was my first book on sociology, but not my first published book. That was entitled *Massachusetts on the Sea;* it was not an ordinary trade book but commissioned and published in 1930 by the Massachusetts Bay Tercentenary Commission.[9] (The Massachusetts Bay Colony, as distinct from the Plymouth Colony, had been founded in 1630.) My co-author was Samuel Eliot Morison, professor at Harvard and one of the greatest American historians. I was invited to do the writing because, beginning with my interest in New England schooners and other sailing ships, I had become something of an expert on the subject. I was really a ghost writer for Sam; he did little of the work. Yet it was still fair that he should be listed as co-author, first, because a large part of the book consisted of my condensation of Sam's classic and much longer book, *The Maritime History of Massachusetts*, and second, his name but not mine would help sell copies.

Yet I did more than condense *The Maritime History*. That book had brought the story down to its climax in the clipper ship era just before the Civil War and stopped there. But seaborne trade itself had not stopped. I did much independent work on the later maritime trade of Boston, working on the manuscript records at the Custom House. I also used this material in a chapter I wrote, "The Harbor and Shipping," for the last volume of *The Centennial History of Boston.*[10]

Such was the beginning of my long connection with the Morison family, cemented by my future wife's having been a classmate and friend of Sam's daughter Emily ("Wendy") at Concord Academy. We were both friends of Sam's first and second wives, his other daughters, his son and sons-in-law, and his grandchildren. Yet my own relations with Sam himself were always ambivalent. I admired him greatly as a writer and historian, but I felt he never really liked me. Perhaps he had reasons.

It is now time to return to Pareto, with two purposes in mind: to account for Henderson's and my own unqualified enthusiasm for the *Traité* in the beginning and for the skepticism I later developed towards some of its arguments. Above all, Henderson found in Pareto a man whose views on science and the scientific enterprise jibed with his own. The generalizations of a science—and Pareto had no doubt that social science could indeed be a science—did not have the mystical status of laws. They were no more than uniformities in the data, which might at any time be modified or upset by the discovery of new and contradicting data. To this, Henderson himself added the notice that most generalizations did not summarize the data precisely but rather approximately— and were not to be despised for that reason. He once startled me by proclaiming in his best magisterial manner that the first approximation to a circle was a straight line. Unless one were prepared to recognize and state the first approximation, neither oneself nor others could arrive at still closer approximations. Henderson was much opposed to striving for too high a degree of rigor too soon. Too high a degree in one area was apt to lead to a decline in rigor in others, like trying to squeeze a partly inflated balloon. It is now difficult for me to separate in my mind Pareto's teaching from Henderson's. Their views overlapped over a wide area but did not coincide—not because Pareto would have disagreed with Henderson but because he simply did not write about some of the matters Henderson taught. Though Henderson was an M.D. who never practiced medicine, he set much store by the qualities of the skilled clinician. For him, science began with the scientist's acquiring an intuitive familiarity with his material, based, if possible, on the necessity he was under of taking responsible action. Many sociologists still have not learned this fundamental lesson. They would rather deal with tables of numbers without first becoming familiar by observation and interviewing with the social situation to which the numbers finally refer.

Henderson also found Pareto's notion of a social system congenial to his own experience. A system is a complex state of mutual dependence among many variables, such that, for instance, a certain relationship between variables x and y holds good for some values of z, etc., but not all. For other values the original relationship may even reverse itself. This is one of the first lessons most scientists learn, though some never do. Henderson himself had struggled with the complex but systematic relationships among variables in his researches on blood. His struggle had made him somewhat skeptical about the conventional methodology of experimental science. The experimental method calls for the scientist's holding the values of other relevant variables constant by physical or statistical means, so as to allow him, by manipulating the values of one variable, the so-called independent variable, to determine its effect on another, the dependent variable. But what if the "other" variables could not be held constant, or if the effort to do so effectively destroyed the nature of the total phenomenon? Henderson's own procedure, at least as I understand it, was not to try to hold constant any of the measurable variables in blood as it passes through its cycle in the body, but to measure at intervals the values of all of them simultaneously, and from these data to construct "nomograms," which showed, for instance, that if the values of any two variables were known, what the simultaneous values of the others would be. At any rate, Henderson felt himself wholly at home with Pareto's treatment of the interdependence of variables in a system, in Pareto's case, a social system.

Another feature of Pareto's sociology that Henderson approved of was his treatment of the equilibrium of a system. Henderson's greatest contribution to research was his account of the acid-base equilibrium of blood. Pareto had written his thesis on the equilibrium of elastic solids, and he was thoroughly familiar with the notion of economic equilibrium. For me there are two aspects of equilibrium: Pareto and Henderson were familiar with both but did not always keep them distinct.

First, if one has reason to believe that a system is in fact in equilibrium, one may use a general equilibrium equation to make up the number of equations, equal in number to the number of unknowns, which will allow one to solve the system of equations, describing a particular kind of phenomenon, so as to obtain determinate values of the variables. I only began to understand this use of a general equilibrium equation when, on the advice of Thomas Kuhn, then a Junior Fellow of the Society of Fellows and later a famous historian of science, I read Ernst Mach's *Science of Mechanics*[11] and found in it examples of this use of such equations. But I do not believe in the use of a general equilibrium equation in sociology, for the obvious reason that no one in the field has ever formulated one.

There is also a somewhat different, though related, notion of equilibrium, which need not require mathematics for its use. Suppose again that a number of variables are in a complicated state of mutual dependence, and suppose further that this mutual dependence occurs within a boundary, either one set by nature, such as the skin of a body, or one drawn arbitrarily by the scientist. Such a system Henderson had to deal with in his study of the blood, and Pareto had put forward the notion of a social system, an idea that was widely and rather uncritically accepted in sociology. It is characteristic of some such bounded systems that if a change, not too great, is imposed on the system from without, the system, by reason of the very interdependence of its variables, will tend to return to the state it would have occupied if the change had not taken place. Examples are the return of the human body after fever to its normal temperature, and the return of a growing child, after it has lost weight through sickness, to the weight it would have reached had it never been sick.

There are analogous but looser examples of equilibrium in sociology. An obvious one is the maintenance in the Soviet Union of a society similar in many ways to the one that would have existed if the Revolution had not taken place. True, private property has in part been abolished, but it is doubtful whether actual work in a Soviet factory is much different from what it would have been under private ownership. Freedom of speech and of the press is still suppressed, indeed even more strongly than under the czars. An elite still governs the nation, not the same elite as of old, but still an elite, and—an important point for Pareto—one much more ready than the old one to use force in governing. Overall, in spite of the Revolution, Russia has remained a bureaucratic police state. Remember that a degree of social equilibrium like this is something we sometimes observe. In itself it explains nothing but rather calls for explanation.

The notion of a social system, like the similar ideas of the British and French social anthropologists, is often a useful guide to research because it makes one look at a society as a whole and the possible relations between its institutions. I used it myself in planning the research for my book *English Villagers of the Thirteenth Century*.[12] It can often be used uncritically, and Henderson sometimes did so. The idea seems to imply that every feature of society is in mutual dependence with every other, so that if any one of them changes, all the others are to some degree affected. That may be true of some systems, such as human bodies, but societies are a good deal "looser," less "organic," less "systematic." Societies have changed greatly in some respects without great changes in others, for instance in the organization of family and kin.

A related difficulty lies in specifying nonarbitrary boundaries for social systems. National states come close to meeting the condition in the modern world and some tribes in the primitive one, but in between are many doubtful cases. Was the Roman Empire ever a social system, though for centuries it was a political one? There are societies that exhibit, often over fairly long spans of time, equilibrium-like features. Yet stability is hardly what strikes us most about human societies over the millennia of recorded history. This is another good reason for not worrying much intellectually about the idea of social equilibrium. There is also a bad reason: that the notion of equilibrium is to be rejected just because of its alleged "conservative political implications." This is a contemptible argument for a scientist to use.

What I found troublesome from the very beginning of my reading of Pareto was the distinction he makes between logico-experimental and nonlogico-experimental *actions*. (Not his parallel distinction between *theories*, with which I have no quarrel.) According to his definition, nonlogical actions par excellence are those that, in the judgment of the actor himself, cause or help cause particular results but, in the judgment of a scientifically trained observer, do not do so.[13] The kind of action that best fits this definition is magic. Thus some people say that dowsing (water-divining) points to a source of underground water. I have had some experience with dowsing, and I am sure that underground water, if found at all, is found by means other than dowsing, including luck and unconsciously registered past experience. Some of the techniques of dowsing allow the latter to take full effect.

In discussing nonlogical actions of this sort, Pareto says: "For Greek mariners, sacrificing to Poseidon and the action of rowing were equally logical means of voyaging."[14] Here Pareto just cannot mean what he seems to be saying. I am a mariner as well as a dowser, and I am utterly certain that Greek seamen cannot have been such fools as to believe they would reach their port *just* by sacrificing to Poseidon; they would certainly have to row. Then sacrificing was not the logical equivalent of rowing, but an addition to it. Sacrifice, the seamen might well believe, would ward off such perils of the deep as could prevent their reaching their port even if they rowed their best. In this way sacrifice might give them confidence, help them perform their voyage, and thus count so far as a logical action. As the British anthropologist Malinowski pointed out, the conditions that give rise to dowsing, sacrificing, and other forms of magic are the strong desires of men that certain results shall occur together with great uncertainty whether they will occur in fact. I shall have more to say about Malinowski later.

Other actions that Pareto certainly claimed as nonlogical do not fit his definition nearly as well as magic does. Thus Pareto certainly considered nonlogical a man's action of volunteering to serve in his country's army in time of war. The man himself would certainly believe that his action might help defend his country. But so, I believe, would a scientifically trained observer. So how does the distinction between logical and nonlogical behavior apply in this case? The fact is it does not.

What Pareto really means by nonlogical, or as we should now say, nonrational, actions are either those that are useless for their intended purpose *or*, like volunteering for the army, appear contrary to the actor's individual self-interest. These are the kinds of actions that give rise to rationalizations, and in rationalizations Pareto, as we shall see, was much interested. The actions Pareto clearly classed as logical were, for instance, those of a skilled engineer, artisan, or merchant when plying his own trade. But these are just the kinds of actions that do not call for rationalizations: they explain themselves. Pareto uses his distinction to make clear that the *Traité* was not going to deal with actions of this sort. Except for this purpose I decided that the distinction was really not very useful. In the meantime I, like Henderson, had thoroughly vexed many people, including my long-suffering father, by gratuitously pointing out to them that some of their cherished actions were nonlogical. My father was not prepared to accept that his volunteering to serve in the U.S. Army was nonlogical.

When one tries to explain why a person has taken one action rather than another, it is really useless to bring in the fact that an outside expert would have told him not to do it or to do it differently. In one sense, people always act logically (rationally); they try to do the best they can for themselves according to their lights; that is, their past experience, their other information, the circumstances they face, the alternatives open to them, and their prospects for success as seen by them. Of course a scientific wiseacre may deem their lights to be dim. But his opinion does nothing to explain their behavior. What we need to know is, if their lights are dim, why they are dim in the particular way they are. Only when we want to teach people to reach their goal more successfully next time, and they want to learn, which is always doubtful, does the question whether their past action was rational become relevant. In the meantime, we do not want to know whether it was rational, but what caused it. This realization led me in time to look for a more satisfactory sociology than Pareto's.

The good that Pareto did me, and can do for others, was negative rather than positive. He forever prevents us from taking, without further evidence, what is written and said about human behavior at its face value. This virtue lies in his discussion of the relations between what he calls the *residues* and the *derivations*. I believe we should now call the *residues* the fundamental values men pursue by their actions and the *derivations* the intellectual processes by which men try to rationalize, that is, attempt to justify, their values and the actions to which they give rise. The *residues* change much more slowly than the *derivations*. If we will but read Pareto carefully, we shall be less often taken in by rationalizations. Since much so-called scientific writing about human behavior and even more nonscientific writing consists of rationalizations, this result may be delightful; for the kind of person who has freed himself from rationalization is one who at last begins to tell us how men do behave, not how they ought to. Not that how they ought to behave is an unimportant question, but we cannot come near to answering it until we know how they do behave. It is idle to tell people to do what they cannot do. But alas! our capacity for believing what we wish to believe—and that is what rationalization does for us—is almost unconquerable. Most of us will be taken in some of the time, though reading Pareto may make the number fewer. Pareto's great virtue is, to use Dr. Johnson's phrase, to "clear your *mind* of cant,"[15] and that is a good place for sound thinking to start from.

Pareto also believed that some *residues* were very different from others. There were two main kinds: the *persistent aggregates* include, for instance, the moral convictions that make men ready to fight to preserve their institutions and societies. Pareto realized, as many liberal intellectuals have realized too late, that this willingness to fight, to lay one's life on the line, is a necessary condition for the stability of a social order, as its absence is an invitation to instability. Of course, it is not the only condition for stability, and obvious willingness to fight may serve the purpose better than fighting itself. Even if one seems to be in a minority in a revolutionary situation, Pareto taught that one should not meekly allow oneself to be led to the slaughter but rather *mourir en brave, les armes à la main*. It is a maxim I have never forgotten, though I am lucky enough not to have had to put it into practice—yet.

I did not really have to learn this maxim from Pareto. I had already learned it implicitly from reading the fascinating books on politico-economic history written by my great-uncle Brooks Adams.[16] My mother, who was one of the few members of her family who could stand him, used to say, "He thought all men should be soldiers and all women, nuns." Ma would add: "Of course it would be difficult to carry out this program." Among the military virtues is a strong infusion of the *persistent aggregates*. In a society and era that, at least in the West, is increasingly pacifist, I am ready to affirm the characteristic values of the soldier and the seaman. Remember that a soldier can display the military virtues without pining for a fight. Unfortunately also a man may be a soldier without possessing the military virtues.

Pareto called the second main class of *residues* the *instinct of combinations*. These include the values that lead to success in invention, science, and business but also—and this was more important for Pareto's theory—to the use of manipulation and ruse, rather than force, in governing. Pareto held that all societies were governed by elites, and the history of these societies depended on the relative proportions of the two classes of *residues* in the elite and the masses. The masses always possessed more of the *persistent aggregates* than did the elite. Thus Pareto anticipated the discovery of "lower-class authoritarianism."

According to Pareto, any elite tended over time to increase its proportion of the *combinations* at the expense of the *persistent aggregates*. It took strong *persistent aggregates* to enable an elite to use force in governing. The use of force might be wholly in accordance with law; it was the failure to use force even though it was lawful that concerned Pareto. His identification of the *persistent aggregates* with the capacity to use force is one of Pareto's most important insights. I feel that what he really meant by the use of force was the ability to make firm decisions and carry them out against opposition. It is really *will* (the *residues*) that counts, for an elite whose will has been undermined cannot present a convincing threat that it will use force if necessary. As an elite loses its *persistent aggregates*, it tends more and more to govern by ruse and stratagem. But these will not keep it in power indefinitely. The government becomes more and more unstable, until a welling-up from the lower classes, with their strong *persistent aggregates*, overturns the old elite and replaces it with a new one with the *residues* needed to maintain a firm social order. Another of Pareto's teachings I have never forgotten is: "History is a graveyard of aristocracies"—a salutary message for someone who thought himself a member of the upper class.

Once the new elite is in place, the old rot sets in again, and the cycle repeats itself. One difficulty with Pareto's theory is that most of the leaders of revolutions do not come from the authoritarian lower class but from the middle. Pareto would argue that at least the leaders of revolution had to possess some degree of the instinct of combinations, which would suggest that they could not come wholly from the lower class. At best Pareto's theory is only a first approximation to the complicated facts. But enough revolutions, past and present, fit his predictions sufficiently well that we had better pay attention to what he has to say. At its crudest his theory dramatizes the struggle between the lions and the foxes in politics.

Pareto was an Italian, though not living in Italy. His *Trattato* appeared near the beginning of the Fascist regime there. In his earlier book, *Les Systèmes socialistes*, he had written one of the best critiques of Marx's *Capital*, though one that was far from wholly hostile. For one thing, he argued that Marx was a better sociologist than he was an economist. Now Pareto declared that the parliamentary governments he knew best, those of Italy and France, were decadent and corrupt. These acts earned for him the accusation that he was an apologist for fascism, that he was "the Karl Marx of fascism." Yet God knows the communists were just as ready to use force in government as Hitler was, and far more ready than Mussolini. In making these charges against Pareto the radicals of the West displayed their usual capacity for deceiving themselves.

The only other evidence that might support the charges is that Mussolini may once have read some of Pareto's work and, when in power, offered to appoint him to the Italian Senate. Pareto never accepted the appointment and indeed died before he could have taken his seat. The true facts, as I believe them to be, about Pareto's political convictions are far more complicated. He had reason to be contemptuous of the plutocratic parliamentary systems. That of Italy folded under pressures created by World War I and that of France in World War II. But neither was he an enthusiast for socialism, though he felt that the plutocratic manufacturers in their greed were asking for it. He never expressed any warmth either towards Mussolini's Italy or Lenin's Russia, and he died before Hitler appeared on the horizon. What he admired first of all in a political elite was its ability to act with some vigor to maintain itself and govern. He was a little less contemptuous of British than of Italian or French democracy; and in this he was again correct, for in World War II, after displaying utter failure of nerve in the preceding decade, Britain was able, if only just, to mobilize enough energy under Churchill to survive World War II.

But it was not enough for Pareto that a government should be able to maintain itself. He was what I shall call an aristocratic libertarian. Personally and emotionally, what he valued was a government that provided for its citizens the maximum of liberty in expression and action. He meant liberty in the old sense, not the humanitarian sentimentalism that passes for liberty with the modern "liberal." Of that he was contemptuous. But liberty, including the liberty to combine with others to pursue common interests—"self-help" as he rightly called it—was something else. As far as I know the only formal statement he ever made about his personal preferences in government was: "I declare myself to be a federalist republican." By this he meant, of course, that he preferred the government of Switzerland, in which he had spent the latter part of his life. Switzerland is a federal republic that has displayed over the years a high degree of both political stability and freedom. I too am prepared to declare myself a federalist republican.

My present view of Pareto's *Traité* is that, with the exception of a few *aperçus* of the greatest importance, it provides the prolegomena to a sociology rather than the substance of one. He helps clear the intelligent mind of cant, but he does not build on the cleared ground. Above all, with the exception of his distinction betweeen the elite and the masses, he is not much interested in what modern sociologists would call social structure. Yet I believe social structure to lie at the heart of sociology. Nor, with the exception of his sneers at corrupt parliamentary governmemts, which do so much to enliven the long pages of the *Traité*, is he much interested in the workings of particular institutions, their changes over time and their variations from one society to another. He was indeed concerned with social systems, but really with only a few of their general features. Reading the *Traité* was a great experience for me and one that I am still prepared to recommend to young sociologists. But I finally decided that I could not build on it directly. It did not lend itself to cumulative growth. I should have to make my own start.

With the publication of the book on Pareto, of which Henderson thoroughly approved, I became, as we would have said under feudalism, Henderson's man. He came to treat me as a sort of son. In summer I used to visit him at his camp on Lake Seymour in Morgan Center, Vermont. Scattered through his property were a number of little cabins, which Henderson had had built according to his own designs, full of neat and ingenious contrivances of his own devising, in which he took much delight. At dinner he fed us a delicious lamb stew, which he kept going continually, adding fresh meat as the old was devoured. Since I was no longer an undergraduate, there was no longer any nonsense about depriving me of alcohol, at least in the form of wine. For swimming in the lake, Henderson wore, beside blue trunks, a cross-striped, blue and white, sleeveless shirt, which made him, with his beard, look like one of the oarsmen in Renoir's painting *Le Déjeuner des canotiers*. What a treat it was to see Henderson addressing himself to chopping down a tree, a long black Wheeling stogie between his teeth. Yet I cannot reconcile the stogie with the fact that Henderson was supposed to be suffering from duodenal ulcer. In his huge gas guzzler of an open Cadillac (or was it a Packard?) we explored much of the beautiful country of northern Vermont and the neighboring Eastern Townships of Quebec. I even took part with the local township in a barn-raising bee, which put me, as did square dancing, in emotional touch not only with my New England past, which was disappearing, but also with my past in Old England.

Like many of my older friends of this period, Henderson urged me to read books that, had I been properly educated, I should have read long before. Sir Francis Bacon's *Essays* I had read at school. Now Henderson made me read the *Novum Organum,* in the wonderful translation by Ellis and Spedding from the original Latin.[17] It makes Bacon's Latin sound like his English. The *Novum Organum* is the greatest book ever written on the philosophy of science. Philosophers now sneer at Bacon's doctrine of induction, yet I have always believed that induction of the kind he recommended does in fact occur.[18] In any event, as Whitehead rightly put it: "The main importance of Francis Bacon's influence does not lie in any particular theory of inductive reasoning which he happened to express, but in the revolt against secondhand information of which he was a leader."[19] Henderson also made me read Montaigne's *Essays,* ultimately in the original French, which I consider, though deliberately unsystematic, to contain the wisest thoughts on the conduct of life—at least by someone who is not a saint—that have been stated in the West. I must also mention Machiavelli's *Discourses*[20]— *The Prince* I had read long before; F. S. Oliver's *The Endless Adventure,*[21] which begins as a life of Sir Robert Walpole and ends, unfinished, with a sympathetic discussion of the behavior necessary to make a man a successful politician; and finally Claude Bernard's *Introduction à l'étude de la médecine expérimentale,*[22] from which Henderson drew some of his own ideas in biological chemistry and the first translation of which into English he stimulated.[23]

Henderson never lost his tactlessness. What saved him was that he was a really great scientist, indeed a great thinker and a great teacher. Persons who came to understand these things, and who succeeded in penetrating Henderson's outer defenses, came to like him very much and to value his company highly. In turn Henderson let down his guard with them. Especially if one were a young man, and Henderson had decided that one had some fire in one's belly, he was endlessly patient in discussing one's problems in research, without worrying about whether they lay within his own particular field of expertise. He had enormous skill in helping one, through discussion, make sure one really knew the questions one was asking and in helping one bring some order out of the chaos of data. Persons belonging to many different disciplines agreed in testifying to this quality in Henderson.

He died suddenly in 1942, after I had been called into the Navy.

NOTES

1. William Allen White, *A Puritan in Babylon: The Story of Calvin Coolidge* (New York: Macmillan, 1938).

2. Vilfredo Pareto, *Les Systèmes socialistes,* 2 vols., 2d ed. (Paris: Marcel Giard, 1926).
3. Vilfredo Pareto, *Traité de sociologie générale,* 2 vols. (Paris: Payot, 1917).
4. Vilfredo Pareto, *The Mind and Society,* trans. Andrew Bongiorno and Arthur Livingston, 4 vols. (New York: Harcourt, Brace, 1935).
5. Joseph A. Schumpeter, *Capitalism, Socialism and Democracy* (New York: Harper, 1942).
6. Crane Brinton, *The Anatomy of Revolution,* rev. ed. ((New York: Knopf, 1975).
7. George C. Homans and Charles P. Curtis, Jr., *An Introduction to Pareto: His Sociology* (New York: Knopf, 1934).
8. Charles P. Curtis, Jr., and Ferris Greenslet, selectors and eds., *The Practical Cogitator or The Thinker's Anthology* (Boston: Houghton Mifflin, 1945), and Charles P. Curtis, Jr., *A Commonplace Book* (New York: Simon & Schuster, 1957).
9. George C. Homans and Samuel E. Morison, *Massachusetts on the Sea* (Boston: Massachusetts Tercentenary Commission, 1930).
10. "The Harbor and Shipping," in *Fifty Years of Boston* (Boston: Boston Tercentenary Commission, 1932).
11. Ernst Mach, *The Science of Mechanics* (La Salle, IL: Open Court Publishing, 1942), pp. 562-76.
12. George C. Homans, *English Villagers of the Thirteenth Century* (Cambridge: Harvard University Press, 1941).
13. Pareto, *Traité,* sec. 151.
14. Ibid., sec. 150.
15. *Boswell's Life of Johnson,* 2 vols. in one (Oxford: Oxford University Press, 1924), vol. 2, p. 496.
16. Especially, Brooks Adams, *The Law of Civilization and Decay* and *The Theory of Social Revolutions* (New York: Macmillan, 1896 and 1913, respectively).
17. *The Philosophical Words of Francis Bacon,* reprinted from the texts and translations, with the notes and prefaces of Ellis and Spedding (London: Routledge, 1905), pp. 256-387.
18. I have recently been confirmed in my opinion by the design of a computer program, naturally called BACON, which will carry out inductions. See Herbert A. Simon, "Unity of the Arts and Sciences: The Psychology of Thought and Discovery," *Bulletin of the American Academy of Arts and Sciences* 35 (1982): 26-53.
19. Alfred North Whitehead, *The Aims of Education and Other Essays* (New York: Mentor Books, 1949), p. 61.
20. Niccolò Machiavelli, *Discourses on the First Decade of Titus Livius,* trans. N. H. Thomson (London: Kegan Paul, 1883).
21. F. S. Oliver, *The Endless Adventure,* 2 vols. in one (Boston: Houghton Mifflin, 1933); and vol. 3 (London: Macmillan, 1935).
22. Claude Bernard, *Introduction à l'étude de la médecine expérimentale* (Paris: Flammarion, 1952). Originally published in 1865.
23. Claude Bernard, *An Introduction to the Study of Experimental Medicine,* trans. Henry C. Green, with an introduction by Lawrence J. Henderson and a new foreword by I. Bernard Cohen (New York: Dover Publications, 1957). Translation originally published in 1927.

8

THE SOCIETY OF FELLOWS

Ahough I had written a book with Charlie Curtis on sociology, I was still not a sociologist but a Paretan. I may have read a few of the sociologists whom the intellectual circles I then frequented recognized as interesting, such as Gustave Le Bon on *The Crowd*[1] and Gabriel Tarde on *Imitation.*[2] They made little impression on me. Of course I had read, as had anyone of my time who had intellectual pretensions, a good deal of Marx, except the early manuscripts. What I had not then read were any of the works of the currently dominant school of American sociology, that of the University of Chicago. It was not fashionable at Harvard. What made me a sociologist was my becoming a member of the Society of Fellows and the experiences that membership brought.

What was the Society of Fellows?[3] Henry Osborn Taylor, author of *The Medieval Mind,*[4] had been in the habit of asking several scholars, his friends, to stay with him in the fall at his house at Cobalt, Connecticut. In the fall of 1925 Henderson and Whitehead had gone to Cobalt, and the conversation had fallen on the subject of graduate education in the United States. The two men continued their discussion on the way back to Boston on the train. Neither was satisfied with the conditions of graduate study, at least for the ablest men. (Neither worried much about the education of women.) The best men needed, of course, ample scholarships, so that worries about money should not interfere with their work. They also needed fewer requirements, fewer hurdles, such as examinations, to jump before they attained the doctorate, if indeed the Ph.D. degree itself was necessary. Instead they ought to be set free to follow up whatever ideas in research or scholarship attracted them. Finally the best men would benefit from conversation with their peers of varied interests and with senior scholars. At that time Harvard offered few institutionalized opportunities for this kind of contact.

This conversation resulted in Henderson's getting President Lowell together with Whitehead and himself for an informal discussion. They found that Lowell's ideas on graduate education fell in closely with their own. Lowell appointed a committee, with Henderson as chairman, to examine for him the nature of an institution that might improve the quality of graduate education. The other members were Whitehead, John Livingston Lowes of the English Department to represent the humanities, and as an unofficial member, Charlie Curtis of the Harvard Corporation, whom at that time I hardly knew. Meetings of the committee began in February 1926, that is, two years before I entered Harvard as an undergraduate.

The committee's report recommended the establishment at Harvard of a body to be called the Society of Fellows. Its design derived partly from the *Fondation Thiers* at Paris and partly from the Prize Fellowships of Trinity College, Cambridge. (Whitehead had been a Fellow of Trinity.) The organization as recommended was almost identical with the one actually established some years later. There were to be two classes of Fellows: a small number of older scholars, the Senior Fellows, who would administer the funds of the society, and at any one time approximately twenty-four Junior Fellows, who would be graduate students or candidates for admission to graduate school. The Senior Fellows were to choose every year a certain number of Junior Fellows, each for an initial term of three years, which might be renewed for a second term. Each unmarried Junior Fellow was to be paid a small stipend and provided with free board and a free suite of rooms at one of the Harvard houses, which were in existence by the time the society was finally established. Married Junior Fellows received a larger stipend in lieu of room and board. In the early days of the society, these emoluments were lavish compared with graduate scholarships in other American universities.

A Junior Fellow was allowed to work on any research project that interested him. At admission the Senior Fellows expected him to describe *some* project, but he was quite free to change his mind later. The facilities of Harvard University were at his disposal, and if his research required money, the Senior Fellows provided him with at least a small grant. The only rule was that a Junior Fellow might not be a candidate for the Ph.D. degree, for it was the special purpose of the society to allow young scholars to escape the stultifying requirements of the doctorate. Because of the difficulty the society later faced in placing its graduates who did not hold the degree, the rule was relaxed. I myself do not hold a doctorate, and I have from that fact indulged myself in much inverted snobbery. A few of the Junior Fellows already had gotten the degree before they entered the society.

Senior and Junior Fellows were to dine together once a week in a special, rather awkwardly designed suite of rooms, consisting of a lounge and a dining room with its own kitchen, which President Lowell had managed to set aside for the future use of the society when Eliot House was built.

After years of trying to find a charitable foundation that was prepared to endow the proposed society, President Lowell finally established it with his own money. Not only had he inherited a great deal, he had, as an exceedingly shrewd investor, made a great deal more on his own hook, and he had no children. The establishment of the society was the last major institutional act he took before he resigned as president of Harvard in November 1932. The society first met at the beginning of the fall term of 1933-34, that is, in the academic year after Henderson had offered his first Pareto seminar. As one might expect, the original Senior Fellows were Henderson, chairman, Whitehead, Lowes, Curtis, until he resigned from the Harvard Corporation, and Lowell, who remained in the society after he had resigned as president. There were also a couple of Senior Fellows, *ex officio,* who did not often come to the dinners.

The Senior Fellows made the selection among the candidates for Junior Fellows. A student might not put himself forward as a candidate, but any recognized scholar at Harvard or elsewhere might nominate a candidate, who was expected to submit specimens of his work, published or unpublished, and, if at all possible, to be interviewed by the Senior Fellows. At the hands of others, this experience was unnerving enough, but at Henderson's it might make the interviewee a candidate for the looney bin, not the society. One story has Henderson's opening an interview by saying to a young scholar: "This is not an examination. No one in this room is competent to examine you. The purpose is for us to get acquainted, and the best way to do that is to talk. So talk!" In fact, the candidate was rendered speechless. Later he was selected.

Someone—it may have been DeVoto, Zinsser, or Curtis, and it is surprising that I have forgotten—had put me forward as a candidate for the society in the first year of its existence. I had run as a poet and had rightly been rejected. My candidacy for the second year was quite another matter. By that time *An Introduction to Pareto* had been published; I had demonstrated my Paretan faith; I was Henderson's man, and Henderson was chairman of the society. I was a good friend of Curtis's. As an undergraduate I had studied under both Whitehead and Lowes. Lowell and Whitehead at least knew who I was. I doubt if Lowes did, which was perhaps just as well, for the lowest grade I had received as an undergraduate (C) was in Lowes's course on English Romantic poetry. If the society were what I wanted, I was in with the right crowd. And it *was* what I wanted. I was still unemployed, or at least unpaid; the Depression still raged, and the society was the best prospect for employment I saw on my horizon. Accordingly when Henderson suggested that I run for the society again, this time as a sociologist, I agreed at once. I had not been able to make anything of myself, but I had learned that if I would only relax and say, "Yes!" others, particularly older men, would make something of me. They did, and I have never regretted what they made. I was elected to the society—it was a sure thing—my term beginning in its second year of operation. I learned of my election in the late spring of 1934, shortly before my father died. I am glad that he did not die without knowing that I was at last employed and embarked on a respectable career.

For the benefit of those who counsel students on the choice of a career, and for the students themselves, let me point out the obvious: my own choice of a career was not really a choice but the nearest thing to pure blind luck. If there had been no Depression and White had been able to employ me in Emporia; if Wheeler had not persuaded Henderson to read Pareto, Henderson in turn, DeVoto, and DeVoto, myself; if DeVoto had not been my tutor; if Henderson had not offered his seminar when he did, and Lowell had not founded the Society of Fellows then, I might very well not have become a sociologist. It is also fair to say that I am not advising all youngsters to leave their choice of career to chance; my case may have been unusual.

Not that in 1933-34 I knew what a sociologist was, except for the example of Pareto, and he became one only late in his life. If I was going to enter the society as a sociologist I had better prepare myself. Accordingly I asked Henderson, in effect, "Master, what shall I do to become a sociologist?" I discovered later that he knew no more about the matter than I did myself, and that he certainly did not propose to consult any of the sociologists, such as Sorokin, who were then at Harvard. Yet his answer was, as always, decided.

First, sociology, if not now a science, might yet become one. Mathematics was the language of science, and a person was a mathematical illiterate who had not proceeded at least through the differential and integral calculus. I had not studied the calculus either at St. Paul's or at Harvard College. Accordingly Henderson ordered me to learn the calculus forthwith. I began to do so under the guidance of Dr. Sebastian Littauer, later a professor of engineering at Columbia, and continued for many years studying the subject by myself. Calculus entranced me with its beauty and power. It has enabled me to understand a great deal of classical physics and economics. Statistics, which Henderson did not suggest that I study, would have been of greater immediate use to me as a sociologist. Even then, calculus is necessary for understanding the intellectual underpinnings of statistics. I now believe that the calculus or some equivalent introduction to higher mathematics is something every educated person, and not just a scientist or engineer, should learn.

Second, German was then the most important foreign language for a scientist to know. St. Paul's had trained me well in German, but I had not kept up my knowledge of it. Henderson ordered me to refurbish my German. The method I adopted, with Henderson's blessing, was to spend the summer of 1934 as a paying guest at Schloss Haunsperg at Hallein, a few miles up the Salzach from Salzburg in Austria. The *schloss* belonged to Graf and Gräfin Thun-Hohenstein, aristocrats who had fallen on hard times with the collapse of the Hapsburg Empire after World War I and the inflation that followed. The year 1934 was fateful for Europe and especially for Germany and Austria. Hitler had come to power; Nazis assassinated Chancellor Dollfuss of Austria while I was at the *schloss*, and we began to foresee and fear some of the developments that led to World War II. To carry out my educational assignment I talked German with my hosts and fellow paying guests. By way of relearning to read German social science, I worked through a great deal of Mommsen's classic *Römische Geschichte*.[5] It is a great book but hardly characteristic of German social science. In it, German is a beautiful language, as it certainly is not in Max Weber. Still my work enabled me to read, if not to enjoy, much of Weber's work before it was translated into English. It also enabled me to read many of the books in German about the Anglo-Saxons and their Continental Germanic origins. I could easily reach Salzburg by bus and thus attend many of the performances of the famous music festival. Though I am not naturally musical, I fell in love with Mozart's operas, especially *Don Giovanni*. In that year Ezio Pinza took the part of the Don with a fine voice and great *panache* in acting. Except for politics, the summer was a delight for me. On my way home I stopped off at Lausanne, went out to Céligny, found Pareto's grave, and piously laid flowers on it:

> *Ut te postremo donarem munere mortis*
> *Et mutam nequiquam alloquerer cinerem.*[6]

Third, Henderson insisted that I should learn historical method, for history, according to him, was the only social science that had a method. I now believe that there is no special historical method other than hard work and the commonest of common sense, but at that time I was ready to do anything Henderson told me to do. His plan was that I should learn historical method by working with Professor Charles H. McIlwain, who taught for many years a famous course at Harvard on English constitutional history.[7] Though McIlwain was a great scholar, I doubt that he had any better idea what Henderson meant by historical method than I had myself. Yet he was a kindly man and willing to do Henderson a favor by taking me on as an unpaid research assistant, especially as I was actually prepared to be of some help to him in the field of English medieval history. At school I had been well trained in classical Latin, which is much more difficult, at least in syntax, than most medieval Latin, and as a former candidate for honors in English literature, I had taken a course that taught me to read simple texts in Old English (Anglo-Saxon).

I met with McIlwain at his house on Francis Avenue, Cambridge, the street on which I now live myself, through much of the academic year 1933-34. He put me to work on the theory of medieval kingship, beginning with the oaths that English kings, from the earliest times and indeed up to the present, have taken at their coronations. He believed that the wording of these oaths reflected important features of the theory. I have forgotten what particular points McIlwain was interested in establishing. Indeed I became skeptical, though I did not tell him so, whether their solemn coronation oaths made any difference at all to the later behavior of the kings. Not that I believe that the theories people hold make no difference to their behavior; Marxism stands as at least one example to the contrary. But Pareto had taught me that behavior was more likely to influence doctrine (the *derivations*) than doctrine, behavior. Whatever my skepticism, I became reasonably expert in interpreting the original sources, and as time went on I became less interested in medieval constitutional theory than in the actual working of medieval institutions.

For instance, one of the prerogatives of an English medieval king was taking possession of goods that belonged to no one else, such as buried treasure, stranded whales, and abandoned wrecks. I became less interested in wrecks than in the practice and risks of medieval seafaring. (Note the maritime theme appearing again.) The kings could seldom make their prerogative good, since the local people could often strip a stranded and abandoned ship clean before the king's officers could arrive on the spot and take possession. For a time I became one of the few persons who knew the difference, which is part of the law of wreck, between flotsam and jetsam. I went on to read widely on the social and economic organization of medieval England, becoming especially interested by Frederic Seebohm's pioneering work, *The English Village Community*,[8] which stimulated the plan for research that I was to carry out while I was a Junior Fellow.

It is amusing for me to realize now that, quite without intending to, I had started out as a social scientist just where my great-uncle Henry Adams had started. In his brief career as the first professor of medieval history at Harvard, he had offered a graduate seminar that resulted in a book of articles by him and his students on Anglo-Saxon institutions.[9] He insisted ironically that his gravestone should record it was he *qui primus explicuit socnam*. (Historians of early England still debate the nature of *sake* and *soke*, legal rights held by some landlords.) But while my great-uncle moved upward from medieval law to the highest achievements of medieval art in his book *Mont-Saint-Michel and Chartres*,[10] I moved downward to plows and field-systems in my book *English Villagers of the Thirteenth Century*[11]—but that did not appear until after I had ceased to be a Junior Fellow. He turned to the sublime, I, not to the ridiculous, but at least the earthy. I wound up less like my great-uncle Henry than like my great-uncle Brooks, who was at his best as an economic historian. (Note also the return here of my Anglo-Saxon theme, my search for historical roots and identity.)

Finally, Henderson arranged that I should take part in an informal course of reading with Professor Elton Mayo, his close colleague in the Harvard Graduate School of Business Administration. Association with Mayo made more difference to my future intellectual development than did any other of Henderson's recommendations. But let it be recorded to my credit that I faithfully followed all of them, and each made at least *some* difference.

Having gotten myself into the Society of Fellows, I must now speak of my experiences there. All the Fellows met every Monday evening during term for sherry in our lounge. (Harvard floats on sherry.) Charlie Curtis's efforts to serve cocktails before dinner were abandoned in favor of the traditional drink. Cocktails are supposed to spoil one's taste for any wine served after them, and very good wine was served at the Fellows' dinners. Though I enjoy most wines, my capacity for making fine discriminations among them had been destroyed forever by the bathtub gin of Prohibition, by this time happily repealed. I suspect that one reason the Senior Fellows ruled out cocktails was the fear that we might become drunk too soon. After sherry we repaired to our dining room, where we sat where we pleased, except for Henderson in the middle of the table, a table long and curved, which barely fitted into the room. There, besides the wine, we got from our own kitchen far better meals than did the undergraduates in the houses. By this time the conversation was lively and we kept it up back in the lounge after dinner. Make no doubt about it, life within the society was in those days opulent. Later, besides the Monday dinners, the Junior Fellows also met once a week for luncheon.

The Senior Fellows were uniformly kind to me, and I got special pleasure from talking to ex-President Lowell, whom I had not known before. Of the original Senior Fellows, Professor Lowes was beginning to get a bit dotty, but I was delighted by his splendidly ambiguous reply to persons who sent him copies of their publications: "I shall lose no time in reading your book!"

Naturally it was the Junior Fellows, my contemporaries, who did most to educate me. In the beginning, their effect was intimidating, which did me much good, for I had closed my undergraduate years at Harvard with the conviction that, even though I might not be a "creative" writer, I was still something special intellectually. Now this last bulwark of my ego was breached beyond repair. Some of the Junior Fellows were older than I, already held doctorates, and were established scholars. Yet none of these external circumstances vouchsafed them their effortless superiority, which was innate. Such, for instance, were Willard ("Van") Quine, who became the greatest logician of his time, and B. F. ("Fred") Skinner, who became the greatest psychologist and made behaviorism respectable. But some of my superiors were of the same age as, or younger than, I. Such was Harry Levin, for years professor of comparative literature at Harvard, whose knowledge of world literature was even then enough to daunt the strongest. Think of being able to talk, without apparent self-consciousness, about Archilochus!

What is more, the differences between us in intellectual productivity became highly conspicuous, because each Junior Fellow was expected to leave a copy of every book or article he had published on a table in the lounge for all to see. It seemed to me that Fred Skinner, for instance, placed a reprint of some new article on the table at least once a week snowing under a person like me, whose publications were still meager, often of only local interest, and hardly original.

I was intimidated, again for my good, in another way. The society was full of first-rate mathematicians, such as Garrett Birkhoff and Stanislaw Ulam, and natural scientists, such as Bob Woodward and John Bardeen. These were scholars of a type with whom I had had no previous contact at all. They brought home to me how limited my previous education, largely literary and historical, had been. My only scientific experience, and that as a field naturalist, was far behind me. These scientists talked about matters I had not even heard of, much less knew anything about.

In the end I got over my feelings of inferiority without forgetting that I had had them. Both the recovery and the remembrance did me good. There was much excellent talk at the dinners and lunches of the society. At least in one's early days as a Fellow, much of it seemed a form of one-upmanship. Like the display of books and papers, it was designed to show how much one knew of esoteric subjects. Yet the man among us who had least to say, John Bardeen, turned out to be the only one to win, at least so far, not just one but two Nobel Prizes. Let that be a lesson to the rest of us chatterboxes! As I became aware of the element of one-upmanship in our talk, I came to feel less humiliated by it. After all, though it may have been in other areas, I had learned to become no slouch at one-upmanship myself; and as over the years I became a more learned social scientist, especially in the notably esoteric field of medieval social history, I was able to hold my own with the rest in showing off. But the better I became at the job, the less I needed to show my skill. The fact was we had all come to terms with one another. I also began, with my friend Jim Fisk, to take a prominent part in the nonintellectual activities of the society by helping to promote some rather drunken dances in our suite of rooms.

I shall speak later and at length about a few of the intellectual issues that I was made to face at least partly because of discussions at the society. Among the hot issues in those days were logical positivism, represented by Quine; behaviorism, represented by Skinner; functional anthropology, represented by Conrad Arensberg, now professor of anthropology at Columbia, who also advocated Percy Bridgman's operationalism in the definition of scientific concepts. I was exposed to a new view of the way science grows by Thomas Kuhn, but that was after World War II, when I was only an occasional guest at the dinners. From Paul Samuelson, now one of the world's foremost economists, I learned, though only in the most general way, about the Keynesian revolution, which was only then just gathering force, in economic theory. But I never became a wholehearted Keynesian. Some of these issues are still hot today.

I was a member of the society from the fall of 1934 through the spring of 1939. These were the great years of the New Deal, and political feeling ran high. I soon discovered that, compared with the men I had associated with as an undergraduate, the Junior Fellows were far more apt to be strong supporters of the New Deal. As far as I knew then, and as I still believe, none of them were communists. They were far less extreme than the real communists of the New York universities, some of whom I came to know later, when they had put their communism far behind them. Instead the Junior Fellows tended to be liberal Democrats or socialists of the Norman Thomas variety. These are the people who will take your money but will not kill you. I had met for the first time a large number of academics of the left, from whom I was not going to escape for the rest of my career as a scholar.

Not that I often wanted to escape. Though I remained a Republican, the liberals did not hold it against me. Most of them I liked as persons, and many had something to teach me. A knee-jerk conservative, I believed, as my father had, in a balanced budget. Paul Samuelson pointed out to me that Great Britain had not balanced its budget for most of the eighteenth century, just when it was initiating the Industrial Revolution and acquiring an empire (but losing the United States). Samuelson shook me at the time, and there are occasions such as war when unbalanced budgets are necessary. Unfortunately they are also addictive. If I had to make a single, once-for-all choice, it would still be for a balanced budget. I became a thinking rather than a knee-jerk conservative. Still, in those days no one would have even considered urging me to become a member of the Harvard Teachers' Union, an organization that was born sickly and died early.

As was to be expected, the Senior Fellows were, on the average and in the early days, a good deal more conservative than the Juniors. Henderson, the chairman, was especially hostile to the New Deal. Harry Levin composed and would deliver to a private audience a magnificent takeoff of Henderson, which required for its appreciation some knowledge of what is now ancient history. Few persons alive today remember even the name of John L. Lewis, then president of the United Mine Workers union and supposed to be the most powerful and radical labor leader of his day. He was tough and vocal, even flamboyant, in backing the interests of his miners, but not really all that radical. And persons who did not know Henderson cannot be aware that he was fond, in almost any connection, of using the phrases "upon the whole" and "in a first approximation." Harry Levin's takeoff, embodying the measured majesty of Henderson's characteristic delivery, ended with the line: "Accordingly it is a reasonable induction from experience that, upon the whole and in a first approxima- tion, John L. Lewis is a—son—of a bitch." Henderson would have used all these words but the S.O.B.

A number of Junior Fellows became my close friends, especially my fellow medievalist and legal historian, George L. Haskins, now professor at the Law School of the University of Pennsylvania, and James B. Fisk, physicist and later head of the world's greatest privately owned research organization, the Bell Telephone Laboratories, at a time when they made their most important contributions to modern technology. Fisk was— alas! he died too young—one of the wisest men I knew. Just before World War II he made me aware of the significance of a German experiment suggesting that it was possible to manufacture an atomic bomb. After the war, he was the first to alert me to the indications, which came from Canada, that traitors had leaked to the Soviets the secrets of the bomb. Close to me also was David Griggs, a geologist now also dead, who I am afraid became infamous within the scientific community by testifying against Robert Oppenheimer in the celebrated investigation of the latter's possible association with communists. Close, too, was Stanislaw Ulam, whose work made possible the hydrogen bomb, Garrett Birkhoff, an- other great mathematician, William F. Whyte, who joined me as a sociologist, and many others.

Two men, both to become professors at Harvard, were more intimate with me later than they had been as Junior Fellows. One was Skinner and the other, Quine.

Over the years, the Society of Fellows has become a great success. It has produced far more than its fair share of distinguished scholars, academic administrators, and even part-time politicians, such as Arthur Schlesinger, Jr., and MacGeorge Bundy. Its membership has included many men who were to become Nobel laureates. Harvard has benefited immeasurably by its presence, since Junior Fellows often became known to their Harvard colleagues sooner than to those elsewhere and thus were invited to take permanent posts here. (But Harvard let Paul Samuelson get away to M.I.T.) It is rare for human institutions to be more successful than might reasonably have been expected. Both the Harvard houses and the Society of Fellows have been so, and be it remembered that President A. Lawrence Lowell was largely responsible for founding both of them.

In the spring of 1939 only one academic year remained of my Junior Fellowship. I had been working hard on the research that was to lead to my book *English Villagers of the Thirteenth Century*. I had also been working hard on reading with Elton Mayo and getting clinical training in interviewing under his guidance. I shall have more to say later about both these enterprises. But I had still published little, and no job was in sight. I am sure that both Henderson and Mayo had tried to get me some regular job in social science, including one at the Harvard Business School, where both had some power; but no offer had come through. Then much to my surprise, late in the spring, Professor Pitirim Alexandrovich Sorokin, chairman of the Sociology Department, offered me an appointment as faculty instructor, the equivalent of the present assistant professor, beginning in the coming fall. Of course I accepted at once. In order to explain—if I am able to explain—how I got this appointment, I shall have to go into my relations with the Sociology Department.

In 1928, the year I entered Harvard as an undergraduate, President Lowell replaced the former Department of Social Ethics with the Department of Sociology. The Social Ethics Department had been, I believe, largely the creation of Richard Cabot. Among American universities, Harvard was late in introducing teaching and research in current professional sociology. Certainly the Social Ethics Department scarcely represented it. While keeping the members of the former department, President Lowell brought in Sorokin, and appointed him chairman of the new department, with the mission of making sociology at Harvard professionally respectable. Sorokin brought with him Carle C. Zimmermann as associate professor.

Sorokin was a Russian by language but he always insisted that he was not one by race but a Finno-Ugrian. He grew up as a poor boy in exceedingly harsh conditions in north-central Russia, but by his own efforts succeeded in getting an education and graduating from the University of St. Petersburg (now Leningrad). He went on to receive a doctorate and later a professorship in sociology there. At the same time he became a prominent speaker on the Socialist, not the Bolshevik, side, and after the first revolution secretary to the premier, Alexander Kerensky. When, in the second revolution, Lenin overthrew Kerensky, Sorokin was cast into the famous Lubyanka Prison. He was fond of saying, "I have been in a Czarist jail; I have been in a Bolshevik jail; I am against all revolutions." In time Lenin had him released from the Lubyanka, and when Sorokin still refused to keep his mouth shut under a tyranny, allowed him to escape from Russia. Stalin would have executed him, and it is surprising that Lenin did not; he did not hesitate to execute others. Sorokin reached the United States and became a professor of sociology at the University of Minnesota.

Though as a Junior Fellow I was in no sense a graduate student in the Sociology Department, yet I had pretensions to becoming a sociologist, and so I wisely called on Sorokin from time to time. In many ways he was a great man. He certainly was a great lecturer, with one of the most beautiful speaking voices, including his Russian accent, I have ever heard. Except for his excellent and pioneering book *Social Mobility*,[12] his ideas did not interest me much. He was then at work on his vast, four-volume *Social and Cultural Dynamics*.[13] This was a work in the genre of Spengler and Toynbee on the cycles of civilization in the West. I have become more and more skeptical of such studies, but I did agree with Sorokin in assessing the modern, or as he called it, the "sensate" society as decadent. And I was entranced with some of the phrases he invented to describe modern culture, especially "physio-dirty."

I became fond of Sorokin and even more of his wife, a distinguished chemist in her own right and, on the side, a talented seamstress. Sorokin once fingered the lapel of a sturdy and stylish coat he was wearing and exclaimed, "See! Made by wife!" The Sorokins gave splendid parties, besides raising a garden full of prize-winning azaleas, at their house in Winchester. There I had a chance to meet the other professors and the graduate students of the Sociology Department.

Though Sorokin was a charming man socially, he could become less so when one fell under his authority. I was not in that position, but if one were, one might suffer. In the tradition of leading professors in European universities, he became, as chairman of the department and with the help of the departmental secretary, a bit of a tyrant.

I also attribute his behavior in part to what cultural anthropologists would call his Russian authoritarianism. Many years later, I was to succeed him as president of the American Sociological Association. One clause of its constitution required the president to "consult" with the chairmen of "sections" within the organization and come to an agreement with them about a particular issue. Sorokin asked me: "Does this mean that, when I'm president I can't just tell them what to do?" I said the clause meant exactly that. "But what if we don't reach agreement, can't *I* decide?" I said that no, he might not, but that men of good will ought to be able to reach a compromise acceptable to all. Sorokin simply could not understand: if one was head of an organization, one had full power over it. I doubt if he ever understood the nature of democratic institutions in the way one does who has been born to them.

Sorokin's authoritarian tendencies may have been exacerbated by jealousy. For a small and young department, sociology by the 1930s had attracted an unusually large number of able graduate students, persons who were later to become distinguished in the profession. There were, to name only a few, Robert K. Merton, Robin Williams, Kingsley Davis, Wilbert Moore, Florence Kluckhohn, and the Rileys, Jack and Matilda. Many of these students wanted to study with Talcott Parsons, who had come to Harvard as an instructor, fresh from Heidelberg and enthusiastic for the work of Max Weber. He did more than anyone else to introduce Weber to American scholars. I have a slight suspicion that Sorokin may have been jealous of Talcott's popularity with the students. At any rate, he was said to have made life administratively unbearable for Talcott.

One of the reasons, I am afraid, that Sorokin came to approve of me was that I was not at least a charter member of the Parsons circle. He had others. I was not a graduate student in the department and so had no occasion to arouse his administrative ire. I was a medievalist, and he highly approved of the European Middle Ages as the very opposite of the "sensate" culture. As an admirer of medieval society, he held in high regard, and rightly so, my great-uncle Henry's *Mont-Saint-Michel and Chartres*, and he knew of our relationship. Yet there was no logical reason why approval of my great-uncle's work should have spilled over onto mine, which was of a very different kind.

There may have been one final reason for what happened. The Sociology Department had few tenured professors, and I suspect that President Lowell did not altogether trust Sorokin's uncontrolled judgment. Accordingly he had set up a committee to make the main administrative decisions for the department. Besides the departmental professors the committee included scholars from elsewhere in the university who were supposed to be interested in sociology. Among these outsiders were Henderson (no surprise), Mayo, Edwin B. Wilson, an old ally of Henderson's and a distinguished statistician at the School of Public Health, and Edwin F. Gay, a former dean of the Business School whom I had met because he had worked on the enclosure of open-fields in England. It is conceivable that Henderson put me forward for the position of faculty instructor, and if he did, he could count on several votes in my favor. But I doubt that he did, for he showed every sign of surprise when I told him that Sorokin had approached me. I believe Sorokin initiated the appointment. Henderson, of course, supported it, and I was duly appointed.

I was the most surprised of all. Naive as I was, I had forgotten that there was even a vacancy in the ranks of faculty instructors, a vacancy opened by Bob Merton's appointment to Columbia. I had forgotten because I could not conceive that I might be a candidate for it, though I had certainly done nothing to spoil my chances. At the end of my second term as Junior Fellow, I was fully prepared at best to be "sold down the river," by which we then meant, quite snobbishly, that I should be forced to take a post at some provincial university, presumably in the South or West. We should never dare to use such language today. In fact no one had offered me a job even in the boondocks. Now, all of a sudden, I was handed a good academic job—good by the standards of the profession— and at Harvard too! Harvard was the best then in a way it will never be again. Once again our little careerist-in-spite-of-himself had enjoyed his usual last-minute good luck.

The very evening on which I heard the good news, "Wendy" Morison, a friend both of mine and of my future wife's, was giving an informal dance in the Morison house at the corner of Brimmer and Mount Vernon Street in Boston. Relieved and elated, I drank more than usual. It was a hot evening in late spring, and I took off my coat in order to dance more vigorously. The noise we made finally brought my old collaborator, Professor Morison, down from his study upstairs. My coatless state offended his sense of propriety, and he handed me my coat to put back on with the simple but imperious words, "Homans, your coat!" That was his right. It was unfair of him to accuse me also of swinging on his chandelier. I had not done so, and if I had, I should have brought it down, but it was still in place. I suspect that Sam sensed the will and took it for the deed.

NOTES

1. Gustave Le Bon, *The Crowd* (London: Unwin, 1909). First English edition.
2. Gabriel Tarde, *The Laws of Imitation*, trans. Elsie Clews Parsons, with an introduction by Franklin H. Giddings (New York: Holt, 1903).
3. See George C. Homans and Orville T. Bailey, *The Society of Fellows, Harvard University, 1933-1947* (Cambridge: Harvard University Press, 1948).
4. Henry Osborn Taylor, *The Medieval Mind*, 4th ed. (London: Macmillan, 1925).
5. Theodor Mommsen, *Römische Geschichte*, 4 vols. (original German editions, 1854-85; many later editions and translations).

6. Gaius Valerius Catullus, *Poems*, No. 101, *Multas per gentes et multa per aequora vectus* (many editions).

7. See especially Charles Howard McIlwain, *The Growth of Political Thought in the West from the Greeks to the End of the Middle Ages* (New York: Macmillan, 1932).

8. Frederic Seebohm, *The English Village Community*, 2d ed. (London: Longmans, Green, 1883).

9. Henry Adams et al., *Essays in Anglo-Saxon Law* (Boston: Little, Brown, 1905).

10. Henry Adams, *Mont-Saint-Michel and Chartres* (Boston: Houghton Mifflin, 1913).

11. George C. Homans, *English Villages of the Thirteenth Century* (Cambridge: Harvard University Press, 1941).

12. Pitirim Aleksandrovich Sorokin, *Social Mobility* (New York: Harper, 1927).

13. Pitirim Aleksandrovich Sorokin, *Social and Cultural Dynamics*, 4 vols. (New York: American Book, 1937-1941).

9

MAYO I: PSYCHOLOGY

When I asked Henderson what I must do to become a sociologist, one of his orders was that I should undertake some informal reading with his colleague George Elton Mayo, usually called simply Elton Mayo. Dean Donham had hoped that Henderson and Mayo would form a team at the Business School. As head of the Department of Industrial Research, Mayo was concerned with the human problems of work; as head of the Fatigue Laboratory, Henderson with the physiological problems. In Morgan Hall, their offices were separated only by space for their genial secretaries, and they were always dropping in on one another. Mayo stimulated my professional thinking more than anyone but Henderson. I say "stimulated" because he did not always influence my thinking in ways he would have approved of. But then I do not believe the best scholars are those who just obey their master's voice.

One of Mayo's charms was that, unlike most of my scholarly friends, he had a mysterious past, some of which he had reason to keep mysterious.[1] Myths grew up about him, which he took no trouble to deny, though the reality when known sometimes turned out to be more prosaic than the myth. Most of the facts I now relate I learned long after his death, and the full story has still to be told. Mayo was born in 1880 in Adelaide, Australia. It looked for a time as if he would turn out to be the black sheep of his distinguished family. For years he did not complete any of the courses of education that lead to conventional and professional success. He studied medicine at Edinburgh, but did not complete the course and receive the M.D. degree. Routine work always bored him, and the knowledge a physician has to commit to memory by rote may have been more than he could bear. Yet like Henderson, who did get his degree, he never lost his respect for the clinical practice of medicine. He worked for a time in London at the Working Man's College, where I suspect he acquired that interest in, and sympathy for, workingmen and women that he never lost. But this work was unpaid. He then visited the part of West Africa that is now Ghana. I long assumed—and Mayo did not disabuse me—that he went there as a British colonial administrator. It now turns out that he meant to make his fortune in the Ashanti goldfields. Instead of gold he caught dengue fever, survived it, and at the insistence of his family returned to Adelaide.

There at last he found his vocation. He went back to the university, became a student of psychology under Sir William Mitchell, graduated in 1910 with honors in philosophy, and won a prize as the best student in his class. (As at Harvard, psychology at Adelaide was then treated as a branch of philosophy.) Mayo was now thirty years old, which is a late age indeed for receiving the bachelor's degree.

The following year Mayo got a position as lecturer in logic, ethics, and psychology at the University of Queensland in Brisbane and later became professor of philosophy there. Psychiatry then hardly existed in Australia, and Mayo as a psychologist began to practice psychiatry, though he had no medical degree—an action that would have horrified physicians in many parts of the world. Among other kinds of patients, he concerned himself with the treatment, often using hypnosis,of soldiers who suffered from what in World War I was called "shell shock." So vivid were his descriptions of these cases that I long assumed Mayo himself had accompanied the ANZAC forces to France. Not at all: he remained in Australia throughout the war and worked with soldiers who had been sent home. He also took private patients, and kept up his interest in workingmen and women. Always a good and relaxed speaker, he often addressed meetings of trade unions to ask their support for the Workers' Educational Association.

I ought to have deduced that Mayo remained in Brisbane through the war, because I knew it was then and there that he and his wife Dorothea became friends of Bronislaw Malinowski—always "Bronio" to them— who was to become one of the world's great social anthropologists.[2] Because he was a native of Poland, then occupied by the Germans in World War I, the British authorities treated Malinowski in theory as an enemy alien, and did not allow him to return to Britain or even, except for short stays, to Australia itself. In practice this meant exile in what was then British New Guinea and included the Trobriand Islands. There Malinowski carried out the studies that set a new standard for thoroughness in anthropological fieldwork. Yet if one can believe his diary, published long after his death, he was bored by every minute of his stay in the Trobriands and loathed the natives he had to work with.

Now Brisbane was the point of departure for British New Guinea, which made it natural for the Mayos to meet him there. While recognizing "Bronio" as in many ways an eccentric, they enjoyed his company, if only because he may have been their only intellectual equal within a thousand miles. After the war, when Malinowski's books had made him famous and he was a professor at the London School of Economics, Mayo continued to keep up with him. Above all, Mayo encouraged his students, including me, to read Malinkowski's books. Such are the accidents, in this case Mayo's living in Brisbane, that bring people and ideas together. One of the purposes of this book is to show how large a part chance played, directly and indirectly, in my intellectual development.

Mayo also became an acquaintance of the other great British social anthropologist and Malinowski's chief rival, A. R. Radcliffe-Brown, usually referred to as "R-B." They too may well have met in Australia, though R-B did his fieldwork on the west coast, not the east, where Brisbane lies. And just as Mayo encouraged his students to read Malinowski, so he encouraged them to read Radcliffe-Brown, especially his first book, *The Andaman Islanders*.[3] R-B's thinking had been heavily influenced by that of the French sociologist Emile Durkheim, and he may have introduced Mayo to Durkheim's work. Mayo also asked us to read a good deal of Durkheim.

As usual a myth accounted for Mayo's coming to the United States. It held that by the 1920s Mayo had become utterly bored with Brisbane, that he suffered what psychologists call a fugue, and at a moment's notice took off for San Francisco with hardly a penny in his pocket, leaving his wife and two daughters behind. In San Francisco he at once happened upon and charmed—indeed he could charm anyone—a member of the Rockefeller family, and with Rockefeller backing went on from there.

In this instance, the myth had some grounding in fact. By 1922 Mayo was dissatisfied with the opportunities for research in Brisbane. The human problems of industrial society had increasingly become his central interest. He had never visited the United States, which had become the leading industrial nation of the world. He indeed landed in San Francisco with little money and had to borrow more in order to stay in this country. He did not meet a Rockefeller but did meet and interest a large number of industrialists, social scientists, and foundation executives. After agonizing delays Beardsley Ruml, director of the Laura Spelman Rockefeller Foundation, persuaded John D. Rockefeller, Jr. to make Mayo a grant of money that enabled him to take up a research post at the Wharton School of Finance and Commerce at the University of Pennsylvania. His wife and two daughters could now join him.

At the Wharton School Mayo carried out some interesting in-plant industrial research and published some magazine articles for the general but well-educated reader. Both attracted the attention of Wallace Donham, the dean of the Harvard Graduate School of Business Administration, who induced Mayo to accept a professorship there in 1926 and teamed him with Henderson. Donham was lucky because, though Henderson and Mayo differed utterly in temperament, they became close friends. Accordingly Mayo had been in the United States, at least during the academic year, for some time before I met him.

Later Mayo stated his program in a letter to Dean Donham that forms an introduction to Mayo's book *The Social Problems of an Industrial Civilization* (1945): "[We] agreed that a research study of human behavior and human relations was eminently desirable. Such a study, if made without presuppositions other than those justified by biology or by the human aspect of clinical medicine, might, we believed, be more productive than a direct attack on labor relations."[4] Note here, first, Mayo's use of the words "the human aspect of clinical medicine" and, second, his proposal that his study of human relations in industry should be "indirect." This meant, in effect, that he was not going to be concerned with "labor relations." It did not mean that Dean Donham neglected to make a "direct" attack on that field, for he appointed Benjamin M. Selekman professor of labor relations. Later I carried out field research for Ben,[5] and we were planning to write a book together when he died of sudden heart attack. Ben had been brought up in a "company" coal-mining town in Pennsylvania and was thoroughly sympathetic with the aims of organized labor.

In pursuance of his research program, Mayo did not originate but took over the direction of what came to be called the Hawthorne Study, because it was carried out at the Hawthorne Works in Chicago of the Western Electric Company, manufacturers of equipment for the American Telephone and Telegraph Company.[6] Mayo's work was financed by a grant of $100,000 a year from the Rockefeller Foundation, a huge grant by the standards of the time. The grant, for a term of years, was renewed, and Mayo used some of it to finance research only indirectly related to the work at Hawthorne. The "data collection" as distinguished from the "writing up" phase of the research was coming to a close by the time I first met Mayo, which must have been in 1933.

When one first laid eyes on Mayo, one noticed first a pale, almost dead-white skin on a very slim body. Then a bald head with a high, protruberant forehead. Soon one discovered that he chain-smoked cigarettes. It was not the fact that he chain-smoked I found surprising, but the way he did it. The cigarette was placed in a long holder, consisting of a set of celluloid tubes, fitting into one another. When one of these tubes had been chewn through or clogged with tar, Mayo replaced it with a fresh one. I never met anyone else who smoked in this way.

Most professors at the Business School maintained their roles as real businessmen by arriving for work promptly at nine A.M.: they might as well have punched a time clock. But not Mayo. He never conformed to a convention he did not find congenial, and as a research professor he was responsible for no regular teaching. He seldom showed up at his office much before eleven, which led some of his colleagues to look down on him as a bit of a charlatan. What he did before this hour I never learned, but I suspect he read a great deal, even in periodicals I did not approve of, such as the *New Republic.*

When he finally arrived at his office, Mayo held court. Anyone who was working in a field that interested Mayo was free to come in and talk about his own work, or indeed about anything else he had on his mind. No one was better than Mayo at helping others to clarify their ideas, even ideas they found difficult to express at all, or at encouraging them to develop the ideas further. In so doing, he took time off to enliven the conversation with comments and stories, sometimes so bizarre that I was sure he had made them up, drawn from his own clinical experience. Thus he could exercise a loose supervision over persons whose work he was responsible for, without its feeling like supervision to them. Indeed he was dedicated to helping people take responsibility for their own work. He did not remain in the office long. Soon after lunch he usually returned home—if home it could be called.

This way of life Mayo continued to follow when in the field. I took no part in the Hawthorne researches, though God knows I wrote more than enough about them at second hand.[7] Still, Mayo took me a couple of times to the plant. He showed me the famous Relay Assembly Test Room, but I noticed that he spent most of his time talking with George Pennock, the head of the plant, whose office was naturally at the highest tower of that huge brick fortress. Mayo did not hesitate to bring me along and Pennock showed no sign of resenting the intrusion, especially as for once I had the sense to keep my mouth shut.

Mayo's chosen role was not to take part in the immediate work of industrial research himself but to maintain the conditions in which others, both employees of the company and members of the research team from Harvard, such as Fritz Roethlisberger and T. N. Whitehead,[8] could carry it out successfully. This was not only a deliberate strategy of Mayo's but in accord with his tastes: he was easily bored by routine, even the routine of research. Specifically, his role was to reassure the top brass at Hawthorne that all was going well and that this foreign body, the research team, was doing nothing to upset the smooth functioning of the plant. Not that any plant operates smoothly for long, and the brass are looking for trouble if they believe it does, but they want to avoid more foul-ups than usual, especially those of new kinds.

I do not believe that Mayo ever returned to Australia. If anywhere, he thought of England as his home; there he returned every summer, and there he retired. In Cambridge one always had the feeling that he was camping out. A man of the world, equipped with every social skill and grace, he never seemed to me much interested in ordinary "social" life and party going. He and Dorothea entertained little, unless a casual lunch with someone like me counted as entertainment. They made one or two close friends, such as Professor Edwin J. Cohn, a pupil of Henderson's, who did more than anyone else to find important applications for the Master's work. They may have seen something of the elder Whiteheads. But they were not conspicuous in the 1930s version of the Cambridge cocktail- and dinner-party circuit.

Camping out for the Mayos usually meant their renting a dingy suite of rooms in the old Brattle Inn, and it was there over tea, once a week in term-time, that he held his informal seminar. His students were some half-dozen graduate students from different fields in the Faculty of Arts and Sciences and the Business School. At these meetings Mayo and his students would discuss in some detail the books he asked us to read, enlivening the meetings as usual with anecdotes, true or invented for the purpose, from his own experience. The books were few in number, and in the course of the years in which he offered the seminar we discussed some of them more than once. Mayo's choice was highly eclectic. In assigning reading he never tried to cover a field thoroughly. Still, our reading included some of the seminal books in modern social science.

Let me take psychology first. We went carefully over Pavlov's famous work on conditioned reflexes, which are now called classical conditioning. A reflex is behavior that the experimenter can produce in the animal at will, as Pavlov produced salivation in dogs by exposing them to the sight of food. In human behavior, operant conditioning is much more important than classical. An operant is behavior that the experimenter cannot produce at will in his subjects. He must wait until they perform it, even if only in sketchy form and then shape (condition) it by reward. Mayo had nothing to say about operant conditioning, though he must have heard of it under the name of behaviorism. Edward Thorndike's "law of effect" had long been known. Perhaps J. B. Watson's gross overstatement of the behavioristic position may have turned Mayo off. But I am sure he was not turned off just because behaviorism was intellectually unpopular. For myself, I was not much interested in Pavlov, and for operant conditioning I had to go to Fred Skinner, who gave it its name and who was my fellow-member of the Society of Fellows. I do not know that Mayo ever met Fred.

Instead we went directly from Pavlov to Gestalt psychology, reading Wolfgang Kohler's *The Mentality of Apes*.[9] Gestalt psychology studied the process by which animals and humans try to make organized wholes (*gestalten*) out of their perceptions. Gestalt psychology led Mayo to Jean Piaget, far less famous then than he became later. Piaget taught that a child first learned, when very young, an authoritarian morality. It was an absolutist morality, to be taken literally, handed down as it was to the child from the father and mother, as Moses brought down from Sinai the Tables of the Law to the Jews. A child was able to acquire a more relativistic or cooperative morality only if he could escape from his family to some body of his contemporaries. From them he would learn that morality was a convention, capable of being changed by those who took part in it, as the players of a game can agree to change its rules. Through this experience an adolescent was on the way to acquiring an adult and mature morality.[10]

Mayo was not interested just in describing the change from one type of morality to another. An adolescent did not make the change automatically, and Mayo was concerned with the conditions that made it possible. A child needed to find a group of his equals he could escape from his family *to*; and such groups might be becoming more rare as industrial society became more disorganized socially. That was the focus of Mayo's interest. Society might be producing fewer and fewer men and women possessing the full panoply of social skills necessary to hold it together. Mayo tended to see the skills as growing out of the cooperative morality, and with Piaget he began to make us think about the mutual relations between the characteristics of individuals and those of their society.

Mayo was at heart a psychiatrist rather than a pure psychologist and, as a psychiatrist, his great admirations were Sigmund Freud and Pierre Janet. Everyone has heard of Freud, one of the most famous—and most overrated—men of the twentieth century. But who has heard of Janet, though in the 1930s he was the dean of French psychiatrists? Mayo asked us to read some of the books of both men, and since Janet is the less well known, let me begin with him. We read and discussed his little book *Les Névroses*,[11] and later on my own account I read *Les Obsessions et la Psychasthénie*.[12] Mayo himself wrote a short book about Janet's work.[13]

Janet made a sharp distinction between the psychoses, which he presumed to have a basis in some physical deficiency of the patient's (though no one knew what it was), and the neuroses, which he presumed to have no physical basis but to have resulted from the patient's experience of life. (Today we should not be quite so sure that the neuroses have no physical basis.) Within the neuroses Janet distinguished between, on the one hand, the hysterias, which by their highly symbolic form, such as the appearance of the stigmata of Jesus Christ, suggested that they were not of physical origin, and on the other hand, more subtle psychotic disorders, some of which Janet called obsessions and which we today should probably call schizophrenia or schizoid conditions.

What Janet did was to describe with the old French thoroughness and lucidity—now lost to French science in the trendy cant of such gurus as Lacan and Lévi-Strauss—the presenting symptoms of the range of neuroses. Nowhere else have I found mental and behavioral disorders described with such a wealth of Linnaean detail. Janet was a marvelous natural historian building on long and rich clinical observations. He was much less interested than was Freud in the aetiology of the disorders, and since he had little confidence that he knew their causes, he had still less that he knew their cures. Mayo reported that Janet had once said of mental patients, "But they cannot be cured!" accompanying his exclamation with a typical French shrug of the shoulders and upturned hands.

Mayo wanted us to read Janet because Mayo felt obsession to be the characteristic mental illness of modern times, and so it is, though we call it obsession no longer. The incidence of hysteria, on the other hand, seems to have declined with increasingly higher levels of education. Reading Janet frightened me in the short, but reassured me in the long run. Like any medical student who reads a text for the first time, I felt sure I suffered from all the diseases described, as indeed I did to some degree. I became a psycho-hypochondriac. I became convinced that my psyche was a festering mass of corruption, and I despaired, especially since Janet had declared there was no cure. Later, with more reading and experience, I decided that if I were mentally ill, at least I was not as ill as Janet's patients or even many of the persons I saw around me. This recognition cheered me immensely and has kept me so. If I am not sane, at least my insanity is well within the normal range. Depressed I have certainly been, yet without ever entertaining a desire to kill myself. I am an obsessive beyond the shadow of a doubt, especially in my frequently high level of anxiety and compulsiveness. Yet these vices bring forth their corresponding virtues. An anxious compulsive is more likely than others to do what he has said he will do and do it when he has said he will. As a sometime administrator, I have found this virtue to be rare among my colleagues and subordinates, but priceless when found—just because it relieves my own anxieties.

Janet provided a naturalist's description of the neuroses. Freud, the other of Mayo's twin gods, was Janet's complement. He did not undertake to survey the range of symptoms but rather to provide, for some of them, an explanation of their occurrences, dynamics, and possible cure. With Mayo we read and discussed a number of Freud's books and papers, beginning, I think, with *Three Contributions to the Theory of Sex*[14] and *The Interpretation of Dreams*.[15] We did not bother with offshoots from the main trunk of Freudian dogma, such as Jung or Adler.

For educated persons living today it is easy to forget how fresh and radical Freud seemed in the early 1930s or how much controversy he inspired. Though Mayo and Henderson were almost always at one with each other, about Freud they agreed to disagree. (Mayo also was easily bored by Henderson's endless references to Pareto, but agreed with him on the importance of Pareto's discussion of "nonlogical" action.) The biologist in Henderson and perhaps something more personal—his wife was in a mental hospital—would have nothing to do with Freud. In my view Freud deserved a better grade of controversy than in fact he got; in the end too many persons accepted his teachings too easily. My own intellectual attitudes towards him were ambivalent from the start.

I was not in the least disturbed by the concept of the unconscious and the tricks it could play, an idea that in the beginning gave so much trouble to so many. I was wholly prepared to believe, for instance, that traumas suffered by children in infancy, traumas that could be brought back to consciousness, if at all, only by hypnosis or free association, could wreak psychic disorder years later in the patient's life. After all, that was a perfectly orthodox finding of behavioral psychology, which was beginning to interest me. Fred Skinner used to say that Freud was a good behavioral psychologist.

From the concept of the unconscious followed Freud's method of psychiatric treatment. Mayo pointed out that Freud had begun by working with the hysterias, which would often yield to hypnosis. (Mayo's shell-shocked soldiers were hysterics.) But Freud soon discovered that most of his Viennese patients could not easily be classed as hysterics or easily be hypnotised. He therefore had to experiment with other forms of treatment, finally coming to depend on the famous method of asking the patient to relax on a couch and "freely associate," that is, bring out any idea, however apparently incongruous or irrelevant, that came into his mind. Freud's method provided the rationale for Mayo's own less-strict method, which came to be called "non-directive interviewing." I could appreciate that these methods might help the nonhysteric bring back under conscious control thoughts and actions that had sunk deep into unconsciousness.

Nor was I disturbed by Freud's emphasis on sex. Mayo suggested, as others had done, that this emphasis, which Freud brought to the explanation of the neuroses, derived from the characteristics of bourgeois society in Vienna before World War I. Mayo was also careful to argue that Freud did not come as a liberator of sexual behavior. Instead he was a bit of an Old Testament prophet, or at least a Victorian moralist, who believed that sexual repression, with its accompanying sublimation, was necessary for preserving civilization. Nevertheless the fact that Freud wrote so much about sex and got people into the habit of thinking about it openly may, without any intention on his part, have led to greater freedom in actual sexual behavior.

Not that I accepted all that Freud had to say about sex. For instance, he postulated a "latency period" between infancy and the onset of puberty in which the child's sexual interests and behavior were in abeyance. I knew damn well from my own preadolescent years that this was not so, and not for one moment did I believe I was a solitary exception. Yet not even Mayo, often a skeptic, ever cast a doubt on the reality of the "latency period."

Worst of all, I could not bring myself to believe in the generality of the Oedipus complex, and that is the very touchstone of Freudian theory. No doubt some persons had experienced it, but I could not believe that I had done so myself or, again, that I was a solitary exception. Therefore the complex could not be universal nor could "working through" it successfully be the key to a viable mental life. Yet he who doubts its universality must be cast from the ranks of the faithful, and I came to consider myself such an outcast. Yet, pusillanimous as I was, I never expressed my doubts to Mayo or to the seminar.

I had certainly felt at times the force of a father's authority and the something less than intimacy with him that accompanied it. I could also feel a mother's complementary nurturant behavior towards her children, though in the case of my own mother I sometimes doubted that she gave us a thought when we were out of her sight. But I could never bring myself to believe that I hated my father because he was my successful rival for my mother's sexual favors. "Aha!" a true believer will say, "you may not have believed it consciously, but you must have done so unconsciously." And I have no doubt that if I had ever undergone psychoanalysis, the analyst would have found it. You can find anything if you *must*.

Yet I had looked hard for my Oedipus complex and its spoor and had not found a trace of them. Not that Mayo psychoanalyzed any of us or required that we be psychoanalyzed. But he did ask a number of us to record our dreams. We were to keep pencils and paper by our bedsides and, as soon as we woke up in the morning, to write down what dreams we remembered we had had in the course of the night. Many people dream little or at least remember little of what they have dreamt. Mayo assured us that with practice we could remember a great deal, and for me that turned out to be correct. Soon I was writing down so many pages of remembered dreams that it got to be boring.

In the record I could find nothing Oedipal. I never dreamt about my father or mother, not at least in a form in which I could recognize them. A true believer might argue that I had been caught too late, that I had already worked through my Oedipus complex, had come out on the other side, and that therefore it would not show itself in my dreams even in disguised form. But a boy who has successfully worked through his Oedipus complex is supposed to identify with his father. Much as I admired my father, the one thing I was sure of was that I did not identify with him: I was definitely different, at least consciously. But a true Freudian believer might find I am more like my father than I think I am.

I could not believe Freud's theory of dreams as the fulfillment of wishes. No doubt some of them were, but in my most frequent form of dream I found myself in a painfully embarrassing social situation. Let an analyst make what he will of that! The wish fulfillment lay not in the dream but in the waking up, which relieved me of my embarrassment. As for the Oedipus complex, my studies in social anthropology gave me still further reasons for distrusting Freud. But I shall speak of them later.

I was always the more interested in Freud the closer he remained to describing his clinical experiences. His abstract theories I always had trouble with. All that stuff about id, ego, and superego seemed to me to repeat in new words a metaphor about human behavior, which did not lack reference to reality but which in Western culture had long antedated Freud. It was so old as to be hackneyed. The most important truth I may have learned from Freud and his disciples is that, in evaluating psychological or social theories, people do not ask often enough whether the theories correspond at all to their own personal experience. Whether or not they do is the first question a social scientist ought to ask, though it may not be the last.

Quite rightly, Mayo did not intend for a moment that the training of social scientists should end in book-learning alone. He believed that they should acquire clinical experience under responsibility, that is, not just firsthand acquaintance with human behavior—each one of us acquires a great deal of that in the ordinary course of his life, if he will only scrutinize it—but the kind of firsthand acquaintance that is driven home by one's taking some responsibility for the behavior of others, by one's having something at risk. The growing social disorganization of the modern world Mayo blamed largely on the failure of leaders at every level to acquire "social skills," and he undertook to see that at least his own students had a responsible clinical experience and with it at least rudimentary social skills.

It turned out that the social skills in question were to be of one kind— and there is more than one kind. As Mayo put it later: "Students are taught logical and lucid expression [I wish they were]; they are not taught that social skill begins in the art of provoking, and receiving, communications from others. The attitudes and ideas thus communicated, by no means wholly logical, will serve to form the basis of a wider and more effective understanding."[16] The "art of provoking, and receiving, communications from others" was to take the form of "non-directive interviewing," Mayo's flexible adaptation of the Freudian couch. The psychologist Carl Rogers independently invented an essentially similar method.[17] And of course wise men and women have learned the art without making its few and simple rules explicit. They are easy to learn but not to practice, because to apply them successfully takes great self-control.

The rules we learned had been made explicit for the program of interviewing many thousands of workers at Hawthorne, which was part of the Western Electric researches.[18] They cannot be repeated too often:

1. The interviewer should listen to the speaker in a patient and friendly, but intelligently critical, manner.
2. The interviewer should not display any kind of authority.
3. The interviewer should not give advice or moral admonition.
4. The interviewer should not argue with the speaker.
5. The interviewer should talk or ask questions only under certain conditions:
   a. To help the person talk.
   b. To relieve any fears or anxieties on the part of the speaker which may be affecting his relation to the interviewer.
   c. To praise the interviewer for reporting his thoughts and feelings accurately.
   d. To veer the discussion to some topic which has been omitted or neglected.
   e. To discuss implicit assumptions, if this is advisable.

Note especially the assumption that authority gets in the way of easy communication. I shall have more to say about this later.

Mayo wanted us to practice this kind of interviewing until it became second nature with us. By what means I know not, he had become a friend of Dr. Joseph Pratt's, who was then head of the Boston Dispensary on Washington Street, near what is now called, but was not then, the "combat zone." Today the dispensary has become the New England Medical Center, run by Tufts University. Pratt and Mayo were sympathetic in their views. Pratt had founded and presided over what he called "The Thought-Control Clinic," an early if not the earliest example of a "therapeutic group." Patients who came to the dispensary complaining of ailments for which the physicians could find no physical basis—and many such patients are always moving in and out of city hospitals—were invited to join the clinic, where under the encouragement of Dr. Pratt they made something like public confessions of their ills and were rewarded by reassurance from other members of the group. I am sure the clinic helped many persons through difficult times.

Each of Mayo's students was to interview the kinds of persons who attended the clinic or might be invited to do so. Before we began, Mayo demonstrated to us how he would interview a patient. I must say he could practice what he preached. No one was better than he at "provoking and receiving communications from others." How quickly under Mayo's guidance, which was really not guidance because it did not in the least inhibit the patient's saying what was on his mind, did the latter begin to pierce the crust of his symptoms and approach what was bothering him underneath. Mayo also demonstrated his method of hypnotizing a patient and making posthypnotic suggestions, but he did not allow us to attempt this technique ourselves. These skills of Mayo's, combined with a—usually—deep insight into the springs of human behavior led me, and many of his other students, to look on him as a kind of sorcerer.

With the rules of nondirective interviewing in our minds, and further guided by Mayo's demonstrations, we were supposed to be ready for our responsible clinical experience. Once a week during term-time, I believe, we went into the dispensary and donned the conventional white jackets of M.D.'s. To be sure this was deception, but Mayo and Pratt believed that patients would not even begin to have confidence in us if we looked like plain civilians. In no other way did we pretend to be physicians. Then each of us was assigned, by some means I never knew, a particular patient, whom at least one real M.D. had examined and certified that the ill of which he or she complained had no physical basis. Each of us was then left alone with his patient to encourage him (in my case usually her) to talk as freely as he liked and in any way he liked about himself and his troubles. A student was to encourage him especially to explore his early history, including details he might have forgotten before the interviewing process dredged them up. Each of us was to meet with the patient for as long as he felt he was getting something out of our relationship. With some patients that meant many meetings. Though we had read much Freud, we were not to act like Freudian psychiatrists and try to interpret to the patient the unconscious mechanisms presumed to be at work behind what he said and did. We were encouraged to make possible interpretations ourselves, but not to inflict them on the patient. We were simply to help him talk freely about himself and his past.

From time to time we discussed our patients with Mayo and what we thought we were learning from them. We did not do so often and usually only if we were running into some special difficulty. As usual I felt that Mayo was often bored by hearing about our patients, though of course we ourselves could not keep our minds off them. Nor did Mayo try to discover how well we were using the nondirective method of interviewing, as Carl Rogers would certainly have done. Did one of us, for instance, by saying the wrong thing at the wrong moment, cut the patient off from pursuing some topic he was eager to pursue? To have provided the ground for such criticism we should have had to make recordings of our interviews. This we never did. Tape recorders were not then in common use. All we did, and that was hard enough, was write down *after* the interview as much of it as we could recall. Obviously we could not recall everything nor even that very accurately. But at least we were practicing interviewing in conditions that, while requiring responsible action on our part, still minimized the harm we could do to our patients or ourselves. Later some of us interviewed in the same way at the Boston City Hospital.

It soon appeared that I, like the other students, was producing "cures" in some of our patients without in the least intending to do so. Mayo had asked us not to get so emotionally involved with our patients that we felt it our duty to try to "cure" them. But the superficial symptoms of some patients disappeared after a few interviewing sessions. We realized that many patients of the sort we were seeing got "cured" spontaneously without anyone's taking any care of them at all. Still, a "cure" was a heady experience, and for several years grateful patients sent me letters. Yet I never acquired the slightest desire to become a psychiatrist or indeed to "do good" to others in any way whatsoever. The greatest good my psychiatric interviewing did was always to myself. Later, I wanted very much to become a good teacher, but I never thought of that as "doing good," and perhaps it was not.

We were lucky to have undergone this experience. In later years I used nondirective interviewing to good effect, but in industrial rather than hospital settings and for informative rather than therapeutic purposes. I am grateful to Mayo for arranging this priceless opportunity for us. I learned to talk to people rather than just collect statistics. A few years later we might not have been allowed to do what we did. Some would have charged us with practicing psychiatry without a license and put a stop to our work. When I told Hans Zinsser, who was of course an M.D., what we were doing, he was not a little shocked, though he did nothing to interfere. Henderson, who was also an M.D., showed no sign of shock, and Mayo himself, who held no medical degree, though he always let himself be treated as if he did, never allowed any convention to get in his way. The one person without whose support we should have been lost was Dr. Joseph Pratt of the Boston Dispensary.

Over the years, as I came to know Mayo better, he used to invite me to have lunch with him. We never made dates ahead of time but always on the spur of the moment. I never invited him: as my superior in status he always invited me. Usually we lunched *tête-à-tête* and not with a third

person, and very characteristically of Mayo, always the outsider, never at
the quite adequate Faculty Club of the Business School but at St. Clair's,
an excellent restaurant that then existed on Brattle Street, just down from
Harvard Square. Perhaps the reason for this choice was that, though
Prohibition had now been repealed, the Faculty Club did not yet serve
alcohol. St. Clair's did, and Mayo and I always opened the proceedings
with a couple of glasses of La Ina sherry—Mayo's choice and never any
other. Much of my education has taken place under the influence of
alcohol.

Mayo and I talked about all sorts of things, though usually not
professional and usually initiated by him and not by me, for I am not
good at small talk, whereas Mayo certainly was. He could be entertaining
about anything. We talked, for instance, about various forms of sports:
horse-racing in Australia, fishing in England. (Mayo never fished in the
United States, and I no longer fished at all.) We talked of the characteristics of the Australian "blackfellows" (the aborigines). We talked at length
of personalities Mayo had known, such as "Bronio" Malinowski, seldom
of our immediate colleagues, though I remember vividly his referring to
one of them as *tout ce qu'il y a de plus bourgeois*. We never talked about
our private affairs at these luncheons. Later I had occasion to ask him
about some of mine, but he treated them in a wholly different context.
Though friendly, we never became intimate. I am sure I furnished him
with some relaxation. After all, through his own training, I had become a
pretty good listener.

These were the 1930s, the years of the Depression and the New Deal,
of "hating Roosevelt" at home, of the Spanish Civil War and the rise of
Stalin and Hitler abroad. Naturally we talked politics, though not as often
as might be expected. Mayo took a more detached view of politics than I
did myself, except where the safety of his adopted country, Great Britain,
was concerned. Even then Mayo was inclined to give almost any British
politician more credit for wisdom than he usually deserved. Mayo was
inclined to view all our troubles as manifestations of an underlying social
disorganization, as "the acquisitiveness of a sick society"—his transposi-
tion of the title of Tawney's book.[19] Mayo may well have been correct, but
his was a view that gave a statesman little guidance on what to do about
immediate issues. He once said of Hitler: "He is restoring by drill the
cohesion of a broken people." No doubt Hitler was doing just that: it is
still an inadequate view of what he ultimately intended. To be fair to
Mayo, I must recognize that he offered the remark before Hitler had
made it clear he was bent on war and holocaust. Mayo made it before we
had begun to take *Mein Kampf* seriously.

Mayo had little to say, one way or another, about Soviet communism, though it was one of the preoccupations of some of the circles we moved in. All too reasonably and without prejudice, he professed not to know how it was apt to come out, and he certainly did not recognize then how far Stalin's regime, like Hitler's, was maintained by terror. His position was characteristic of many liberal and well-educated persons both here and in Europe. In this respect my own views were both in advance of Mayo's and more accurate. But I did not argue with him.

Unlike me, Mayo was not a conservative in grain. He held no doctrinal views against unionism or against socialism, at least as embodied in the British Labour Party. Because he carried out so much of his work in a capitalist organization, the Western Electric Company, and because the "human relations school," which he was credited with having founded, was so much interested in making modern industry work more effectively precisely by making it more human, leftists took him to be a mere apologist for business. Their view was superficial. From Mayo's youth he had been active in the field of workers' education; he got along splendidly with individual workingmen and women and with union leaders, even the most radical—which did not mean he agreed with all they said. Much of the research I later carried out under his direction we carried out not under the aegis of any capitalist organization but rather that of Phil Murray and the Steel Workers' Organizing Committee, the predecessor of the current steel workers' union. Mayo was interested in training a wiser elite, one better skilled at maintaining human cooperation, than any he saw before him in the 1930s; but he had no preconception about where the new elite was going to come from; it might perfectly well come from the unions.

Mayo struck me as one of the few persons I knew who was a true man of the world. It was not just that, like Odysseus, he had known many cities and learned the customs of many men, though he had. Rather he had learned, as most of us never do, to be at ease with himself and to make others feel so too—to be tactful, never out of countenance, never afraid of conventions but never outraging them without reason, and effective in bringing out, without embarrassment, what was innermost and most sincere, even if often misguided, in all kinds of men and women.

Mayo's greatest weakness, except perhaps for an engaging touch of easy boredom, lay in his writings. In them he did not practice what he preached. He would jump from the most clinical, down-to-earth descriptions of research to the wildest generalizations. These were not theoretical generalizations: it is possible by a leap of the imagination to move from clinical observations to propositions about the general characteristics of human behavior. But Mayo's generalizations were not of that sort; they concerned the current sociopolitical scene. Consider the following statement of his: "If our social skills had advanced step by step with our technical skills, there would not have been another European War."[20] In fairness to Mayo, let us recognize that others made remarks of a similar kind. In one sense, the statement was true by definition: since war is a breakdown of social relations between nations, it implied that some persons are unequal to dealing with strains in social relations. In another sense, the statement was meaningless, since Mayo did not go into the clinical, in this case historical, details of the situation that brought on the war, nor did he specify what skills he had in mind, except for increased skill in communications. Hitler communicated clearly enough, had we but listened. And would mere skill on the part of Western leaders in communicating with Hitler have prevented his doing what he intended from the first to do? The answer is No: not their words but their actions alone counted, and Mayo had nothing to say about communicating through actions. Nor did he ever mention intelligence as a social skill that could be nourished, the kind of intelligence that might have led the Big Four at the Versailles conference to heed the advice implied by John Maynard Keynes's book *The Economic Consequences of the Peace*.[21] And is courage a social skill?—the courage that might have shamed the premiers of France and Great Britain into calling Hitler's bluff when he invaded the Rhineland in defiance of the Versailles Treaty? That might have toppled him from power, and it was their last chance of doing so, short of war. Perhaps Mayo took courage, resolution, and intelligence for granted, and perhaps they cannot be taught. Skill in giving and receiving communications is indeed an admirable skill. Yet Mayo's generalization from it was not only wrong but reached in violation of his own maxims: it was not even remotely based on clinical experience. History is a highly clinical experience.

What had I gained from Mayo so far? I had become a friend, though not an intimate, of a charming man, and also a man with astonishing and penetrating intuitions into the behavior of individual human beings. He had taught me an essential tool for social scientists, one that I think all should be trained in: the nondirective interview. But I must make one of Mayo's failures clear, because it had a big effect on my future. Though I found most of the reading in psychology he assigned interesting and even in some points essential, he did not put me into contact with a psychology that was both general and handled the most profound tendencies of human behavior. I did not find a psychology satisfactory to me until much later. I was already in touch with it but did not know it. Remember that it was not just psychology Mayo trained us in. There was also social anthropology, to which I now turn.

NOTES

1. For Mayo's history, see Elton Mayo, *The Social Problems of an Industrial Civilization*, with a new foreword by J. H. Smith (London: Routledge & Kegan Paul, 1975). But see especially Richard Trahair, *The Humanist Temper* (New Brunswick, N.J.: Transaction, 1984).
2. See Bronislaw Malinowski, *A Diary in the Strict Sense of the Term* (New York: Harcourt, Brace & World, 1967).
3. A. R. Radcliffe-Brown, *The Andaman Islanders* (Cambridge: Cambridge University Press, 1933).
4. Elton Mayo, *The Social Problems of Industrial Civilization* (Boston: Harvard University, Graduate School of Business Administration, 1945), p. xi.
5. See Benjamin M. Selekman, Sylvia Kopald Selekman, and Stephen H. Fuller, *Problems in Labor Relations*, 2d ed. (New York: McGraw-Hill, 1958), pp. 625-700.
6. The single most important book on the Hawthorne Study is F. J. Roethlisberger and William J. Dickson, with the assistance and collaboration of Harold A. Wright, *Management and the Worker* (Cambridge: Harvard University Press, 1939).
7. See especially George C. Homans, *Fatigue of Workers*, Report of the Committee on Work in Industry, National Research Council (New York: Reinhold Publishing, 1941).
8. See especially, T. North Whitehead, *The Industrial Worker*, 2 vols. (Cambridge: Harvard University Press, 1938).
9. Wolfgang Kohler, *The Mentality of Apes* (New York: Harcourt Brace, 1927).
10. Jean Piaget, *The Moral Judgment of the Child* (London: Kegan Paul, Trench, Trübner, 1932).
11. Pierre Janet, *Les Névroses* (Paris: Flammarion, 1915).
12. Pierre Janet, *Les Obsessions et la Psychasthénie*, 2 vols. (Paris: Alcan, 1919).
13. Elton Mayo, *Some Notes on the Psychology of Pierre Janet* (Cambridge: Harvard University Press, 1948).
14. Sigmund Freud, *Three Contributions to the Theory of Sex*, trans. A.A. Brill (New York: Nervous and Mental Disease Publishing, 1916).
15. Sigmund Freud, *The Interpretation of Dreams*, trans. A.A. Brill, (New York: Macmillan, 1913).
16. Elton Mayo, *The Social Problems of an Industrial Civilization* (Boston: Harvard University, Graduate School of Business Administration, 1945), p. 13.
17. Carl Ransom Rogers, *Counseling and Psychotherapy* (Boston: Houghton Mifflin, 1942).
18. Roethlisberger and Dickson, *Management and the Worker*, pp. 270-91; for the rules, see p. 287.
19. Richard Henry Tawney, *The Sickness of an Acquisitive Society* (London: Allen & Unwin, 1920).
20. Mayo, *Social Problems of an Industrial Civilization*, p. 123.
21. John Maynard Keynes, *The Economic Consequences of the Peace* (London: Macmillan, 1919).

10

MAYO II: SOCIAL ANTHROPOLOGY

The field besides psychology that Mayo chiefly asked us to study in his seminar was social anthropology, especially the work of two members of the British school, Radcliffe-Brown and Malinowski. Mayo's choice was not determined by their being friends of his. They were also the two most distinguished social anthropologists of their generation, though Clyde Kluckhohn would have added the American, Franz Boas. In the work of Radcliffe-Brown we concentrated on *The Andaman Islanders*[1] and in the work of Malinowski, on *Argonauts of the Western Pacific*.[2] We also dipped into the work of less important anthropologists such as that of Malinowski's pupil, Raymond Firth, and above all into that of the great French sociologist Emile Durkheim, who, though not a professional anthropologist, had written a book that had much influenced Radcliffe-Brown.[3]

It may seem curious that from this reading Mayo did not intend us to learn except in passing about anthropology as a science. He wanted us first to learn the characteristics of what he called an "established society" and its difference from modern society. He believed that the Andamans, though much degenerated under white influence, had once been an established society and that the Trobrianders still were one. He wanted to establish a baseline from which modern societies had departed. He did not believe for a minute that modern societies could or should become "established" again, but neither that they could continue on their present course without wrecking themselves. Mayo yearned for a third form, an "adaptive society," which would combine the virtues of the other two: the integration of the "established" with the flexibility of the "modern."

For instance, in Trobriand unlike modern society, ordinary economic transactions were sustained by ritual, or, as Pareto called it, nonlogical action. Thus on the eastern coast of New Guinea and the neighboring islands, including the Trobriands, a set of ports were linked together in a ring, the so-called *kula* ring. From time to time each port would dispatch, amid great excitement, a fleet of big outrigger canoes laden with trade goods and bound for one of the ports on either side of it in the ring. There a trader from the fleet had a local partner with whom he exchanged two kinds of goods: ordinary commodities and ritual ornaments of no practical use. The other ports in the ring were linked by similar expeditions.

The ritual ornaments were also of two kinds, one of which circulated from partner to partner around the ring in one direction, the other in the other. No trader might keep any ornament indefinitely: partners traded ornaments with one another amid great excitement; many of them had become famous and their mere possession, however brief, gave a trader prestige. This ritual exchange provided the expeditions with an interest out of all proportion with the much more bulky but purely utilitarian exchange accompanying it. Thus in the eyes of both Malinowski and Mayo nonlogical actions in an established society like that of the Trobriands supported logical ones by supplying them with an extra reward. This was not true of the modern world and for that reason, Mayo argued, modern people made their economic behavior less fully a part of a whole life.

Radcliffe-Brown joined Malinowski in asserting that the rituals of a society helped maintain its other institutions. Mayo asked us to read with special care the chapters in *The Andaman Islanders*,[4] in which Brown tried to show how the symbols of ritual made reference to the features of both the physical and the social world that were of importance to the natives and how therefore the manipulation of the symbols helped maintain the social organization. Malinowski had argued that economic ritual had helped maintain everyday economic exchange. Brown extended the idea to a whole society. In so doing he had simply taken for granted that the manipulation of symbols would have the predicated effect; he offered no explanation why it should do so. The effect did not hold good of ritual alone: every feature of society by reason of its relations with other features contributed to the maintenance of the social organization as an ongoing whole. This idea was not unlike Henderson's notion of a system in equilibrium.

Let me now look back on what was happening to me. As usual our reading in the seminar had led me to look rather aimlessly into other books in anthropology. And even from the books Mayo assigned I ceased to learn what he wanted me to learn. Forgotten was the difference between an established and a modern society or the need to establish an adaptive one. My reading, especially in Malinowski and Radcliffe-Brown, had led me in a different direction, in fact into two theoretical controversies in anthropology, one over what was called *functionalism* and the other into what I call *culturalism*. Both controversies became big influences on my later thinking.

Let me consider functionalism first. I believe it was Radcliffe-Brown who first gave it this name, so let us start from his definition. Here it is: "The *function* of any recurrent activity, such as the punishment of a crime, or a funeral ceremony, is the part it plays in the social life as a whole and therefore the contribution it makes to the maintenance of the structural continuity."[5] Note the *therefore*. This definition seems to imply an explanation of an institution: an institution becomes a feature of a society because of the part it plays, through its relation with other institutions, in the maintenance, that is, the survival of the society.

But wait! As I got into the problem I discovered that there were many forms of functionalism. Thus Radcliffe-Brown and Malinowski both called themselves at one time or another functionalists, and yet Malinowski's functionalism was different from, and simpler than, Radcliffe-Brown's. The difference is best illustrated by their controversy over magic. Here is Malinowski:

> An interesting and crucial test is provided by fishing in the Trobriand Islands and its magic. While in the villages on the inner Lagoon fishing is done in an easy and reliable manner by the method of poisoning, yielding abundant results without danger and uncertainty, there are also on the shores of the open sea modes of fishing and certain types in which the yield varies greatly. . . . It is most significant that in the Lagoon fishing, where a man can rely completely on his knowledge and skill, magic does not exist, while in the open-sea, full of danger and uncertainty, there is extensive magical ritual to secure safety and good results.[6]

Malinowski's explanation came close to using folk-psychology. A person who undertakes an activity dangerous in itself, its results uncertain but if successful valuable, is likely to feel anxiety. He feels that he ought to try to *do* something, anything, which may include superstitious action. If the action is followed by success, as sooner or later it must be, as rain-magic in the long run is followed by rain, then he is likely to repeat the action; the magic allays his anxiety, and allows him to pursue his fishing with confidence. He soon learns to rely for success not on magic alone but also on continuing to fish. This explanation is not far different from the behavioristic one. More important, for Malinowski the function of magic is the reward it brings to individual men. I shall call it *individualistic* functionalism.

In his Frazer Lecture, published in a little book entitled *Taboo*, Radcliffe-Brown set himself the job of producing a different theory of magic from Malinowski's. His example was the ritual performed by mother and father in the Andaman Islands before the birth of a child. He wrote:

> I think that for certain rites it would be easy to maintain an exactly contrary theory, namely that if it were not for the existence of the rite and the beliefs associated with it, the individual would feel no anxiety, and that the psychological effect of the rite is to create in him a sense of insecurity and danger. It seems very unlikely that an Andaman Islander would think it dangerous to eat dugong or turtle meat taboo during childbirth, if it were not for the existence of a specific body of ritual the ostensible purpose of which is to protect him from these dangers.[7]

Superficially, the situation of Andamanese childbirth looks much like that of Malinowski's fishing: in most societies, successful childbirth is much desired, but it is attended with uncertainty and therefore with anxiety. In these circumstances as in the Trobriand fishing, the persons concerned perform a ritual, in this case a taboo on the eating of certain foods, not considered at all dangerous under ordinary circumstances. But Radcliffe-Brown will have none of this argument:

> The alternative hypothesis which I am presenting for consideration is as follows. In a given community it is appropriate that an expectant father should feel concern or at least make an appearance of doing so. Some suitable symbolic expression of the concern is found in terms of the general ritual or symbolic idiom of the society, and it is felt generally that a man in that situation ought to carry out the symbolic or ritual actions or abstentions.[8]

If most people in a society feel an emotion on a particular occasion and show it, sooner or later they will feel that all people in that society ought to show it. The display has become a norm. But Radcliffe-Brown had more in mind than that, and this is where his kind of functionalism comes in. In a given community, why is it appropriate that an expectant father should show concern, aside from the reasons I have given? I think many functionalists of Radcliffe-Brown's sort would have answered as follows. For a society, including the Andamanese, to survive, its members must take the greatest care at childbirth. The ritual of childbirth emphasized its importance and accordingly had become one of the institutions of Andaman society. Its function was its contribution to the maintenance of that society. A chief difficulty with functionalism was that it could not cite the mechanisms by which institutions came so conveniently into existence in order to maintain a society. Indeed functionalism was a type of theory designed for societies for which we had little or no written history: these were the "primitive" societies. When we had anything like a written record of how an institution came into being, social scientists forgot all about functionalism—or should have.

The difference between Malinowski's functionalism and Radcliffe-

Brown's was the following. For Malinowski the function of an institution was what it did for individual persons; for Radcliffe-Brown, what it did for society. Accordingly, just as I have called the former's functionalism *individualistic*, I shall call the latter's *societal*. I remember having a fierce discussion of Radcliffe-Brown's functionalism with my friend, colleague, and anthropologist in the Society of Fellows, Conrad Arensberg, in my rooms at Kirkland House after one of our dinners. But he did not remain a functionalist. I also wrote a paper trying to reconcile the positions of Malinowski and Radcliffe-Brown.[9] Mayo approved of the paper. Underneath I remained a skeptic about societal functionalism.

The second theoretical issue that my reading in anthropology got me into was what I call culturalism. It was exacerbated by the appearance in the 1930s of the "culture and personality" school of Abraham Kardiner, Margaret Mead, Ruth Benedict, and others. My friends Clyde and Flossie Kluckhohn were members.

I had always believed, without giving it a thought, in the folk saying "Human nature is the same the world over." Of course there were superficial differences between the behavior of Japanese and that of Americans, but at a deeper level we shared the same physical and social characteristics because we were members of the same species. I was astonished when I found the "culture-vultures" laughing at my folk wisdom. Clyde Kluckhohn once said to me that if one were asked why the behavior of members of one society differed institutionally or otherwise from that of members of another, all one could answer was, "because of the culture." Though I had not yet begun to think about the nature of explanation, I considered this a singularly poor one. All it amounted to saying was that the reasons people in a given society behaved as they did was that the older generation had taught them to do so. But why that particular way rather than another? That was the real question. It was the same kind of answer later anthropologists gave me when they tried to explain institutions by the norms the members of a society required themselves and fellow members to live by. This begged the same question: Why these particular norms and not others? Moreover cultures changed. I had learned from Malinowski's great *Crime and Custom in Savage Society*[10] that natives, just like moderns, did not obey the norms unless they had sufficient inducement to do so, and if the inducements changed, as they well might for all sorts of reasons, the natives' obedience to norms would change too. If Clyde's answer was not an answer, what could I offer instead?

One of the books I had read on my own hook was Firth's thorough and beautiful field study of the society of a small Polynesian island called Tikopia.[11] In it I read a detailed description of the *avunculate*, so called by anthropologists after the Latin word *avunculus*, which means specifically "mother's brother." Through Norman French we get our word *uncle* from it, though it originally meant only one kind of uncle. The avunculate appears as an institution in many societies, particularly those that we call patrilineal and that vest jural authority over his children in the father. Between a boy and his mother's brother or brothers, and if he has none, between him and male kinsmen on his mother's side of the family whom he calls by the same kinship term as the "real" mother's brother, a relationship grows up that is especially close, warm, familiar, and free. The details differ from society to society, but the overall resemblance remains.

Firth was not the first to describe the avunculate, nor did I first read about it in his book. I believe the first to describe it was the great Roman historian Cornelius Tacitus in his *Germania,* which appeared in 98 A.D. *Germania* is an account of the Germanic tribes with which the expanding Roman Empire was beginning to come into contact along the Rhine-Danube frontier. I had read it in connection with my work on Anglo-Saxon institutions, for the Anglo-Saxons were Germans in origin. Tacitus wrote: "Sisters, children mean as much to their uncle *[avunculus]* as to their father: some tribes regard this blood-tie as even closer and more sacred than that between son and father, and in taking hostages make it the basis of their demand, as though they thus secure loyalty more surely and have a wider hold on the family *[domus].*"[12] *Domus* refers not just to the physical house but to the social one, the family.

The usual explanation of the avunculate we owe largely to Radcliffe-Brown.[13] The father holds jural authority over the son. Jural authority, since it implies the right to punish, tends to inhibit emotional closeness between father and son. The mother's brother in patrilineal societies holds no such authority, yet is obviously identified with the boy's mother, whose behavior towards him, like that of most mothers in most societies, tends to be nurturant. In Tikopia as in other societies, an older man may provide certain kinds of nurturance that a mother may not. Women are not admitted to the painful initiation ceremonies the boys must undergo, and a mother's brother holds the boy's hand, so to speak, as he goes through them. Indeed in some societies the kin-term for mother's brother means literally "male mother." The avunculate takes the form not only of actual behavior but a norm of what behavior ought to be. Boys are taught how to behave towards their mother's brothers and vice versa. No doubt many of them do not feel the sentiments the norms call for, but still put on an act of doing so, for fear of punishment for violating a tribal convention. Note that this, like Malinowski's explanation of fishing magic, is a psychological explanation of a social institution.

Norms develop in a number of ways. In cases like the present, I suspect but cannot prove that the process is something like the following. Members of families living in a uniform environment, with a simple technology and division of labor, tend to evolve the same general kind of family organization. The organization may include a definite locus of jural authority in the father; and by the explanation offered above, many such families will tend to develop the same general pattern of interpersonal relations, including the avunculate. But what many families do in fact becomes in time what every family ought to do. That is, it becomes a norm, and the elder generation teaches it to the younger, thus reinforcing what the tendencies inherent in the social organization originally brought about. Of course if the circumstances underlying the organization change, the interpersonal relations sooner or later change too.

Statistically, the classical avunculate tends to appear patrilineal societies, those in which one belongs to the group one's father does, societies that vest jural authority in the father, and in which his patrilineage supports his authority. It appears in every continent and over widely separated periods of time. Compare Tacitus's Germany with Firth's Tikopia. Indeed the distances in time and space are so great that few of the societies possessing the institution can have borrowed it from the others. This means that it must have been independently invented several times, and this for me was a crushing blow to the culture-vultures. True, in the most general sense every culture was unique. Yet the avunculate implied a single human nature in another sense, that, given similar circumstances—and in the case of the avunculate the circumstances were similar—it produced similar patterns of behavior in different societies. Human nature *was* the same the world over. Sensible people have always known it. My job has often been to draw social scientists back to common sense. They have not always appreciated my good deed.

My suspicions were confirmed by the society which by that time I knew best: Malinowski's Trobriands. Its organization was very different from that of Tikopia. It did not belong to the patrilineal group but to another with far fewer representatives, though still distributed over more than one continent, an organization that anthropologists call by the ghastly name of matrilineal-avunculocal.[14] In these societies a boy belongs to a matrilineage, that is, a group to which his mother and his mother's brothers also belong. Though he spends his childhood with his father and mother, his father holds no jural authority over him. Instead, when he draws towards puberty, he leaves his father and mother and moves to the village where his mother's brothers live; hence the term *avunculocal*. At that time he comes under their authority. Under these circumstances, he tends to develop just the same kind of warm and close relationship with his father that a Tikopia boy develops with his mother's brother. By a flash of induction, which I am sure was not original with me but felt like it at the time, I saw that both cases, Tikopia and the Trobriands, followed the same rule. Crudely put, it was that close and warm relations tended to fall on the side of the family away from the man who held jural authority over a child. And if the same general assumptions about human nature, if applied to different given conditions, predicted different patterns of interpersonal relations, one more blow was dealt to the views of the culture vultures, to the notion of the absolute uniqueness of cultures.

What the anthropologists could not explain was why some societies were patrilineal-patrilocal and others matrilineal-avunculocal (and there were other types). To know that, one would have had to know how the societies had developed as they did, that is, to know their histories. Primitive societies tended to be short of history, but when we had a little social history, as I was beginning to have of English social history, it tended to support the theory. The Anglo-Saxons had possessed the avunculate. As non-kin organizations, governmental, commercial, industrial, had arisen, the patrilineage had disappeared and the power of the father had declined. Accordingly the avunculate had declined too, though traces of it persisted as late as the sixteenth century. Now it has wholly disappeared. This was just what we might have predicted. Again, at least if we followed the data on kinship, it still looked as if human nature was the same the world over, in the sense of producing generalizations that held good of many cultures. Now it was incumbent on someone to explain why these generalizations held good.

My study of kinship in the Trobriands and Tikopia had the side effect of further undermining the little faith I still had in Freud. After all, the underlying Oedipus complex should be the same in both societies: in both the son should be the father's rival for the mother's love. But the manifest behavior was very different in the two cases: the father-son relationship was ambivalent in Tikopia and in societies like Vienna that Freud studied, in which the father was in theory the boss. But in the Trobriands the relationship could not be closer. Perhaps a hatred of the father-rival still lay deep in the Trobriand unconscious, but where was the couch that could bring it to the surface? I suspected that, in the case of the Oedipus complex, human nature was *not* the same the world over, and that authority might in this case be more important than sex.

Note that both issues, the functional and the cultural, were concerned with the relation between the behavior of individuals (human nature) and the norms (culture) of the societies to which they belonged. I shall recur to this issue over and over again.

The third issue that my reading and discussions in social anthropology brought to my attention was of a very different kind: it was methodological rather than substantive. Mayo had nothing directly to do with this issue.

In the early days of my Junior Fellowship, W. Lloyd Warner joined the Harvard Anthropology Department fresh from a study of a tribe of "blackfellows" called the Murngin, who lived on the northwest coast of Australia.[15] Warner had undertaken the study under the stimulus of Radcliffe-Brown, who had himself analyzed the social organization of Australian aborigines. When Warner came to Harvard, his link with Radcliffe-Brown put him into contact with Mayo, and they became friends. It was believed that Warner helped persuade Mayo to change the format of the last of the Western Electric researches, the so-called Bank Wiring Observation Room. Unlike the earlier researches, the investigators were to use neither an experimental design nor pure interviewing. As far as possible they were to leave the group undisturbed and study it, as anthropologists would study a primitive tribe, by observation backed up by interviewing.[16] In my view this study became the best study of a working group ever made.

In return, Mayo, still interested in the differences between an established and a modern society, helped Warner get a grant for a field study of a modern industrial community, which Warner, one of the most energetic of men, was more than ready to undertake. The city he chose was Newburyport, Massachusetts, then a center for shoe manufacturing. It was not too large—for even then social studies were expensive—and not too far from Cambridge, while still remaining outside the orbit of Greater Boston. Over the years Warner and his colleagues published six volumes on the research, entitled the Yankee City Series.[17] To disguise its identity, the researchers had referred to Newburyport as Yankee City. Since the disguise has become an open secret, I shall call the city by its real name.

Warner might not have chosen Newburyport had he known it was the hometown of the greatest satirical novelist of the time, John P. Marquand. In his novel *Point of No Return* there is an entertaining but not savage caricature of a social anthropologist doing field research in a New England community.[18]

Warner recruited a number of graduate students in anthropology to carry out field research in Newburyport. Two of them, Eliot D. Chapple and Conrad M. Arensberg, were close friends of each other, and I knew them both well. Warner became interested in understanding the societies in Europe from which many of the citizens of Newburyport had come, and sent Connie, with another anthropologist, Solon T. Kimball, to make a study of a rural community in County Clare, Ireland.[19] It was an excellent study, and it suggested many ideas to me when I myself came to study rural England in the Middle Ages. Connie could be very persuasive, and it was under his influence that another member of the Society of Fellows, William F. Whyte, Jr., gave up his original subject, economics, for sociology and carried out another of the splendid field studies that marked the era, a study of a group of young men of Italian origin in the North End of Boston. Whyte reported his research in his book *Street Corner Society*.[20] Ever the parasite, I used it later, together with Tikopia and the Bank Wiring Observation Room, in my own book *The Human Group*.[21] Warner eventually moved to the University of Chicago. Now he is dead.

What came to bother Chapple and later Arensberg was the lack of rigor with which the results of social research could be made and reported. Among the books all young men who pretended to belong in the intellectual avant-garde during the 1930s were supposed to have read was *The Logic of Modern Physics* by Percy Bridgman, professor of physics at Harvard and later a Nobel laureate.[22] Bridgman expounded the doctrine of *operationalism*: a concept was defined by the operations used to measure or identify it. A proposition that included a variable not operationally defined was meaningless. Much later Braithwaite taught me the fallacies of operationalism.[23] It has much to be said for it, but a theory cannot be built with operational statements alone. As Mayo would have put it, the idea is "hard-boiled but half-baked." But at that time even Henderson was shaken: I myself was a true believer, and Chapple and Arensberg were fanatics.[24]

The question this last pair posed for themselves was: What is the variable in social science research that is most ripe for operationalization, and how does one go about doing it? The variable they chose they called *interaction*. In fact interaction included a whole class of variables: in conversation how long and how often did a given person speak; how often and how soon did he initiate talk or other action, either at the beginning of a conversation or after a pause; with how many persons within a given place or time did he interact, and for how many did he initiate the interaction? Chapple invented a machine, the *interaction chronograph*, that recorded some of these data automatically. Some interesting propositions could be tested with it. For instance, in interaction with a stooge, specially trained to interact with a person on certain kinds of occasions and at certain rates, the person who talked often and interrupted the stooge regularly, that is, one whose interaction rate was higher than the stooge's, often turned out to be an effective salesperson. Chapple tested the proposition in a Boston department store.

Eliot and Connie revealed their views to me, because I knew they were on to something and asked them to do so. I doubt if they would have done so spontaneously. They were a bit condescending: I was not a really hard-nosed social scientist. I agreed with them that interaction was a class of variable ripe for operationalization. The trouble is that persons who have discovered something tend for a while to be able to see only that. Eliot and Connie began to talk not only as if they believed interaction ought to be operationalized but also as if it were the only variable that needed to be used to analyze social behavior, or at least the only independent variable. There I could not follow them, but they started me asking myself what other classes of variable ought to be added to interaction. I came up with two, which I called *sentiment* and (God forgive me!) *function*.

With the first, Connie himself had, as usual, helped me. He had suggested that I read J. L. Moreno's *Who Shall Survive?*,[25] which had come out as early as 1934. Its title had nothing to do with the contents of the book. I later read a much better book, *Leadership and Isolation* by Moreno's pupil and research assistant, Helen Hall Jennings.[26] Both described the nature and purpose of what they called the *sociometric test*. It had no more right to that name than did many other methods of measuring human behavior. But they used it first, and their name has stuck. Unlike the complicated machinery of the interaction chronograph, the sociometric test is a simple questionnaire. The investigator asks each member of a group to list the other members of the group in the order in which he or she would *like* to join them in some particular setting or task, such as living in the same house with them, doing housework, working with them at some task outside the house, or spending leisure time with them. The results of the tests could be used to construct various secondary measures, such as the number of mutual choices, the number of first choices a particular member received, the relationship between choices on different criteria, etc. Since I assumed that liking was a sentiment, I decided, with the sociometric test in mind, to make *sentiment* the first of the classes of variable I would add to interaction. Also, without any formal use of questionnaires, the Western Electric researches and other good studies of small groups had often discussed interpersonal sentiments. Let us finally not forget common sense: sentiment is an obviously important part of human behavior.

My third class took a longer time to come to me, because it was really residual. There was an enormous number of kinds of actions people performed that might or might not require interactions with others or express interpersonal sentiments. Many such actions could be measured, but the problem of their variety became manageable because in most studies only a few of them needed to be taken into account. One example was output: the number of certain physical objects a factory worker produced within a unit of time. Measures of output had figured prominently in the Western Electric researches. This large and varied class of variable I originally decided to call *function*, which was madness itself, because it added yet another meaning to that already ambiguous word. Note that interaction is without specific content; it is a measure of the frequency with which social behavior occurs, but the behavior may be of any kind, though it is most often talk. *Sentiment* and *function* added content to interaction.

Following Henderson I assumed that, within a given group or society, each class of variable would be mutually dependent with members of other classes, but I did not try to specify the propositions stating the actual relationships between the variables. This made what I had created a conceptual scheme, not a real theory. As Henderson used the word, a conceptual scheme is a statement of the variables that need to be taken into account when studying a phenomenon, usually with some further assumption that the variables are mutually dependent in a system, but not specifying the propositions linking the variables. A conceptual scheme is now sometimes called a paradigm. Other scientists use conceptual scheme to mean a real theory. I shall have more to say about theory later.

My first sketch of my threefold classification appeared in the last chapter of my *English Villagers of the Thirteenth Century*,[27] where it was wholly out of place; but I wanted to put it on record as soon as possible, because I might not get another chance, as I was pretty sure the Navy would soon call me to active duty, which it did in May 1941.

Such was the state of my reflections on social science when I left Harvard for the Navy. Though I have done much useful and enjoyable fieldwork, the purely intellectual issues I have since then worked *at*, though not *through*, derived largely from what I read first with Mayo and later on my own account. But let me repeat: these were not the issues Mayo himself was interested in. In an earlier autobiographical sketch, I put the matter as follows:

> Given the chance, I have always deserted anything that had contemporary practical importance or that might lead to reforms. I have deserted the twentieth century for the thirteenth, social pathology for primitive kinship, industrial sociology for the study of small groups. It may have been mere escapism; my nerves may have been too weak for the modern world. More likely I was reluctant to change a world that, on the whole, was behaving so well towards me. But I have found a description of the syndrome that is more flattering to me and that may well be true. I have come to think now—I did not see it then—that what never failed to interest me was not sociology as an agency of change or as a means of understanding my

immediate environment but sociology as a generalizing science. What were the best possibilities for establishing generalizations? What were the main intellectual issues? What was the subject really about? By what handle should we lay hold on it? A science may naturally turn out to have practical applications, but it certainly does not grow just through its practical applications. The modern world offers plenty of material for generalizations about social behavior, but it is not the only world that does. Thus the briefest look at primitive kinship showed plenty of generalizations lying embedded in the matrix of fact and crying for formulation. So did industrial sociology if one forgot about reforming industry and thought only of the opportunities its captive groups provided for studying social behavior at first hand. If the emphasis was on science, what made a particular subject matter important was simply the chance of exploiting it intellectually. Did the vein lie near the surface?[28]

NOTES

1. A. R. Radcliffe-Brown, *The Andaman Islanders* (Cambridge: Cambridge University Press, 1933).
2. Bronislaw Malinowski, *Argonauts of the Western Pacific* (New York: Dutton, 1922).
3. Emile Durkheim, *The Elementary Forms of the Religious Life* (London: Allen & Unwin, 1915).
4. Chs. 5, 6.
5. A. R. Radcliffe-Brown, *Structure and Function in Primitive Society* (Oxford: Oxford University Press, 1951), p. 30.
6. Bronislaw Malinowski, "Magic, Science,and Religion," in *Science, Religion and Reality,* ed. J. Needham (New York: Macmillan, 1925), p. 32.
7. A. R. Radcliffe-Brown, *Taboo* (Cambridge: Cambridge University Press, 1939), p. 39.
8. Ibid., p. 33.
9. George C. Homans, "Anxiety and Ritual: The Theories of Malinowski and Radcliffe-Brown," *American Anthropologist* 43 (1941): 164-72. Reprinted by permission in George C. Homans, *Sentiments and Activities: Essays in Social Science* (New York: Free Press of Glencoe, 1962), pp. 192-201.
10. Bronislaw Malinowski, *Crime and Custom in Savage Society* (London: Kegan Paul, Trench, Trübner, 1926).
11. Raymond Firth, *We, The Tikopia* (London: Allen & Unwin, 1936).
12. Cornelius Tacitus, *Germania,* in *Dialogus, Agricola, Germania,* trans. William Peterson and Maurice Hutton (London: Heinemann, Loeb Classical Library, 1932), p. 293.
13. A. R. Radcliffe-Brown, "The Mother's Brother in South Africa," *South African Journal of Science* 21 (1924): 542-55.
14. See especially Bronislaw Malinowski, *The Father in Primitive Psychology* (London: Basic English Publishing, n.d. [1927?]).
15. W. Lloyd Warner, *A Black Civilization* (New York: Harper, 1937).
16. F. J. Roethlisberger and William J. Dickson, with the assistance and collaboration of Harold A. Wright, *Management and the Worker* (Cambridge: Harvard University Press, 1939), pp. 379-548.
17. W. Lloyd Warner et al., *Yankee City Series,* 6 vols. (New Haven: Yale University Press, 1941-63).

18. John P. Marquand, *Point of No Return* (Boston: Little, Brown, 1949).
19. Conrad M. Arensberg and Solon T. Kimball, *Family and Community in Ireland* (Cambridge: Harvard University Press, 1940).
20. William Foote Whyte, *Street Corner Society* (Chicago: Chicago University Press, 1943).
21. George C. Homans, *The Human Group* (New York: Harcourt, Brace, 1950).
22. Percy W. Bridgman, *The Logic of Modern Physics* (New York: Macmillan, 1927).
23. Richard B. Braithwaite, *Scientific Explanation* (Cambridge: Cambridge University Press, 1953).
24. Eliot D. Chapple with the collaboration of Conrad M. Arensberg, "Measuring Human Relations," *Genetic Psychology Monographs* 22 (1940): 3-147.
25. Jacob L. Moreno, *Who Shall Survive?* (Washington, DC: Nervous and Mental Disease Publishing, 1934).
26. Helen Hall Jennings, *Leadership and Isolation*, 2d ed. (New York: Longmans, Green, 1950).
27. George C. Homans, *English Villagers of the Thirteenth Century* (Cambridge: Harvard University Press, 1941).
28. George Caspar Homans, *Sentiments and Activities: Essays in Social Science* (New York: Free Press of Glencoe,1962), pp. 9-10.

11

MEDIEVAL ENGLAND

In the course of my work with McIlwain on English constitutional history, I read, as usual, other texts than those he had assigned and developed interests different from his. Among other books I ran into Frederic Seebohm's *The English Village Community*,[1] the earliest, I believe, description of what came to be called the "open-field" system of medieval agricultural organization. This impressed me with the manner in which all its elements, technical and social, seemed to fit together, which both Henderson and the social anthropologists had told me they ought to do if the system were to count as a social system.

The Senior Fellows expected a candidate for a Junior Fellowship in the Society to have some research project in mind that he might carry out if elected. Wisely, they did not hold him to his plan if he changed his mind, but they expected him at least to have thought of one. When I became a candidate, I proposed to make an anthropological study of an historical society, rural England in the thirteenth century. I chose the thirteenth century because I knew it was the earliest century from which enough documents survived to make it possible for me to approximate a study of most of the aspects of society in their relationships with one another, such as anthropological field research called for. Although my work with Mayo had a greater influence on me in the long run, I spent at least half my time as a Junior Fellow doing the research for, and writing my book *English Villagers of the Thirteenth Century*.[2] In this work I received little guidance but much encouragement and other help from Edwin F. Gay and especially Norman S. B. Gras, both experts in English economic history and both professors at the Harvard Business School.

So far so good, but, as I have suggested earlier, there was a deeper reason for my interest in specifically English institutions. I was a Yankee New Englander. Though we did not use the term then, I was a Wasp, a White Anglo-Saxon Protestant. My immediate ancestry, except for the German Crowninshields, was English in origin. And it looked in the Boston of my childhood as if the Yankees, as we then called all New Englanders of colonial ancestry, were an endangered species, threatened demographically, politically, and culturally by what we were pleased to call "the newer races," especially the Irish, whom we ourselves had originally encouraged to cross the Atlantic in order to build our railroads and tend our looms. I felt no hostility towards individual Irish, particularly Irishwomen; after all, they had had a big hand in bringing me up. But I was worried, as earlier generations of Yankees were not, about my English, or more generally, my Nordic inheritance. Almost as soon as I learned to read easily, I had become an enthusiast for the Norse sagas. In studying medieval England I was not just applying the ideas of modern social anthropology to an historical society, I was also bolstering up a threatened identity. I had felt the latter strongly when, with my parents and my sister Fanny, I made my first visit to England in the year before I entered Harvard College. In studying medieval England, I was again, as we should say now, looking for my roots.

Let me turn now to the practical problems of research. My first job was to read the secondary sources on my subject, which were numerous and good, for they included men of the caliber of Sir Paul Vinogradoff and especially Frederic William Maitland, one of the greatest of all English historians both as a thinker and a writer. My next job was to read the published primary sources, those edited from the original manuscripts. Harvard had had a long and distinguished succession of scholars in English medieval history, beginning indeed with my own great-uncle, Henry Adams; and perhaps for that reason the University Library had a nearly complete set of the published primary sources, including those published by the county record societies, some of which had produced excellent work. What happy hours I spent in my carrel on the south side of Widener Library, next to the stacks of books on English history! Even the printed sources proved to be so numerous that I decided, if I were even to come within sight of finishing the job I had set for myself, I should have to concentrate on certain kinds of sources but not all. I decided to concentrate on two of them: first, the manorial custumals, which purported to record the customs, that is, the food- and money-rents and the work services due from the peasant tenants to the lords of their manors, who were often great ecclesiastics, such as the abbot of Ramsey Abbey. Such a lord might hold as many as twenty manors, often in different parts of England, so there would be twenty different custumals, from which one began to get an idea of regional variations in custom. Unfortunately, the custumals compiled by the officers of different lords also differed greatly in the richness of detail they recorded and therefore in the degree to which they were a help to me.

The second class of documents I decided to concentrate on were the rolls of the manorial courts. A lord of a manor had the right to hold a court, the hallmote, usually every three weeks, which at least his unfree (villein) tenants were bound to attend, and to appropriate to his own use the fines levied in the court. A manorial court roll was the record a clerk kept of the actions taken in the court. Some of the entries were routine and of little interest, such as the fines levied for absences. But some were of the greatest interest. Since I wanted to study rural society as a whole, I knew, from the teachings of the anthropologists, that I should have to pay particular attention to kinship. About some of the more intangible aspects of kinship, the rolls had little to say. On the other hand, they contained entries describing how manorial juries decided disputes concerning the inheritance of land, and inheritance of land lies at the very heart of kinship in an agricultural society. Again, since court rolls survived, though in unequal numbers, from manors in most parts of England, I could begin to get an idea of regional variations in customs of inheritance. It turned out that my greatest original contribution to knowledge in this field was my survey of these customs. In much of my other research I was going over materials that earlier scholars had exploited. I added some details but that was about all. Indeed one of the reasons for paying particular attention to the court rolls was that scholars had tended to neglect them, with the exception, of course, of the great Maitland, who with his usual perspicacity had edited one volume of them.[3]

A class of documents that I in turn chose to neglect was the manorial account rolls, which recorded, as the result of a yearly audit, the income and outgo from the manors of particular lords. Some of these rolls were extraordinarily detailed, even recording just how many eggs were sold in a given year and for what price each. My neglect of the account rolls meant that I paid rather little attention to purely economic matters, which may have been a pity, since the thirteenth century was a period of economic inflation, and prolonged inflation has effects not only on the economy but also on social organization. I ought also to have considered what the sheer mass of the records implied. If the lords were prepared to spend so much money on what was, after all, a big item of administrative overhead, they must have made enough gross profit to carry the overhead. Towards the end of the century their profit margins may have come down.

It is interesting that we possess from this period far more detailed information for hundreds of rural communities in England than for any of the equivalent communities in, say, China, though there were plenty of landlords in China, and China was then, as it still is, many, many times more populous than England. Was it English legalism that made for all this record keeping? Was it that England, compared with China or indeed with France, had enjoyed longer periods of internal peace? Invasions, civil wars, and revolutions are great destroyers of records. Or was it simply that the English records were kept on parchment, while the Chinese, if kept at all, must have been kept on paper. Parchment is nearly indestructible, unless long soaked in water. I have opened court rolls that looked as fresh as they did when they left the clerk's hand more than six hundred years before. But paper goes to pieces unless it is treated with special care.

By the spring of 1936 I had pretty well run through Harvard's supply of published documents of the kinds I was interested in. I then had to go to England to read as many of the original manuscripts as possible. Logistically, the Society of Fellows with a small grant made possible my stay there. I also took off well supplied with letters of introduction to medieval scholars and with what were then called "dago dazzlers," formal letters to which the Harvard seal was affixed, directed to whatever institutions they might concern, and certifying that I was a responsible scholar, worthy of their help. In England letters of introduction were more useful than "dago dazzlers." The English were not dagoes, nor were they easily dazzled, and London was the capital of what was still a great empire.

I knew that the largest collections of manuscript court rolls and custumals, though not of course the only ones, were in London at the British Museum and the Public Record Office on Chancery Lane, near the Law Courts and the Inns of Court. I got myself a cheap room with bed and breakfast, the latter usually a kipper. Indeed I occupied a series of cheap rooms, finally winding up on dreary old Bryanston Street behind the Marble Arch. But life in London turned out not to be as dreary as I had feared at first it might be. A couple of my friends turned up and shared my squalor by living in the same house. We were now in full Depression, and Depression, while hell for the workingman, was bliss for me, because my money went so far. I could afford to attend the ballet at Covent Garden every so often and to dine well once a week, usually at L'Escargot in Greek Street, Soho, then one of the best restaurants in London.

With one exception, the personal letters of introduction Professor Gras had written for me turned out to be of no use at all. I presented one to R. H. Tawney, who was a great economic and social historian. Theoretically he was also a great believer in brotherly love, but he took not the slightest interest in me or my project and gave every hint that I was wasting his time, as no doubt I was. I soon took my leave and never met him again. Perhaps his brotherly love did not extend to capitalists, which my clothes certainly proclaimed me to be; perhaps it did not extend to Americans. In France I presented a similar letter to Marc Bloch, then at the height of his power and influence as a medieval social historian. He too paid not the slightest attention to me and got rid of me as soon as he decently could. I wonder whether I now give the same impression to younger scholars who come to me for guidance. I bet I do, and the reason is that I feel I have no guidance to give. That may well have been the most parsimonious explanation of the behavior of both Tawney and Bloch.

I should have become wholly disillusioned by letters of introduction, if Gras had not also introduced me to M. M. ("Munya") Postan and his wife, Eileen Power, both then, I believe, holding posts at the London School of Economics or some other branch of the University of London. Both were historians of the medieval economy and worked closely together. Eileen, a woman of great charm as well as intellect, died young at some time before the end of World War II—a great loss. Munya was a short man, who peered at me quizzically from under shaggy red eyebrows. He was not of English but of Franco-Bessarabian origin, though by the time I knew him he had lost almost all trace of a foreign accent.

Eileen and Munya had no more reason to be kind to me than had Tawney or Bloch, but they were kind—very kind. They lived in Bloomsbury, though not as inside members of the famous Bloomsbury set, of which Wyndham Lewis had shown so much contempt, and they invited me to parties there. Munya asked me to speak to his seminar at the Royal Institute for Historical Research. I assumed that in England occasions of this sort would be highly formal, so I dressed up for it by putting on a stiff collar with my business suit. When Munya showed up in an old sweater I blushed to the ears, but he did not seem to be embarrassed by this ugly duckling, the opposite of a worldly duckling, he had taken under his wing. He even appeared to be interested in my developing ideas about English medieval society, though he never fully agreed with them. His own ideas were more "economic" and less "social" than mine, a good counterpoise, which made my defense of my own less stupid than it would otherwise have been. We remained friends afterwards, and later I became a friend of his second wife, Cynthia. For many years he was a professor at Cambridge University, and has recently died.

My last introduction was of a very different kind, but none the worse for that. For this one I was indebted to my mother. I received a standing invitation to escape from London on weekends to Stepleton House near Blandford in Dorset, one of the loveliest of English counties. Stepleton House was the home of an American, Mrs. James Donald Cameron, who deserves a biography in her own right. She was born Elizabeth ("Lizzie") Sherman, the niece of John Sherman, United States senator from Ohio, who gave his name to the famous Sherman antitrust act, and of the great

Union General William Tecumseh Sherman, who led the march through Georgia, proclaimed that war is hell, and did something to make it so.

Elizabeth was married off, while she was still a young woman, to James Donald Cameron, United States senator from Pennsylvania, a much older man. The rumor was that she was married much against her will, the price of a political alliance between the two senators. The truth may have been more prosaic: her uncles may simply have believed that the match was advantageous for her, socially and financially. She bore one daughter, whom she idolized.

When my mother as a young girl first visited her uncle Henry Adams in Washington, after the suicide of his wife, Clover Hooper, she met and admired Mrs. Cameron, who was one of the beautiful, ultrasmart women, leaders of Washington society, who were apt to drop in for a late breakfast with Uncle Henry, to regale him with the latest gossip, which he loved. Mrs. Cameron was not only beautiful but very intelligent. My mother became a younger friend of hers and remained so.

When he was apart from Mrs. Cameron, great-uncle Henry not only wrote her often but also wrote her some of his best letters.[4] He certainly fell in love with her, and after the death of her husband I suspect he wanted to marry her. She had, in my opinion, the good sense not to accept. I feel certain also that they never had an "affair" in the physical sense. But they remained devoted friends. I did not meet her until she was an old lady, but I can attest that she kept her charm until the end, and I can well imagine the devastating spell she must have cast when in her prime.

Her beloved daughter Martha had married Sir Ronald Lindsay, the son and brother of Earls of Crawford, chiefs of Clan Lindsay—if the Lindsays count as a clan in the Highland sense of the word. Like other younger sons, Sir Ronald had made a career in the British Foreign Office. Indeed he became British ambassador to the United States during the Hoover administration, when my uncle Charlie, as secretary of the Navy, had some dealings with him. Martha had died young, leaving no children. Sir Ronald had not married again and, as I understood it, Mrs. Cameron bought Stepleton House and lived in it to provide a country home for him.

My mother had kept in touch with Mrs. Cameron. We had stopped briefly at Stepleton House on our trip to England in the summer before I entered Harvard. When I was about to return to England to do my research, Ma wrote Mrs. Cameron and gave her my address in London. She asked me down for a weekend and later extended the standing invitation. I always wondered whether she had consulted Sir Ronald before taking this rash act, for I was pretty sure he considered me a pain in the arse. But I did not worry about this and took full advantage of Stepleton as a refuge from London weekends.

Stepleton House was a small but elegant country house, mainly, I think, of the period of Queen Anne, set in the bottom of a valley under rich trees on a fine, flat English lawn, where we took tea on sunny summer afternoons. I imagine that the place would be rather dank in winter. The house had its own chapel, in which Mrs. Cameron had installed a beautiful memorial to Martha.

I would take the train at Waterloo Station in London and be met at Salisbury in some style by Mrs. Cameron's chauffeur and limousine. Then we would drive the rest of the way to Stepleton across Cranborne Chase. As a great hostess, Mrs. Cameron both went out of her way to keep me amused and also left me plenty of time to amuse myself, which I was well able to do in those surroundings. Stepleton lay right under Hod Hill, which is crowned by an Iron Age earthwork or hill-fort, just like the ones I had read about in school in Caesar's *Gallic Wars*. What is more, there was, within the earthwork, the square outline of what had been a Roman camp. Not far away was Hambledon Hill, a much greater fort, with a triple ring of huge earthworks, and still further away, Maiden Castle. I could imagine these great bare grassy hills, now silent and empty except for a few sheep, once full of the livestock, women, and children of the natives, while the slopes and crests of the walls rang with the shouts and clash of weapons of attackers and attacked. I felt how far back the history ran, whose physical remains I was looking at: the defenders of these earthworks and the Roman legionnaires who attacked them had died before the people I considered my ancestors, the Anglo-Saxons, speakers of a Germanic language, had even begun to turn Britain into England. From Stepleton House I wandered on foot over much of what is now considered Hardy's Wessex. The trouble was that I did not much enjoy Hardy's novels. It was Alfred's Wessex, not Hardy's, that interested me.

I often planned to take a walk before breakfast but was just as often foiled by the butler. Yet I am glad to have met with a fine, imperturbable specimen of that old English institution before it disappeared forever. On my early visits, I brought with me only two pairs of trousers, one of which was unsuitable for walking because they were the dress trousers that went with my dinner coat. (Of course, we always dressed for dinner.) Before I was supposed to be awake, the butler would sneak into my room to pick up my ordinary trousers and press them, intending to return them to me with hot water for shaving. He thus left me with no trousers at all in which I might take a preprandial walk, and I had to stay in bed. Yet I cannot fault the butler for doing his duty, and on one occasion he saved my social face. On the first leg of the trip to Stepleton, that is, on the London underground on the way to Waterloo Station, a pickpocket had nabbed my wallet. I had enough silver in my pocket to buy my ticket to Salisbury, but not enough for my fare back after the weekend. I explained my embarrassment to the butler and negotiated a small loan from him, which I repaid, with a suitable tip, on the next weekend. Our butler had maintained the finest traditions of Jeeves.

My main social problem at Stepleton was Sir Ronald Lindsay. His defining characteristic seemed to be that he would not make the slightest effort about anything, certainly not about me. His superiority, if he had it, was the most effortless I have known. Considering the matter later and dispassionately, I am not sure he had any duty towards me. Was he not supposed to be on vacation and thus resting? At any rate, he made no effort. After dinner it was Mrs. Cameron and I who kept the conversation going, so far as it was kept going at all. Yet 1936 was, to say the least, an interesting year in European politics, and Sir Ronald, through his connection with the Foreign Office, must have been well informed. Yet he said little or nothing.

I had been brought up in the belief that, besides huntin' and shootin', "good political talk" was the rule in English country houses, and I was bound that I should do my share. Accordingly on one of my earlier weekends I came down to Sunday breakfast with Sir Ronald. As was the custom at breakfast, the men ate alone, helping themselves to various goodies, including kedgeree, which were kept on hot-plates on the sideboard. Sir Ronald said nothing, not even, I think, "Good morning." Primed by kedgeree, I felt I must say something and that in what I considered to be the country-house tradition. What I said was more or less this: "The Egyptian situation seems fraught with interest, does it not, Sir Ronald?" (I knew he must know something about the Egyptian situation.) His eloquent answer was a grunt. He may have been one of those persons who just do not like to talk at breakfast. He may have had his fill of foreign affairs and just wanted to get away from it all. To be charitable, I must suppose he had some ability, or he would not have become British ambassador in Washington (but that does not quite go without saying). Finally, he may have come to dislike Americans (but his wife and mother-in-law were Americans). I was not alone in my opinion of him. My father, who had met him and was a good judge of men, shared my view.

Mrs. Cameron was quite unlike Sir Ronald. She could not have been kinder to me, and she was both a kind and a brilliant woman. When I was not walking, she took me in her limousine in long drives around the country, taking care to explain to me what I was looking at, such as Corfe Castle. Such of Wessex as I did not cover on foot I covered in her car.

She also took me to parties, usually not dinner parties but tea parties, and I could sense the respect in which the county families held her, though she was an American and an outsider. I remember especially one crowded tea party she took me to, held at the huge country house of some nobleman for the purpose of supporting the work of the local visiting nurse. As I recall the scene, there were three enclosures in which tea was dispensed, one for the gentry, which included Mrs. Cameron and myself, one for the farmers, and one for the farm laborers, each with their respective families. It almost reproduced "Ullathorne Sports" in Trollope's *Barchester Towers*. Always the research sociologist, I disgraced Mrs. Cameron by asking our hostess, who must have been at least a countess, some impertinent questions about her peculiar customs. But Mrs. Cameron never chided me. I am glad to have known Dorset intimately and to have seen the traditional life of the English landed gentry before taxation killed it forever. Mrs. Cameron died during World War II.

Let me now return to my manuscripts, which were, after all, the reason that I was in England. The hours were not long at either the Public Record Office or the British Museum. One was not admitted before 10 A.M.; one had to leave by, I believe, 4:30 P.M., and naturally one was not allowed to take the manuscripts home to work on them during the evening. What is more I took a reasonable time off for lunch in a cheap restaurant, such as a chophouse in Fleet Street at the southern end of Chancery Lane. As far as hours were concerned, there was no way I could kill myself with work.

These research libraries provided printed lists, called calendars, of the manuscripts in their possession, but for what were considered fairly unimportant manuscripts, like manorial court rolls, a calendar indicated nothing about their contents but gave only their dates and the manor or group of manors they originally came from. One would hand an attendant a slip, requesting the manuscript one wanted, and he soon brought it to one's table. In those days there was not a huge number of scholars competing for the use of manuscripts.

Physically, the manorial court rolls were just that: a single strip of parchment or several stitched together, rolled up, and tied with a piece of red tape. The use of red tape to tie up rolls is in fact the origin of our expression for the sins of bureaucracy. The rolls were kept in Latin, but a Latin whose constructions were often English. I did not have to remember the classical use of the infinitive in indirect discourse. Instead the clerks used a *quod* clause, as in the English, "He said *that* . . ." I had studied some medieval palaeography in the year before I went to England. What I had to master most thoroughly were the standard abbreviations for groups of Latin letters, which made a kind of shorthand out of the sentences in rapidly written manuscripts, which the court rolls certainly were. I also had to learn, for instance, the special Latin words for agricultural objects and practices, which often do not appear in ordinary Latin dictionaries. Luckily many of them were just Latinized forms of Middle English words.

The court rolls seem to have been written down while the court was sitting, though some landlords had registers compiled of especially important entries copied from the original rolls. Cheap clerks wrote the rolls; the more skillful ones had more important duties than serving in manorial courts. But though the clerks generally wrote badly, at least all of those trained in a particular period of time had been taught to write in the same way. Individuals varied less in their style of handwriting than they do today—if indeed anyone writes longhand any more. These characteristics of the rolls allowed me after about two weeks of practice to read them at least as rapidly as I could a letter from my mother, though I must admit her handwriting was not of the plainest. The landlords must have considered their custumals to be of more enduring importance than their court rolls, for they were much better written and accordingly easier to read.

Speed of reading was crucial for the researcher, entirely apart from the shortness of the hours of work. In those days manuscripts could not be reproduced by photography nearly as cheaply as they can today, and thus kept for study at the scholar's leisure. We had to take notes directly from the manuscripts, and since the curators did not let us take notes in ink for fear that we might blot—or, horrors! even alter—the manuscripts, we took notes in pencil. I took mine on 5" x 8" filing cards, which I then placed under suitable headings in cardboard boxes. Other characteristics of the court rolls made note-taking easier than it might otherwise have been. Like court records today, they were kept in a pretty well standardized form, corresponding presumably to the standard order of business in the court itself. Accordingly one soon learned to skip over the parts of the record that were of only routine interest to the scholar and concentrate on copying those that concerned important suits between villagers. Even so, during the working day, I was kept as busy writing as the clerks had been who had kept the rolls in the first place.

With what excitement I untied the red tape around each new court roll, hoping I should find in it some single entry—some single entry, mind you—that might confirm a pet theory or throw a new beam on the darkness of medieval life! No one who works on modern sociology, where data are so plentiful that they become mere statistics, can know the joy sheer single facts can be of their own sweet selves. And facts they were. Manorial court rolls came as close to providing hard data as any historical records in existence. They were legal records. Of course there must have been perjurers in court then, as there are now, but in those villages where everyone knew everyone else and his or her business, there must have been far fewer perjurers who could get away with their perjury without challenge.

Particularly delightful was the discovery of facts that one had expected to find because they were consistent with facts one already knew. One example was the following. In a large number of English villages—I shall go into this matter at greater length later—the holding of a villager descended at his death or retirement to one and only one of his sons. The other sons had to get out, often with a "portion," presumably in money, from their father's movable property, not his land. Many of them did get out, by picking up a vacant holding or being apprenticed to a tradesman in a borough. But I suspected that some, for want of motive or opportunity, would choose to stay in their old home. What rule would then govern their behavior? It seemed to me that the only rule consistent with the preservation of unigeniture would be one that required such sons to remain unmarried, so that if they did produce children these would be bastards and thus unable to put forward a claim to the holding. With what joy I finally ran into an entry that stated perfectly clearly the rule I had predicted.

I discovered something new about almost every aspect of social life, but the subject to which I had most to contribute, because cases concerning it were, for obvious reasons, particularly apt to be recorded in manorial court rolls, was peasant customs for the inheritance of land. Many of them were similar to those of the common law as discussed in the great book by Pollock and Maitland, *The History of English Law before the Time of Edward I*.[5] Indeed the peasant customs may have been influenced by the common law, but it was at least something to have shown that the customs of peasants, who were often unfree serfs, resembled the rules of the common law, which was essentially the law applicable to freemen.

What was more important, I found that I could advance with some confidence a generalization linking variations of customs of inheritance with variations in other features of English society. This generalization popped out at me by Baconian induction after scanning a large amount of data. I held no theory that would lead me to look for it. Or rather, the anthropologists had taught me that every institution of a society was related to every other, but not just how they would be related in particular cases, and this was a particular case.

What was the generalization? Among the most crucial institutions of medieval society, not only in England but elsewhere in Europe, were its field systems, the ways in which agricultural technology was socially organized. If we leave aside the so-called highland zone of the North and West, the rest of England was dominated by two different kinds of field systems. H. L. Gray, in one of the classics of English economic history, *English Field Systems*[6]—written, by the way, while he held a post at Harvard—had roughly delineated the boundaries between the two. When I say "dominated" I mean that a particular system was much the more common in a particular area, but not that it was universal even there. The ability of peasants to find particular solutions to special local conditions is great, and it must be if they are to survive.

A strip crossing England from the northeast to the southwest coast was dominated by one form or another of what scholars of my time called the "open-field" system of agriculture. In the sixteenth century Englishmen called it the champion husbandry, the word *champion* being their corruption of the French *champagne*, which means "open field." It is perhaps better called the "common-field" system, since other systems may have looked just as "open." Under the various forms of this system, the houses of a village were apt to form a compact unit, clustered together or strung out side by side on both sides of a village street. This was the "town." The tilled fields of the village lay outside the town, divided into two, three, or sometimes more great sectors. The rotation of crops was applied to these sectors as wholes, and any villager holding land in one of the sectors was obliged to plant the crops assigned to it in any given season. Indeed the sectors were sometimes called "seasons." A villager normally did hold land in each of the sectors, usually an approximately equal amount in each. I do not want to go into details, especially as the system allowed, as of course it had to do, much flexibility in adjustment to local conditions.

With his usual clarity, Sir Francis Bacon gives us the "feel" of the common-field area as it still existed in his time. He wrote in 1606: " . . . for in the champaign countries of England, where the habitation useth to be in towns, and not dispersed, it is no new thing to go two miles off to plough part of their grounds; and two miles compass will take up a good deal of country."[7]

To the southeast of the "champaign countries," notably in Kent—which we must remember was the English home of the Homanses—and in East Anglia, especially the counties of Norfolk and Suffolk, a different kind of field system prevailed, which I shall call simply "nonopen field." In this area, as Bacon and others suggested, settlement was much more likely to be dispersed in small clumps of houses, which we are justified in calling hamlets, or even in single big houses standing alone. Although the crop rotations might well be the same as those used in the common-field areas, they were applied to smaller units, to the land around a single hamlet or farm house. Even when villages existed, as they did in parts of East Anglia, the rotation of crops was not applied to the great sectors of the village fields. Instead the fields were divided into smaller quarters or "precincts" and the crop rotations were applied separately to each of the precincts.

The discovery I made was that there was a high correlation between differences in field systems, differences in patterns of settlement, and differences in the customs of inheritance of villagers' holding of land. In the areas of England dominated by common-field systems, for instance, the usual rule was that a peasant holding of land passed by descent to one son of the last holder. In the nonopen field areas, a peasant holding normally descended to all of the sons equally, who might physically divide their shares or continue to work the holding jointly. For obvious reasons, we have come to call the former impartible, the latter partible inheritance. The generalization was not absolute but statistical—not that I ever took the time to do the necessary statistics: the correlation was obvious by inspection. And it has stood up well under the scrutiny of later investigators. In modern times, with changing agricultural practices and changing legal rules about landholding including the right to leave land by will, the differences and accordingly the correlation have disappeared.

I later became aware of other differences between the two areas. Besides differences in patterns of settlement, there were differences in the nature of the units of local government, and in the names given these units, to the peasant holdings themselves, and even to different social classes among the peasantry.

In one way, all these discoveries were very satisfactory. Indeed they thrilled me. Henderson and the social anthropologists had told me to look for social systems, and one sign of the existence of social systems was that the institutions of one were systematically interrelated and different from those of another. Did not, therefore, the common field and the noncommon field form two distinct social systems? My teachers had told me what to expect, and, by God, they were right.

And yet, and yet, and yet . . . ! What I thought I had discovered simply raised new questions. After all, why should there be two systems? And though they differed systematically in a number of ways, they did not differ in all, and the ways in which they resembled one another may have been more important than those in which they differed. Above all, the people in the two areas spoke the same language with only minor dialectical differences. (The upper classes in my century presumably still spoke French among themselves.) The geography of the two areas was the same, in that both showed similar variations in terrain and soil: in this respect the differences within each area were greater than the differences between them. Though a county like Kent displayed great physical variation, the county was still subject to a single rule of partible inheritance. And the same held true of agricultural technologies. The people in each area knew identical technologies; the differences between them lay less in technology than in the way technology was geared to social organization. Again and again, English scholars have tried to attribute the differences between the two systems to technological or geographical factors or some combination of the two. Again and again they have failed, but it's dogged as does it, and they keep on trying. One could make a better case for the importance of these factors in highland England: a rugged terrain and a pastoral economy were unlikely to encourage a common-field system. But I was concerned with the lowland.

I finally decided that the mistake these scholars made and, at first, I myself was making came out of a too narrow interpretation of Marx or some other form of the economic interpretation of history. I myself was introduced to these ideas by reading the books of my great-uncle Brooks Adams, especially *The Law of Civilization and Decay,*[8] as much as by Marx. Marx was quite correct in emphasizing that, in studying a society, one should put the greatest weight on the means of production and on the social relations of production they implied. That was not the difficulty here. But we had unconsciously drawn the further conclusion that, with one set of geographical and technical conditions, one and only one kind of social organization could be associated. There might be environments so severe that they allowed only one kind of social organization: the Eskimo might be an example. But now I had reason to doubt whether our assumption was justified in general. Two or more different types of social organization might be equally well adapted to a single type of geographical and technical environment. Marx of course would have argued that the common field and the noncommon field were not really all that different; in his language both, in the thirteenth century, were feudal economies. Yet if we stopped to think, as of course we did not, we could find supporting evidence for my generalization all around us. Thus the Soviet Union and the United States employed essentially the same technologies both in agriculture and in industry, and yet their social organizations differed greatly and in many ways. The reasons they differed lay, of course, in their different past histories.

This reasoning set me free, in the sense that I need no longer worry over the mere fact that lowland England in the thirteenth and, I supposed, earlier centuries supported two somewhat different social systems. There could perfectly well be two or even more. But my recognizing the possibility still did not answer the question why there were in fact two. That question I did not take up again until I returned to Harvard after World War II, and the answer I found to it, while better than nothing, was never wholly satisfactory. I did not realize that I already had a clue.

When I wrote up the results of my research for my book *English Villagers of the Thirteenth Century*, which appeared early in 1941, I decided to concentrate on the common-field area, because its institutions, then as now, were better understood than those of the noncommon field, though I did point out that both existed and were different. When my manuscript was ready for publication, the United States was still suffering from the Depression. My book was big and expensive to publish, and the Harvard University Press was unwilling to publish it without a subsidy. But in those days the subsidy did not have to be large. Professor Henderson and, I believe, Professor Roger Merriman of the History Department approached my richest relative, my uncle Charlie Adams, with the request that he provide the subsidy. He did so, and here was a bonus I received for my many years of serving as a member of the crew of his racing yachts. The year 1941 was a bad time for the book to come out. In World War II no one was interested in the thirteenth century. For years it sold slowly, but the press finally did sell out its original edition, and later editions have maintained ever since its tenuous life in print.

I received still another bonus from the book. Shortly after World War II, I received a letter from a certain Hugh Reynolds in London, who pointed out that I had made a mistake, the nature of which makes no matter here, in describing what lawyers call "the curtesy of England"— the rights of a widower in land held by his wife in her own right. It seems to have been called the curtesy of England because English law was more courteous towards the widower—allowed him greater rights—than other countries were. Mine was an utterly stupid mistake: I had read the appropriate documents and should have known what the correct provisions of the rule were. But somehow I managed to write them down wrong. I suppose all historians have blushed at some time or another at making mistakes of this kind. I am sure I am not alone.

Reynolds's letter pointed out my error most politely, and I replied, making no effort to defend myself but abjectly confessing my sin. Reynolds turned out to be a most able and respectable London solicitor, who of course knew all about the curtesy. We kept up a correspondence on all sorts of subjects, which lasted the rest of his life. When I visited England after the war, I presented myself at his invitation at his flat in St. John's Wood. I remember the look of astonishment, mingled with a little disappointment, that passed over his face when he first saw me. He had expected to see a much older man, seasoned by many years of medieval scholarship, with whom, I fear, he believed he could feel more at home than with one so much younger than himself. I also looked younger than I was. In spite of his first disappointment, Hugh, his wife, and his three daughters could not have been kinder to this rather noisy American. They entertained me, my wife, and even my own daughters on my later visits to their homes in London and on the Norfolk coast. One of his daughters, Susan, has herself become a distinguished social historian of medieval England. Hugh Reynolds was the finest kind of Englishman; to have known him and his family has been one of the great rewards of my life.

During my absence from Harvard in World War II I did not give a thought to English social history. When I came back, my interest returned with a rush, though it was always to be a sideline with me. I had left with a nagging question: Why should the customs of the common-field parts of England differ from those of the noncommon field, and differ in many ways besides the field-systems themselves? Geography and technology did not seem to account for the differences. What came to me after the war was a possible historical answer, on the analogy of the explanation of the differences between the United States and Soviet Russia. Had the different customs been brought to England by Germanic invaders who already differed in their Continental homelands? I realized that this could not be the final explanation, but it might serve as an intermediary link. Unfortunately we knew far less about the Germanic invasions than we did about the histories of the United States and Russia. We were dealing with the darkest part of the Dark Ages. Still, we knew something and might find out more. If one thought the hypothesis worth pursuing, the obvious step was to study the earliest descriptions of the institutions in those parts of Continental Germania from which the invaders had come. In recent years, the English economic historians, with their native insularity and their utter fixation on economic and technological explanations, had failed to take any step in this direction—with one exception.

The exception was J.E.A. Jolliffe, professor of history at Oxford, whose book *Pre-Feudal England: The Jutes*[9] appeared in 1933. I was especially interested in the Jutes. Although we ordinarily speak of the English as Anglo-Saxons, the Venerable Bede in his great *Ecclesiastical History of the English People*,[10] which he wrote in Latin in the first part of the eighth century, stated in chapter 15 that England was invaded in the fifth century by three Germanic peoples and not two: Angles, Saxons, but also Jutes. What is more, he said that the Jutes were the earliest invaders, under the leadership of Hengest and Horsa (suspicious names because they mean respectively male and female horse, and the horse may have been the totemic animal of the Germanic peoples). The Jutes had invaded

Kent; indeed Hengest and Horsa were supposed to have landed just a mile or two from Ramsgate, from which long afterwards my Homans ancestor had come to New England. Bede said that Jutes also settled in southern Hampshire, and independent linguistic evidence confirmed him. For obvious reasons, Bede thought that the Jutes had come to England directly from Jutland, the name still given to northern Denmark, and indeed Jutes must have lived there at some time, though not necessarily at the time of the invasions.

Jolliffe made a careful study of the earliest records describing the social organization of Kent, and then, skeptical of the Jutland hypothesis, looked at the social organization of the homeland of the Franks—their homeland before they conquered and gave their name to France—which lay just across the Channel from Kent in what is now Belgium and in a belt extending over to the Rhine. He found distinct similarities between Kentish custom and that of the Frankish homeland, and he partly convinced me he was correct. The inference was that the peculiarities of the custom of Kent could be explained if Franks, or at least a people whose custom resembled that of the Franks, had invaded Kent in the great wandering of the peoples that both created and followed upon the collapse of the Roman Empire in the West.

Kent was a part of noncommon-field England, but it was not the only part. In the lowlands, the other main part was East Anglia, especially the counties of Norfolk and Suffolk. The custom of East Anglia was not identical with that of Kent but resembled Kent more than the custom of common-field England. For example, the rule of inheritance in East Anglia was that land was partible among the sons of the last holder, like the Kentish rule called *gavelkind*.

If Jolliffe could find a part of continental *Germania* whose custom resembled that of Kent, where might I look for one whose custom resembled East Anglia? The more I thought about it, the more I felt that an obvious candidate was Friesland.[11] There is still a part of the Netherlands and West Germany called Friesland, and in the Dark Ages it had been larger, a "Greater Friesland" extending, due east from East Anglia, along the southern coast of the North Sea perhaps from the mouth of the Scheldt as far as the Anglo-Saxon country at the base of the Danish peninsula. On the south it abutted on Frankish territory, so that, if continuity was an argument, their customs might have resembled one another.

Not only is there still a Friesland, but there is still a Frisian language (*Fries*). What is more, linguists had long known that it was the language most closely related to English. There was even a jingle that brought out the similarity:

Good butter and good cheese
Is good English and good Fries.

Not even modern Dutch, a descendant of Frankish, resembles English as much as Frisian does. Yet we must remember that in the Dark Ages all the languages in the area, including the languages of the Angles and Saxons, were no more than dialects of one another.

There was even a little documentary evidence that Frisians, as well as the traditional Angles, Saxons, and Jutes, had invaded England in the Dark Ages. Procopius of Caesarea, a great Byzantine historian, and writing, be it noted, more than a century before Bede, had stated that in his time Britain was inhabited by *Angloi* and *Frisoi*. Byzantium was a long way from England, but Procopius might still have good reason to be well informed. Frankish ambassadors had come to the Byzantine court; they would certainly have known something about England, and Procopius, as a man about court, might well have heard the ambassador's accounts.

Inspired by information of this sort, I made a deeper study than any I had made so far of the early institutions of East Anglia. On the other side, I looked for evidence about Frisian institutions of the earliest date from which a large enough body of records had survived. Since I was no longer a Junior Fellow and had neither time, training, nor money to find and work on the original documents, presumably mostly in the Netherlands, I looked for the best secondary source I could find, which was one cited by the great French historian Marc Bloch. As I read the book, I found it described a society that seemed to me to have astonishing similarities with the society of medieval East Anglia. Even the names of some of the social classes and tenement-units were the same. Again I shall not go into details. But nothing in my intellectual life, except perhaps my discovery in my childhood of the land snails on Eagle Island, has given me more pleasure. And yet how important was it? Really of no importance at all. Thank God, it is not the importance of a discovery but the mere fact of having made it that gives me joy.

In lowland England the institutions of Kent and East Anglia resembled one another without being identical. Bede believed that Jutes invaded Kent but also that the Jutes came from Jutland. I now felt sure that Frisians had invaded East Anglia in the Dark Ages. I later found that I was able to connect the Frisians with the Jutes on the Continent too. For *Beowulf* and *The Fight at Finnsburg* describe a group of Jutes actually living in Friesland and not in Jutland, and it places the only other Hengest mentioned in the early sources—if it is not indeed the same Hengest who invaded Kent—in Friesland too.[12] My personal search for roots was at an end. Coming from the Isle of Thanet in East Kent, the Homanses could well have been of Jutish origin. I leave them looking out across the North Sea from Friesland. I cannot trace them back any further.

In short my explanation of the social differences between common-field and noncommon-field England was that in the Dark Ages (fifth century A.D.) two groups of Germanic peoples, bearers of slightly different cultures, had invaded England. The Angles and Saxons, with later reinforcements in the North by Danes, had founded common-field England; the Frisians and Jutes, perhaps arriving a little earlier, had founded noncommon-field England. We should not be called merely Anglo-Saxons but Anglo-Saxon-Friso-Jutes.

Of course my theory required some mad assumptions. The characteristics of neither East Anglian nor Frisian social organization were recorded in any detail before about 1200 A.D., and yet the Germanic invasions of England occurred around 500. I had to assume that local social institutions had maintained themselves well enough on both sides of the Channel for their similarities to be recognized after a passage of no less than seven hundred years. I emphasize local social institutions. There certainly had been great political changes and—greatest change of all—the Germanic peoples had been converted to Christianity. Yet I was still ready to make the assumption for local institutions and for conditions in the Dark Ages. We knew of still more striking continuities. Thus the Germanic institution of the *comitatus*—the band of warriors accompanying a leader in battle, rewarded by him and feasting with him in peace—reported by the Roman historian Tacitus in his book *Germania*[13] in 98 A.D. reappears, apparently unchanged, in the Anglo-Saxon *Beowulf*. Here again the continuity is of the order of seven hundred years.

My explanation would account for the distribution of local custom in medieval England but of course it was not a final explanation. It only pushed the problem back into continental *Germania*. Why should the Anglo-Saxons, on the one side, and the Friso-Jutes, as I called them, on the other, have developed somewhat different institutions *there?* That question, I suspect, will never be answered. After all, I had little enough evidence to support my own narrower explanation.

I am afraid English historians have not accepted my theory except by grudgingly admitting that Frisians may well have invaded Britain. But that is rather less than admitting that East Anglian institutions resemble Frisian ones, and that the invaders must have established them there. Still, and with little justification, I remain pleased with my discovery.

After my return to Harvard at the end of World War II, my interest in the English peasantry provided me with another bonus, probably more important for my general intellectual development than my pursuit of the Friso-Jutes. The Harvard Department of History had once been strong in the field of European medieval, and especially English medieval, history. After the war, with the retirement or death of some of the grand old men in the field, like my old mentor McIlwain, the department was no longer so strong. History, moreover, had been opening up types of studies somewhat different from the political, constitutional, and legal ones that had been dominant earlier. The History Department did not propose to abandon its old interests, but it was prepared to stick its toes into the cold waters of the new ones. Another way of putting the matter is to say that some of the old boundaries between history and other social sciences, such as economics and sociology, were beginning to break down.

At some time in the late 1950s, Oscar Handlin, who knew all about my work on the English peasantry of the thirteenth century, asked me if I were interested in offering a course in the History Department on English medieval social and economic history. His invitation carried weight, since he was then chairman of the History Department, was an excellent social historian himself, and indeed had just escaped becoming officially a sociologist. I found the invitation flattering, as some historians then, and even later, were contemptuous of sociologists. I told Oscar I was indeed interested, though I was not well prepared to teach such a course then, except of course for the thirteenth century. But preparation for teaching about other centuries by reading and keeping up with current publications would come as I went along. I have never worried about whether I was prepared to teach any subject in the social sciences.

Beginning, I think, in 1957 I offered a course entitled English Social History: 400-1642, and I did so every other year until I retired. I enjoyed teaching it more than any other course I taught at Harvard. The year 1642 is, of course, the date of the opening of the English Civil War, but I always told my students that the course was really about the twelve hundred years between the Germanic invasions, which began about 400 A.D., to the founding of Harvard College in 1636, as if the latter were the "far-off divine event" towards which all English history moved. Still more accurately, it was, since it covered such a long time, a sketchy history of English institutions between the two great English overseas invasions: the Germanic invasion from the Continent, which made England England and not Britannia, and the largely English invasion in the seventeenth century of the eastern seaboard of what is now the United States.

"Social and economic" meant what I wanted them to mean. In practice, I did not try to deal in depth with political events unless they had big social and economic effects, which, for instance, the Norman Conquest most certainly did. Nor did I try to deal with constitutional and legal issues, such as those raised by Magna Carta, because Professor Sam Thorne of the Law School was ably dealing with them. Of course I made exceptions. To understand, for instance, some of the social and economic developments, I had to provide my students with elementary information about the various legal provisions governing the tenure of land. But within these limits I was free to talk about what I thought was important.

Teaching the course forced one big change in my thinking. I had designed *English Villagers of the Thirteenth Century* to be a cross-sectional study: it was to describe peasant society as it existed within a limited period of time. It disregarded change. Now I had to consider what is pompously called the dynamics of history. I had to consider long-term changes in social and economic behavior and institutions. Above all, I found myself trying to explain these changes. Was history really just "one damn thing after another," or could one make sense of it? This is, of course, the big question that has troubled historians over the centuries.

Looking back over my more than forty years of interest in English medieval history, I am sure we have made much progress. We can make more sense by far of what happened than we used to make, and we have done so without any of that thrashing about concerning theoretical issues that has marked so many fields of social science. One reason for our progress is that we have been, as social and economic historians, dealing mostly with the behavior of fairly large numbers of people in similar positions and holding similar interests. It is much easier to explain the behavior of such categories of people than that of single individuals in very special kinds of positions. Thus it is easier to explain why English landlords over the centuries changed their strategies of estate management than why William the Conqueror managed to win the Battle of Hastings or even why he undertook to invade England at all.

In the second place, the problems of medieval history are not especially relevant to those of the modern world. Accordingly medieval history has been largely free from those ideological conflicts that have plagued so much of the interpretation of modern history. There are, naturally, medieval historians who call themselves Marxists, and much to my amusement, a Soviet historian quoted Lenin in apparently conclusive refutation of the method I used in *English Villagers*.[14] But upon the whole I do not observe that medieval historians who call themselves Marxists behave very differently from other medievalists. They have been controlled by our tradition of sticking pretty closely to the manuscript sources, which are far richer than most nonmedievalists realize.

Though, as I have said, medievalists seldom talked about theory, history does have a problem with theory. There have always been historians who claimed that history has no theory at all. History has a theory, but like much of sociology its major premises remain unstated, so that it remains implicit. True, there are no "iron laws" of history, such as

Marx and my great-uncle Brooks Adams were sadistically fond of enunciating. Instead, the laws of history, like the laws of the other social sciences, are the laws of psychology, that is, the laws of the behavior of men and women as members of a particular species, otherwise called human nature. The so-called iron laws, when they hold good at all, follow from these more general psychological laws under particular given circumstances.

When I saw changes taking place in medieval England, I always saw persons acting, not organizations, institutions, or "society," though their actions created and maintained for a time all of these things, which also provided some of the contingencies for the further actions of persons. Of course, some of the persons concerned were numerous, placed in similar circumstances, and acted in similar ways, so that one did not have to follow the fortunes of every particular individual but only those of the category. The actions of persons were also constrained by the actions of other persons, so that the resultant effects might well be different from those any one of them had envisaged. But the general propositions used to explain their behavior remained the laws of psychology. What I believed to hold good of the explanation of English history I could not help believing held good of all history. England was no exception, though the English sometimes talked as if they were exceptions to everything. I shall not here pursue further the problem of the explanation of social behavior, since that problem first came alive for me in another connection.

NOTES

1. Frederick Seebohm, *The English Village Community,* 2d ed. (London: Longmans, Green, 1883).
2. George C. Homans, *English Villagers of the Thirteenth Century* (Cambridge: Harvard University Press, 1941).
3. F. W. Maitland, ed., *Select Pleas in Manorial and Other Seignorial Courts,* vol. 1 (London: Selden Society, 1889).
4. *The Letters of Henry Adams,* ed. J. C. Levenson et al., 3 vols. (Cambridge: Harvard University Press, 1983). The biography of Mrs. Cameron has appeared at last: Arline Boucher Tehan, *Henry Adams in Love* (New York: Universe, 1983).
5. Frederick Pollock and Frederic William Maitland, *The History of English Law before the Time of Edward I,* 2d ed., 2 vols. (Cambridge: Cambridge University Press, 1911).
6. Howard Levi Gray, *English Field Systems* (Cambridge: Harvard University Press, 1915).
7. Francis Bacon, "Certain Considerations Touching the Plantations in Ireland," in his *Works,* ed. Basil Montagu, 15 vols. (London: Pickering, 1825-1834), 5: 169-85.

8. Brooks Adams, *The Law of Civilization and Decay* (New York: Macmillan, 1896).

9. J. E. A. Jolliffe, *Pre-Feudal England: The Jutes* (Oxford: Oxford University Press, 1933).

10. *Baedae Opera Historica,* trans. J. E. A. King, 2 vols. (Cambridge: Harvard University Press, Loeb Classical Library, 1954).

11. For the argument and evidence presented in the next few pages, see George C. Homans, "The Frisians in East Anglia" in my *Sentiments and Activities: Essays in Social Science* (New York: Free Press of Glencoe, 1962), pp. 158-81. This paper was amended and reprinted from *Economic History Review,* 2d Series, 10 (1957): 189-206. See also G. C. Homans, "The Rural Sociology of Medieval England," *Past and Present,* No. 4 (1953): 32-43, and "The Explanation of English Regional Differences," *Past and Present,* No. 42 (1969): 18-34.

12. See *Beowulf and the Fight at Finnsburg,* ed. Fr. Klaeber, 3d ed. (Boston: D. C. Heath, 1950), pp. 232-34.

13. Cornelius Tacitus, *Dialogus, Agricola, Germania,* trans. William Peterson and Maurice Hutton (London: Heinemann, Loeb Classical Library, 1932), p. 283.

14. E. A. Kosminsky, *Studies in the Agrarian History of England in the Thirteenth Century,* ed. R. H. Hilton, trans. Ruth Kisch (Oxford: Blackwell, 1956), p. 39.

12

SAILING WITH UNCLE CHARLIE

My recent chapters have been largely devoted to my "intellectual" interests, using "intellectual" in the narrow sense of that word. The next six may provide some relief. Like everyone else I have had many interests besides intellectual ones, and they have certainly concerned my intelligence if not my intellect. The next two chapters provide a sample—though only a sample—of my worldly interests in the 1920s and 1930s. The four that follow deal with my part, a small one but important to me, of the greatest experience of my generation, World War II. Even if my life during these years was largely nonintellectual, if indeed under stress I showed by my behavior that I could disregard the lessons I thought my mind had mastered, that too contributed to my education: I learned how quickly cerebral control may be undermined. I have already spoken often of my uncle Charlie. I turn first to describing the activity in which I came into closest contact with him.

The historians spend their time talking about every great Adams except the one I knew, my mother's brother, Charles Francis Adams, the third of the name. I cannot speak of his career as treasurer of Harvard College, as secretary of the Navy in the Hoover administration, as the leading citizen of Boston in his day. I can only try to describe what it was to serve as one of the crew of his yachts. My excuse is that his career as a racing skipper was the greatest of his careers, the only one in which he reached supremacy. For some fifty years he was acknowledged to be the ablest helmsman in Massachusetts Bay and, if the ablest there, the ablest on the East Coast—though Long Island Sound may have had its reservations—and if the ablest on the East Coast, then so also in the world. He was, moreover, supreme in every kind of boat, from the little Herreshoff S-class to the cup defenders: in 1920 he had, in *Resolute*, successfully defended the America's Cup. Here was a new kind of excellence for an Adams, for to the earlier members of the family competitive sport may well have seemed frivolous, even British. But if new, still excellent. Let those who do not know what it is to be a seaman argue that in Uncle Charlie his race had lost its bite.

I never sailed with Uncle Charlie on the big boats, but I did sail with him as one of his crew most summers from 1923 through 1940 in the R-class sloops, designed by W. Starling Burgess, *Lightning, Dandelion,* and, greatest of them all, *Gossoon,* in the Q-class *Bat,* and finally in the 8-meter *Thisbe.* All of them, I suppose, were between thirty and forty-five feet long overall. Almost every year we were champion in our class at Marblehead, our most dangerous opponent being Frank C. Paine in *Gypsy* of his own design. In the smaller boats, those of the R-class, two of us went as crew, I and Uncle Charlie's son, Charles Francis ("Chas") Adams, who became president of the Raytheon Corporation. In the larger boats we added a third, usually my other cousin, Thomas Boylston Adams, who became president of the Massachusetts Historical Society. In short, we were all Adamses, crew and skipper. As the smallest and lightest hand I was usually assigned the work with jib and spinnaker, requiring less muscle but, by that token, more brains.

For many summers Uncle Charlie had lived—if it can be called living—in a wooden barracks, hugger-mugger with Perkinses, Hunnewells, Lees, Thorndikes, and other Adamses, forming a sort of advanced communist experiment like Brook Farm only more successful, called The Glades Club. "The Glades" may suggest something lush: it is in fact a bleak promontory jutting out from the South, or proletarian, Shore of Massachusetts Bay inside Minot's Ledge Light and outside Cohasset harbor. Uncle Charlie kept his boats moored behind The Glades in a hole affording slightly greater depth of water than elsewhere over the sandy bottom.

The Glades is some eighteen miles across the Bay from Marblehead, where we raced. Every Saturday Uncle Charlie sailed his boat over to Marblehead in time for the race in the early afternoon and then back again afterwards. Note: he *sailed* her. He could well have afforded a motorboat to tow him, but he sailed. No other boat in our classes sailed from anywhere: they stayed in Marblehead; and I suspect that no other skipper would have been prepared to sail our distance. The result was that we got more experience in handling ship and sails than did the others, who only went out for the afternoon to race, and far more experience in keeping her going in light airs. We had to keep her going if we were to get to Marblehead in time to eat and back to The Glades in time to sleep. But we got something more than experience: to the imagination of at least one boy we were, compared to our opponents, the hardy, the bold, the true mariners. It was we, not they, who followed the sea and carried on the traditions of sail.

Looked at objectively, the task of getting a racing yacht back and forth across the Bay under sail in summer was by no means arduous. In all my years with Uncle Charlie we always reached Marblehead in time for the race, and almost always in time for lunch before it; and as for getting home, I spent only one full night aboard, when fog, blowing in before an easterly, surprised us halfway across and made it doubtful that we should find the entrance through the Cohasset ledges. We ran in under old Boston Light and then anchored in Hull Gut till morning, when the weather cleared. It is fair to admit that if the weather was bad enough we did not try to sail over partly, I think, because Uncle Charlie's boats were not at their best in a blow. For the record, our fastest run across the Bay was made in *Bat* from Marblehead in one hour and three-quarters under trysail and small jib before a fresh northwester. Our average run was, I suppose, somewhere between four and five hours.

The weather on the less typical passages included northwesters in the early fall when the Bay was, in Uncle Charlie's words, feather-white, and the salt dried and crusted on our faces in the sun as we beat up to Marblehead, reefed, and rainy northeasters—again a head wind—when we had the choice of getting soaked on deck or sick below. More characteristically the winds were gentle, southeast by day, westerly by night.

We met at The Glades float a little after seven in the morning, and rowed out in the dinghy, our oars puddling and breaking the rafts of eelgrass combed out by the ebb tide. Looking overboard one could sometimes catch a white flash against the bottom where a flounder shifted berth and showed his underside. To the west against the coffee-colored Cohasset rocks the water was pale blue, but to the east and seaward golden and hazy under the sun. Still heavy with sleep, we set the working sails and ran out with the last of the night breeze. Then while some of us slobs were apt to go back to sleep on deck, Uncle Charlie puttered.

But it was puttering with malice in it. When people tried to explain Uncle Charlie's racing record, they spoke of his touch at the helm. That was what they could see; what they could not see was his tireless obsession with anything that would help the boat sail faster—not just the big things like the slow agonies of breaking in a new mainsail or statesmanlike conferences with the yard men about the state of the underbody but also all the little things most yachtsmen did not bother about. He spent some time on his boat every day in summer, rowing off to her after he got back to The Glades from a long day in State Street, righting crimes against speed.

His method was characteristically elimination rather than addition. He was, above all, death on superfluous weights. When he bought a boat secondhand he went over her with a screwdriver taking off useless gadgets and dumping them unceremoniously overboard. A whole stove once went overboard in this fashion—and with it any suggestion of hot coffee. All cushions and mattresses always went the same way: should anyone want to lie down, there were always the sail bags, which were in fact much more comfortable. He would have been glad to get rid of the heads, and the boats he had built for himself never had one. Even for crowded waters, a canvas bucket was just as good. In brief, he was, in his care for speed, the supreme rationalist, the supreme functionalist.

He was indeed a bit of a Puritan. Anything that did not directly contribute to our salvation, even if innocent in itself, was suspect. No one cared less for the elegancies of yachting. He never shined brass. He seldom coiled a line. When we hoisted the mainsail below deck, we let the halyard lie where it dropped. If it came in all right, he argued, it would, left undisturbed, run out all right again. Our furls had only to be good enough to let the sail cover be put on. Nor did Uncle Charlie insist, as Admiral Morison did, that the stops be tied in neat bows on top of the sail. He did not care for fancywork like a golden groove along the sheer-strake. The appearance of the vessel was nothing to him so long as the paint in contact with the water was smooth. We were a working ship: the others could go in for the beautiful.

In the same way telltales were a superstition and contributed, however little, to friction. At night we ran, quite illegally, without lights, for lights prevented the helmsman's seeing what he ought to see. In the days of Prohibition this suspicious feature of our behavior led Coast Guard cutters to overhaul and hail us, until, I suspect, they got used to our presence in the Bay on Saturday nights. Finally, Uncle Charlie never insured his boats, and never lost one, though the moorings off The Glades were pretty well exposed to northeasters. The loss of a vessel would, in his mind, have paid him off fairly for being a damned fool.

Not long after we cleared the land the offshore westerly would die. Then we slatted gently over the smooth sea, waiting for the standard summer southeaster to make. We would first see its scattered cat's paws to windward; then they were all around us, bringing freshness to the golden summer. The water would begin to whisper under the bow. With luck we could set the spinnaker and count on reaching Marblehead with time to spare. To starboard we left the red lump of the Boston lightship, to port our halfway mark: the grey pillar of the Graves lighthouse, crossing the tracks of the ships bound in and out of Boston. In the early days these sometimes included a coasting schooner. Later the wooden draggers from the Georges Bank were more prominent, trailing stinking clouds of diesel smoke, and mackerel fishermen towing seine boats almost as long as themselves.

At Marblehead we came to our moorings, took off the working sails, put on the racing sails—we were always heaving sails up on deck—and went ashore for lunch at the Eastern Yacht Club. Uncle Charlie's approach to the clubhouse was in some ways his finest moment, and the only one when I ever suspected him of self-consciously acting the reverse of self-consciousness. An old navy seaman's duck cap, its brim reversed, might be pulled down over his noble beak; then came a pullover sweater, and finally a pair of knickerbockers, left unbuckled perhaps and drooping below the knees, held up by a sail stop instead of a belt, a stop passed not through the belt straps but below them, so as to hitch the knickerbockers up. The effect was as little nautical as possible, and put Uncle Charlie at once oneup on the gentlemen in white flannels and yachting caps on the piazza.

How shall I reproduce the smells of an old-time yacht club before it became just another country club: smells of tarred marline, manila rope, and new cotton duck, of large, dark, high-studded rooms fitted with varnished woodwork and straw matting, of the sea breeze blowing through open transoms and slatted doors, of clam chowder and blueberry pie?

After lunch we dumped our spare sails into the dinghy and were off to the starting line off Marblehead Rock. If there was one department of yacht racing in which Uncle Charlie fell short of excellence it was in starting. He was never very bold or skillful at getting the best berth at the windward end of the line. Indeed I never felt he liked, as so many racing skippers do, maneuvering at close quarters. He would get into a luffing match if one were forced upon him, but his heart was never in it. I suspect he felt it was irrational, bringing in factors outside the sheer speed of the boat. In starting, at any rate, Uncle Charlie seemed to be content if at the gun he was somewhere near the line with his wind clear.

Since the commonest wind at Marblehead in summer is south to southeasterly, the first leg of a race is usually to windward. This is the point of sailing that brings out the greatest differences in ships and helmsmen, and in this point lay Uncle Charlie's skill. He counted on getting ahead on the windward leg and holding his lead on the run or reach that followed. He did not expect, except by sheer luck, to pass another boat off the wind, though he was certainly afraid of being overhauled himself. Nor was he at his best in strong breezes, which demanded crude methods. His supreme expertise lay in coaxing a ship to windward in light airs—and at Marblehead in summer the winds are light: the place fitted the man. Like all great magicians he was credited with powers he did not possess. People thought he had the gift of finding the strongest breezes, but in this he was no better than other skippers.

Indeed there were no special tricks of wind or current at Marblehead that gave an advantage to local knowledge. Uncle Charlie never sailed any extreme course on the mere gamble of picking up a favorable slant. Even when he was, for once, behind, he seldom went off wind-hunting. I do not mean he did not care about finding the breeze: he certainly did. All I mean is that he was above all a rational sailor. Since he ought to be able to beat any boat sailing under the same conditions as his was, the best strategy was to stay with the rest of the fleet, and especially his chief rivals, rather than leave them and look for a breeze. To the usual maxim "Stay between the leading boat and the mark," he added the rule "Stay with a boat you're beating."

And he did beat them. Besides what I have called his rationality, his only gift was a superb sensitivity to the helm and the trim of the sails, as if he were a delicate machine that could register to ten decimal places when the ship was doing her best. Characteristically he sat to leeward watching the jib, the tiller over his shoulder, holding it, as he could in these beautifully balanced yachts, between thumb and forefinger, as if to pick up and read its least vibration. Occasionally he would say in a low voice: "Ease the jib a hair," or something of the sort. And however bad our start—and it was seldom really good—we found ourselves before long well up in the fleet or leading it.

During a race there was little conversation. Unlike some skippers, Uncle Charlie did not seek his crew's advice unless things were going very badly. For our part we volunteered no suggestions, but simply reported the movements of our competitors and the sighting of the windward mark. Our efforts in the matter of strength and skill were not always distinguished. In the early days I myself weighed less than a hundred pounds and added little pull when getting in the main sheet. But we were always willing, proud of our boat and our record. Uncle Charlie, moreover, assumed we would do our best. He found it embarrassing to praise us, as to express most other sentiments, and seldom did so, except for some truly outstanding feat, when I think he praised us out of duty, not desire. I once got a "Good work!" for setting the spinnaker without a hitch in a northeast blow when the ship was putting her nose down under the seas. But neither, since being inarticulate works both ways, did he blame us, not even when I managed to fall overboard from the forecastle at the start of a race in a nearly flat calm.

In demeanor Uncle Charlie was normally the calmest of men. In his younger days he had acquired a reputation for hard swearing when his blood was up, and I was often asked whether he swore at us. He did not: perhaps he felt that his son and nephew were sitting ducks for abuse. But there were times when he got, shall I say, excited and behaved rather unlike the cool skipper that the code of the sea demands. There are, in my experience, such times for every skipper. For him they were apt to come when we had rounded the weather mark for the run to the finish, and another boat was close astern. As one of us went forward to struggle with the spinnaker, he would appear to jump up and down in the cockpit, not shouting so much as passionately exclaiming: "Hurry, boys! Hurry up! Oh hurry!" These vivid comments did nothing to speed the setting of the spinnaker. They were irritating distractions in a ticklish job. Nor did Uncle Charlie nourish any intellectual doubts that we were doing our best. It was just that for once the tension got too much for him.

For Uncle Charlie wanted above all things to win. Beneath the calm exterior, surely at times of a type that justified an Englishman in claiming the Yankees to be the coldest of men, lay a passion for victory, at least in racing. Much trusted and respected though he was as a financier, I doubt that in this field he felt the same passion. Like his father, he must often have felt that he did not want to be bothered. Racing was different. He enjoyed sailing for itself, but there was no nonsense that racing was a way of getting a pleasant afternoon sail. Once when one of our opponents withdrew from a race for reasons that seemed to us quixotic, and so allowed us to score a win, Uncle Charlie remarked quietly: "I like to win boat-races." (*Boat* was pronounced *bot*.) He was lucky in wanting to win what he was good at winning, and we were lucky too. He set before us an example of the passion for excellence that, in whatever unlikely places it may show itself, is still the thing in the world to be most cherished.

Back to the weather mark. At Marblehead the last leg of a race is usually a run before a failing breeze. It is not the point of sailing that separates the men from the boys, in boats or skippers. Uncle Charlie harbored no illusions that he could, except by sheer luck, overhaul any boat on the run to the finish, and he went over, so to speak, to the defensive. His preoccupation was not to pass but to avoid being passed. He would sight astern, holding at arm's length his thumb erect, with his index finger against it, to measure the angle subtended by our nearest pursuer's mainmast, and so determine, by comparing two successive observations, whether she was gaining. I never found out how he remembered where, against his thumb, his finger had stood on the previous occasion. Under these circumstances the finish line came as a blessed relief.

With the end of the race our opponents' work was done. Ours had hardly begun; we had to work the ship back across the Bay. We returned to Marblehead harbor, bent on once more our working sails, and got under way again. By this time our late rivals were sitting on their piazzas, knocking back the first of many cocktails. Towards them our attitudes had all the ambivalence of working stiffs eyeing the fat cats of the bourgeoisie. No doubt they were to be envied their costly pleasures. On the other hand the moral superiority was unquestionably ours. Ours was

all that beauty
Born of a manly life and bitter duty.[1]

Yet as we rounded Marblehead Rock, it was hard to sustain enthusiasm for the great tradition. Not only was the wind failing, but it was ahead. Much experience to the contrary, it did not seem possible that we should beat our way over to the South Shore. When we had made enough offing, we put the ship over onto the port tack and started a long board towards Nahant. At this point Uncle Charlie turned her over to the crew and went below to sleep. He threw himself flat on his back on the sail-bags and at once began snoring, mouth open. He had the gift, shared we are told with other great men, of relaxing swiftly and completely when his responsibilities were at an end. He was, by the way, far ahead of the other great men of his time in his inability to refrain from going to sleep in the midst of public speeches. But even in sleep he retained his preternatural sensitivity. He would feel the ship check her way, wake up and call to the cockpit: "She's all in the wind, George." Or, "You can bring her up a hair." In the same way he could sail her by the way she felt, even in black darkness and light airs.

By suppertime our prospects were usually cheerless enough. The onshore, day breeze had died. The ship slouched over the seas, sails slatting in the gear, blocks banging, somewhere between Nahant and the Graves. The sun was sinking in smoke over Boston, and the sea resuming its eternal cold, eloquent of shipwreck in the North Atlantic. Having slept his fill, Uncle Charlie would stick his head out of the cabin, make a tour of the horizon, sniff, and announce by way of encouragement, "Fair wind on t'other tack, bye-'n-bye."

Then we piped—if that is the word—to supper. This usually consisted of club sandwiches, sardines, and invariably of bananas, the brown parts of which Uncle Charlie would cast overboard, saying: "Why make a sewer of your stomach?" He ate with slightly exaggerated champings of his jaw and lips. Except sometimes for a thermos-full of soup or cocoa, never, I think, anything as stimulating as coffee, it was a cold supper, and the only other liquor aboard was a bottle of Poland Springs Water, referred to by my cousin Tom as *Eau de Pologne*.

Uncle Charlie never touched alcohol. He once asked me how many members of my class at Harvard had been ruined by drink while still in college. As members of the Prohibition generation, many of us drank hard, but "No," I said, "none of us has been ruined by the stuff." He implied that several of his class had been. His was the era at Harvard of the Gold Coast and the California millionaires. "Billy" Hearst, he said, always kept outside his door a bucket of whiskey, together with a tin dipper, to which anyone was free to help himself if so disposed. Uncle Charlie did not try to stop people's drinking, nor failed in good fellowship while others drank, but no member of his crew would have considered bringing a bottle aboard: it would have been too uncomfortable.

If Uncle Charlie ever became conversational it was at supper. He would ask us what we were doing, especially, as a former treasurer of Harvard, what we were doing in the years we were attending the College. He liked to talk about the prospects of the football team and the crew. He even asked who the great professors were, once saying wistfully that it must be a great satisfaction to spend one's life doing something on? was really interested in. Would he have liked to spend his life boat-racing? He had served on the Harvard Corporation under two presidents; both were able—though Lawrence Lowell in his youth had been conceited—but Eliot was one of the greatest men he had known. In what ways Eliot was great he did not undertake to explain.

Uncle Charlie, though a rationalist, was in no sense an intellectual. He had had two famous intellectual uncles, one of whom, Brooks, he certainly regarded as a crank, and two members of his crew were intellectuals in grain. These experiences had not led him to share the vulgar anti-intellectualism of the common businessman. His was rather the healthy attitude of the nineteenth century, which did not regard intellectuals as a different breed of men. His view may have resembled that of his father, John Quincy Adams II. When my mother as a little girl asked him why her uncles, Henry and Brooks, spent their time writing, he answered simply—and accurately—"I suppose it amuses them." It was perfectly legitimate to amuse one's self.

So Uncle Charlie did not talk about books or ideas. Indeed he was not a reader, though he liked to have his wife, my aunt Fanny, read *to* him of an evening as he fell asleep. They seldom, I think, read novels, certainly not the novels of my literary enthusiasms. I once urged him to read *Moby Dick* but I am afraid he never even started it. I doubt that he was much interested in the drama of human personality, which did not mean in the least that he ever failed in his devotion to his friends. He would talk about the abilities of his contemporaries and their qualities of judgment, but not about their souls. In following this rule, he began with himself, he did not talk about himself; gentlemen did not do so. Human beings were, no doubt, capable of anything. Why they should be so was their business, not his. One could only try to deal with them, and then only when it was absolutely necessary, and all one might use was honesty, courtesy, some good fellowship, and a great deal of silence. What intrigued him were not the human passions but the spectacular problems of coping with the physical environment. Politics had too much of the irrational about it, but he enjoyed reading, for instance, about arctic exploration and naval warfare. He became an expert on the Battle of Jutland, and when he was secretary of the Navy he liked to discuss the proper use of aircraft carriers in a potential war against Japan. On subjects like these he was exceedingly interesting and exceedingly acute. Not until his imagination was captured did his mind go to work.

His taste in the arts was that of the American people as a whole. He did not look like their epitome but he was just that. He enjoyed musical comedies and almost any movie. When we stayed at the Eastern Yacht Club for Race Week, we would row across the harbor in the evening and walk to the local movie house to see anything that was showing. To only one of the finer arts did he respond: he liked to look at paintings, though he seldom in fact did so, and he had developed firm and unconventional tastes—unconventional at least for the 1930s. While his crew submitted their orthodox, avant-garde enthusiasms for Rembrandt or El Greco, he maintained the position that Franz Hals was the greatest of painters. Franz Hals *is* a great painter, and Uncle Charlie was not being vulgar.

During his service as secretary of the Navy under President Hoover, Uncle Charlie was often indiscreet with us, or perhaps he worried less about security than people do today. He once discussed the problem of bribing Japanese admirals, and told how he had detected a British ambassador lying twice in one morning. His statements were astonishingly matter-of-fact; it was not in moral outrage that he mentioned the ambassador but, if anything, in recognition of human foolishness. He was in fact opposed to the taking of moral stands that could not be made good by force. Accordingly he deplored the refusal of his colleague, Secretary of State Stimson, to recognize the Japanese conquest of Manchuria, as well as Stimson's refusal to use information gained through cryptography that had broken foreign codes. But this same high respect for physical realities and his lack of imagination about human passions led Uncle Charlie, at the outbreak of World War II, to believe that Britain was finished, and that the United States should stay out of the war in Europe. Pearl Harbor ended all that. The Japanese war was the one he had been preparing for, with all too little in the way of funds, while he was secretary of the Navy. So while we were slatting around off the Graves we were never, in those days, very far away from great affairs and the Adams tradition of statesmanship. But what we dramatized I am sure Uncle Charlie did not. Self-dramatization was the last thing he was given to—except perhaps in making his entrance to the Eastern Yacht Club. He never saw himself, or wished to see himself, as a statesman.

He disliked the New Deal in almost all its forms. Indeed he failed to understand what it was *about*. In the middle of the Depression he once remarked that he had driven a good deal around the Commonwealth of Massachusetts and that the workingmen appeared to him to be reasonably well clothed and housed. Yet he never expressed the fear and hatred of Franklin Roosevelt so current among businessmen of his class, never talked about "that man in the White House" or told any of the scabrous jokes—but then he never told jokes at all. Anyhow, Franklin Roosevelt was a Harvard man. Nor did he mouth the catchwords of "free enterprise." I doubt if he was aware of economic doctrine, whether Adam Smith's or Maynard Keynes's, which did not mean in the least that he was incapable of wisely investing his own and other people's money; he certainly was not caught in the stock market crash. No doubt he believed that the country would get out of the Depression more quickly by saving than by spending, but he stated his views as a matter of good judgment, not good doctrine. No doubt Franklin Roosevelt was a demagogue; no doubt he was taking advantage of the Depression to get votes—but then it was the nature of politicians to try to get votes. No doubt he was bad for the country, but the country was, at bottom, wise and would with experience get over the New Deal. Above all, Uncle Charlie never expressed that most vulgar of sentiments, the complaint that he was being personally hurt by the New Deal or increased taxes. If he was a conservative, he was an aristocratic conservative, though no one was less likely than he to think of himself as an aristocrat. On the other hand, he rarely expressed criticism of businessmen, and certainly not of businessmen as a class. He could never have said, as my father did, "In bad times the country is ruined by the politicians; in good times by the bankers."

Naturally Uncle Charlie spoke about seafaring. He had a long story that ended with the wise and rhythmic line: "If you ever gets ashore, and I guess you never will, don't you never cuss no more about the weather." And he described sailing out from The Glades in his youth to a Boston bark that had dragged anchors during a northeaster and slid up onto the West Shag ledges. The skipper was somewhat discouraged, not only by his immediate situation but by the circumstance that his wife had died off the west coast of Africa and was now below, pickled in a barrel like Lord Nelson. You can see that Uncle Charlie's view of seafaring was less than romantic. He was not given to scorn, but if anything could rouse his scorn it was hearing that someone "loved the sea." No one but a damned fool could love the sea. He had once signed on with a friend of his to take a schooner down south in winter. They were dismasted in a gale and spent two days expecting the ship to go to the bottom at any moment. In itself, the sea was cold, fearful, and treacherous.

Though he had a sense of humor and could reach a kind of quiet gaiety, Uncle Charlie's conversation was never consciously funny. Its quality was quite different. Whatever our actual ages, he always took for granted that we were his equals, indeed that we were just like him, sharing his sense of what constituted good judgment. This was flattering and good for us, but sometimes hard to live up to, as two of the crew were in fact emotional romantics, closer to Shelley than to Uncle Charlie. Finally, since he was human, he could be fatuous, as in his great statement about a Boston businessman: "He'll go far if he don't bust." But fatuous was the last thing Uncle Charlie usually was.

If supper did much to relieve our cheerlessness, the wind did more. Though we never believed in it ahead of time, we usually did get a fair wind on t'other tack. The night breeze, the offshore breeze began to make, breathing of all the heavy, hot summer of North America. It blew high in the air and did not show on the surface of the water at all, which remained unbroken. As if at some secret pressure the sails fell asleep, and we gathered way with a hiss like softly parting silk. We came about and began to move up under the South Shore, the lights and music of Paragon Park at Nantasket Beach coming off to us with an incongruous suggestion of human frivolity.

Sometimes we had to anchor or lie to at the entrance of the Cohasset channels, waiting for the flood tide to give us enough depth of water over the shoals. More often we picked up the ledges, lying black in the moon-glade, and went right in. We shot up to our mooring-buoy—Uncle Charlie was an effective though not an elegant buoy-shooter—getting our sails down as we did so, for our racing yachts did not lie to a mooring well with sails hoisted. A quick furl, and we were in the dinghy, rowing in to The Glades, phosphorescence dripping from our oars. If we were early enough, some of the natives were still sitting after dinner on the back piazza, swatting mosquitoes and arguing whether they could see Thatcher's Island lights, as they had done, by way of passing an amusing evening, for fifty summers gone.

NOTES

1. John Masefield, "Ships" in "Miscellaneous Poems" in *Poems* (New York: Macmillan, 1925), vol. 1, pp. 105-108.

13

DINING WITH Ba

Was it Talleyrand who said that if one had not known the old regime, one had never known how sweet life could be? For myself I may say that if I had not known Ba, I should hardly have known that sweetness either. But *sweet* was not the word for Ba, and I never loved him as I did Hans Zinsser, but he had sweetness in him, and was a man to be both enormously respected and enjoyed. My sisters and I learned to call him Ba when we were children and kept on doing so after we grew up. He was in fact Robert Shaw Barlow, my father's partner in the Boston law firm of Hill, Barlow, and Homans. I have already mentioned him several times, especially in connection with my failure to be elected to the Porcellian Club at Harvard.

Ba was the eldest son of Francis Channing Barlow (1834-1896), who rose from serving as a volunteer in a New York regiment to holding the rank of major-general in the Civil War. His intelligence and fighting qualities led to his rocketing to the top. He was the "boy general," not only because he was so young but because he looked younger than he really was. He is supposed to be represented, in a celebrated painting by Winslow Homer, as the Union officer grasping a big sabre and interrogating a tall Confederate prisoner with long flaxen hair. (He carried the sabre, not to slaughter the enemy but to beat his own stragglers on their butts with the flat of it.) Twice he had been left for dead on the field of battle, once at Antietam and again at Gettysburg. Ba used to tell the story that at Antietam a medical corpsman found his father stretched out on the ground and asked him, "What can I do for you, my poor little drummer-boy?" Whereupon Barlow managed to snarl, "Drummer-boy! Jesus Christ! I'm a major-general!" (I think in fact he was a brigadier at the time.) At Gettysburg, where he held the right flank of the Union line on the first day as long as he could—and that was long enough—he was found and rescued by no less a person than General Gordon of Georgia, leading the advancing Confederate troops. There is a monument to General Barlow at Gettysburg.

At the end of the war, General Barlow returned to New York, where, in his words, he "practiced law in the morning, golf in the afternoon, and adultery at night." There Ba himself was born. He is supposed to have looked much like his father, with the same dead-white skin and the same jowls drooping from thin cheeks. And had he not lived in a time of peace, Ba himself would have made a good officer: imperturbable, bold within the limits of what was possible, realistic in his appraisal of what men were capable of, but ready to hold them up to at least that standard.

Ba attended Harvard College, graduating in the class of 1891. There he became the inseparable companion of Francis ("Swelly") Bangs. In later years Ba lunched with Swelly and his wife, "the Czarina," every Sunday of his life when he was in Boston. As a member of the Porcellian Club, he also became a friend of my father, who graduated in 1894.

Already a connoisseur of the various forms of fleshpot, Ba was also something of an intellectual, without working hard enough to turn himself into a scholar. He introduced himself to George Santayana, then a young instructor in philosophy. In his autobiography, *Persons and Places*, Santayana records long sessions of drink and talk with Bangs and Barlow in the house of the Zeta Psi fraternity, now the Spee Club, my own. He says of Ba: "Bob was a satirical lover of the frail sex and frequented all levels of female society, approaching the dear creatures with a cold eye but with gallant inclinations. He allowed himself no exclusive passions, and remained a bachelor all his life. . . . Boldness pleased him in thought and war, no less than in love; any man of character had his respect who dared speak the truth and shame the hypocrites. With this taste, sharpened and fed by legal practice, for he became a lawyer, went a certain gentleness of aspect and manner, equable, lazy, and a bit sleepy."[1]

I do not remember a time when I was not aware of Ba. Though always kind to children, he did not pay much attention to them until, as he said, they were old enough to be interesting to talk to. So he sent me a present every Christmas but paid little other heed to me until I reached my teens. But I saw a good deal of him: indeed he was highly visible. He would show up to dine and spend the night at our summer place, incongruously dressed—but as he always dressed—in a grey homburg and a formal dark suit, wearing a stiff, stand-up collar, of a type old-fashioned even then, its points apparently supporting his pasty jowls, indeed, as it seemed to me, painfully impaling them. My mother used to say that Ba would visit us only when she had engaged a new cook whom Ba suspected might be skilled at preparing one of his favorite dishes. Though my mother and he were devoted to one another, they both recognized her indifference to anything distinguished in the way of cuisine. With these tastes, she failed to keep her cooks up to Ba's standard, so he did not dine with us often. Once per cook was usually enough.

I used also to see Ba at the offices of Hill, Barlow, and Homans at 53 State Street. His office was filthy, even by comparison with those of the other partners. There he labored in a stagnant cloud of pipe smoke, in semidarkness, the shades drawn, surrounded by piles of papers everywhere on desk and floor and apparently never touched. Later I heard that only the hardiest of secretaries would work for him. His method of summoning one was to shout down the corridor, "Send me one——!" using one of the even now less printable four-letter words.

As a lawyer, Ba took little interest in such matters as the Sacco-Vanzetti case, which preoccupied other members of the firm. I doubt, indeed, that he took a scholar's interest in the law or was ambitious for advancement in the profession either by appointment to the bench or by achieving recognition as a leader of the bar. But that did not prevent his being a first-class lawyer. In the firm he was the specialist in personal and domestic problems of all kinds, such as divorce. He claimed that he was the best will-drafter in Boston, and I have no doubt that he was. Within the scope of his interests, he had a powerful mind, clear and spare in its statements, with no nonsense about it at all.

I did not come to know Ba well until I entered Harvard College. Then he became mildly interested in what I was writing for the *Advocate* and the *Harvard Graduate's Magazine*. More important was the problem of getting me into the Porcellian Club. I have reported his extraordinary claim that if I did not join the Pork, I should never meet an attractive woman. It was the only truly silly remark I ever heard him make—but we are all allowed to make at least one, just to keep us human. He atoned for it later by introducing me to my future wife. Ba had met her and her sister at the Bangses—"Swelly" was their great-uncle—and asked the two of them to dine with him, my friend George Haskins, and me. He made the girls toss a coin to determine which one would have which man as a date for the evening. My present wife won.

Though in theory I was a broken man, Ba did not hold it against me when I failed to "wait" for election to the Porcellian Club. Instead I saw him more and more often, until by the middle of the 1930s I was dining with him, when I was anywhere near Boston, about once a week. Our dinners were of two kinds. I might dine with him alone. He was ready to enjoy plain food, but even his plain food was apt to be a little out of the ordinary. So he might take me off to some Boston restaurant whose specialty he was fond of: to the Parker House for broiled tripe, to Jake Wirth's for pig's knuckles, to the Copley Plaza for oyster crabs. Then we might move on to something like the ballet, to which indeed he introduced me. Or I might dine with him at the Somerset Club, usually before the Saturday evening concert of the Boston Symphony Orchestra. We arrived at the symphony so full of champagne that we could not do full intellectual, though we did full emotional, justice to the music. For the moment I shall say no more about our dinners tête-à-tête and turn to his more characteristic mixed parties.

In my time, whatever may have happened when he was younger, Ba did not entertain, nor was he entertained in, company of his own generation, whether male only or mixed. He was a member of none of the small dining clubs for men, partly intellectual and partly social, that flourished so luxuriantly in Brahmin society. Nor, though a bachelor, was he in demand by hostesses as an "extra man." When Ba, for instance, visited my father and mother, he came alone. The strong could take Ba by himself and enjoy him, but he made uncomfortable the least common denominator on which a larger gathering must be built. He told us that in the old days, when placed at dinner next to some young woman he had just met, his opening gambit was always to turn to her with a leer and ask, "I suppose you think *you're* attractive?" He must have been bored by "society," and he in turn may have shocked it, the men as much as the women. The things they took seriously enough to talk about he may not have taken seriously himself, and those they took too seriously to talk about at all he may have been all too ready to discuss, and discuss with the veils off. As Santayana knew, he was prepared to "speak the truth and shame the hypocrites," prepared, perhaps, to emphasize just those truths which were most apt to make others look like hypocrites. They must have felt him to be so down to earth as to be at least rude and at most dangerous. In short, I doubt that he was welcome in polite society.

What Ba did enjoy in his later years was entertaining the younger generation. He really liked the young: they had not lost their electricity. Their elders were beyond saving: the young he might hope to bring up to share his interests. He wrote to Santayana after the publication of the latter's *The Last Puritan*,[2] and Santayana wrote back (Ba gave me a copy of the letter): "Your first letter especially, in which you describe your mode of life, surprised and interested me, because that is not the way in which I should have pictured you as living in your old age, but rather the way I should have chosen for myself, if I had stayed in Boston and been free to live there after my own fashion. A bachelor apartment is a pleasant position opening conveniently into a club, and relations kept up naturally with young people, who are agreeable anywhere, but in America, at least in my time, the only people with whom one could establish frank and unprejudiced communication. And now the younger generation seem to be better informed, and better spoken than the average of our own time."[3] I am not sure that my generation, when it was the younger generation, was really all that interesting, but it is pleasant to remember that Ba and Santayana thought so.

His *habitués* were apt to be sons and daughters of friends of his, their wives and husbands if they had them, their lovers if they had not, and other young men and women they in turn felt were in the Barlow style and introduced to the circle. Plenty of otherwise splendid persons were not in the style: a taste for Ba was a special taste, not easily acquired. Notable among the regulars were, besides the girl I was to marry, the two Boyden sisters, cousins of mine: Hallie Ohl and Anstiss Williams. I myself brought in my friend George Haskins from the Society of Fellows at Harvard. In the 1930s Ba must have entertained the young at dinner at least twice a week in little groups of six or so.

Ba had lived for years in an apartment consisting of one of the upper floors of 41 Beacon Street, looking over the Common from Beacon Hill and just above the Somerset Club, which owned the building and rented apartments only to members. Ba's apartment was spartanly furnished, except for the bathroom, which was fully equipped for soaking in a hot tub and reading at the same time. Some of the rooms were bare of everything except rows of gallon jugs full of martinis, which Ba mixed months in advance and allowed to age. At first it seemed surprising that a man who held such well-developed tastes in food, drink, tobacco, and women should be so little concerned with his material surroundings and even his comforts in the form of decor, furniture, and pictures, but he believed in concentrating on essentials, and most mere "things" were not essential. And though he was a great reader, he did not allow himself to accumulate a library of his own. He got much of his reading matter from the Boston Athenaeum, a private library further up Beacon Street.

The *convives* of the evening gathered in the living room, if that is the right word for it, for no one but Ba could have borne living in it for long. The walls were, as one of us pointed out, the color of excrement. The only picture I remember was Audubon's "Canada Goose" from the Elephant folio. Though Ba never took any exercise whatever in the years I knew him, never ever walked when he could find a taxi, and took no interest in any sport, he had been in his youth an avid duck hunter, and that may explain the goose. Nor do I remember any rug on the floor. Though there must have been one, the effect was as if there were not. Around the wall stood nondescript chairs.

Right in the middle of the room, like a pulpit facing the congregation, stood a smallish golden-oak desk, covered mostly with Ba's pipes. From behind it he dispensed his premixed martinis, never before dinner any other drink. They were of the old-fashioned sort, made three and not six to one with sweet and not dry vermouth, and shaken very hard, not by Ba but by one of the men present, until the silver shaker was covered with frost. Ba had heard of the purist doctrine that martinis should be stirred and not shaken, lest the gin be bruised, but was skeptical of it, as he was of most doctrines, especially purist ones. Perhaps because they had been left to set for so long, their flavor was unlike that of any other martinis I have tasted, but I found them delicious. Drink in hand, we settled down to an hour of talk and laughter.

Ba spoke rather deliberately, even hesitantly, because he had trouble with his dentures, which would give off clicks from time to time, and not because he was at a loss for a word. Excellent legal draftsman that he was, he could always say exactly what he meant. His sentences were far more coherent than ours. He never monopolized the conversation. Indeed his stated ideal for us was that of Rabelais's Abbey of Thelème: *fais ça que voudras*. But there were certain subjects we did not talk much about. If they came up, Ba would not so much change the subject as let it drop. Thus we seldom talked about sports. Though there were philosophers among us and though he himself had been interested in philosophy in his youth, we did not talk much about philosophy or other academic subjects. Ba always asserted that he was a social philosopher, and we certainly talked social philosophy according to Ba's definition of the subject. Indeed we talked about little else, but that was anything but philosophy in the technical sense.

And though these were the days of Jim Curley in Massachusetts, the New Deal in the nation, and fascism in the world, and though politics were much on the minds of some of us, we did not talk about politics as if we took them hard. Ba's view was: "So long as the politicians leave us liquor and tobacco—and they will have to—we shall do all right." He was not worried. He never was obsessed, as were at that time so many of the men he knew, with hating Franklin Roosevelt because he was about to rob them of their money. He quoted a remark made by a lisping member of the Coolidge family: "Someday the pwoletawiat is going to wise up and take away my pwopetty," but he quoted it only with amusement. We told lewd jokes about Eleanor Roosevelt only because in those days most such jokes were recast so as to bring her in.

With sport, money, politics, and of course religion left out, what remained for us to talk about? One guess would be enough. We talked about sex, not so much sex in the raw as the predicaments it creates in the relations between men and women, for homosexuality was not among our interests. If he was a social philosopher, what Ba taught was the social philosophy of sex.

Ba never married. He always claimed that the only woman he ever loved had married another, but he did not expect us to be convinced by his excuse. It was difficult to imagine Ba married: he valued his independence too highly. For him, one of the few generalizations that admitted of no exception was that all husbands were henpecked, and those of us who were married bore out its truth by agreeing with him so long as our wives were present. Ba did not hold our condition against us: since we should have known what we were getting into, our fate was no more than we deserved, and it might even do us good. But it was not for him. His nightmares took the form of dreaming he was married and waking up in screams.

Ba had much advice to offer on the conduct of relations between men and women, although another of his generalizations stated that no one took advice unless it coincided with what he was ready to do anyway, and then he did not need it. One of his favorite maxims was: "What he (or she) doesn't know won't hurt him (or her)." This was hardly new. The difference was that Ba took it, and others like it, very seriously, not just as things to say in order to show that one was properly cynical, but as the bases of planning; not just as rationalizations to be used after the fact, but as rationality itself. His philosophy was highly practical, fitted for men and women who proposed to do as much as they could of what they liked, while causing the least possible trouble for themselves or, it is fair to say, for others.

The fact that Ba never married did not mean, as Santayana recognized, that he was uninterested in women. He was interested in the whole range of women from courtesans to ladies. Indeed his interest had been supposed at one time to be uncontrollable. The story was that, in his youth at a dance in a private house, he had pursued a debutante upstairs with rape too obviously in mind. In the 1890s this was shocking behavior. In his dinners alone with me, but never in our general gatherings, he would tell me some of the details of his seductions, both of society women and of others encountered casually in such places as railway stations and restaurants, including members of the class he referred to as "female drummers." He never told me their names or let slip details by which I might have identified women I knew, and I am glad that I do not hold in my weak hands the honor of revered Boston grandmas. For the benefit of at least one otherwise happily married woman of society he had rented a room in the Hemenway Street area, where she would meet him for an hour a day between her other social engagements. Talking with Ba at these times was like talking with Casanova. To a naive person like myself, he gave quite a new idea of the underside of Victorian and Edwardian morality. More important, he gave me an idea of the power of something other than love in bringing men and women together, the power indeed of something other than sheer good looks, for Ba can never have been really handsome. Ba was not boasting, though he no doubt enjoyed having someone to go over these memories with. Nor was he lying. Neither about sex nor about anything else did he give the slightest impression that he was embroidering on the truth. Simple truth was what concerned him and what, he felt, most people would not admit. In dealing with facts he was rather plonking than otherwise. Nor did he ever moralize about what he or others did. The behavior he described was wholly natural and only what was to be expected, if only we would recognize it as such.

At the general gatherings the discussion of sex never became as personal as this. We had to show some pretence of gaiety and wit: mere grossness and the use of dirty words were out, but anything else went. We told some of the better limericks and invented new ones. George Haskins even produced limericks in Latin. We told stories. There is something wrong with me, and I cannot tell stories of any kind, but I do remember the ending of one of Ba's. At a certain point, Mandy says to her old husband, "Silas, I do believe you're boasting." But shortly afterwards she comes back with, "Hand me my dentures, Silas, I want to bite you!" Since we were Bostonians, we had to bring in our ancestors even in the matter of sex. We revered George Crowninshield, Jr., a collateral ancestor of several of us, who was supposed, quite incorrectly, to have enjoyed, aboard his yacht *Cleopatra's Barge*, the ultimate favors of Napoleon's beautiful sister, Pauline Bonaparte Borghese, the subject of Canova's famous reclining nude. We discussed with the lightness that befits serious topics, the theory that a man has only a certain number of shots in his locker, and that prolonged abstinence gives temporarily greater powers. Ba held that it did not, citing his own disappointment upon his return from a long hunting trip. Finally, we loved the moments when sex comes most crazily into literature. One of our favorite sports was reading aloud Swinburne's *Dolores*, with its lovely bogus rhetoric:

> As our kisses relax and redouble,
>   From the lips and the foam and the fangs
> Shall no new sin be born for men's trouble,
>   No dream of impossible pangs?

Some readers might conclude that he was just a dirty old man, or even that he was a corrupter of youth—but if this was corruption, I fear that we were corrupt before Ba got at us. And he was too intelligent not to have more to offer. His was rather the disabused frankness, which does not expect much of people—or, better, *does* expect things of them that they won't admit—and which we encounter in a Yankee fisherman from Cape Cod or the coast of Maine. With that sort of man he often said that he could talk more freely and honestly than he could with many proper Bostonians.

The same quality of the tough old Yankee, but at another level, attracted Ba to Justice Holmes. One may well imagine that Ba had few heroes, but Holmes was one of them, and a close friend too. It was not Holmes the legal thinker who attracted Ba—Ba cared little enough for that sort of thing—but Holmes the man; and Holmes, for his part, may have found in Ba an intellectual who shared his more earthy assumptions rather more fully than did, for instance, another friend of his such as Harold Laski. The two must have met while Holmes lived in Boston and became chief justice of Massachusetts; indeed Holmes moved Ba's admission to the bar, and they kept up their friendship after Holmes left Boston for the Supreme Court in Washington. Ba was never one of Holmes's regular correspondents, but he visited Holmes every summer when the latter came to spend his vacation at Beverly Farms. Indeed Holmes spoke of Ba's "prescriptive right"[4] to stay overnight as one he did not generally extend to others. The references to Ba in Holmes's letters suggest that the two did not spend much time on the law. Thus in 1907 Holmes wrote to Lewis Einstein: "Bob Barlow (son of the General) has just left here. I delight in his talk. He really studies literature with an unobstructed eye and seasons the results with most improving slang. . . . It is a great privilege to be allowed to associate with the (relatively) young on equal terms."[5] Again, Laski wrote to Holmes in 1917: "I agree with Bob Barlow who said that apart from theology and sex there is really nothing to talk about,"[6]—and Ba did not talk about theology. The friendship of Holmes and Ba did not require agreement for its maintenance. In literature they agreed on the greatness of Tolstoi but not on that of Balzac. Holmes thought that there was "too much of the boor and snob about Balzac with all his genius."[7] They disagreed even about Homer. Thus Holmes wrote to Einstein: "Barlow, who is a more accurate critic than I, insists that the great things keep their greatness and defy the effect of repetition of the motif; that Homer would give the same delight if the Iliad were written today. It does to him. To me it is a feeble joy. I prefer the modern and complex."[8] Ba often spoke of Holmes to us. I remember especially his telling us of the comment Emerson had written on a paper of Holmes's, when the former was a professor and the latter an undergraduate at Harvard. Holmes had undertaken to attack Plato, and Emerson's comment was: "When you strike at a king, you must kill him."

When we were with Ba, we discussed much the same kind of subjects that he did with Holmes. After sex, our next great topic was literature, especially French literature. Ba's vacations from the law took the form of his disappearing to Paris for at least a month in the spring. He did not do so in my time, but my father told me he had done so for many years before that. From what he talked about, we guessed what he did there: he took part in unspeakable orgies in gilded palaces of sin. No doubt we let our imaginations run too far, for he certainly also went to the best restaurants, concerts, and theaters. He had attended, for instance, and enormously enjoyed the first appearance in Paris of the Russian ballet under Diaghilev, and even kept his programs, which were themselves works of art. This was unusual for him, for he was not given to accumulating mere things.

Whether through his visits to Paris or still earlier experiences, he had become much interested in, and knowledgeable about, French literature, especially the novelists from Choderlos de Laclos to André Gide, but also some of the romantic poets; and we used to have readings from Musset's[9] *La Nuit de Mai* or *La Nuit d'Octobre*, with its great tirade:

> *Honte à toi qui la première*
> *M'as appris la trahison . . .*

He was also an admirer of the Russian novelists, to whom French literature had led him and whom he read in French: Turgenev, Tolstoi, and Dostoevsky. Given Ba's usually rather straightforward tastes, I was surprised by his interest in Dostoevsky, even in *The Idiot*. He had also read much of the literary criticism of the nineteenth century, such as that of Sainte-Beuve, and many of its memoirs, so that his talk about the novelists was mixed with the gossip, scandal, and personalities of the period, from Adah Mencken (of whom he had a picture) to Georges Sand and the Duc de Morny.

When I first came to know Ba well, much of what he said went over my head. I was familiar with English literature but not with French, and Ba sometimes sounded as if he were the reverse. With a very few exceptions, he seldom talked about writers in English. He was never one to praise a book just because it had a reputation. If he said he enjoyed one, you could be sure he really did. In spite of his admiration for most French novelists, he never said a word in favor of Proust. And the only modern novel in English I remember his praising was John O'Hara's *Butterfield 8*. But he was a great fan of Bernard Shaw's, went to all of his plays, and fondly exhibited a postcard the great man had sent him in response to a letter of his.

When Ba became aware of my ignorance of French literature, he naturally asked me if I could read French. I said I could not, and he went on: "But you must have studied French in school?" I had studied it for ten years. "Nonsense then," he said, "of course you can read French." He was quite right: I could. It was just that the blue-pencil marks my teachers made on my written translations had persuaded me that I could not. Ba's notion of a refresher course in French was to order me to try Casanova's memoirs: "You will soon find that you can read French, and you must not bother about looking up every word, though you must understand what is meant by *l'heure du berger avait sonnée*." It means that the girl is about to fold.

I tried Ba's prescription and found it worked. Under his guidance I then went through a long course of reading in the French novelists, beginning with Balzac's *Le Père Goriot* and his other stories of young men on the make, then going on to Stendahl, *Le Rouge et le noir* but not *La Chartreuse de Parme*, which was not to Ba's taste, to Flaubert, *Madame Bovary* but not *L'Education sentimentale*, which I later came to enjoy more, then to a great deal of Maupassant and Zola, especially *Nana*, and some of the books that are not classed among the great ones, such as *Le Nabab* by Dumas *fils*. We ended with Gide's *L'Immoraliste*. By that time I had long been able to go on by myself. Like Charlie Curtis and Mrs. Frederick Winslow, Ba urged me to learn Greek. "Greek literature isn't like the literature in other languages," he insisted. "In most languages the best poetry is the most difficult, but the best Greek poetry is the easiest to read." He meant Homer. I am not sure that Ba was right in thinking it the easiest, but I learned enough Greek to read Homer, and I now have Ba's copy of the *Iliad*, which Holmes had given him, as I have Charlie's copy of Catullus.

Thus Ba contributed greatly to my education as he did to that of others. Not that this was the purpose he set for himself. He wanted to contribute to our pleasure, not our education, and he never urged us to read a book he did not think we would enjoy. His own taste, though sound, was obviously not very distinctive, except perhaps his rejection of Proust. Perhaps the thinly disguised homosexual passion was not much to his interest, and the drama of snobbery, the other theme at the heart of *A la recherche du temps perdu*, certainly was not. Nor when he talked about books was his conversation self-consciously "literary," though I remember his discussing the originality Balzac had shown in his description of the *pension* in *Le Père Goriot*. He was more apt to tell anecdotes about the authors and the men and women in real life that their characters were supposed to represent. Nor did he think the worse of any of his young friends if they were wholly uninterested in literature. All he asked of them was something he called "electricity." But when the company at the cocktail hour was of the right sort, we talked a good deal about classical literature in an appreciative but gossipy way.

It was now time to go down to dinner. Along the wall beside the long straight stairs of 41 Beacon Street ran an *ascenseur* of a type I have never met elsewhere. It ran in a groove along the wall—how it stayed on the wall was never clear—and it had two flaps that could be folded down to make seats for passengers. There was a great deal of giggling over which girl should be allowed to ride with Ba on this machine, the theory being that the two seats facing one another allowed, and even required, the passengers to rub knees.

We then took a few steps down Beacon Street to the Ladies Dining Room on the ground floor of the Somerset Club. This consisted of a couple of rooms decorated with white and gold woodwork vaguely suggestive of the eighteenth century and furnished with red plush *banquettes* along the walls in the manner of a Parisian restaurant, all protected by an outer stone wall from the gaze of passers-by on the street. Here we always sat at the same corner table. I am afraid that by this time we were apt to be a bit noisy, but if the other diners suffered, they seldom complained.

We usually started dinner with oysters, even if they were not in season. Ba believed in dousing them with both horseradish and tabasco, and he taught us to make Barlow sandwiches: two oyster crackers with a layer of butter and a dash of tabasco in between. For the main course we were not allowed to choose for ourselves from the regular menu. The Somerset Club was served by a great chef, François Lombard, and Ba took full advantage of him. For all his guests he ordered in advance some dish of which he was fond and which he had reason to believe they would enjoy too. He was no snob about food and did not insist that we confine ourselves to the classical French cuisine. His choice ranged from Porter House steak and *filet mignon sauce béarnaise* to slightly more exotic dishes such as capon *en casserole*, sweetbreads *sous cloche*, shad roe, and even venison steak with wild rice and chestnut dressing. His taste in food was peculiar only in his conviction that no one could be seriously interested in vegetables, except perhaps fried eggplant or really fresh asparagus, and accordingly we got no vegetables or salad unless they happened to be an essential accompaniment of the main course. For drink we usually had champagne, especially the "flat" champagne that Ba favored—champagne from which most, but not quite all, of the bubbles had gone. The conversation, though still lively, was now less likely to be devoted to sex, as a courtesy to the other diners who were apt to be rather more proper Bostonians than we were. Instead, we turned naturally to the subject of food and the great personalities associated with it, such as, in the United States, "bad" Sam Ward. (There was also a "good" Sam Ward.)

Ba allowed us to choose our own desserts, but again he was apt to steer us away from ice cream or fruit and towards a cheese savory or a Beacon omelet, a type of small omelet *flambée* which was a specialty of the Somerset Club. Then coffee and back to No. 41, with more giggling about the *ascenseur*.

Here we topped off with brandy or, more often, *marc de Bourgogne,* which had, as Ba was not original in stating, the aroma of new-mown hay. At this point we were beginning to be talked out or slowed down by a plethora of good food and drink. In any event, the evening now took a different turn. Ba was a lifelong lover of music. He was one of the generation to which Wagner had come as a miracle of beauty. I believe he had even made the pilgrimage to Bayreuth. But he was far from being limited to Wagner. I have spoken of our going to the symphony concerts together, and he took me, as a matter of musical piety, to hear Paderewski play on his last visit to Boston. Snifters of *marc* in hand, we adjourned for music into Ba's bedroom. This was as stark as the other rooms in the flat, furnished with a couple of straight-backed chairs and a plain iron bedstead, luxurious in neither springs nor mattress. Again, I remember only one picture, never identified but Dutch-looking, of a cottage beside a dark and romantic pool. Here we listened to some of Ba's records played on his already out-of-date Victrola, often one of Mozart's concertos, of which Ba was very fond, or Beethoven's "Emperor" concerto as rendered by Yehudi Menuhin.

We did not confine our music to passive listening. Ba had both the records and the librettos of several operas. We would choose some section of an opera and divide the parts among ourselves. One girl and one boy — and there was much controversy over which ones—would lie on the bed propped up with pillows, while the others would group themselves around on the hard little chairs, and we would sing from the libretto guided by the music of the opera from the Victrola. Our favorites for this purpose were *Don Giovanni, La Bohème,* and *Traviata,* but we sometimes tried to sing the "Spring Song" from *The Valkyrie.* Anyone listening to us would have been appalled by our singing, since few of us had good voices—though we had plenty of volume—and some of us hardly had an ear, but we managed to enchant ourselves. Indeed we felt that there could be no more romantic way of ending an evening. Eventually we got ourselves home as best we might.

Robert Frost, himself a tough old Yankee like Ba, used to say that in order to enjoy life, one had to be a bit coarse. Dining with Ba we were just exactly a bit coarse. The emphasis fell unashamedly on the simple sensuous pleasures, with no tincture of the sentimental guff and guilt that are the curses of modern conversation. And we had our due reward. How we enjoyed ourselves! And we owed it all to Ba.

NOTES

1. George Santayana, *Persons and Places,* 3 vols. in one, *The Middle Span* (New York: Scribner's, 1963), 2:98-99.
2. George Santayana, *The Last Puritan* (New York: Scribner's, 1936).

3. I do not know the whereabouts of the original of this letter or even whether it still exists.

4. *Holmes-Laski Letters: The Correspondence of Mr. Justice Holmes and Harold J. Laski, 1916-1935,* ed. Mark DeWolfe Howe, 2 vols. (Cambridge: Harvard University Press, 1953), 2:1166.

5. *The Holmes-Einstein Letters,* ed. James Bishop Peabody (New York: St. Martin's Press, 1964), pp. 30-31.

6. *Holmes-Laski Letters* 1:92.

7. Ibid. 2:879.

8. *Holmes-Einstein Letters,* p. 25.

9. Alfred de Musset (1810-1857).

14

THE NAVY I: *HAZEL, ACCENTOR,* AND *YMS 59*

At Harvard College I had belonged to the Naval Reserve Officers Corps and graduated with an ensign's commission in the Naval Reserve. I had inherited a seafaring tradition; I had seafaring experience, though under sail; my uncle Charlie had been secretary of the Navy (1928-32) during my college years. More important, perhaps, the program in "Naval Science" consisted of one course a term, one-fourth of the courses a student was required to take, together with pleasant summer cruises; and none of the courses, except for navigation, was demanding, which allowed me extra time for my literary pursuits. After being commissioned, one could get promotion, though slowly in the peacetime reserve, by attending weekly drills. I attended none, so that by the time the entry of our country into World War II loomed ahead, I was still an ensign, and still subject to recall to active duty whenever the president chose to declare a state of national emergency. I had volunteered for active duty at the time of the fall of France. Not until a year later, in May 1941, was I actually called, presumably because the Navy had not yet built enough new ships to need reserve officers. My orders to report to the Navy Yard, Boston, for a refresher course reached me at New Castle, Pennsylvania, where I was interviewing unemployed steelworkers. I rushed home at once. The New Castle research was never finished and never published. My unemployed were reabsorbed by new war industries.

When back in Boston, I paid a courtesy call on Professor Ferguson, then dean of the Faculty of Arts and Sciences, to report that I must resign from Harvard. He was kindly, but at the end of our interview said something like this: "Mr. Homans, it is my duty to inform you that there is no tenure vacancy in the Sociology Department until [as I remember it] 1950." In 1941, 1950 seemed an eternity in the future. By the way the war was then going, I judged I was unlikely to survive it, so Ferguson's words did not touch me deeply. But I did understand that, if by chance I should survive, I was unlikely to come back to a job at Harvard.

While still being given refresher training, the Navy allowed me a forty-eight-hour leave to get married to Nancy Parshall Cooper. We are still married.

After finishing our course at the Boston Yard, the Navy assigned all of us refreshed reservists to ships under construction, so that we should be familiar with them when they were ready for sea. The Navy had many ships built on the Great Lakes, provided of course that their draft was not too great to let them escape to salt water, by way either of the Chicago Drainage Canal, which led to the Mississippi, or the Lachine Canal, which led to Montreal and tidewater on the St. Lawrence. I was assigned as prospective executive officer (second in command) of U.S.S. *Hazel*, a net-tender then being built at a yard in Lorain, Ohio, which was experienced in building the huge ore carriers that carried iron ore from Duluth to the steel mills further down the Lakes.

Can there be a type of naval vessel whose duty is duller than a net-tender's? She is designed to put in place across the entrance to major ports the heavy steel nets that prevent submarines from entering the ports underwater, and to open and close these "gates" for friendly vessels. To handle such great weights, the chief physical features of a net-tender are a powerful windlass and two "horns" at the bow, joined by a big sheave, to carry the chain holding the net. Net-tending is a safe but sedentary occupation, and I am glad that, as we shall see, I never had to take part in it.

Hazel rated three officers, all of us reservists. The engineering officer, Lawraston Riggs, was a mining engineer in civil life and a fine man, systematic but tactful, sometimes under heavy stress, in pointing out my mistakes. But the skipper, who had been a stockbroker, had a problem: he was very jittery. Quite honestly he confessed to me before we set sail, bound down through the Great Lakes and St. Lawrence River, to be fitted out at Portsmouth, New Hampshire: "George, I want you to know that, though it is against Naval Regulations, I have a case of whiskey in my cabin. I can't face this voyage without it." I never detected him under the influence, nor did he offer me any of his liquor. More important, he did not trust his junior officers enough to allow them to practice ship-handling. This is a great mistake, because a skipper may be relieved at any time, and then he must certify that one of his junior officers is in all respects prepared to assume command.

At first Nancy and I stayed at the Elks Hotel at Lorain, until we kept being woken up by couples let in for half-hour stands—though *lays* would have been a better word—in the neighboring rooms. Then we took a room in the house of a Syrian couple, who took good care of us, though we slept on sheets made out of old flour sacks stitched together and breakfasted on unleavened bread.

The voyage from Lorain—officially from Cleveland where we were commissioned—around to Portsmouth was the pleasantest I ever took in the Navy. It was early autumn. It was interesting going through the locks of the great Welland Canal, and later through the little Lachine that took us to Montréal. There was no St. Lawrence Seaway then, and we had to pass through the Lachine so slowly that Riggs could keep up with us with his bicycle on the towpath. We were not yet at war, so that we did not have to take elaborate precautions even after we reached salt water.

From my point of view the only serious drawback was that my wife and the captain's mistress (he married her later) followed us in the latter's car and seemed to be able to find us every night when we were in port, even when I tried to keep from them all knowledge of our movements. This was very bad for the ship's morale, for the crew did not enjoy similar privileges. They certainly had wives, but apparently no cars.

At Montréal, where tidewater begins, we took on our river pilot. We did not need one, since the river is so deep and *Hazel* was so small that the piloting could, and effectively was, left to us. Yet all ships were required to take pilots. Ours turned out to be French-Canadian and genially anti-English. He spent his time in the pilothouse telling scabrous stories about the British royal family. The French-Canadians were strongly opposed to Canadian participation in the war. I myself was hissed in the streets of Québec city, I suppose because my American naval uniform was mistaken for the similar British one. Ours was, I think, the first American warship to come down the river.

The pilot left the pilothouse from time to time for a spot abaft the funnel, where he had himself a swig of brandy and returned with stories still more scabrous. Since this irregular behavior made no difference to us, we took no action about it. When we berthed at Tadoussac at the mouth of the Saguenay, he claimed that he had an aunt who lived there and would spend the night ashore with her. She too seemed to have been well supplied with liquor. At Father's Point, where outbound ships drop their river pilots, we dropped ours into the tender in a cargo net.

The pilot had added to the joy of life. Besides, the voyage down the St. Lawrence had been beautiful, the steep north shore a wall of red autumn leaves.

In the rest of the voyage we met with two bits of bad weather. We spent most of one night at anchor in the Northumberland Strait under the lee of Prince Edward's Island. Then we passed through the Gut of Canso between Cape Breton Island and the mainland of Nova Scotia. And just off the southern cape of Nova Scotia a strong but luckily brief gale struck us. *Hazel* rolled so heavily that her sea suctions came out of water. The sea suctions are the openings in the hull that allow cooling sea water to reach the engines. Without cooling water, the engines tend to overheat and must be slowed down, leading to loss of control of the ship. Had the gale been stronger or longer we might have been in serious trouble. But the next day was calm and we berthed safely at the submarine base at Portsmouth.

After leaving Cleveland I became more and more certain that I had sprung a hernia. I acquired it through no heroic efforts on behalf of the Navy but through fits of sneezing brought on by hay fever in Ohio. It became more and more uncomfortable to stand watches, and I spent more and more time in my bunk when off duty. The naval medical officer at Portsmouth confirmed me in my diagnosis and got me a medical discharge from *Hazel* and sent me to the Naval Hospital at Chelsea, Massachusetts, to get my hernia repaired. This was rather an agreeable interlude than otherwise. Near me in the hospital was a supply officer who suffered from a nervous breakdown brought on by the pressures of preparing for war. The physicians treated him with a combination of gin and hot baths, both in unlimited quantities. He used the gin to give daily parties for his friends among the other patients, including me.

I was home convalescing or rather at a party given by my friend David Crockett at Ipswich on Pearl Harbor day, December 7, 1941, and home also for Christmas. Soon after, when declared fit for duty, I was not sent back to *Hazel*, nor, thank God, to net-tending of any kind.

Such was my first tour of active duty in the Navy. The second was very different, if only because the United States was now at war. I was ordered aboard U.S.S. *Accentor*, a ninety-seven-foot wooden minesweeper, as executive officer. (In case you do not know it, an accentor is a bird, just as hazel is a nut, not a girl.) She was under the command of Gordon Abbott, a son of friends of my family's and one of the best commanding officers I ever served under. He continued in the minesweeping service and, I believe, commanded the ships that swept Tokyo Bay in preparation for the entrance of the Pacific Fleet and the surrender of Japan.

Accentor was equipped for sweeping the moored mines that had been standard in World War I and exploded by contact with a ship's hull but not, I think, for the more sophisticated magnetic and acoustic mines with which the Germans were then plaguing the British. When I came on board, *Accentor* was employed sweeping the main ship channel out of Boston towards the lightship, my old sailing ground. That continued for only one more day. Before I could become familiar with ship or crew, the skipper was granted leave, which made me for the first time a commanding officer, and at the same time *Accentor* was ordered to Portland, Maine. Casco Bay had temporarily become an anchorage of the Atlantic Fleet. *Accentor* and her like were now to sweep the channel into Portland.

Getting *Accentor* into Portland was child's play for an old coast-of-Maine cruiser like me. But how about bringing her alongside the wharf at

Portland? Though I could have done the job under sail, I had no experience of handling vessels under power. Skipper Abbott had had no time to teach me. I knew the theory from studying the standard textbooks. But the practice? Moreover one has less control over a single-screw vessel like *Accentor* than of twin-screw ones, which my later ships were, for at slow speeds the single propeller has a tendency to make the stern of the ship crawl sidewise. I thought of turning the job over to the new executive officer, who I was told was experienced in fishing trawlers. I rejected the thought on the grounds that such action would reveal the skipper's lack of either skill or courage and thus undermine morale. I was quite mistaken. Later I saw regular-Navy officers delegate shiphandling jobs they could not cope with themselves to their juniors who could, and do so without appearing to lose face. Never hesitate to admit one's incompetence not only in knowledge but in action! At any rate, I brought *Accentor* alongside the wharf in Portland under my own orders. Either I brought her in too fast or did not back her down soon enough and cracked a couple of strakes in the bulwarks near the bow. But we made it, and this was a small price to pay. Though the Navy never held it against me, I can remember the look of horror that passed over my executive officer's face. Yet he wisely said nothing. And for once I learned from experience. Never again did I have serious difficulties with ship-handling. Indeed it became one of my few real strengths as a naval officer. And on later ships, when I myself had inexperienced executive officers, I took pains to teach them and allow them to practice the tricks of the trade.

Casco Bay has several minor entrances besides the channel to Portland. From time to time one or another of the sweepers was ordered to patrol one of these entrances at night, lest enemy submarines should penetrate them. Unfortunately there was little a sweeper of the *Accentor* class could do to stop an enemy. If the submarine tried to come in under water, we had no underwater sound gear (sonar) with which to detect her. If she tried the surface, we had no radar: it was only just beginning to be installed on the larger ships. We should have to do what we could with night-glasses, and they were of no use in a Maine fog. Moreover, if we did contact a submarine, she was better able to sink us than we, her. We could raise the alarm, but the loudest alarm would be our own explosion. Patrolling an entrance meant of course moving at random up and down and across it. With the problem of outlying reefs it was a hard job of piloting. I discovered from my fellow skippers of minesweepers that they did not patrol an entrance at night but anchored in the fairway and set a sharp watch. I followed their example.

This was my first encounter with a common pattern among the small ships in the early days of the war. They were asked to carry out duties they were not then equipped for. This certainly undermined the morale of their officers and men. At its worst it led to disobedience to orders: to anchor in a channel is not to patrol it. But giving such orders may have improved the morale of our superior officers. The orders covered, as we say, their arses. If anything did go wrong—and it seldom did—they could point out that they had used to the best advantage all the ships they had under their command.

It was the end of December and cold in Casco Bay. Ice froze on our gear. I suffered from an obscure disease that was particularly inappropriate for seamen: earlier I had become allergic to cold, salt spray; and in Casco Bay all the exposed parts of my body and many not exposed broke out into itchy, oozing, red welts. Though I applied liberal amounts of a certain grease, the welts spread. I was beginning to think of reporting myself to our medical officer as unfit for duty, when I was saved. Captain Abbott returned from leave, and I received orders to report to the Naval Mine Warfare School at Yorktown, Virginia, and subsequently to take command of one of a new class of wooden minesweepers, called YMS (yard minesweepers), then under construction at Jacksonville, Florida. So ended my second and shortest cruise in the Navy. Never again did I serve in cold northern waters, and so never again did I suffer from my allergy.

Nancy and I rushed south by car and sooner or later found quarters, made congenial by the presence of other reserve officers and their wives, on the main street of Williamsburg, not far from Yorktown. Gasoline rationing had cut off most of the tourists and we had the historical monuments all to ourselves.

At the Mine Warfare School I received the best instruction in science I had had since my early days studying evolution at Browne and Nichols School. The Mine School undertook to train us to deal with the new types of mines and to use them ourselves. We started with fundamentals: two intensive courses, one on electricity and one on magnetism, both magnificent intellectually and pedagogically. I forget who taught electricity, though he was first-rate. Magnetism was taught by Howard Aiken, who was to build, without the benefit of the transistor, which had not yet been invented, the first modern computer at Harvard. A terror, both socially and intellectually, Aiken was the best teacher I have had the luck to be taught by. I still remember most of what he taught, which is rare for any course. The school also put us through various practical exercises in the York River and planning exercises ashore. I ended by knowing what the new minesweeping machinery was supposed to do, but not how it was made. I could not, for instance, repair the simplest breakdown. Engineers were supposed to do that.

After a pleasant winter, Nancy and I again motored south along the coast to Jacksonville, Florida, where my new command, *YMS 59*, was being built. She was not being well built: her timbers were insufficiently seasoned. That I did not discover until later. In its rush to acquire a mass of small auxiliary vessels—a need it had not envisioned in peace time—the Navy was making use of every single yard able to build a ship that could float, however briefly, on salt water. Accordingly the quality of the work done varied greatly from yard to yard.

It is difficult now to recall the fear, indeed among those directly concerned with shipping, the panic, when the German submarines ran wild along our Atlantic coast in the early months of 1942. Especially dangerous was their sinking of tankers bringing oil from Texas to the Northeast. The Navy had not yet organized air patrols and had not enough escort vessels with which to organize regular convoys—the tactics that eventually solved the problem. In the meantime the cities of the East Coast, including Jacksonville, were blacked out, lest the loom of their lights should silhouette ships and thus improve the aim of a submarine lying to seaward of them. Hard pressed themselves, the British even sent over some of their own escorts to help out. But for some time our coasters sailed singly and took their chances.

Nancy and I had rented a cottage on Jacksonville Beach, blacked out like the rest of the city. One night we were sitting in the dark looking over the calm sea, when a tanker was torpedoed and went up in flames only a mile offshore. That gave me to think what might be at stake in antisubmarine warfare.

When it came time for *YMS 59*, after launching, to proceed to the big naval base at Charleston, South Carolina, for fitting out, the Navy did not allow us to take the direct course over the open Atlantic. Instead, to keep us safe from submarines, it routed us through the Inland Waterway, inland, that is, from the necklace of islands that screen the Georgia coast. This turned out to be a pleasurable by-product of the submarine scare. I had nothing to do, for we took on a special pilot to get us through the sometimes tricky channel, and I could spend my time admiring the picturesque scenery.

When we reached Charleston, Nancy and I got ourselves a room on the Battery (pronounced Bat'ry) at the southern end of the peninsula on which Charleston lies and spent our spare time exploring the beautiful eighteenth-century southern end of the city.

I myself turned out to have little spare time. Fitting out a ship is usually a straightforward matter of taking on light equipment, ammunition, stores, and crew. Not so with *YMS 59*. Ours was the first of our new class of minesweeper to arrive in Charleston, and she presented the base with problems it had never faced before, for we were equipped to sweep the new acoustic and magnetic mines. An acoustic mine sunk a ship when the noise of her engines passing over it activated an electric trigger that set off a huge charge of explosive right under her keel. In theory, acoustic mines could be easily, if tediously, swept. *YMS 59* was equipped with a noisemaker, which we lowered over the bow and then turned on to project forward and underwater a racket that would explode the mine ahead of the sweeper. The only trouble was that both acoustic and magnetic mines could be set to explode only after a random number of passes over them, so that one had to keep on sweeping. One of the theories of mining is not that it sinks ships but that it ties up much of the enemy's equipment and personnel which he could otherwise use to better purpose. Mines could be laid by submarines and, in waters close to Germany and Japan, by air.

The problem presented by the magnetic mine was more difficult to cope with. Every vessel, even a wooden vessel if it contains an engine, may be considered a piece of soft iron, and every piece of soft iron is surrounded by a magnetic field. When this magnetic field passes over a mine laid not too deep below it, and sensitive to magnetism, this again triggers an explosive charge that breaks the ship's bottom. The British immediately thought of one way of dealing with such mines. It was called degaussing after Karl Gauss, the German investigator of magnetism in the nineteenth century, and after the gauss, the unit of magnetic force that bears his name. An electric current can create a magnetic field. Degaussing a ship consisted in wrapping her in wires in such a way that, when an electric current was passed through the wires, it neutralized the magnetic field under her bottom. The trouble with degaussing big ships was that it was expensive and unreliable.

Degaussing was supposed to let a ship escape magnetic mines. It did not get rid of them. Ships like ours were supposed to do this. The method used was to stream astern of the sweeper two "tails," actually big electrodes, one longer than the other, and then with a specially powerful generator aboard the ship pass a heavy current through the electrodes, which set up a magnetic field between the tails. When this field passed over a magnetic mine in sufficiently shallow water, it was supposed to explode the mine.

But unlike sweeping acoustic mines, sweeping magnetic mines required that they should explode astern of the sweeper. This necessarily meant that the sweeper herself would have to pass over the mine safely first, and no doubt in the course of her career of sweeping would have to do so often. Accordingly the sweeper would have to be degaussed with special care, until the strength of the magnetic field under her own keel approached zero. I doubt that the Charleston Navy Yard had had much experience with any degaussing, and ours was the first sweeper of magnetic mines its engineers had to deal with. Thus they were forced to make us their guinea pig.

Many fools have told me that the physical sciences are exact sciences in the sense of being able to make exact predictions. Except for some aspects of astronomy and for the other sciences under controlled experimental conditions, this is not true. One of the most important understandings I acquired at the Naval Mine Warfare School was that it was not true. What is more, I learned that one may have full confidence in the theory of one's science, in this case electromagnetism, and still not be able to make exact predictions from it, for predictions are made by applying a theory to given conditions, and one may not know enough about the given conditions in particular cases. I now had to face one of them.

I soon discovered that the engineers at the Navy Yard—or any other scientists for that matter—could not predict the magnetic forces, or *signature* as it was called, under the keel of *YMS 59*. If they could, I suppose they might have speeded up the process of degaussing us. The trouble is that the magnetic field of a piece of iron such as a ship has many determinants and they change over time: the chemical composition of the iron, the location and heading on which the ship was built, the amount of pounding she has received from workmen and from the seas, the latitudes and longitudes over which she has voyaged, etc. A ship acquires a magnetic field, from the earth's magnetic field, for instance, and what she has acquired earlier helps determine what she will later. That is, magnetic *hysteresis*, as it is called, is an historical science, and from historical sciences—geology, evolution, personality development, and others—it is notoriously difficult to make exact predictions. Usually it is impossible to retrieve the necessary data from the past, and if it were possible, it was certainly impossible in those days to process the data so that they would yield exact information promptly. Scientists knew the general theory of magnetism, but at least as far as magnetic minesweeping was concerned, theory was a blind giant.

Though *hysteresis* gave me intellectual comfort, since sociology, too, is an historical science, practically it led to boredom. Incapable of predicting the magnetic field of *YMS 59*, the engineers sensibly resorted to measuring it empirically. This was done by "running the range." The range consisted of huge coils of wire, attached to appropriate meters, laid down under the waters of Charleston harbor. The minesweeper passed on a standard course and speed over the coils, which registered the strength of her magnetic field as she passed. The engineers required her to make pass after pass, day after day. The trouble with this was that the skipper—that is, I—had to see that she followed exactly the same course every time, or the results would be worthless. What with continually changing conditions of wind and tide, this exacted very careful attention to inshore navigation, usually called piloting. A job like this, which is both highly repetitious and demanding of close attention, becomes very boring. I became very bored with "running the range."

What was worse, the results obtained from running the range convinced the engineers that their original wiring design for degaussing *YMS 59* was inadequate. They ripped out the old wires and put in new ones in a different pattern. It seemed that for weeks the ship was a spiderweb of wires. And then we had to run the range some more.

The climax came in the early evening sometime in May or June of 1942. One of the engineers caught me on the phone at home on the Bat'ry and ordered me to get *YMS 59* under way and run the range again, this time in darkness. The Bureau of Ships had set a deadline for completing our degaussing by a certain day, and a few more passes before midnight would just let the engineers meet the deadline. I was relaxing with my first bourbon. All except the watch (one-third of the crew) had been granted liberty: I would have great trouble rounding them up. Though in theory I could have gotten the ship under way with the watch alone, running the range accurately at night would have been exceptionally difficult. I explained all this on the phone to the engineer officer. He insisted, and then I refused to do it. I had disobeyed an order. No doubt he could have raised hell with me if he had taken my case to the admiral, but he did not, for I heard no more about the matter. No doubt BuShips would tolerate some small delay: we duly ran the range the next morning. I can only hope that our sufferings on the range made life a little easier for the YMSs that fitted out at Charleston after us.

We were now "in all respects ready for sea" and temporarily berthed at the small-craft base on the Ashley River. (The confluence of the Ashley and Cooper rivers forms Charleston's harbor.) We had been out on some training exercise and were returning to base. I had the ship nicely lined up to come alongside a certain slip. This was a bit tricky, because we had a strong current under our stern, and I was pleased with myself. At this point a uniformed figure appeared on the slip and ordered me by megaphone to back out and come alongside a different slip. Furious at having my excellent ship-handling thus wasted, I grabbed my own megaphone and without thinking shouted back, "You can go to hell!" Still, with some difficulty I backed the ship out and brought her alongside the other slip. When I got ashore I discovered that the officer I had damned was none other than the commanding officer of the base, whom incidentally I had known earlier at Yorktown. Quite properly he chewed me out, but I never discovered that he—kind man—took any other action against me. From my fellow officers this exploit won me the sobriquet, duly inscribed on a certificate, of "Go to Hell Homans!" But having now both disobeyed an order and cursed a superior officer, I was beginning to understand how wise I was not to have undertaken, as I had planned in my youth, a career in the regular Navy. Temperamentally I was unfitted for it. I should never have scaled the heights and made admiral. As it was I doubted whether even in the reserve I should move up in rank.

15

THE NAVY II: ARUBA-CURAÇAO

The first cruise of *YMS 59* was a short one. For reasons I have now forgotten, perhaps simply to give us a shakedown, we were ordered to go south along the coast to Savannah and then return to Charleston. I found the naval station at the entrance to the Savannah River on a blacked-out coast in the middle of a moonless night. Although all navigational aids, like the lights ashore, were shut off, and our ship had no radar, this was not really much of a feat. But as I stood on the bridge while we were coming to an anchor I heard a voice from the darkness of the forecastle below me saying, "By God! He made it!" in tones of intense surprise.

My crew had as yet no great reason to feel confidence in me or the other officers, yet confidence helps determine such vital matters as obedience to orders. The problem was not limited to our ship. No crew at first felt confidence in any of the reserve officers who commanded the small-craft or "spit-kit" Navy. The difficulty did not lie, as it did in the big ships, in the relations between reserve officers and regulars (called "ring-twisters" after their Annapolis class rings), because there were no regular officers in the small-craft Navy. Our difficulty lay rather in the relations between us reserve officers and the regular enlisted men, many of whom had long records of service in much larger vessels, and for whom assignment to the new small craft meant a comedown in both physical and social amenities. They knew their business, at least in the older naval technologies. Did we know ours? Clabby, our chief boatswain's mate, fell into this category. He had been master-at-arms, that is, chief of police, on a big ship in the Pacific. And now what was he? I doubt that he began to feel much confidence in me until I once demonstrated that I could get the crew to stream paravanes, the first step in sweeping moored mines, without a foul-up and without his help. Anyone who could set a big spinnaker on a racing yacht could stream paravanes. Unfortunately my troubles with Clabby did not end with paravanes.

He taught me some things it was good for me to know about the unofficial ethos of the old Navy. At Charleston I caught him picking up a coil of hawser left unguarded on a ship lying alongside us, and I took him to task. He could not be brought to understand that he had been doing any wrong. Rather it was his positive duty to the ship to snap up, when he could, any such unconsidered trifles as spare gear that might at some time come in handy. No wonder spare parts and gear sank in secret hoards as into a quicksand and put a real strain on the ability of the United States to supply its armed forces. Though I made Clabby return the hawser and thus, I am sure, convinced him that I was a fool, I did not otherwise discipline him. Perhaps I should have turned the blind eye altogether.

We came back from Savannah in daylight and calm weather. Under these conditions, every bit of driftwood on the surface was visible. How far the German submarine campaign along the East Coast had demoralized the crew they showed by reporting—as it seemed to me then— every bit of driftwood as a periscope. From my station on the bridge, I thought I recognized the wrack for what it really was; and so great a nuisance did the reports become that I finally issued Ship's Order No. 1: "Indiscriminate cries of 'submarine' not directed to the bridge will not be tolerated." When I got back to Charleston and reported to the admiral, I made the mistake, by way of passing the time, of telling him that on the way back from Savannah members of my crew had reported many things as submarines which I was sure were not submarines. I thought he would be sympathetic. Instead, he chewed me out, declaring that whenever anything was reported to me as a submarine, I ought to have made an "emergency attack" on it with my depth charges, even if, lacking sonar, I could not have made an effective attack on the submarine unless she were fool enough to keep her periscope raised. I might at least have reported the alleged sightings by radio, but I had not done even that. Once more I had run into the unstated, but for obvious reasons not always observed, doctrine of the Navy that, if an action might be militarily useful, one ought to take it, even if the chances of its really being useful were vanishingly small. Skipper Homans was not piling up a record as a zealous officer. Nor was he learning to keep his mouth shut.

Finally, towards the beginning of June 1942, *YMS 59* was dispatched on what was to be her regular duty assignment. Specifically we were ordered to take her to San Juan, Puerto Rico, where I was to report to Commander, Caribbean Sea Frontier. We were to stop for supplies at various ports along the way, the first being Miami. One night off Cape Canaveral in Florida, now famous as Cape Kennedy, Chief Clabby woke me up to report that not one but two torpedoes had passed under the ship. I was sure that this was nonsense; at most the two torpedoes must have been porpoises. No sensible German submariner would have wasted two torpedoes on us when more valuable targets, such as tankers, were within reach. Moreover, the torpedoes, if shot in earnest, would have sunk us. Nevertheless, mindful of my latest chewing-out, I felt that this time I must do something, however silly. So I spent the rest of the night dropping all our depth charges, at a cost of thousands of dollars to the United States Navy, over an area of the sea in which a submarine conceivably might have been if it had tried to torpedo us and then escape. Depth charges make splendid big bangs under water and shatter a calm surface like glass. I had made my "emergency attack."

When we got into Miami I reported these events to the operations officer, as I was bound to do. How they managed to get interpreted as they were I do not know. But about a year later the Navy began to send us what were called "wreck charts." These purported to show the location of vessels sunk in shallow water, because sonar could easily mistake them for submarines and thus lead to their being uselessly depth charged. One such wreck chart showed *YMS 59* on the bottom right off Cape Canaveral, where the alleged attack upon us had taken place. But the Navy sent the chart *to YMS 59*, which was still very much afloat. Let not thy left hand know what thy right hand doeth.

From Miami our orders were to proceed independently to Guantanamo Bay, the United States Naval Base on the southeast coast of Cuba on the Windward Passage. On the first morning after leaving Miami, Chief Clabby woke me up to report that the ship's cook had refused duty or even to get out of his sack. No doubt he was both seasick and hung over from drinking in Miami the night before. I always seemed to run into trouble with cooks aboard my ships. They made a big difference to morale, but theirs was a hard job, especially on ships like *YMS 59*, which usually carried only one of them, and he could not quickly be replaced. What to do now? Could nondirective interviews and human relations help me? No, they took too long. Anyhow under the pressure of anxiety, anger, and impatience one is apt to forget what one has learned about treating men as "ends in themselves." *Video meliora, proboque, deteriora sequor.*[1] According to Naval Regulations, I should have had the cook up before Captain's Mast, the local court aboard ship, and given him one of the conventional punishments. But that too would have taken too long to solve the immediate problem, which was getting the crew their breakfast. Furious, I myself filled a bucket with cold sea water, went below to the crew's quarters, and dumped it over the cook as he lay in his berth. At least I did the job myself and did not ask anyone to do it for me. Under this dousing, the cook leaped out of his berth, and I thought he was going to throw himself overboard. Instead, he came to his senses and cooked breakfast. The cook was at heart a good man, and I gave him no further punishment.

On the north coast of Cuba, on our way to Guantanamo, we got our first taste of what was to plague us off and on for our whole time in the Caribbean: pitching into the short but heavy chop built up by strong easterly trade winds. At about this time I was reading Sam Morison's life of Columbus, *Admiral of the Ocean Sea*,[2] and I could at once appreciate the frustrations Columbus and his fellow seamen faced in trying to claw to windward under sail in these waters. In the end *YMS 59* herself was to be disabled by the trade-wind chop.

When we reached Guantanamo, I discovered that my days of independent coasting were over, and that I should have to take over the burden I was to carry for most of my time in the Atlantic: the escort of merchant ships. Four YMSs, all bound for San Juan, were assigned the job of convoying to that port, by way of the north coast of Hispaniola, an aged Cuban freighter christened *Libertad*. (Remember that Cuba was a friendly, indeed an allied, nation then.) Since I was the senior officer of the YMSs, I had the job of commanding the little convoy. This responsibility I did not relish at all. German submarines were known to be active off Puerto Rico. Only one of the YMSs was fitted with the sonar gear necessary to detect the presence of a submarine under water, and her officers were not trained in its use. Finally poor old *Libertad*—alas, she brought us no liberty!—could only just manage to make five knots over the ground, a speed much too slow to make it worth her while, if she were ever to reach San Juan, to steer a zigzag course so as to throw off the aim of an attacking submarine. I thought she was a sitting duck, and so she was, yet I was responsible for her. For a whole week we steamed towards our destination and encountered no vessel whatever, either on or underneath the surface of the sea. Yet I was so anxious—a paralyzing condition from which I never became altogether free—that, though I lay down on my bunk from time to time, I am pretty sure I did not go to sleep for a whole week. When we reached San Juan it did not seem to me that I felt tired, but instead slaphappy and extremely irritable. I felt the need to complain about something to the admiral commanding the Caribbean Sea Frontier, who was referred to as "Genial John," precisely of course because he was *not* genial. A wise old officer of the staff persuaded me not to do so. I wish I had had him by my side on other occasions. A useful side effect of this experience was that, having gone without sleep for a week and survived, I lost all worry, which had been once strong in me, about being able to go to sleep. Sleep, it seemed, made little difference.

During the convoying of *Libertad* I began to acquire the attitude towards combat with the enemy that I was to maintain throughout the war. Admirable as are the narratives in Sam Morison's *History of the United States Navy in World War II*,[3] he regularly makes a psychological assumption that I find dubious. He assumes that the officers and men of the Navy were, to a man, burning to kill Japs or Germans, as the case might be. As Admiral Halsey, I think, exclaimed: "Kill Japs; kill more Japs; kill still more Japs!" This attitude may have been held by some of the regular officers, who for years had been training for combat, and whose professional advancement depended on it. But I doubt that it was held even by all the regulars, and it was certainly not characteristic of my friends among the reservists—not that we talked about it much.

Naval Regulations required that, once a month, I, as commanding officer, should call the ship's company to quarters and read to them "The Articles for the Government of the Navy." I especially enjoyed the article stating that anyone "who pusillanimously cries for quarter shall suffer death" or—an anticlimax—"such other punishment as a court-martial may prescribe." I was pretty sure that, if I got into combat, I would not pusillanimously cry for quarter. If I did so, it would have to be over the radio, since I should not face the situation to which the article was originally designed to apply: two frigate captains, their ships under shortened sail and no further apart than the proverbial biscuit-toss, hailing one another in English between broadsides. No doubt we would do our best if combat were forced upon us or required by our duty, and I am sure we should have given a good account of ourselves. We would not go out of our way to avoid combat, but neither would we welcome it. Other things equal, let someone else fight the Japanese or the Germans. Our feelings and also our guilt were strengthened by the news we were beginning to get about the state of the war in the Pacific. Indeed it was not until after our victories at Guadalcanal and Midway that we began to believe we might win the war. In the meantime, come victory or defeat, we in YMS 59 knew that our assignment in the Caribbean, with all its vexations, was highly desirable, because reasonably, if not wholly, safe. We were to be envied. This attitude remained mine, not only while I commanded YMS 59, which would have stood no chance against a German submarine, but also later when I commanded a ship that could have fought one on equal terms.

In fact we never made contact with a submarine, though there often were submarines in our neighborhood. One of these occasions was upon us. From San Juan, three of the YMSs, including 59, were ordered to the United States Virgin Islands for some inadequate and brief training in antisubmarine warfare. Late one night, when we were berthed in the harbor of Charlotte Amalie, the naval officer in command ashore woke me up and said something like this: "An American Liberty Ship, sailing independently, has just been sunk at approximately such and such a position off the entrance to the Anegada Passage. [The Anegada Passage is the most northeasterly of the entrances to the Caribbean and comes in just south of the Virgin Islands.] The survivors are in lifeboats. I want you to get under way at once, find them, pick them up, and bring them back here. We believe the submarine is still somewhere out there. She probably won't waste a torpedo on you, but she might gun you. Good luck!" Submarines carried deck guns, usually heavier than the 3-inch, 50-caliber gun on the forecastle of a YMS. Even in a gunfight on the surface, we were apt to come out worse than the submarine unless we managed to be the first to get in a lucky hit. And there was no reason to believe that the submarine would be so stupid as to stay on the surface. With these last cheerful words ringing in my ears, I took the ship to sea.

By dawn long swells were piling into the passage, but with little wind behind them, so that we were able to make good progress. Using a powerful though simple search plan, that of simply steering straight across the entrance to the passage, we succeeded in finding all the lifeboats, which were the more visible for being under sail, and picking up the survivors. They were glad to get on board, though without our help they would have easily reached the British Virgin Islands, as the weather was good, the wind fair, and the distance small. The survivors included the whole crew, for the German skipper had surfaced and ordered all hands to take to the boats before he sank the ship. He took the risk of being found by our air patrols.

The German skipper had a disturbing reason for letting the merchant crew off so easily. When I talked with the ship's master, he told me the submarine skipper had hailed him from the conning tower and told him what port his ship had sailed from (New Orleans), where she was bound (Egypt), and what her cargo consisted of: munitions for the British Army in the Western Desert. The submarine skipper had no business knowing any of these things. He was waging what we were to call psychological warfare. He was trying to persuade the merchant mariners that German naval intelligence was omniscient, and that therefore their destruction was inevitable. The Liberty Ship was sailing without escort. Convoys, which were to be part of the answer to the submarine threat, were, for lack of escort vessels, not yet fully organized. The submarine skipper story was successful in helping further to undermine my morale, which was already low. But in spite of the warning with which we had left Charlotte Amalie, *YMS 59* made no contact with the submarine.

At about this time, which must have been early in July 1942, the Navy informed us of our permanent duty assignment, so far as anything in the Navy is permanent. The three YMSs then at Charlotte Amalie were to report to a new command, subordinate to the Caribbean Sea Frontier, called Commander All Forces Aruba-Curaçao (CAFAC). Ours were, I think, the first American ships assigned to CAFAC. At that time I had not heard of Curaçao except as an excellent sweet liqueur, now distilled in France though originally made on some West Indian island. But where was the island? I had not even heard of Aruba.

The three islands of Bonaire, Curaçao, and Aruba then belonged, with other islands in the Caribbean, to the Netherlands West Indies. The Dutch, when they commanded the greatest sea power on earth, had occupied them in the sixteenth century. They had nothing to recommend them but their location. One thinks of the islands of the West Indies as covered with lush vegetation. Not so these islands: hardly any rain falls on them. I still do not understand how they could have grown the oranges from which the liqueur is made. But the location of the islands was and is crucial. They lay only an easy day's (or night's) sail from the coast of Venezuela, then part of the famous Spanish Main, that is, the northern mainland of South America. And I mean *sail*. Even in our time little native schooners kept the islands supplied with fresh produce, complete with cockroaches. Since this was wartime, they sailed without lights, and when on night patrol we were always in danger of running them down.

So located, and with their few harbors easily defensible, especially the harbor of the capital, Willemstad on Curaçao (named of course after William of Orange), the islands provided Dutch ships with splendid bases for piracy against Spain in time of war and smuggling with the Main in time of peace, for Spain tried to prevent the ships of other nations from trading with its colonies. The islands were, and are, "free ports," with no customs duties paid on cargo entering or leaving them. Over the centuries they had acquired a very mixed population: Whites, especially Sephardic Jews, descendants of those who had fled to the Netherlands to escape the Inquisition in Spain and Portugal; Blacks, products of the slave trade, red Indians from the mainland, with later additions of Chinese and Indians from India, descendants of indentured servants imported in the nineteenth century to such other islands as Trinidad and Jamaica. The islands had even developed a language of their own, called *papiamento,* a mixture of Hispanic, Dutch, and no doubt other languages.

The islands must have led a sleepy existence when Venezuela and Colombia freed themselves from Spain and the great days of piracy and smuggling ended. What revived their importance was the discovery in the early days of the present century of huge deposits of petroleum around and in the shallow waters of the Lake of Maracaibo, not far away on the Venezuelan coast. The question was where the Maracaibo crude was to be refined. It probably could have been refined most cheaply at Maracaibo itself. But the water over the bar at the entrance to the lake was too shoal to allow the passage of oceangoing tankers in order to load the oil. An alternative might have been to pipe the crude to deep-water ports elsewhere in Venezuela. The oil companies rejected this solution because, I believe, they did not trust the long-time dictator of Venezuela, Gómez, to obey the rules of capitalism. They were afraid he might seize the refineries if they built them in Venezuela itself. They had just been burnt by the nationalization of oil by the revolutionary government of Mexico.

But the Dutch, one of the most capitalistic of nations, they felt they could trust. Accordingly they adopted the following solution to their problem. Small shoal-draft tankers, called "lake tankers" because they could cross the bar at the entrance to the Lake of Maracaibo, picked up cargoes of crude oil there. It then took them less than a day's steaming to reach the islands of Curaçao or Aruba, about sixty miles to the north. The great Anglo-Dutch combine, Royal Dutch Shell, built a refinery in back of the harbor at Willemstad, Curaçao, and Standard Oil of New Jersey, through its subsidiary, the Lago Oil and Transport Company, another at the eastern end of Aruba. At one time this was the largest refinery in the world. Lago had also created an artificial harbor, San Nicolaas, convenient to its refinery, by blasting a channel through the outlying coral reef. The lake tankers brought the crude to these harbors. Then ocean tankers picked up the refined oil. The harbors at both islands were deep enough to accommodate them.

At the opening of World War II, these two refineries supplied a large part of the oil needed by our European allies for both military and civilian purposes. Thus they were of capital strategic importance. The Netherlands, which the Germans had surprised and conquered in the very first days of the blitzkrieg, was unable to defend them, just as she had been unable to defend her great East Indian empire from the Japanese. There was a Dutch Naval Command at Willemstad, controlling no planes, a few small ships, and one cruiser, *Van Kinsbergen*, handsome but useless for meeting the immediate needs. Only the United States could begin to protect the Dutch islands or indeed the rest of the West Indies from German submarines or surface raiders. Accordingly it undertook to provide the vital air patrols and later, as they became available, the necessary small escort vessels. Hence the proposed establishment of CAFAC and the assignment to it of the YMSs. We were far from being ideal for the purposes in hand. After all, we were minesweepers, not escort vessels. But we were the nearest available approximations.

In *YMS 59* I led—if that is the right word—our two sister ships across the Caribbean from north to south, from the Virgin Islands to the Dutch headquarters at Willemstad.

The harbor of Willemstad is surely among the most picturesque in the world. At the entrance stands the old Dutch fort, guarding a channel which is more like a street, for it is hardly wider than one and is bordered by old Dutch houses with high, stepped gables, painted in pastel colors. Just inside the channel from the fort lies a pontoon bridge, which allows people and vehicles to pass from one side of the channel to the other, but which can also be swung open as if on a hinge to allow ships to enter and depart. At the inshore end the channel opens into a basin, where the refinery and later the so-called U.S. Section Base were located.

Because CAFAC as an American command existed largely on paper, we came at Curaçao briefly under the control of the Netherlands navy. Besides its pleasures and practicalities, seafaring has always meant tradition to me, and I now was part of the Dutch tradition, of the great admirals like Piet Hein, the only man to capture the whole Spanish plate fleet, of Van Tromp and de Ruyter. I always got on well with officers of the Dutch navy, partly because defeated, undermanned, and tired, they did not insist on keeping us busy when it was not clear that keeping us busy would do any good. This was un-American.

Still there was enough to do in the early days, which passed in a kind of haze of fatigue, the kind of fatigue I had undergone in escorting *Libertad* and does not make one go to sleep. I was not familiar with the local geography, and naval routines were nonexistent. Part of the trouble was my own fault. I had not yet qualified my engineering officer for standing deck watches, so that my executive officer and I stood watch and watch. This was standard practice for the watches on the old sailing ships. At first I could not understand how they could have borne the strain, because my anxiety still prevented me from going to sleep at once when I went off watch. I got used to the routine in time, but at first I think I was sometimes close to being out of my mind.

Whenever I did fall asleep in those days and nights of light-headed fatigue, a recurrent dream possessed me. So far as I remember my dreams at all, I seldom recognize that their themes recur. Now I dreamt over and over again that I was exploring with my ship a coast far to the south, which no White man had ever seen before. On that coast I found and penetrated far up a great river, at the entrance of which lay a charming, small, walled city full of people in narrow streets. I do not know what a Freudian would make of this dream. It was not in the least threatening but rather both realistic and romantic. I wanted to explore that coast in my waking hours.

Out of my mind or not, I somehow escaped any disasters in those early days at CAFAC. We helped escort tankers in and out of Curaçao to the "main convoys," which the U.S. Navy had organized at last to sail through the middle of the Caribbean between Guantanamo and Trinidad. At Guantanamo a northbound convoy was picked up by another convoy to New York; at Trinidad a southbound one by another destined for Africa or Brazil. Finally I discovered that *YMS 59* was specifically to report to Aruba, some sixty miles west-northwest of Curaçao, and I did so when I was ordered to take a single ship from a main convoy into San Nicholaas. I kept station on her through a soft, dark southern night, my eyes clamped to those wonderful 7 x 50 nightglasses on which I depended for more than a year. For me they were the most blessed instrument man had ever invented, and I still cannot believe that he has improved upon them. Of course we had no radar, which was to make child's play of station-keeping.

But station-keeping was not my main problem. That was to find Aruba in the dark. Of course I knew where it was on the chart but I had never seen it by daylight, and at night it was thoroughly and totally blacked out. Not a light showed. Luckily the coral reefs that encircled the island did not lie far offshore, so that I could pick up the loom of the main body of the land with my glasses before I was entangled in the reefs. Even so my troubles were not at an end. I still had to find the signal station at the harbor of San Nicholaas and get permission by flashing light to enter. With later experience, these difficulties disappeared.

At Aruba our ship came under the command of a naval reserve officer who had formerly served, I believe, as harbormaster for the Lago Oil and Transport Company. In our more discouraged moments we claimed that we were working for the Standard Oil Company of New Jersey and not for the U.S. Navy. Socially, the enlisted men fared ill. San Nicholaas was a squalid town, which offered them little but bars and whorehouses. Perhaps that was all many of them wanted. As for the officers, they too would have suffered, if the families of the American managers of the refinery had not gone out of their way to offer us hospitality, and if our ship had not soon been joined by other YMSs, almost all of whose officers I liked.

At Aruba we were at once faced with several problems of logistics, which the Navy naturally had not warned me about. I do not want to go into the details of the naval pay system. It is enough to remember that, except for pittances of "emergency pay," getting the ship's company of a small ship paid depended on the presence of their pay accounts within walking distance, and when we reached the base at Aruba ours were, I believe, still back in San Juan. Of course many of the crew had made over large shares of their pay to their dependents, who always got their money on time. But we all kept some part of our pay for our own use as pocket money, even if there was not much we could spend it on. Without our pay accounts we could not get even that.

I thought I could improve the morale of the crew and enlist it in my support by making a big issue about pay with the authorities ashore. I would "stand up for my men." I soon discovered, in the long run to my advantage, that standing up by the mere use of strong language—and I could make mine strong indeed—produced little of the intended effect. Indeed, if you kept it up, you looked more and more like an ass. What was wanted was not strong language but successful action, and the former need not lead to the latter. If you could not get that, you had much better shut up, even if your crew remained unpaid. Otherwise you would only lose the goodwill both of your crew and of the administrators ashore. In its own good time the Navy got our pay accounts to us, but by that time I had lost the goodwill at least of the administrators.

Besides pay, there was food (chow). At Aruba we were at the very end of the chow line. There was no naval supply facility. We were supposed to be supplied by the Air Force, which had established a base for patrol aircraft. Naturally it was inclined to supply us with only those items of which it had more than enough for its own men. For a time the single such item seemed to be mustard pickles, and for weeks, as I remember it, we sustained life on mustard pickles alone. My memory must be overdramatizing, for can mustard pickles in fact sustain life? That problem, like pay, worked itself out in time.

On the other hand, the base at Aruba was not equipped to carry out anything more than the most minor repairs to our ships. For repairs, we had to go to Curaçao, and that we always looked on as a holiday. The need for certain repairs recurred regularly. Driving *YMS 59* hard against the heavy trade-wind chop wore out the piston rings on our diesels. That meant "blow-by" and loss of power. Then we had to go over to Willemstad on Curaçao to install new rings.

The Navy stationed the YMSs at Aruba to perform military duties. Minesweeping, the only one we were fully equipped to perform, was the one we performed least often, and then only to show we could still go through the motions. It was silly to sweep the entrance to San Nicholaas. Aruba was only the top of a mountain that rose steeply to the surface from enormous depths. Two hundred yards off the entrance, the depth of water was already too great for mines to be effective. I was fond of saying that the undersea slope was so steep that a mine laid there would roll down to the bottom, thousands of fathoms below. Nevertheless our commander ashore did perfunctorily order us from time to time to sweep the channel. It was nasty work, since the sludge of oil in San Nicholaas was always so thick that the gear, the decks of the ship, and naturally the officers and men soon got fouled up with it. We certainly never exploded a mine, and I think only four mines were swept in the whole Caribbean in the course of the war, and none of these was anywhere near Aruba and Curaçao.

If we did not do what we were equipped to do, we did what we were not. Shortly before we arrived at Aruba a German submarine had lobbed a couple of shells into the refinery, starting fires that were soon put out. I never understood why submarines making a determined attack could not have destroyed the refinery altogether and thus denied much oil to the Allies. Oil is obviously highly flammable; the refinery was right on the edge of the coast; the coast was steep-to, so that a submarine could get within close range under water before she had to surface in order to fire her deck gun. True, Aruba was well within the islands that ring the Caribbean; air patrols were now maintained from these islands, so that a submarine was in danger if it surfaced anywhere within the ring. Yet, as we shall see later, at least one submarine penetrated safely as far as Curaçao.

I finally guessed what may have been one of the reasons German submarines never made another attack on the Esso refinery. From time to time a Spanish or Vichy-French tanker would arrive unescorted and anchor inconspicuously at the other end of the island from the refinery, where she would take on oil, presumably from lighters. The Allies may not have wanted to drive the Spanish into the arms of the Germans by denying them oil, so they allowed the Spanish and the Vichy-French just enough oil to keep their economies going; and the Germans spared the refinery from which the oil came. Even war has its accommodations.

Yet our superior officers insisted that one of the jobs of the YMSs was to protect Aruba against a renewal of this kind of attack. Accordingly from time to time they ordered one of us to spend the night patrolling around the island. This was not difficult to do. Our excellent night-glasses easily kept us in contact with the coast. But would our patrolling answer its purpose, or indeed any purpose at all? We had depth charges but no way of locating a submerged submarine to drop them on. We could shell a submarine on the surface—and she us, probably to even deadlier effect—and a submarine would indeed have to surface in order to shell the refinery. But we were ordered to patrol around the whole island, and if a submarine waited until we were at the other end, she would have been able to get in a good shelling before we got back. If our superiors were afraid a submarine might land a party of saboteurs, they never told us so.

Accordingly we did not take our patrolling very seriously, nor did *YMS*

59 present a military appearance as she slowly circled the island through the night. Our laundry hung out to dry, and fishing lines trailed astern on the chance that we might eke out our diet of mustard pickles. Fishing was one of our few useful activities. Though our commanders ashore were sometimes hard on me, I do not think I was hard on the crew of *YMS 59*. Perhaps I was not hard enough.

If we were very lucky we were sent to spend the night, for reasons I have now forgotten, at Oranjestaat on the south coast at the other end of the island from San Nicholaas. Oranjestaat possessed the only natural harbor on the island—a small creek—and therefore it was much older than San Nicholaas. I could never make out what the inhabitants of Oranjestaad did to make a living. Their houses and gardens lay unseen behind high walls. What gave the place its charm was the sense of mysteriousness and secretiveness that Conrad conveys in "A Smile of Fortune"[4] for a town on some island of the Indian Ocean (Mauritius, Reunion?). Unhappily there were a great many rats at Oranjestaat, and it was very easy for them to get on board. We never wholly eradicated either cockroaches or rats.

The YMSs also had the duty of picking out of the southbound main convoys from Guantanamo to Trinidad those tankers that were bound for Aruba in ballast and escorting them there. By the same token we had to deliver tankers that had loaded oil at Aruba to the northbound main convoys from Trinidad to Guantanamo. From Guantanamo most of the tankers proceeded in a series of convoy legs to a final destination in the British Isles or at worst Murmansk. I am afraid that in the early days their usual fate was torpedoing and the loss of all hands by fire or drowning. Since sailing in either direction the main convoys passed north of Aruba and south of Curaçao and thus between the two islands, these particular escort assignments were usually short.

We maneuvered the tankers in and out of the main convoys, at least in daylight, by hoisting flag signals chosen out of the British-designed "Merchant Ships Signal Book" ("Mersigs" for short), which I enjoyed greatly. It was less logical than the signal book of the U.S. Navy and allowed us to send a greater and more human variety of messages.

Detaching the ships from a main convoy was easy, at least in daylight. At night, since we had no radar, it was difficult to find the convoy. When we did we simply made a signal—and if one is a true salt one always "makes" a signal—that meant: "Ships bound for Aruba, follow me!" Getting ships bound out of Aruba joined up to a convoy was much more tricky, and it often fell on me, as the senior skipper of the YMSs, to do so. Let us assume that six tankers were full of oil and ready for sea and that three YMSs were available to screen them out to the main convoy. Our commanding officer ashore first called a "Convoy Conference" to be attended by all the skippers, merchant and Navy. At the conference he specified that I was to command the local convoy and then discussed the prospects for the main convoy and any special procedures that were to be in force for the occasion. No one ever raised the question whether the YMSs were able to provide any protection for the local convoy. I suspect that some knew we were not but said nothing about it, for the dangers they were apt to run into locally were as nothing to what they were to encounter later crossing the North Atlantic. If some thought we really were able to provide protection, our function was purely psychological. To persuade men they are safe, even when they are not, is surely not bad for their morale.

Of course our own officers and men did know how weak we were and often wondered what we were doing at Aruba and Curaçao. By now the ships that escorted the main convoys were equipped to give them some real protection, not to beat off a repeated and determined attack but to make it dangerous and costly, since they were actually able to sink a submarine. Not us. It was conceivable, but not really believable, that the mere sight of a screen of YMSs inspired such terror in a German skipper that he dared not attack ships we convoyed. German naval intelligence must have had a pretty accurate notion of our capabilities. And if submarines were ready to attack convoys escorted by destroyers and corvettes in the North Atlantic, they were not likely to be deterred by YMSs in the Caribbean. The fact remains that no tankers were ever sunk when in one of our local convoys. After a terrible slaughter of ships around Trinidad in March 1943, the submarine menace in the West Indies faded away.

After the convoy conference, the tankers sortied and formed a column, with the YMSs ahead of them to provide a screen. From my ship I maneuvered the whole by means of Mersigs. From Curaçao the main convoy took a northwesterly course, from Aruba our little convoy, a southeasterly one, so that the two convoys approached one another at the sum of their speeds. That left me little time for maneuver when we sighted the main convoy, which we had to do with our glasses since we had no radar. The trick then was to swing our whole column of tankers around some 180 degrees by a series of Mersigs, at such speeds and courses that they formed one of the outboard columns of the main convoy. At that time our duty was at an end. We signaled "Good Luck!" to our ships, which, God knows, they were to need later in the North Atlantic, and took off back to Aruba. I much enjoyed this kind of operation. Since a tanker turns slowly and requires a long turning-radius, the operation of joining our column neatly up to the main convoy required some judgment and timing. I was quite good at it. For other reasons I should never have made admiral, but had I become one, I should at least have been able to maneuver a fleet.

In the end one tanker exposed whatever pretensions we may have had to providing antisubmarine protection. In the early months the tankers had been old and slow, and the YMSs, if they had to, could make about fifteen knots and stay ahead of them. Later a new and faster generation of tankers began to come off the ways. One day I was ordered to take a single one of them out to meet a main convoy. She took off at her top speed, which was several knots faster than ours, and by the time she joined the main convoy, *YMS 59* was several miles astern. Here we were obviously of no military use at all.

Our uselessness, and our near isolation in Aruba from regular naval discipline, tended to make some of us a little "asiatic." That is the word the Navy gave to men who had spent too long a tour of duty on the old Yangtse patrol in China. It means someone who has become a little strange or irrational for lack of contact with normal human beings, that is, with Americans. Here is one example. An officer of a sister ship and a great friend of mine got into the habit, when he had to interview a member of the crew, of drawing his loaded service-issue 45-caliber pistol and laying it on the table before him, saying to the seaman: "Now we can talk more comfortably!" And I had been taught about "social skills"! Yet through all the frustrations and ambiguities of our duty, we all remembered that we were in a good berth: we thought of Guadalcanal, Tarawa, and now the Murmansk convoys.

Our third main task was to escort the small fleets of lake tankers that departed every morning from both Aruba and Curaçao bound for Maracaibo to load crude oil. We, of course, were responsible for the Aruba fleets. The YMSs never reached Maracaibo itself. We would escort our outward-bound fleet across to the peninsula of Paraguaná on the Venezuelan coast, dominated by the big round mountain called the Pan de Santa Ana, and then continue along the south coast of the peninsula until we met the lake tankers that had left Aruba the day before, loaded at Maracaibo, and were to return with us to Aruba. As usual we were performing no useful military task, unless we gave comfort to the crews of the lake tankers. But it was often pleasant work, especially on winter mornings, when the trade wind blew lightly but brought a freshness to the tropical air. Along the coast we saw flights of flamingoes and, out on the calm sea, giant rays with "wings" some twelve feet across would break water, leaping and falling back.

We were most pleased when we were ordered to sail independently for Paraguaná. *YMS 59* made, I think, the first rough survey of Amuay Bay on the peninsula. The question was whether the bay could be made into an emergency harbor of refuge for the lake tankers in case of a big submarine attack, but nothing was done to carry out the plan. At the time we made our soundings the shores of Amuay Bay were empty save for goats and thornbush. After World War II a huge refinery was built there.

Our favorite port on the peninsula was Bahía Boca de las Piedras not far south of Amuay Bay, where the Gulf Oil Company had an installation and a small pier to which we occasionally brought a ship. There was also a settlement of fishermen. I admired greatly the classic lines and decoration of the houses they had built out of the simplest materials, largely adobe.

At one time we arrived at Las Piedras and found a Venezuelan gunboat, vintage about 1900, alongside the pier. She was painted white and gold, and her officers and men were in white and gold uniforms. Our own shoregoing uniforms were elegant also, but at sea we all, officers and men, wore dungarees or khaki shorts and usually stripped to the waist. As I brought *YMS 59* alongside the pier in this costume, yelling out my orders as usual, the Venezuelan officers must have looked on us as uncivilized *yanquis*, but we were the better seamen. The gunboat was even less useful for the purposes of modern warfare than we were, and she got under way from La Guaira, the port of Caracas, only once a year. She was a pure token.

Along the coast between Amuay Bay and Las Piedras was stationed a unit of Venezuelan coast artillery. To it an American liaison officer had been attached who did me many good turns. Once he drove me in his jeep through the trackless thornbush that covered the slopes of the Pan de Santa Ana until we reached a settlement called Muruy. It had a big white church of the standard Spanish baroque design fronted by a huge dirt plaza, which was surrounded by a few adobe hovels and almost no inhabitants. It gave me one of my most eerie historical impressions. Muruy had, I believe, been founded within twenty-five years of Columbus's discovery of America and a whole century before the founding of the Massachusetts Bay Colony. And here it still was, without even a road leading to it. I felt how grandiose had been the designs of the Spaniards for their conquests in the New World, and how often their civilization had failed to take deep root.

For all hands, in their different ways, the greatest charm of Las Piedras was social. To me the American boss of the Gulf installation could not have been kinder. For the enlisted men what made Las Piedras enchanting was that it was effectively without law. It had Zulia beer and willing girls but no police, at least no incorruptible police, and these conditions created the perfect liberty port. I should have had a mutiny on my hands if I had allowed liberty to less than two-thirds of the crew. With the rest I did not have enough men both to stand watches on the ship and man a shore patrol, which would itself have probably succumbed to the fleshpots of Las Piedras. Sometimes when we were, without warning, ordered by radio to get under way at once, I was unable to round up all the liberty party. Some of them failed to get back to the ship, so widely and obscurely had they gotten themselves shacked up ashore. I suppose I should have reported them to naval headquarters as absent without leave, but I never did, counting on picking them up on our next visit to Las Piedras. We always did pick them up; we had no permanent AWOLs; my unorthodox policy—really not a policy, for I doubt if I could have done anything else—seemed to have worked.

Only one potentially unpleasant incident marred the enchantments of Las Piedras. Once I was woken up at night with the news that Chief Clabby had been arrested. I have said that there were no incorruptible police in Las Piedras. That was just the trouble. Men alleged to be customs officers watched at the head of the pier to see that we smuggled nothing ashore. American money was no use in Las Piedras; the men had to take tangibles ashore to pay for their beer and their girls, and they had little money anyhow. The joys of Las Piedras were to be had only by barter. The cost of bribing a customs officer to look the other way did not seem to be high. Even so Clabby had not paid the minimum. Perhaps a chief paid a higher tariff than an ordinary seaman. What was worse from my point of view was that Clabby had proposed to use as his *valuta* government property, to wit, a can of Spam. Spam passed as currency on the coast of Venezuela. Clabby had no business having Spam in his possession, and misappropriation of government property the Navy considered, and still considers, to be a serious matter.

I pulled on an orthodox uniform and found Clabby sitting on the ground in the local jail, which consisted simply of a large fenced-in square of dirt, open to the sky. This was not cruel or unusual punishment, since on the Paraguaná peninsula it hardly ever rains. On the theory that I was bound to do the best I could for my men, I determined to "spring" Clabby. But I knew no Spanish. I managed to get hold of my friend the American liaison officer to act as my interpreter. Just as important, he got hold of the so-called *administrador*, who was the one official who held any power in Las Piedras, and that power was arbitrary. An *administrador* was a kind of local governor, not elected but appointed from Caracas, the capital. He never came from the district he governed, lest his local ties should corrupt him. Our *administrador* was an *andino*, a man from the Andes mountains, as were most of the bureaucrats of Venezuela in my time.

The *administrador* was good enough to show up, and through my friend I put to him the following argument: "Tomorrow my ship must tow a target for the Venezuelan coast artillery to practice shooting at. [This was true.] Without the service of this man who is now in your jail, my ship will be unable to tow the target. [This was a lie. Though streaming targets was in Clabby's department as chief boatswain's mate, we could easily have done the job without him; it was child's play for any seaman.] Our failure to tow the target will be a serious disappointment for the coast artillery, which I am sure you will not wish them to undergo. So will you please release your prisoner? I assure you that the United States Navy will discipline him." I offered the *administrador* no bribe; I had none to offer him. I do not know that he believed my argument: he struck me as an intelligent man. But he released Clabby under my recognizance. I suspect that he wanted no trouble with the Americans—Caracas might intervene—and did not know what to do with Clabby. He may have felt he could not treat him as he would an ordinary Venezuelan prisoner, which I suspect would have been pretty roughly. I myself did not punish Clabby severely: perhaps I awarded him a few days' loss of liberty, and I reported nothing about the misappropriation of government property. He had just been an ass.

The Duke of Wellington once said: "I don't know whether our soldiers terrify the enemy, but they certainly terrify me." That was the way we felt about our allies, the Venezuelan coast artillery. Towing targets for them to shoot at was our least favorite duty. They were notoriously inaccurate, so that we could never be sure they would not put a shell through the ship instead of through the target, which we towed at what should have been a safe distance astern. They certainly would never have been able to do what they were supposed to do: hit a hostile ship that appeared off the coast. I suspect that the morale of the whole Venezuelan army was low, even though they had inherited the tradition of Bolívar's intrepid troops. They were our allies, but I doubt whether they saw any compelling reason why they should be. In my time the soldiers were still conscripted by press gangs, which would wait for men as they left the movie theaters. One Venezuelan general ordered his gang: "See that nothing escapes me, not even a cat!" At least on the day following Clabby's arrest and release the coast artillery succeeded in avoiding making a hit on our ship but missed the target too.

Once CAFAC sent us to the big American base at Chaguaramas on the beautiful northern coast of Trinidad, just inside the steep islands of the "Dragon's Mouth," the northern entrance to the Gulf of Paria. I think CAFAC sent us there as much to give us a little "rest and recreation" as to effect some minor repairs to the ship. We sailed from Aruba as "tail guard" astern of a main convoy, an ignominious position but one which accurately reflected our military value, for submarines did not have the speed under water to catch up with and make an effective attack on a convoy from astern. That was why the real escort screen was always ahead of a convoy.

We enjoyed ourselves in Trinidad, and then were ordered to proceed independently back to Aruba. That is, we were to sail alone, but the Navy set us a course to follow through the middle of the Caribbean. Since I liked coasting—there is always something to see—I disobeyed orders and sailed along the northeastern coast of Venezuela, passing inside the high and beautiful island of Margarita, called so of old by the Spaniards by reason of its pearl fisheries, and inside the dry reef of Tortuga. All went well. I do not know what the Navy might have done to me if a patrol plane had sighted YMS 59 off her prescribed course. In the ship's log we reported what we had actually done, but in the ordinary course of affairs no one looked at logs. Note that I was learning the charms of disobedience to orders, partly through much sailing alone and not in company and partly through getting away with it.

I have spoken of our regular duties and irregular pleasures. Now I must speak of our disasters, or rather *my* disasters, for the captain is the man who, fairly or unfairly, must take final responsibility for anything that goes awry on his ship, just as he must be the last to leave her if she goes down. My disasters were largely associated with Willemstad, Curaçao, the headquarters of CAFAC, which was too bad, because otherwise Willemstad was far more attractive than Aruba.

In the early days, when I was still overtired and more than usually irritable and when I still thought I must "put up a fight" for my ship, I got into childish quarrels about minor matters with one of the American administrative officers of CAFAC. I do not think I was the only one of the two who was childish, but I must admit my share. I find in my records a copy of a letter this officer wrote to CAFAC in which he stated that a letter I had written him "shows a discourteous, impertinent, disrespectful, and insubordinate attitude." It is true that I have a knack of writing "strong" letters, letters which state my position in a forceful way but, to my mind, imply nothing more. I have discovered that the people who receive these letters not only consider them "strong" but also insulting. I had not yet learned—and still have not learned the lesson so thoroughly that temptation does not sometimes get the better of me—the practical wisdom an anonymous naval officer embodied in a set of verses one of which was: "They prosper who burn in the morning the letters they wrote overnight." In this case CAFAC expressed itself satisfied with the rejoinder I made to the charges brought against me, but I am sure they got into my record and did it no good.

The worst disaster in my naval career also occurred early in our stay at

Aruba-Curaçao. It was brought about by our nagging consciousness of our military inferiority to German submarines. This preoccupation may seem irrational now, since we never did make contact with a submarine, but it did not seem irrational in the fall of 1942. We could not detect the presence of a submerged submarine. Our only hope of avoiding disaster was to surprise one on the surface—but what reason had we to hope that a submarine skipper would let himself be surprised? What is more, a U-boat carried a deck gun of heavier caliber than ours. We would have to get in the first shot and, even then, make a direct hit. In order to get in the first shot, we kept our deck gun loaded at all times when at sea. This was contrary to regulations, because the motion of the ship tended to loosen the shell from the cartridge while both were in the chamber, leading to possible disasters, whose details I shall forgo. Nevertheless my other officers and Chief Clabby allowed me to be persuaded that our only hope lay in adopting this irregular policy. We avoided loosening the shell from the cartridge only to encounter another kind of disaster, whose possibility no one had mentioned to me.

Our deck gun was mounted on our raised forecastle just forward of the bridge and pilothouse. The Bureau of Ordnance had originally developed this gun as an antiaircraft defense for the big ships of the fleet. It had been superseded by more efficient guns, so that there was a surplus available for small craft. It was as large a gun as a ship of our size and construction could well have carried.

One morning we were departing Willemstad, I think to pick up a ship from a main convoy and take her into Aruba. As usual when we were going to sea, I was at the conn on the bridge. The bridge of boats had opened; we had passed through and had almost reached the open sea, when Chief Clabby asked me, according to protocol, for permission to load the deck gun. The chief threw a shell into the chamber; the breechblock slammed closed before it could have been closed by the lever intended for this purpose—and the gun went off. There was no chance even to pull the lanyard of the trigger. Nothing like this had ever happened to us before. I could not have been more startled, especially as, standing on the bridge, I was only a few feet abaft the gun. When I gathered my wits about me, I discovered that the gun had been trained so precisely fore-and-aft that the shell had knocked off the top of the jack-staff on the stem of the ship. That's what one gets by trying to make one's ship look smart! But I could not see that any other damage had been done, so I concluded that the shell had passed harmlessly out to sea, and I continued with my sortie. The Dutch fort, of which we were abeam, signaled to ask what had happened. I signaled back what I thought had happened, and was allowed to go ahead with the operation.

When I got into Aruba a day or two later, I discovered that CAFAC was to convene a Board of Inquiry to investigate the affair, for it turned out that the shell had not flown harmlessly out to sea. It was not a solid shot but a high-explosive shell made to be set off by the arming of a fuse before hitting the target and exploding. Perhaps hitting the jack-staff had both armed the shell and deflected it. At any rate, it had exploded *astern* of the ship. Why it should have done so I never could discover, for the gun was aimed straight forward, towards the open sea. And there it had killed a poor civilian in a small boat—the only man, incidentally, I ever killed in the course of the war. It was a most unlikely series of events.

The Board of Inquiry partly absolved me. Ordnance experts, it appeared, had long known that if the springs were not adjusted exactly right, the shock made by the closing of the breechblock of the 3-inch, 50-caliber gun might trip the firing pin and set off a shell in the chamber. Chief Clabby indeed was aware of this feature of the gun and testified that in the Pacific Fleet it was deliberately exploited to make antiaircraft fire from the gun more rapid because semiautomatic. But Clabby was good enough to testify that he had never informed me of this, nor had any ordnance expert done so. Accordingly in one sense I could not be held responsible for what had happened. On the other hand, the question remained why the gun was loaded at all, which was certainly my responsibility. The Board of Inquiry recommended that I be not brought before a court-martial, but that the board's findings be made part of my record, which was looking worse and worse.

A less severe disaster overtook me when I was ordered to change my berth at the harbor of San Nicolaas in the middle of the night by backing out of one slip and coming alongside another. The purpose was to make room for another vessel. In backing out one of my propeller blades hit a coral head and bent, making one of our engines run so rough as to be unusable. This was an accident I could have avoided, had I not been in such a hurry to get the job of changing berths over with. All the crew, including me, had been waked up and we wanted to get back to sleep. My naval mistakes were almost always the result of impatience.

Repairs to the propeller blade required our going over to the main base at Willemstad, and I was looking forward to a long spell of liberty there. But I reckoned without the ingenuity of the U.S. Navy. I should have known better by this time. Not long before, when in charge of a main convoy from Trinidad to Guantanamo, the old gunboat, U.S.S. *Erie*, had been torpedoed just off Willemstad. This was one of the few occasions when we got hard evidence that submarines penetrated the central Caribbean. The skipper of *Erie* managed to beach her before she sank, and her remains now rested on the rocky coast of Curaçao west of

Willemstad. Though with only one propeller *YMS 59* was no longer fast enough to escort tankers, we were, until our other propeller was repaired, quite fast enough to patrol the waters offshore of *Erie*, and that is just what CAFAC ordered us to do for many weary days. This made no military sense whatever. *Erie* was obsolete before the war began. No German submarine would try to pump more torpedoes or shells into her; she presented no further threat to them. *Erie* was worth less to the Navy than it would cost to get her off, if indeed that could be done. In fact her remains are still there.

But there are principles other than military ones that help explain the behavior of the Navy. One I have already mentioned: keep your arse covered. But I suspect that other, more general, and Calvinistic principles were at work, such as: the devil will always find work for idle hands to do; or even the behavioristic one: never reward anyone for a mistake he has made, that only makes it more likely that he will do it again. Perhaps the sight of the crew of *YMS 59* luxuriating in idleness on the beach was believed to undermine the morale of the other YMSs. At any rate this was the dullest and most useless duty I ever performed in the Navy.

Our final disaster was not my fault at all, nor did the Navy try to blame it on me. Like so many wooden vessels ordered hurriedly in the heat of procuring small craft in preparation for the war, *YMS 59* was built of unseasoned wood. In time her frames and planking shrank, so that we had to take up on all the bolts that held them together. More important, we had been forced to drive her so hard into the chops of the trade wind that she had begun to get out of shape. Between the drive shaft of each of our two diesels and the corresponding propeller was a reduction gear, which literally reduced the revolutions per minute of the former to that of the latter: the two operated most efficiently at different speeds. The diesel shaft and the propeller shaft were designed to lie parallel to one another. When they got out of line, the reduction gear was naturally the weak point where something was likely to give. And that was just what happened: we stripped one of our reduction gears and limped over to the now-existing U.S. Section Base at Willemstad for repairs. The ship could be brought back into something like her original shape by the classic method used on old barns: passing rods through the hull, connected by turnbuckles, which could be swayed up to bring the ship back to her lines. But the base had no spare reduction gear, so one was ordered from the States. That would take time. We were no longer ordered to patrol offshore *Erie*, so for once I could look forward to a period of little duty. The period turned out to be longer than I expected. For another YMS that needed a reduction gear stole ours off the pier at Miami, where it was all ready to be shipped to us. And I had made a stink about Chief Clabby's stealing a mere coil of hawser! A second reduction gear ultimately reached us.

I used my liberty to good purpose. From time to time during the long watches of the night at sea, my mind turned back to the intellectual problems of sociology. When they came to the surface I always found that I had made progress: an unconscious dialogue had been going on in my mind between what I considered to be the typical facts of my science and the intellectual framework in which they might be organized. In my last long stay at Willemstad, in a rush of what seemed like inspiration, as grass suddenly springs up from the desert after the first rains, I made a detailed sketch of a paper I later published entitled "A Conceptual Scheme for the Study of Social Organization."[5] This in turn included the main ideas that went into my book *The Human Group*.[6] But neither was published until after the war, and this was still the year 1943.

In the words of the old sailing-ship chantey:

> *The times are hard and the wages low,*
> *Leave her, Johnny, leave her!*

Some of us old-timers in Aruba and Curaçao were long overdue for relief. Many of the officers and men who had been with us since Charleston had left already, including both of my original junior officers, to be replaced by others now pouring out of the naval training schools. I had granted leave to many men, and from leave they seldom returned, but were assigned to new construction in the United States. From time to time the Navy sent me replacements for certain categories of enlisted men, leaving me to choose whom I would in turn release for reassignment. Under these circumstances one was always tempted to hang on to one's best man and release one less able. It never paid to yield to the temptation. A skipper can do nothing more crucial for maintaining morale than to be fair. Release for reassignment usually carried with it those most coveted of rewards, leave and a trip back to the States. Those who had best served the ship best deserved those rewards. What is more, if one let the best man go, one usually discovered that the person next in line was better qualified to take his place than one had expected, especially as he in turn could now be confident that his own good work would have its reward.

Finally in the summer of 1943, after more than a year under the command of CAFAC, I too requested leave and was granted twenty days in the continental United States. I left Aruba for the last time on August 7, 1943, together with my friendly enemy, Chief Clabby. I believe we were the last of the original ship's company of *YMS 59*. We knew that times had changed when we sailed from Aruba to New York without convoy aboard one of the new fast tankers, *Esso New Orleans*. A submarine could not catch up with us even from abeam, and therefore could not sink us unless we just happened to cross her bows within torpedo range. We enjoyed a calm, pleasant voyage under the command of a splendid Scottish skipper of the old stripe. I enjoyed all to myself a huge stateroom just below the bridge, while Clabby berthed in the crew's quarters. Clabby and I shook hands and said good-bye somewhere on a pier in Bayonne, New Jersey. In my absence I was relieved of command of *YMS 59*, my current executive officer being fully qualified to take charge of what was left of her. Something was left, for I saw her later in Pearl Harbor. Thus ended my third cruise.

Notes

1. Publius Ovidius Naso, *Metamorphoses*, bk. VII, lines 20-21.
2. Samuel Eliot Morison, *Admiral of the Ocean Sea: A Life of Christopher Columbus* (Boston: Little, Brown, 1942).
3. Samuel Eliot Morison, *History of United States Naval Operations in World War II*, 15 vols. (Boston: Little, Brown, 1947-1962).
4. Joseph Conrad, "A Smile of Fortune," in *'Twixt Land and Sea Tales* (Garden City, New York: Doubleday, Page, 1923), pp. 3-88.
5. George C. Homans, "A Conceptual Scheme for the Study of Social Organization," *American Sociological Review* 12 (1947): 13-26.
6. George C. Homans, *The Human Group* (New York: Harcourt, Brace, 1950).

16

THE NAVY III: TRINIDAD-RECIFE

After twenty days' leave spent at my new home in Cambridge, I was ordered to report to the Submarine Chaser Training Center at Miami, Florida. My days as a minesweeper were over—quite rightly, as I had swept no mines and had spent my time in antisubmarine escort work. I was now to get some real training for the job. Nancy joined me and shared the squalid pleasures of Miami Beach.

While I was at home I had a long talk with Clyde Kluckhohn, who with his wife, Florence, had become friends of mine at Harvard before the war. He was now, I think, a full professor of social anthropology. He told me little of the discussions that were to lead after the war to the founding of the Department of Social Relations. But he did suggest that there was likely to be a position open for me at Harvard and urged me to get out of the Navy in order to take advantage of this opportunity, which might not come again.

Naturally I was interested. If there was one thing I was interested in then it was my professional—and I did not mean naval—advancement, though naval officers would still have said that "I had my finger on my number." In 1941 the dean of the Faculty of Arts and Sciences had told me that, war or no war, there would be no vacancy for me at Harvard until 1950. Now it looked as if all that had changed. But how to get out of the Navy while the war was still going on?

To get an answer to this question I consulted my uncle Charlie, who after all had been secretary of the Navy and knew many of the men who were now high in the Navy Department. He agreed to try to help me, made an appointment for me to call on the Chief of the Bureau of Personnel in Washington on my way south to Miami, and gave me a personal letter to him. I duly called on him and he turned down out of hand my request to resign from the Naval Reserve. He and others in the Bureau of Personnel were polite, but I could still sense that they felt some contempt for me. They were right, as I see it now. The war still looked as if it was far from being over. The Western allies had not yet landed in France. Though we were not aware of it at the time, the back of the

German submarine campaign was broken, but many thousands of American marines, soldiers, and sailors were still to die in such places as Iwo Jima and Okinawa. In spite of having served many months at sea, I had done so in a relatively safe berth. What right had I to ask for release when my fellow officers and men were still dying? I really do not believe that I tried to resign in order to escape danger. My reason lay rather in my selfish desire to push my academic career. This is my one mistake in the Navy of which I am wholly ashamed. I made plenty of other mistakes, but I did not consider them moral mistakes. Incidentally, this was the single time I visited Washington in the course of my naval service.

By now the Navy had really learned how to train its reserve officers. The Submarine Chaser Training Center was a good school. Though it did not provide the admirable scientific background of the Mine Warfare School, it did train us thoroughly and practically in the use of the new antisubmarine equipment: radar and sonar (the underwater listening and echo-ranging device). With the new ships thus equipped we had a reasonable chance both to locate a submarine above or below the surface and to sink her. This made all the difference to morale.

I did well at the school. I always did well at *schools*. And on graduation I was asked my preference for my next assignment. With my present seniority, rank as lieutenant, and past experience, I could aspire to becoming executive officer (second in command) of one of the new small escort destroyers (DEs), with the hope of succeeding to the position of skipper before long. Perhaps I was wrong in not making that choice, but I had grown fond of command and did not want to wait for it. In this case it would have to be command of a smaller ship than a DE.

What I did get command of was U.S.S. *PCE 842*. PCE means Patrol Craft, Escort. The Navy never built many of them. They were originally designed as minesweepers, and only a few were converted to escort vessels. They were about the size of British corvettes: some 800-tons displacement, 180 feet long, carrying, besides the usual depth charges, a 5-inch gun on the forecastle and several smaller antiaircraft guns. Unlike *YMS 59*, a PCE was built of steel, looking both broad of beam and rather top heavy, with a capacious flying bridge, from which the watch officers and I conned. I often thought that a PCE might roll over in a heavy gale but I never heard of one's doing so. A PCE was driven by two heavy diesels of the sort used in the engines of freight trains. Unlike the engines of *YMS 59*, they were well up to the work demanded of them, but they still could not move the ship at more than fifteen knots, which meant that we should be limited to escorting slow convoys. We were equipped with both sonar and radar.

A PCE was a reliable ship. Her one weakness lay in her evaporators, the machines that convert salt water into fresh. On a YMS we had no evaporators, as we never went on long voyages and could count on getting enough fresh water in our tanks before going to sea. On *PCE 842* we were to remain at sea for weeks at a time; we might well be forced to depend for fresh water on the evaporators, and they were always "crapping out."

We had what seemed to me a huge ship's company of about eighty men and nine officers, including me. By this time the training centers were turning out more officers than the Navy knew what to do with. As I discovered later, none of my officers had ever been at sea before, except for one, a New Englander, who was a yachtsman like myself. Most of them were middle westerners, born nowhere near tidewater. Still, there was an old story in the Navy that if one wanted to get the best officers and men, one sent a man inland carrying an oar, and not until no one recognized what it was did one begin recruiting. (The story is older than the Navy: it appears in the *Odyssey*.)[1] One advantage of all these officers was that I myself no longer had to stand regular four-hour watches, as I did in my previous ships, though of course I took the conn upon getting under way, coming into port, and attacking submarines, or what were reported to be such. I enjoyed a huge and comfortable main cabin, together with a "sea cabin" just below the flying bridge, where I slept when at sea.

The Navy detached me from duty at the Submarine Chaser Training Center on November 16, 1943, and sent me to Chicago, where the ship was being built, by way of the naval station at New Orleans, where she would ultimately be fitted out. The Navy also sent to Chicago a few key members of the new crew, officers and men, so that they could become familiar with the ship as she was being built, and note any deficiencies. The Pullman Standard Car Company, maker of the famous Pullman cars in the great days of the railroads, was building the ship in South Chicago. I noted in our heads (bathrooms) some of the fittings I had become familiar with while traveling in Pullmans. The company did a good job with *PCE 842*, which did not prevent my making some of my usual snooty remarks to my temporary commanding officer, who was in charge of inspecting naval construction in the Chicago area. In one way or another I am sure these remarks got into my record. Nancy and I stayed in a hotel near the University of Chicago and I went to the yard every day. My blood had been "thinned," as folk medicine calls it, by a year and a half in the tropics, and I have never felt so cold in my life as I did that winter in Chicago, especially when we took the ship out into Lake Michigan, only partly cleared of ice, for trials in January.

When construction was completed, the ship went on down the

Mississippi, by way of the Chicago Drainage Canal, under the command of a pilot. I was ordered to proceed directly to New Orleans, where I was to meet her at the naval station and we took on the crew and the rest of the gear. I much enjoyed my weeks at New Orleans, living as a paying guest in the house of one of the kindest of old Southern families. I approve of New Orleans. One of my best friends among YMS skippers, Wally DuBourg, had also come from there.

It was now that I made another bad mistake, but I was learning, if far too slowly, and this was the last one I was to make as a naval officer. When we had completed fitting out *PCE 842*, a set of naval inspectors came on board to put her through her official sea trials, whose purpose was to determine whether her hull and gear, and especially her engines, met the specifications laid down in her design. Usually a ship's official trials are carried out in the open sea, where there is plenty of room, but New Orleans is far up the river from the sea. Our trials were held on an empty stretch of the Mississippi below New Orleans. Here the river is more than a mile wide, but still a mile is not an unlimited stretch of water. The skipper of the ship is in command during the trials; the inspectors only tell him what the tests shall be, watch and measure speeds, etc.

PCE 842 passed all her preliminary trials without trouble. The final trial required my taking her at full speed through a figure-eight course, with the rudder first being put hard over to one side and then to the other. It should have been obvious to the meanest intelligence, and it was to me, that where the ship started on a maneuver of this kind would determine where she ended up. With my usual impatience to get an irksome job over with, I did not calculate carefully enough where we should start, and in the middle of the second half of the figure eight I realized that if we kept on, the ship would hit the bank. I backed the engines full, but even so we slid gently into the Mississippi mud of the shore. Nothing was to be seen except miles of marsh and waving reeds. I heard the chief boatswain's mate on the forecastle saying, "This does not look like a good liberty port to me."

It did not have to serve as one. We had not hit the mud hard enough to stick. We backed the engines and the ship readily slid off. Tests showed that no damage whatever had been done to hull or gear. The inspectors, kind men, made no comments. On the next attempt, which I started at a different place, we completed the figure eight successfully, and the ship was accepted. I do not believe the inspectors even mentioned the grounding in their report.

The mistake I made was that *I* did. I should have disobeyed orders, as I had in the past. But I did not. Naval Regulations require that all groundings be reported in writing, and this is just what I did. Writing! I wrote far too easily. It seemed to have no effect. No board of inquiry met; I was not reprimanded or relieved of command, but I bet that report got into my record. I was impatient at the wrong times and conscientious at the wrong ones too.

In spite of the troubles I brought upon myself, I had by this time gotten rid of an illusion with which I had entered the war: that as an intellectual I was bound to be incompetent in practical affairs. I had really believed in the myth of the absent-minded professor. Now I had concluded that I was just as "practical" as the average of my fellow officers. True, I was not equally interested in all sides of my temporary profession. I had never been one of those real American boys who enjoy taking cars apart and putting them together again, and I never became much interested in the details of mechanical and electrical apparatus, though I had to listen carefully when told of their failures. But this was a question of interest, not practicality. I was interested and competent, when my impatience did not intervene, in such matters as rigging, ship-handling, and fleet-maneuvering. I was even learning to be an adequate, though never popular, administrator. My fellow commanding officers treated me as one of themselves and never even referred to my being an academic and a Harvard man. On this evidence I decided that though the academic profession was still the right one for me, I could in a pinch make my living in a number of other professions, except perhaps medicine—*the Homans profession*. That I had become conscious of a more generalized competence gave me a great sense of freedom. Provided I survived the war, I was going to make my way.

After our trials, we went down the Mississippi to its mouth in charge of a pilot. Near sunset, we dropped the pilot, went to sea bound for Key West and Miami, and set the first watch. In spite of the fact that few of the officers had been to sea before, nothing went wrong in a night of calm weather. In fact I had an excellent set of officers, though I was unreasonably hard on some of them. At Key West and Miami we went through our "shakedown cruise," culminating in a final series of tests carried out at Miami by officers of the Submarine Chaser Training Center. These tests did not concern themselves with the physical capabilities of the ship but with the military training of her crew. Could we be reasonably expected to be able to do what we would be asked to do? We passed the tests, though without distinction, and were certified as ready for duty. Quite rightly, the Navy had made all the procedures for testing and training the crews of a small craft more formal than they had been when I first went to sea in *Hazel* and *YMS 59*. Indeed in those days no one had tested us at all.

Our assigned duty took me back in the direction from which I had come at the end of my last cruise, that is, to the South Atlantic and away from the main theaters of war. We were to serve on the convoy run between Trinidad and Recife, just around the bulge of Brazil; and as a first step we were ordered to report to the naval base at Trinidad. Accordingly in the middle of March 1944 *PCE 842* sailed independently, following for much of the way the course we had taken in *YMS 59*, but this time without any responsibility for a *Libertad*. We enjoyed a particularly beautiful day running south through the Mona Passage between Hispaniola and Puerto Rico. The sea was dead calm and the visibility high, so that every reef, island, and peak stood out in preternatural clarity. In my experience the Caribbean had been more apt to provide a strong trade wind, a sharp chop, and a smoky haze, like a "smoky southwester" in Buzzards Bay. At the naval station at Chaguaramas in Trinidad, which I had visited earlier in *YMS 59*, I reported for duty as an escort of the next convoy bound southeast for Recife.

Among the links in the convoy routes that now crisscrossed the Atlantic was one running from Trinidad at the southeastern corner of the Caribbean along the northeastern coast of South America past the mouth of the Amazon, around Cape St. Roque, the bulge of Brazil, where part of the convoy usually broke away for Africa, and winding up at Recife, just south of the bulge. I wish it had gone further, but it did not. At Recife the Brazilian navy took over the convoy and dispersed its ships to ports in southern Brazil. As a result we never got to Rio or even to São Salvador da Bahia.

Similarly on the run north we took over the ships of a Brazilian convoy and forwarded them from Recife to Trinidad. Recife means "the reef," and is the capital of the Brazilian state of Pernambuco. Indeed it is itself often, though wrongly, called Pernambuco. The U.S. Navy had a base at Recife, which was the headquarters of the South Atlantic Command, the Fourth Fleet under Jonas Ingram, a really genial admiral. Besides other duties, such as patrolling the gap between South America and Africa against the passage of German surface raiders, the Fourth Fleet was in charge of the convoy run back and forth between Trinidad and Recife. *PCE 842* was assigned to the Fourth Fleet and this run.

In many ways this was a sensible assignment for our ship. The merchant ships on the run were slow, mostly old Liberty Ships, so that a PCE could easily patrol ahead of them. The run was long, and made still longer southeast-bound by the heavy current that sets westward along the northeastern coast of South America, continuing through the Caribbean, and finally shooting out through the Straits of Florida to become the Gulf Stream. This was the current, together with the southeast trade winds, that made the south-bound sailing ships in the old days so fearful of "falling to leeward of Cape St. Roque," that is, falling to the northwest of the cape. Against the combined wind and current they would find it troublesome to get back and around the bulge of Brazil. Accordingly they stood well over towards the coast of Africa before changing course to the southwestward to reach across the southeast trades.

The merchant ships could make about eight knots through the water but, against the current, only about five over the ground, which is slow going. Eastbound it took a convoy about twenty-one days to get from Trinidad to Recife. This made it again appropriate to assign PCEs to the run, for we had good endurance at sea, except for the fickle evaporators. It took a convoy only about eighteen days to make the run in the other direction.

What the Brazil-bound merchant ships carried I do not know; what they carried back from Brazil I certainly do. About half our northeast-bound ships carried coffee, that is, about five ships, each with ten thousand tons of it, per voyage. My jobs in the Navy consisted in providing the Allies with the two commodities they needed most to win the war: oil and coffee. The U.S. Navy, at least, could not have fought the war without coffee. My Crowninshield ancestors would have understood: they made their first fortune out of pepper and coffee.

I enjoyed coasting, and our voyages between Trinidad and Recife were coasting voyages in the technical sense that we were never more than a hundred miles from the coast and sometimes much less. But we might as well have been in mid-ocean. From Trinidad past what were then the Guianas, British, French and Dutch, past the great estuary of the Amazon and almost down to Cape St. Roque, the coast was low and marshy. One could hardly see it before one was on it. By the same token, the continental shelf here was broad and shallow, so that one could be well out at sea and still have only ten fathoms of water under the keel. This had the advantage of limiting the ability of a submarine to operate submerged. At the widest part of the continental shelf the great Amazon River poured out through many mouths the largest volume of water of any river in the world, so that, again, one could be well out of sight of land and still be sailing through water as muddy as the Mississippi at New Orleans, often studded with tree trunks, brought down, it may be, from the Andes, thousands of miles inland. For one who likes his water blue, this kind of seascape is depressing.

The weather was equally peculiar. We left Trinidad in the northeast trades, with their long, smoky swells, and the flying fish taking off around our bows. Unhappily we soon lost the trades and entered the doldrums, which lie along the equator across the mouth of the Amazon and stretch over the Atlantic to the African coast. In my reading about sailing ships I had of course heard about the doldrums, and how their light and baffling winds made it hard work to get through them under sail. They were bad enough for the crew of a power-driven vessel. The windless air was stifling; huge thunderheads stood up all around us, and, as it seemed to me, dumped heavy rain squalls upon us about once every quarter-hour. Sometimes in the distance we saw a waterspout, a kind of small sea tornado, but none ever hit us. The weather added to the depression created by the water of the Amazon. What a joy it was, as we got down towards Cape St. Roque, to pick up the first, fresh, sparkling breath of the other trade wind, the southeast, which then stayed with us to Recife. There it is an onshore breeze and, though only a few degrees south of the equator, keeps Recife in July and August cooler and fresher than Cambridge, Massachusetts.

Yet the doldrums, through which we were to pass so often, had their compensations. Between the great towers of cloud, the sunsets over the unseen mouths of the Amazon were often of a brief but astonishing beauty. The practice in warships at sea in World War II was to go to General Quarters, that is, fully man the action stations, for some half-hour at daybreak and again at sunset. The theory was that ships were most vulnerable to submarine attack at these times, since they were silhouetted against the sun on the horizon. At General Quarters my station of course was on the flying bridge, and there I had a loudspeaker, which I neither had nor needed on *YMS 59*. I also had a captive audience. When appropriate, I enjoyed calling out to the crew at these times, "The attention of all hands is drawn to the beauty of the sunset!" The crew may well have judged that I was crazy or "asiatic," but those are not altogether bad impressions for a skipper to give, for a person who is a little uncanny is also unpredictable, and attention must be paid to him. I will also bet that no one else had ever called the attention of the members of the crew to the beauty of anything.

On my first voyage south to Recife, I crossed the equator and thus became a "shellback." We put on the usual ceremony. King Neptune, who was one of the crew, had to show some tact to one of his initiates who was also his commanding officer. He awarded me a certificate, some of whose clauses reveal the views the crew took of me, naturally the more favorable ones. Among more standard charges, the certificate brought two special charges against me. One was "whispering" and the other, "murdering the English language." As for whispering, I have always had a loud voice and used it. My fellow commanding officers of YMSs used to say that they could detect the approach of *YMS 59* from half a mile away simply from hearing the yells that came from my bridge as I gave orders.

The other charge is more favorably ironic: I doubt that the members of my crew had ever heard as good English as they did from me.

Now let me speak of our main business. In the campaign that came to an end in March of 1943, the Germans had sunk many ships around Trinidad. The wreck-charts were studded with their hulls lying in shallow water. But we arrived a year later. The main campaign was over. Still, individual submarines, not wolf packs, occasionally attacked the Trinidad-Recife convoys, and from time to time naval intelligence, its information based on sources not revealed to me, reported the possible presence of a submarine on our course; but as usual my ship never encountered a submarine though we had some interesting scares. The submarine threat had not declined so much that the convoys were abandoned.

By this time, the organization of a merchant-ship convoy had become standardized. It consisted of several columns of merchant ships, ahead of which in a fan-like formation the naval-escort vessels were deployed, each occupying a sector of the front and patrolling it with random changes of course, so as to confuse the aim of a submarine. In our case the escort consisted of about five PCEs. This so-called screen remained ahead of the convoy from one beam to another of the leading merchant ships in the outboard columns, but not astern, for it was nearly impossible for a submarine to catch up with a convoy from astern. In command of both merchant ships and escorts, and usually sailing in the leading merchant ship of the central column, was the so-called convoy commodore, usually a naval officer of higher rank than ours, called back from retirement. The senior officer of the screen, who was supposed to command the escorts, usually had little to do in that capacity. During daylight, small lighter-than-air aircraft, called blimps, provided us with air cover. Our sailing so close to the coast made this possible; the blimps could be stationed at small hangars scattered along the mainland.

The convoy commodore also called upon the escorts from time to time to perform various training exercises. One of them was to simulate fueling at sea, an operation that enabled the great American fleets in the Pacific to keep the sea for months at a time. One had to bring one's ship close aboard another, supposed to be a tanker, and then hold this position by maintaining the same course and speed as the other, so that if one were alongside a real tanker, the hoses could be passed and the oil pumped. On the part of the ship to be refueled, this required close cooperation through voice-tube between the skipper on the flying bridge, the helmsman just below him in the pilothouse, and the engine-room crew, which had to produce just the right number of rpm to keep the ship moving at the exact speed of the tanker. *PCE 842* and her skipper became recognized as being particularly good at this operation, getting into the correct position quickly and maintaining it steadily. When impatience or impudence did not get in my way, I could be quite effective as a naval officer.

My main business remained sinking submarines or at least protecting convoys against them. If a sonar (or indeed other) contact was made with a submarine, the skipper was supposed to take the conn and make the attack with the advice of his "antisubmarine warfare officer." The two also spent many hours together when ashore working out on an "attack trainer" which simulated the movements of ship and submarine on a screen and allowed an instructor to criticize the skipper's commands. Since a submarine could not attack from astern, it had to attack the convoy from ahead. The speed of advance of the convoy added to the dash toward the convoy by the submarine allowed a skipper only a few minutes in which he could make an attack, between the time of contact and the time the submarine had penetrated the screen. During daylight hours I was generally awake and easily available for dealing with a contact. But submarines usually attacked at night, and then I slept in my sea-cabin, just below the flying bridge, with only my pants on. I might have only a few minutes to go from deep sleep to mortal combat.

I soon discovered that several objects sounded on the sonar as if they were submarines but were not. Often the officer of the deck woke me up quickly and roughly—he had to do so—with the ominous words, "Captain, we have a contact!" I rushed out to take the conn and make an attack, when at the last moment our antisubmarine officer would say, "Sorry, Captain, it's only a school of blackfish." Blackfish (or "pilot whales") are mammals of the whale family, larger than porpoises but smaller than the great whales. At a distance, a school of blackfish made a sound on the echo-ranger of our sonar much like that of a submarine, but on closer approach the sonar would pick up the characteristic clicking noises with which these intelligent animals talk to one another. What a comedown! Back to the sea-cabin and to sleep, if sleep were possible after the excitement of a contact.

On only one occasion did we make what seemed to be a real contact. It did not dash towards the convoy, but it might still be a submarine, so we informed the convoy commodore by voice radio, maintained the contact, which required our leaving the screen, and proceeded to make several attacks in the most approved manner. We dropped many thousand dollars' worth of depth charges, setting off many splendid big bangs. So splendid were they that I was afraid the shock would trip a circuit breaker and stop the engines while we were still dropping charges: one would really be a damn fool if one blew one's stern off with one's own TNT, that is, if one was hoist with one's own petard. But the contact, instead of splitting into a cluster of echoes, as it would have done if it had been a real submarine and we had succeeded in hitting it underwater, or being blown to the surface, the supreme triumph of any antisubmarine warrior, as he can then prove he has made a kill, continued to sound just as it had done when we made our first attack.

At that point we decided to check the ship's position on the chart, which we had neglected to do in the excitement of the contact. Of course we could not be sure of our position within a matter of yards, but we were northwest bound, just around Cape St. Roque; the bottom was shallow but rocky; we had not reached the muds of the Amazon estuaries, and the chart recorded an underwater reef close to where we might have been. Since the great westerly current was flowing over it, the sonar would record it as having relative motion just like a submarine. We finally abandoned our vain attacks and took off after the convoy, now many miles to the westward of us. When we made our report, including our recorded data, to the unit in Washington that evaluated submarine attacks, it concurred in our judgment that what we had been attacking was not a submarine. When we passed that way later in the other direction, I was told that some members of the crew had referred to the reef as "Homans's folly." I should be proud to have any reef named after me, folly or not. And better "Homans's folly" than "Norman's Woe!" After all we had, for once, done just what the book told us to do. That our attack was unsuccessful was a detail. Most attacks on submarines, real or imaginary, were unsuccessful.

In spite of the exercises the convoy commodore put us through and the occasional contact, time at sea on these really long voyages often hung heavy on my hands, especially as I no longer had to stand regular watches. I reviewed my calculus by taking a standard, nonelementary textbook to sea with me. In the course of time I worked all the problems, finishing the last one just as the war ended: it was appropriately the problem of finding the formula for the volume of a *torus* or anchor-ring. After my first visit to Recife, I learned at least to read Portuguese, the language of Brazil. For someone like me who already knew French and Latin, learning to read Portuguese was easy. Learning to speak it well was another matter: the vowels are nasal and tricky. But I read Camões's *Os Lusiadas*,[2] the great epic of Vasco da Gama's voyage, and Euclides da Cunha's *Os Sertões* (The Backwoods),[3] a classic account of a famous peasant revolt in the desperately poor backlands of northeastern Brazil, behind Recife. I also read Gilberto Freyre's books on the social history of the Northeast, especially *Casa-Grande e Senzala*[4] (Big House and Slave

Quarters). Freyre was a native of Recife, which is, so to speak, the capital of the Northeast, as Boston is the capital of New England. On the strength of his being a fellow sociologist and a Columbia Ph.D., I made Freyre's acquaintance and visited him with great pleasure at his house in Apapucos outside Recife. As a political opponent of the then current dictator, Getulio Vargas, he was kept under not very stringent house arrest.

It is now time to describe Recife, our base, the port to which we brought and from which we took our convoys. It was the only city in Brazil I ever saw. Its name comes from the reef, now strengthened into a breakwater, which makes its small harbor. Alongside the breakwater lay a Brazilian battleship of World War I vintage, which never moved and could not have done so, but whose guns might have provided some coast defense, I suspect about as effective as the Venezuelan coast artillery. We escort vessels made fast to a long quay, which was also a main street, across from the breakwater.

Recife had, I believe, been originally founded sometime in the sixteenth century by a member of the great family of Albuquerque, relatives of the admiral who had destroyed the Arab fleets off Hormuz and thus won for Portugal about a century of control over the Indian Ocean. The Dutch had briefly conquered the city at the height of their seapower at the beginning of the seventeenth century. The Portuguese then recovered it, and on the coastal lowlands developed a typical plantation economy producing sugar by slave labor in the form both of local Indians and of Blacks imported from Africa. This was the society Gilberto Freyre described. Sugar was still in my time grown in the neighborhood of Recife, and the waterfront streets still held its sickly smell. A very different economy, of free peasants barely maintaining their subsistence, obtained in the higher country inland from Recife, subject to fierce droughts. This was the country described by Euclides da Cunha. I never reached it.

Recife was not a particularly attractive city. In terrain it was flat, but compensated in part for its flatness by a few interesting internal waterways, which had earned for it the thoroughly exaggerated title of "the Venice of South America." It possessed a few of the extravagant baroque churches, decorated with blue tiles (*azulejos*), which were so marked a feature of old Brazil. But just as Recife could not compare with Rio in its natural setting, so it could not, I am told, compare in baroque churches with São Salvador da Bahia to the southward.

More attractive than Recife itself was Olinda, the original settlement, now a suburb. It was built on a hill and was our first landfall when we came in from sea. Covered with old, decaying white houses behind high walls, it gave me the same feeling of the life in death of an old society that, in their different ways Oranjestad in Aruba and Muruy on Paraguaná had done.

I thought I knew what poverty was, but I did not until I got to Recife. It was awash with desperately poor people living in mere shacks along the beaches and other slums. To my eyes, they were nothing like the poor but self-respecting fishermen I had known in Bahía Boca de las Piedras. Instead they seemed to me the corrupt poor, the *lumpenproletariat* of Marx. I may well have been mistaken, as I had little contact with them. Let me speak instead of the bourgeoisie, with whom I did have some contact.

I was introduced to Recife society at the *Clube Portuguesa*, which at regular intervals put on dances to which American naval officers had standing invitations. Many of us attended in our white, starched, dress uniforms. There I encountered a culture more different from that of the United States than any I had yet known. I felt I had entered some provincial capital of France under the Third Empire. The girls in their very best dresses sat in a semicircle around the dance floor, each attended by a chaperon—I do not know the Portuguese for *duenna*—an older woman dressed in severe black and apparently speechless. Having sighted a beautiful or interesting-looking girl, one approached the duenna, bowed, and requested in one's sketchy Portuguese one's desire to dance with the girl under her protection. One was never refused, but one had to go through these motions. During the dancing, it was perfectly proper to talk to one's partner in such Portuguese as one could muster up or in whatever other language both understood: in my case this language always turned out to be French, not English. It was not proper to "cut in" as we did in the United States in those days, or take the girl off the floor; and after the particular dance ended, one had to return the girl to her chaperon. The music was good; I became a good dancer of the *samba* (it is an easy dance) just as I had become a good waltzer in Boston.

The dances offered me special pleasures besides the dancing itself. To an historian, such as I was, particularly a naval historian, it was exciting to hold in one's arms a female Magellan (Maghalães) or Albuquerque. The two Albuquerque girls were very beautiful, tall and willowy, with the *matte* white skin of the northern Iberian aristocrats. Descendants of the Visigoths perhaps?

To a sociologist, it was interesting and enjoyable to be able to dance with women of almost every color or physical type, from pure Whites, like the Albuquerques, to practically pure Blacks. For the first time in my life I danced with a Black woman. Indeed persons of White European, Black African, and native American origin—and every combination of these three—could become members of Recife "society," at least as represented by the *Clube Portuguesa*. I picked up the veiled impression that the whiter one was, the better, but no one was excluded on the grounds of color alone. Though no doubt one was excluded if one could not afford to learn and maintain the manners of the local bourgeoisie, color itself did not count. One could meet women a little more informally at the British tennis club, but the chaperons were still on hand.

With very few exceptions these contacts with women went no further. Members of the bourgeoisie never invited American officers to their homes until they had satisfied themselves by thorough inquiries that the officers in question were, first, unmarried, and second, had either inherited money or had good prospects in life once the war was over. I made no secret of the fact that I was married, so naturally I was not invited, but there were plenty of unmarried officers who never saw the inside of a Recifian home. True, I had visited Gilberto Freyre, simply as a fellow sociologist. I was told that a few American officers had married local girls; I never personally met one.

On my side, I tried from time to time to invite women I had danced with or met at the "British" club to have luncheon in the wardroom of our ship, making it clear that the duennas were invited too. This kind of party could not be more innocent; it would give my officers pleasure, and our Navy certainly would not have disapproved. The reply to my invitations was inevitable and uniform: "*Os costumes de Pernambuco não permitem*" (the customs of Pernambuco do not permit it).

I once asked an attractive and especially intelligent young woman called Jacqueline Ayres what she did with her time in Recife. She said that on most days she was allowed out of her house only for a short walk and then only in company with another girl. I knew she had received part of her education in Paris. (None of the women had been educated in Great Britain or the United States.) So I asked her whether in Paris she had been kept under the same restrictions. No, she was allowed much more freedom there. I decided it was hell to be a young woman in Recife, and I guessed it was not much better to be a married one, at least if one abided by the rules. I also knew that in all societies there were methods of getting around the rules. I imagine that by now the *costumes* themselves have changed. Modernism must have been stronger than even the bourgeoisie of Recife.

Besides these amusements (or nonamusements) of the bourgeoisie, we sometimes attended parties of a very different kind, held at a place called Beberibe, a short distance inland from Recife. The dance hall consisted simply of a big thatched roof, open to the jungle on all sides. From the Navy both officers and men attended, and from the Brazilians all sorts of men and women—except the bourgeoisie. In contrast to the *Clube Portuguesa,* there were no duennas, no introductions, for the time being no social classes. Everyone was on his or her own. One might dance with any woman one could persuade to dance with one. And the band was marvelous, especially in the fierce beat of the *marcha de Carnaval.* In Latin-American countries Carnival is the time of relaxation that precedes the austerities of Lent. Every year Brazilian musicians compete in writing *marchas* to be played in the coming Carnival. Beberibe came close to being an orgy. I never enjoyed dancing for its own sake more than I did there.

I must at last speak of the morale problems I met with—and often created—on *PCE 842,* for morale problems should be closest to the interests of a sociologist.

One fact colored my behavior as skipper throughout our convoy duty. When I first arrived at Recife I found I had been "passed over" for promotion from lieutenant to lieutenant commander, while all the other officers of my rank had been promoted. In the wartime Navy promotion through the rank of lieutenant was pretty much automatic; it depended on time spent in a lower rank. The method of promotion to higher ranks was different. The Bureau of Personnel convened in Washington special boards consisting of officers whose rank was just above that of the candidates for promotion, so chosen because they were presumed to be more familiar than were more senior officers with the special conditions the candidates had faced. They reviewed the records of the candidates and decided which were to be promoted. There is no perfect way of deciding promotions, but this has always seemed to me as effective and fair a one as has ever been devised.

Accordingly I must not blame the board for failing to promote me. Consider my record: it showed one killing of a civilian (admittedly not altogether my fault), two groundings, and several snooty letters to administrative officers ashore. The board had to compare this record against thousands of spotless ones. Had I been a member of the board I should no doubt have reached the same conclusion. And had I been an officer of the regular Navy, being passed over would no doubt have ruined my career, in the sense that I probably should never have made admiral. As it was, the chief practical difference being "passed over" made was that many officers, hitherto my juniors, were now my seniors. I could no longer be escort commander, but that was a small loss. Nevertheless, and quite irrationally, my failure made me morose, and I took it out on some of my own officers. I was not passed over again.

I felt that I had treated my officers and men in *YMS 59* much too easily. Conditions in Aruba and in Las Piedras had allowed me to. *PCE 842* was to be different: she was to be a "taut ship." I instituted a regular captain's inspection even when at sea. (As the old saying went, "There are no Sundays off soundings.") But most skippers had given up this naval practice while at sea in wartime. It offered me a chance to go over every part of the ship, and each part was the responsibility of one of my officers. Since I could always—literally always—find something wrong, captain's inspection gave me a chance to work off my spleen on officers whose personal characteristics happened to vex me. These had nothing to do with their abilities as naval officers. To a man, they were effective and conscientious. Their virtues spoke loudly in favor of the middle class in the United States. But for reasons I could not make conscious I just did not like some of them. "I do not love thee, Dr. Fell: the reason why I cannot tell." I did nothing to hurt their careers; I just exercised on them my high capacity to be verbally nasty. I ought not to have done so. Yet the PCE *was* a taut ship.

I was also beginning to understand the social isolation a ship's captain suffers on long voyages. As Captain Marryat wrote, and he had had plenty of experience, "being captain of a ship may truly be designated as *solitary confinement*."[5] Though I took my meals with the other officers in the wardroom, I no longer shared their lives as I had with the officers of YMS 59 by standing watches just like theirs. And in that ship we were hardly ever more than a night away from base: my officers could escape from me. Now we were at sea for weeks at a time, while I held the powers of a petty tyrant. I began to understand how serving as skipper could make men not a little mad, whether in the form of a Captain Queeg or in that of a Captain Ahab. To have power and to be isolated from men of equal or superior power is bad for a man. Power corrupts and isolated power corrupts absolutely. I also began to understand from my own experience what I had learned from anthropological texts: the strongly ambivalent attitude subordinates hold towards persons in authority over them.

None of this made me a popular skipper, but I was cheered to discover that I was not alone in this respect. When, after three weeks at sea, we finally made fast at Recife, my equals, the commanding officers of the other escort vessels, and I, who of course had not seen one another during the long voyage, at once got together in the Hotel Grande for drinks, and when we were in our cups, we never failed to agree in the most maudlin fashion that "Nobody loves me aboard my ship!"

But there were degrees in not being loved. I came to a conclusion that Herman Melville had reached long before in *White-Jacket,* his account of his voyage home from the Pacific as a seaman aboard an American frigate. His conclusion was that naval officers who came from the South were naturally more at their ease in exercising authority, and therefore less likely to antagonize their subordinates, than officers from the North, like me.[6] Melville accounted for the difference by the degree to which officers had been used to exercising authority. Southern officers from their earliest days held command over the unfortunate Black slaves or their modern descendants. We northerners had no such experience, felt a bit guilty about exercising authority, tended to overplay it when we were forced to use it, and needed some time to come to terms with it. If this explanation is correct, it illustrates one, perhaps the only, good feature of a caste society. If power corrupts, there may also be something, sometimes, to be said for effortless superiority.

The beginning of wisdom for a man in command at sea, or indeed anywhere, is to learn that, though one is in theory a tyrant, there are always some orders one cannot get obeyed. The orders one does *not* give are the most interesting ones. The greatest weakness of *PCE 842* lay in her evaporators, which were always "crapping out." When they did so early in a voyage, I wondered whether the engineers could repair them in time, and, if not, whether we had enough fresh water in the tanks to keep us going until we reached port, and I tried to hit upon ways of conserving water. Work in these humid tropics made for much sweat; naturally the men were always taking showers, and for washing fresh water is far superior to salt. Over the loudspeakers I decreed that no more fresh-water showers were to be taken, and I gave the reasons. Was my order obeyed? It was not. Not even if we had carried marines on board, and I had set one as sentry over every shower faucet, would the order, I suspect, have been obeyed. Nor would the exercise of the skills of human relations, such as nondirective interviewing, which Mayo had taught me, have made the slightest difference. Only if we had in fact run out of fresh water and as a result had been forced to forgo showers or even to go thirsty would the crew have obeyed such an order in the future. I have often wondered whether anything but direct experience ever teaches humankind. I often hoped we should run out of water, but we never did. Accordingly the crew never learned the risks we ran, and I earned nothing but ill will for my efforts to take utterly reasonable precautions.

In the same way I have often wished that those of my students who call for a new kind of society to be brought in by a violent revolution—if no blood is shed, the revolution cannot be real—would actually experience such a revolution and the regime that follows upon it. Not lectures, not "listening," as we used to listen to patients, but only actual experience would have taught them, and then they would have learned too late.

A skipper must learn not only that his orders are often not obeyed, and that in the future he should not give such orders; he must also learn that he himself cannot survive without some cooperation from his crew, and that they must give it freely.

Even a ship as small as ours is divided into subgroups by the special tasks they perform, the two largest being the men who work on deck, sometimes called the "deck apes," and the men who work on the engines, called the "black gang," though they are not as black as they used to be in the days of coal-fired boilers. Besides standing their regular watches, in our case four hours on and eight off, all the members of the crew normally "turn to" for other work during daylight hours. This is especially true of the deckhands under the chief boatswain's mate, for the battle against rust on a ship is relentless and unending. On the other hand, the work in the engine room in the tropics was very hot, and perhaps our dependable diesels did not require much work to be done on them. With the permission of the engineering officer, members of the black gang not on watch were not required to "turn to," and they took to lolling about on deck, where, at least in the trades, there was always a breeze. The sight of their taking their ease infuriated the deckhands, who were breaking their arses at chipping and painting. The bosun complained to me. Acting with my usual impulsiveness, I decreed that members of the black gang not on watch should "turn to" forthwith.

My reaction precipitated a counterreaction. A delegation of the black gang, supported by the chief machinist's mate and the engineer officer, waited on me to protest in their turn. This time I showed some sense: I did not fly into a temper and act as if I had a mutiny on my hands. Instead we talked and finally worked out a compromise: members of the black gang not on watch would not be required to "turn to"; on the other hand they would not flaunt their leisure before the deckhands; while off watch they would stay below, in their bunks if they so desired, but they would not be visible and therefore infuriating on deck. As far as I know the compromise worked. But I should have consulted the persons concerned before I gave the order and not afterwards. Military organizations are geared to emergency action, and in emergencies orders must often be given precipitately and obeyed without question. The danger inherent in this kind of organization is that persons in command may come to treat all situations as if they were emergencies.

My last example of a disciplinary problem was of a different kind. Perhaps out of sheer bad luck I tended to run into trouble with my ships' cooks. While *PCE 842* was lying alongside the quay at Recife, one of my officers drew my attention to the fact that our current cook was enticing Brazilian civilians aboard the ship to do much of his work for him, and paying them off in cans of Spam. As in Venezuela, Spam served as currency in Brazil. Unfortunately it also remained the property of the

U.S. government. On the surface, the case called for severe disciplinary action. On the other hand, two of my officers argued that the cook's problem was really medical. One was a commissioned officer who, before entering the Naval Reserve, had had training in social work. The other was our chief pharmacist's mate, who, while not being a commissioned officer, was the head, so to speak, of our medical department. A rumor was abroad that he had once held an M.D. but had lost his license by performing an abortion. (Remember that this was in the year 1944.) Dramatically, the rumor ought to have been true, but I suspect it was not. Both officers I considered wise men. The chief had diagnosed the cook's problem as anemia, which left him with so little energy that he had to get others to do his work.

The two officers persuaded me, and therefore, instead of taking disciplinary action, I sent the cook ashore to the small American hospital. But the doctors there refused to accept him as a patient suffering from physical illness and returned him to the ship. I was sure that they were mistaken, but what was I to do now? I felt strongly that to keep the cook on board and let him go on as he had been going would set a very bad example for the ship's company. The medical option closed, I felt I must adopt the disciplinary one. Perhaps we could have found a third, and still better, option, if we felt we had time. But at the moment the only way I could get the cook off the ship was to call a court-martial that would award him a bad-conduct discharge from the Navy. We held a court-martial, with the former social worker acting as defense attorney for the cook. In spite of his efforts, the court decided in favor of discharge. I felt then, and I still feel, that I did deliberate injustice to an individual in order to safeguard the greater good of the organization. In my small way, I had done injustice "for reasons of state." This kind of choice is forced on one more often, the higher one rises in an organization. Accepting responsibility for it is one of the heaviest burdens of command. At least his bad-conduct discharge got the cook a trip back to the States.

Whether a person in command does harm to people inadvertently, or out of sheer bad temper, or for reasons of state, he is bound, if he has not wholly lost his humanity, to feel guilty. I would not have him become hardened, though that is all too likely to be his fate. At the same time I would urge him, if he can, to get his guilt under control. For the need to expiate his past guilt may cloud his judgment and lead him to overcompensate, the next time he faces a moral decision. I wish I could tell him how to get his guilt under control. I know no method that will guarantee success. Every commander must try to find his own. All I can do is to warn him that the problem will force itself upon him.

On August 22, 1944, at the end of a convoy passage from Recife to

Trinidad, I was relieved of command of *PCE 842* and sent back to the States for leave and further assignment. My excellent executive officer, Lieutenant W. W. Smyth, was fully qualified to take command. I am sure that some of my officers were glad to see me go. At any rate, I walked down the pier at Trinidad without once looking back at the ship, and then flew to New York. Thus ended my fourth cruise in the Navy. I had done harm, as in giving our cook his discharge, but I felt that decision was forced upon me. Otherwise, I had made no major mistakes since New Orleans. I have always kept warm memories of Brazil and Recife, which have helped me forget the boredom of escorting slow ships through the doldrums.

NOTES

1. Homer, *Odyssey*, bk. XI, line 125.
2. Luiz de Camões, *Os Lusíadas*, first published 1572 (many editions).
3. Samuel Putnam, *Rebellion in the Backlands*, trans. from Euclides da Cunha, *Os Sertões* (Chicago: University of Chicago Press, 1949).
4. Gilberto Freyre, *Casa-Grande e Senzala*, 4th ed., 2 vols. (Rio de Janeiro: José Olympio, 1943).
5. Frederick Marryat, *Newton Forster or The Merchant Service* (many editions), ch. 1.
6. Herman Melville, *White-Jacket*, ch. 34.

17

THE NAVY IV: THE PACIFIC

My last tour of duty—of course I did not know it was to be my last—began by looking as if it were to be much like the others. I thought I was apt to continue in small ships in antisubmarine escort duty and probably in an unimportant theater of war. As far as combat was concerned nothing could have been quieter than the South Atlantic in 1944. Instead I was assigned to a wholly different kind of duty and wound up in the very center of the naval war, that is, the Pacific.

The reason I thought I was going to continue as before was that, after the usual brief leave, I was ordered to report for a refresher course to the Submarine Chaser Training Center at Miami. As usual I did well, and the officers at the center thought I might get a higher command in antisubmarine warfare. I might even aspire to the command of a frigate, a name revived to describe a large, slow, escort vessel, about the size of a destroyer escort, and designed for long-distance convoys. Instead, on November 22, 1944, I was ordered to report to the Beach Battalion School, Amphibious Training Base, at Oceanside, California, just north of San Diego, for training, as it turned out, as a division beachmaster. I was going to leave the escorts for what we called the "amphibs" and to leave the sea to carry out my main duty on the beach.

We seagoing officers looked down on assignment to the amphibs as a fate worse than death. Especially we all thought that service as beachmaster meant almost certain death. I wondered whether the Bureau of Personnel was punishing me for my past sins. As we used to say, "I must be on their shit list." A later and cooler judgment suggested that this diagnosis was almost certainly wrong. It is very bad policy to punish a man for his past sins when he has already been thoroughly punished. That will destroy any hope he may have for recouping himself by doing his new job well. And the job of division beachmaster, though unpleasant enough, was exceedingly important, and required good men if it were to be done well. Moreover, my so-called "fitness reports" had been looking much better recently.

More likely, the Navy recognized that the Germans' submarine campaign was broken, partly because all their important bases on the French coast were now in Allied hands. No more officers were needed for antisubmarine work in the Atlantic, and in the Pacific, for reasons not clear to me, Japanese submarines had never been a great menace. On the other hand, in the Pacific many officers were needed for amphibious warfare, especially for what the American military services were anticipating as being the culminating campaign of the war: the great assault on the main islands of Japan. Only a very few persons knew that the atomic bomb might allow us to escape that encounter, which could not help being drenched in blood.

What was a division beachmaster? First, in the organization of the Amphibious Forces, a transport division (Transdiv), if it was like the one I was to join, consisted of seven ships. All of them were converted "Victory" cargo ships, displacing 15,000 tons each. Five of them were "attack transports" (APAs) designed to land troops. For this purpose they carried outboard, on davits, a number of landing craft. In an assault, these were lowered into the sea and filled with troops. On orders, they formed a line, rushed for the beach, and, when they hit it, they lowered their bows like ramps, and the troops charged ashore. Then, lightened of their load and, it was hoped, unscathed by enemy fire, the landing craft were supposed to retract from the beach and return to the mother ship for more soldiers. The two other ships in the division were "attack cargo" ships (AKAs) designed to land heavy military materiel rather than troops.

Each ship of the division carried a small beach party, largely equipped for communications. In an assault on a hostile beach, the beach party went ashore with an early wave of the assault troops, took charge of the section of beach assigned to it, and in communication with its division beachmaster, the captain of its ship offshore, and the commander of the troops moving inland—the beach party might in fact of course be pinned down by enemy fire—tried to see that traffic moved smoothly across the beach, that bottlenecks were cleared, and that the troops ashore got what they needed when they needed it. If the beach party under the ship's beachmaster did not do its job well, it could create the most deadly foul-ups, and foul-ups were almost certain if the enemy were able to prevent our troops' crossing the beach. The Japanese would certainly try to do just that. For this period the beach party would be as much under fire as the soldiers. Even if our infantry did succeed in moving inland, the enemy might still shell the beach from a distance. In short, the job was both important and dangerous. Its only advantage was the short period a beach party remained in action. If the assault failed, its members were likely to die. If it succeeded, they were unlikely to stay on the beach more than a day or so: they withdrew as soon as their ship had unloaded troops or cargo.

A commodore, a rank just below rear admiral, which the Navy had revived for the duration of the war, commanded the seven ships of a transport division. And the commodore had a staff. The operations officer was in effect the chief of staff, with the duty of drawing up plans and carrying out the routine administrative duties of the command. Other members of the staff included an intelligence officer and the division beachmaster. The staff also included a small complement of enlisted men, mostly communications specialists (radiomen) or administrative (yeoman) types. The staff sailed on one of the APAs of the division, which was specially fitted with a flag bridge, above the ship's own bridge, containing communications equipment. If the division was operating as a unit, either at sea or in an assault, the commodore gave his orders from this bridge.

I was to be division beachmaster on the staff of such a transport division commander. In an assault my duty was to go ashore and "coordinate" the work of the individual beach parties of the ships of my division. In this capacity I was never sure under whose command I should fall: my own commodore or the beachmaster on the staff of the next higher echelon, the squadron. This potential duality of command is characteristic of line-and-staff types of organization, about which I was later to lecture so often. And no doubt I should have to work with both these officers and with the commanders of the assault troops. Accordingly there was no reason to question my need for communications support.

In an assault I should probably go in with the fourth wave of troops— and that is a mighty early wave. I too would take a beach party ashore with me, consisting of radiomen and signalmen. I would also take ashore my own jeep, equipped with especially elaborate communications gear and built to be driven through several feet of sea water without flooding. Its most conspicuous feature was an exhaust pipe that stuck several feet up in the air, that is, out of the water. In this jeep I could, in theory, move from one part of my beach to another. It was my movable command post ashore. As matters turned out, my jeep gave me a great deal of pleasure, not by meeting the purpose for which it was designed but for sightseeing. Finally, it should be clear that a beachmaster and his party, when not engaged in an assault, real or practice, had nothing whatever to do.

Though I could intellectually appreciate its importance, I did not look forward to the job of division beachmaster one little bit. I thought of myself as a seaman and especially as a sea captain. Now I was to become a sort of landsman and a staff officer to boot. Since I had been brought up on the coast of New England, I knew a great deal by experience about beaches, surf, and tides, but I felt that nothing else prepared me for being a beachmaster.

Nor was I encouraged by my experience at the Beach Battalion School at Oceanside. It was far inferior to both the Mine Warfare School and the Submarine Chaser Training Center. It was really only a depot for officers and men waiting for assignment to ships not yet ready for them. I did at least meet the men who would form my beach party, but we had little to do. Our only training consisted in making several landings through the surf on the beaches of Camp Pendleton, the great Marine base on the West Coast. Those landings at least made us familiar with the way the small landing craft behaved. But that was all, and it was cold work in the winter. One thinks of southern California as warm. Not in the winter. Apart from the landings, every evening a cold fog penetrated our quarters, which were inadequately heated. Happily we did not stay at Oceanside long. It had done nothing to persuade me I could master a beach. But then—let it be said now—I never did have to master a beach except in training exercises. But this was becoming my regular experience: I had never tended a net, swept a mine, or fought a submarine, though I had been meant to do each of those tasks. And as so often before, so now with beachmastering. Yet I did not miss in retrospect what I had so much dreaded in prospect, for I drew experience from each of these jobs, though it was not the experience the Navy intended.

On January 30, 1945, I embarked on what proved to be my last cruise. Though I was now sure the Allies would not lose the war, I was not sure when, if ever, they would win it. The Germans had just proved in the Ardennes that they could strike back, and we had hardly laid a hand on the Japanese main islands.

Specifically I reported to Commander Transport Division 69 to be a member of his staff as division beachmaster. The staff berthed aboard the designated flagship of the division, U.S.S. *Randall* (APA 224), then lying in San Diego. I liked the other members of the staff, especially the intelligence officer, Joe Estes, who joined us later and who became after the war a federal judge in Texas. Above all I liked my commanding officer, Commodore Paul R. Glutting, USN, who, strangely enough, had been one of my instructors way back in the Harvard ROTC. That experience did not seem to have left him embittered towards me. I had not always got on easily with my commanding officers, but I always got along splendidly with him.

Shortly afterwards, *Randall* went to sea, and for the few months that remained of the war I saw a good deal of that other ocean, the Pacific. For some time the remaining ships of our division did not mobilize under our command, and *Randall* was employed independently on various odd jobs. Under these conditions, she did not come under ComTransDiv 69 but remained under that of her own skipper, so that our staff in theory had nothing to do. But by this time I was well aware of American naval doctrine and knew that having nothing to do did not mean doing nothing. Sure enough, Commodore Glutting soon had us standing regular watches on the flag bridge, looking at the sea, which was of no use, since the ship's officers, on the bridge below, were already keeping a lookout, and writing up a log, which was of no use either, since the ship's watch officers already kept one. I did not hold this against the commodore, I knew all officers of the regular Navy would behave in this way. But I did resent going back to standing regular watches after the freedom I had enjoyed in *PCE 842*. After my naval experience I have decided that the single unalloyed human good is a whole night in the sack.

From San Diego we sailed to the famous Pearl Harbor on Oahu, and then with a miscellany of other vessels conducted a perfunctory landing exercise on the lee side of the island of Maui, on the beaches of the giant extinct volcano Haleakala. There I went ashore with my beach party in the midst of xerophytic scrub like that of the Paraguaná peninsula.

From Pearl Harbor *Randall* sailed independently, on some errand I have now forgotten, to Kwajalein atoll in the Marshall Islands. It is the largest atoll in the world and surely one of the world's extraordinary sights: a circle of coral, the coral itself perhaps a hundred yards wide at its widest and perhaps five feet high at its highest, but the whole circle enclosing a lagoon perhaps fifty miles long, so long at least that one could not see from one end to the other. I have forgotten whether we returned to Pearl Harbor, but if we did so we sailed west again to Eniwetok, an atoll almost as large as Kwajalein. There for the first time I felt the overwhelming force of the American military effort, which I had certainly not felt on the coasts of South America. Eniwetok was crammed with shipping as far as the eye could see. We also went to Ulithi and Guam, I have forgotten in which order.

Above all, we went to the island of Iwo Jima, where I first saw action, though I did not take part in it. There the American marines had just carried out one of the most famous and bloody assaults of the Pacific campaign. We thought we needed the island to facilitate the attacks of our Flying Fortresses on Japan. Except for this fact it had no importance at all. It had no harbor; ships simply anchored on the lee side. It was only four miles long, just long enough to hold an airfield. And it cost us 25,851 marine casualties. I thought of Hamlet's question about the expedition Fortinbras was making to Poland, in order to

> *fight for a plot*
> *Whereon the numbers cannot try the cause,*
> *Which is not tomb enough or continent*
> *To hide the slain.*[1]

I thought of these lines especially when the body of a Japanese soldier floated past the ship. Iwo Jima had not been large enough to hold *him*.

The atmosphere of the island was eerie. The whole area is volcanic underwater, and as we approached the island I saw smoke rising out of the open sea, where presumably a volcano was active in the depths and slowly building up a new island.

Thank God! We were not part of the original assault on Iwo Jima. I should have hated to try to master one of those short, steep beaches of black volcanic sand. Instead we brought in Army troops to replace the marines who had made the original assault. The island was under our control, but fighting was still going on, as marines with flamethrowers blasted the last of the Japanese out of the caves and tunnels they had carved deep into the rock.

Let me change to a very different kind of subject. The mores of the Pacific Fleet were very different from those of the Atlantic. It sometimes seemed as if never a law of God or man—certainly not of the Navy—ran west of Pearl Harbor. The difference was especially clear in the matter of liquor. According to Naval Regulations, no drinking of alcohol, except for medicinal purposes, was to take place aboard an American naval vessel. Of course one might drink ashore, and there was plenty of good liquor in the West Indies and Brazil. The British sent some of their best liquor there in order to build up their foreign exchange. The rules of the British Navy itself were different from ours. Aside from the traditional tot of rum, it allowed officers off watch to drink in the wardroom, and when we were in port in company with British ships—and we often were both in Charleston and the West Indies—their officers positively plied us with liquor with every intention of getting us drunk. But in the Atlantic Fleet, so far as I knew, the rule against drinking aboard ship was still strictly enforced, with the exception of the skipper of *Hazel*.

But the Pacific Fleet was different. The Navy had established a few officers' clubs ashore, but they were so crowded that, when one at last reached the bar, one ordered six drinks at a time, because one might never be able to reach it again. What made the Pacific different from the Atlantic Fleet was drinking at sea. A few of us aboard *Randall*, both from the ship's officers and the staff's, got into the habit of having a few drinks together in the evenings when we were off duty, the alcohol coming from the medical stores. I remember enjoying this relaxation, but I do not remember the conversation except that it was earthy. One reserve officer, brought up on a farm, described eloquently the pleasures of sexual intercourse with sheep. One advantage the Navy certainly provided me with, though fieldwork in Pennsylvania had begun to do it: I learned about men and seamen, not just the Brahmins of Boston or the rich of New York, but a whole range of American, perhaps even human, types.

Randall went back to San Francisco, my first visit to that great city, and underwent minor refitting at Oakland across the Bay. I stayed aboard for a time while the commodore and other officers took leave. Here I was particularly aware that the strain of war was beginning to tell on me. I do not mean the strain of combat, for I had not undergone any of that, but the fatigue with which endless watchfulness and responsibility can poison a nature that was, like mine, anxiety ridden to begin with. I was particularly short-tempered at this time, and I recognized it for the kind of short-temperedness that goes with being overtired. Eventually I too got a short leave and went all the way across the continent in June 1945 to North Hatley, Québec, where my wife was spending the first of many summers.

Then back to *Randall*. On this cruise, she wound up at Buckner Bay, Okinawa, in the Japanese Ryukyu Islands, southwest of the main islands. The marines had assaulted a short time before our arrival, and the Japanese were still stubbornly defending the southern end of the island. *Kamikaze* planes were beginning to make their suicide attacks on the warships in our screen around it. Over 200,000 men were killed or wounded in the course of our capture of this bit of land, which is a lot of men, even though Okinawa is a good deal larger than Iwo Jima. The battle for Okinawa was the bloodiest in the history of the United States. As at Iwo Jima, we were not engaged in the first assault, but brought in replacements. And this time we had the other ships of our division with us. It was clear that, unlike Curaçao, Aruba, Trinidad, and Recife, I was getting close to the heart of the matter.

I went ashore to look over the part of the island nearest the ship and in our hands. Into the low hills of Okinawa, over the centuries, the natives had sunk a large number of burial vaults, each belonging, I believe, to the members of a particular clan. Stone arches made the entrances to these vaults conspicuous. I inspected one of them briefly, and found that our men, in their compulsive search for souvenirs, had been prepared to rob the dead, even the very recently dead, and even of quite trivial grave-goods. No doubt if the Germans had won in the Atlantic they would have robbed my ancestors in the Sears Chapel in Longwood or even the Homans tomb in Dorchester. Oh! the yearning for souvenirs, the yearning for something tangible to show that one had really been to a place like Okinawa! For reasons not clear to me I never shared the yearning for souvenirs, and therefore I was free to make moral reflections. What could one do, I wondered, with this people, the Americans, who, supposedly civilized, were still ready to rob graves, indeed to take jewelry from the very bodies of the dead. It was not as if only a few crooks had engaged in the dirty business: a large number of otherwise decent men had done so. I knew that the Americans had great qualities. No greater courage was shown by men in battle than by those who beat the Japanese out of the Pacific Islands. But they also had these other traits. I doubted that anything any number of persons tried to do would ever make a "great society" out of them—not that they would make a worse society than many other people, but at best they would be far from perfect. In trying to control them, their government should limit itself to matters of the most obvious and proved necessity. Anything else they were absolutely sure to evade. I amused myself in a wry way by thinking what America would be like if it ever came under the control of Communists. What a problem the commissars would have on their hands!

At Buckner Bay, all of the ships of our division were together under our commodore's command, and we in turn came under the command for the first time of the next echelon above us, the admiral commanding the squadron. It had its own squadron beachmaster, my superior when on the beach. The squadron commander quite rightly ordered a practice landing on the shores of Buckner Bay, and for the first and only time I actually mastered a beach—if "mastered" is the right word. I was bored; I was highly irritable, and perhaps for these reasons I was not conspicuously good at my job, though I made no obvious mistakes. It was high time the squadron got some serious training, though we did not know then that the effort was wasted.

Our intelligence officer had informed me that our division with, of course, several others, had been assigned to take part in the next major operation of the war, the great and final assault on the main islands of Japan. Our specific target was the southern island of Kyushu. I forget now whether we were to take part in the first assault or come in with reserve troops. I had no relish for mastering a beach in either case. The Japanese would defend the beach itself with their usual tenacity. What is more, the island rises steeply from the coast into mountains, so that, even if our arms achieved the greatest possible success on the first day, the Japanese would still be able to shoot down from the mountains to the beaches for several days more. And on the beach I should have to stay, a sitting duck. My bet was that I should also become a dead duck.

On the last day before the war ended—and we still did not know it was about to end—I saw my younger brother, Bob, for the first time since the war began. He also had been a naval officer but had served only in the Pacific. He was not a flyer, but a deck officer in one of small aircraft carriers converted from merchant ships and sometimes called "jeep carriers." His ship was anchored like ours in Buckner Bay and he came aboard for dinner. That evening, the very last of the war, I heard for the first time shots fired in anger at a ship I was in. Japanese bombers attacked the shipping crowded into Buckner Bay. Our ships could not risk getting under way, so great were the chances of collision. But that very crowding allowed us to "make smoke" successfully. The ships put up a huge pall of thick oily smoke over the fleet, so that the Japanese bombers, unable to pick out individual targets, could only make a hit by sheer chance. In the darkness and smoke I heard several explosions that sounded as if they were near us but none did any damage. On the other hand, the battleship *Pennsylvania* on the outer edge of the screen was hit, but not sunk, by an aerial torpedo.

I knew I was saved from death on a beach on Kyushu when we got the news the next morning of the Japanese surrender. I had been saved by the atomic bombs dropped on Hiroshima and Nagasaki. Just before the war began, my physicist friend Jim Fisk, of the Society of Fellows, later chairman of the Atomic Energy Commission, and president of the Bell Telephone Laboratories, had told me about an experiment made in Germany—I think it was the one carried out by Lise Meitner—which suggested the possibility of atomic fission and all that it implied. But during the war I had given no thought to the atom. Several of my scientific friends were engaged in one way or another in the development of this bomb; but I did not meet them during the war, nor would they have told me what they were doing if I had. Now what Jim Fisk had told me about had suddenly returned to save me.

Intellectually I realized at once that a new epoch in history had begun. What interested me more at the moment was my own emotional reaction to the bombs. Not for a minute did I believe the theory, which became current later even among scholars whom I otherwise respected, that the Japanese would soon have surrendered anyway, persuaded by the terrible fire raid, as lethal in itself as one of the bombs, with which Admiral Halsey and the Third Fleet had recently raked the east coast of Japan. Nor did I nor do I believe that dropping the bombs as a demonstration on some uninhabited island would have brought the Japanese to surrender: we did not have enough bombs to take any such chance with them. Instead I have always agreed with Admiral Morison's argument that the Japanese military were determined to defend their home islands and believed that the casualties they could inflict on our invading troops would cause us to give up our invasion and negotiate a peace.[2] The slaughter on Iwo Jima and Okinawa would be as nothing to that on the home islands. Nothing short of demonstrating the power of the bombs on the scorched bodies of some hundred thousand of defenseless civilians would have induced the emperor to intervene and stop the war. Even so it seems to have been a matter of touch and go whether he would be successful.

I must say, though with some shame after many years of hindsight, that the morality of dropping the bombs never bothered me in the slightest at the time. Indeed since then the question of morality seems to have been raised only by persons who were in no danger whatever of invading Japan. But no such detached position could ever be mine. What were the lives of a hundred thousand Japanese compared with my own, which I was sure I should lose on some Kyushu beach? The fact is they were *nothing*. It is one thing to make moral judgments in the safety of Cambridge or Washington, quite another to make them when one is looking down the barrel of a gun. I have always blessed President Truman and Secretary Stimson for their decision to drop the bombs. I think their judgment was correct in fact and in morality: they saved a million American lives. When I was first called to active duty, I was sure I should not survive the war. Now, by the best of luck I had done so. Indeed I had hardly even had a brush with danger. Amazing!

I took advantage of peace and a brief period of inactivity to use my amphibious jeep for a purpose it was never intended to carry out. I took it ashore and explored the island of Okinawa. The northern part of the island was almost untouched by war and to my eyes, tired by the sea, very beautiful. I saw craggy inlets, to the banks of which clung crooked pines, and in which gnarled fishermen were casting nets. Until then I had not believed that the Japanese prints and drawings I had seen from my youth could have represented real landscapes.

When the war ended the rush for home began. The speed with which the government of the United States demobilized its armed forces seriously weakened its ability to negotiate with the Soviet Union, just when we were beginning to feel the first chilly breaths of the Cold War. The government could not have done otherwise: the reservists and draftees demanding demobilization would simply have brought so much political pressure to bear on Congress that the executive branch, against its better judgment, would have had to cave in. Cave in it did. The war ended, the boys just "wanted out" and out they went.

In the course of the war, a group in the War Department, under the leadership of Professor Samuel L. Stouffer, who was later to be my colleague in the Department of Social Relations at Harvard, had conducted various psychological and sociological studies in the Army, which then included the Air Force.[3] I believe this was the first time the academic discipline of sociology had ever been applied to military affairs. Among other things, the group had administered an elaborate questionnaire to a sample of officers and men, asking, in effect, what would be the fairest way for the Army to decide the order in which men should be discharged when the war came to an end. Upon analyzing the results of the questionnaire, the group recommended that the Army adopt the so-called point system for discharge, and both the Navy and the Air Force adopted it as their policy too. By this system, a man scored so many points for months of active duty, for months outside the continental United States, for months under combat, etc. A man who had accumulated a certain number of points could ask for separation as soon as the war was over, and others could ask later when they had built up a high enough score. Once one had accepted the purpose of the point system, which was demobilization, one had to admit that Stouffer and his group had done a good job. By and large the soldiers, sailors, and airmen accepted the system as fair, and fairness on the part of those in command has a great deal to do with maintaining high morale on the part of their subordinates.

By the end of the war, I had accumulated more than enough points to claim immediate separation, but so had others of the staff, especially Commander Coffin, the operations officer. Though I had more points for active duty than he did, he was older than I and of higher rank. (I had been promoted to lieutenant commander, without further difficulty, in September 1944.) Commodore Glutting let Commander Coffin go soon after the war officially came to an end. I too yearned to go and claimed it as my right. But the commodore turned me down. The point system had a catch, as such systems must always have if they are to adjust to real conditions. A commanding officer was authorized to refuse to release a subordinate, even if the latter had the requisite number of points, provided that the C.O. would certify that the subordinate was a "military necessity." There was nothing unrealistic about this catch, for as we shall see, the Navy still had plenty of work to do. Accordingly when I asked the commodore why he was not releasing me, he replied that he was keeping me as a military necessity. In a wry way this was a great compliment, indeed the only one I received during my naval career. No one else had ever remotely hinted that I was a military necessity: indeed the general idea some of my superiors had conveyed to me was that they could fight the war very well without my help. Accordingly I pressed the issue and asked Commodore Glutting why he considered me a military necessity. He replied, "If you weren't around, who would we have to talk to the admirals?" Without my realizing it, I had acquired the reputation of speaking up to officers of higher echelons than ours ("the admirals"), pointing out to them both the advantages and difficulties we would encounter in carrying out the plans they had in mind for the division, and if necessary, persuading them to modify the plans. I could organize good arguments, and by this time I could do so without insulting the admirals. The very qualities—a willingness to speak and write to my superiors in strong language—which had done me so much harm at the outset of my naval career, was doing me a different kind of harm at the end—except that as usual it turned out to be anything but harm. As an Annapolis man and a regular officer, I also suspect that Commodore Glutting had been trained by long years of experience not to talk up to the admirals. But as for me, where was now my ideal of myself as a seaman? Of what account were my abilities in ship-handling and maneuvering small fleets? I was a military necessity just like the most ordinary academic or lawyer, because I could *talk*! With the departure of Commander Coffin I became, as senior staff officer, operations officer (chief of staff) as well as division beach-master.

So far in my naval career I had not encountered any really bad weather except for the short, sharp gale that struck *Hazel* off the south coast of Nova Scotia. Now I was to go through not one but two typhoons. (A typhoon in the Eastern Hemisphere is the same kind of thing as a hurricane in the Western.) I had experienced ashore the great hurricane of 1938 in New England and was well aware of the terrible forces these tropical storms could mobilize and release. Now the higher command had ordered our division to move from Buckner Bay on the east side of Okinawa over to the west coast. Since there was no harbor capable of taking us in, we anchored in the open sea, together with hundreds of other ships, large and small, destined, we supposed, to embark occupation troops for Japan and for China and Korea, where the Japanese had also surrendered.

On one lowering, ugly-looking day, the admiral in charge of the ships around Okinawa suddenly made us a signal by radio to prepare for a typhoon. The warning came much too late—I believe the weathermen had calculated that the storm would miss the island—and hardly had we received it, when heavy rain, one of the first manifestations of a typhoon, fell upon us. The admiral then ordered us, together with all the other ships on the west coast, to get under way at once, proceed westward, and ride out the typhoon in the East China Sea. He did not have time to assign different courses to each unit, so here were hundreds of ships, of all sizes and in all kinds of units, all getting under way and putting to sea at once. By now the rain—the rain came before the wind—had reduced visibility to less than a hundred yards and was coming down in such sheets as to render our radar almost useless. Somehow we got the ships of our division under way and in line ahead, using some such crude signal—and only crude ones could be used—as "Get under way and follow me!" The trouble was that scores of other units were doing the same thing and taking their own chosen courses to the westward. It seemed to me, standing on the flag bridge of *Randall,* that collisions, with heavy loss of life, were inevitable.

Indeed I soon glimpsed, coming through the wrack, the leader of a column of landing craft smaller than ours, steering a course that intersected ours. There was not time for either column to signal or maneuver, and again I was sure that one of our ships would hit one of theirs and, since ours were much larger, sink her. But no, by sheer good luck, the ships of the two columns threaded one another like the interlocked fingers of two hands, and the other column disappeared once more into the wrack. I burst into hysterical laughter: no other reaction was possible.

When, without further narrow escapes, we got out into the offing and had plenty of sea-room, we sailed back and forth along a single course for a night and the better part of two days until the weather moderated and we returned to Okinawa. Offshore, the rain lessened but the wind and sea got up, which is the way with tropical storms. I must say I enjoyed myself. In a sailing ship or a small craft I should have feared for my life, but though *Randall* rolled heavily I had no fear that she would sink. From her bridge I could in safety simply watch the sea at the time of its greatest wrath—and it is something to watch. I could follow the great seas lazily rising up alongside and, as if with a tap, staving in the bottoms of our landing craft, high above the waterline. Only one incident unnerved me. The Japanese had filled the East China Sea with fields of moored contact-mines to discourage our submarines from penetrating their sea-routes. The typhoon must have carried one away from its moorings; it had bobbed to the surface and was drifting with wind and sea. Our lookout sighted it, and so did I, on our port bow close aboard, so close indeed that any effort to maneuver the ship to avoid it would have come too late. Had it hit us, it would have blown a huge hole in our bow, which, in a typhoon, might have been enough to sink us. But I watched the mine slide harmlessly astern just off the side of our ship. Though I had never swept an enemy mine, at least I had seen one.

On the last night the weather cleared. Our radar could keep track not only of our own ships but also of other units, all now making their way back to Okinawa. I could maneuver our division by voice radio so as to keep us out of the way of the others. In the morning the commodore mildly chewed me out for not waking him at midnight to let him take over his share of the task. (The staff was shorthanded by then.) But why should not our commodore, who was getting on in years, enjoy a full night in the sack? For myself I enjoyed maneuvering ships in formation, and I knew I could do it well. Why should not I have my fun?

The next morning, with the sun out full and a great sea still running, the swells dark blue—wine-dark—at the base but feather white at the breaking crests, reminded me of the greatest of Japanese color prints, a copy of which hangs in my study, Hokusai's *Mount Fuji Seen through the Great Wave off Kanagawa*. Later, I believe off Manila, we went through a second typhoon. We were getting bored, and it was attended by none of the exciting features of the great Okinawa typhoon.

After our return from the typhoon I was temporarily detached from the staff of the division and sent to the Fourth Marine Division, encamped in the northern part of Okinawa, to act as a liaison officer and help with the planning of the next operation, which of course was not going to be a warlike one. Our ships, together with many others, were to land the marines at the Taku Bar at the head of the Gulf of Pechili in China. The Taku Bar was the port of the great city of Tientsin, and the marines were going to take Tientsin over from the Japanese.

I messed with the officers of the marine division. They were perfectly polite to me but utterly detached. They could take no interest in this outsider who did not know what war meant. I felt that from Guadalcanal to Okinawa they had seen too much, lost too much, felt too much. They were bone-weary, deadened, and wished only for silence. I was abashed in their presence: they were the elite, the regulars, the professionals, the real soldiers.

In the course of organizing the landing, I discovered in myself a capacity for planning complex operations and embodying the plans in clearly written orders. I might have made an exemplary staff officer, if only I could have gotten myself under enough control to accept criticism of my plans from my superior officers and rewrite them in accordance with their ideas. A good staff officer must accept this distasteful feature of his duty, even if he knows full well that his own ideas are better than those of his superiors. I doubt that, even so late in my naval career, I could have mustered up this control.

Some persons might explain by my academic experience my capacity to write clear-cut orders for different units so that their activities would neatly dovetail together—provided of course that the orders were obeyed, and some of them never would be. I knew better. I knew that many academics, though crammed with knowledge, could never write a plan down clearly or fit its parts together. I was more inclined to explain my capacity genetically: my father would have made an excellent staff officer, just as he did make an excellent lawyer. The qualities needed for the two activities are not dissimilar.

I did not myself land at the Taku Bar. Since our landing was unopposed, lesser beachmasters did that. Indeed we were welcomed by the local Chinese. But in the course of reviewing, as part of the job of planning, the intelligence information the Navy had put into our hands, I discovered that there were parts of the Chinese coast on which our landing of troops was considered inexpedient unless utterly necessary, because Chinese Communist guerrillas controlled these parts, and might make trouble of some unspecified kind. I had felt my own first chilly breath of the Cold War.

The next assignment of Transport Division 69, and my last as operations officer, was the most interesting. We were ordered south from Okinawa to Hong Kong with a brief stop at war-ravaged Manila. I remember specially passing the great wall of mountains that makes the off-shore, eastern coast of Formosa. The word means "beautiful" in Portuguese. The Portuguese were the first Westerners to see Formosa: it is now Taiwan. We passed part of the coast at night and saw the great slopes studded with little points of light. These were fires made by the descendants of the aborigines, not the later Chinese invaders, burning brush in order to clear land for their gardens and fertilize the soil. We anthropologists call this technique "slash-and-burn" or even "swidden" agriculture.

Off Hong Kong I saw my first junk under sail: from close aboard I saw she was armed with old brass cannon, which took me back to the sixteenth century. I saw the city itself on its famous and beautiful harbor. Were it not for the long row of European banks and commercial houses along the waterfront, I should have thought myself back in the Middle Ages, with the long streets full of bright signs in Chinese characters, where handicraftsmen worked in the open in full view in the fronts of their shops. But the Navy had not sent us to Hong Kong to see the sights.

At the end of the war, the Allies had assigned to Generalissimo Chiang Kai-chek sovereignty over all of China because he had been an ally himself, however little he may have done to deserve the name. His problem now was to make his sovereignty good, especially over those industrial parts of North China, such as Manchuria, which the Japanese had controlled. It was the job of our division, together with others, to move the troops Chiang had available in South China up to the North. These were troops, I believe, that had served on the Burma Front, that is, in tropical forests.

They came aboard our ships at Kowloon, on the mainland across the harbor from Hong Kong. They were dressed in khaki shirts and shorts, in the big straw hats of Chinese peasants, and for footgear in sneakers, presumably supplied by the United States of America. They brought with them no heavy equipment such as artillery. Machine guns they did bring, their parts disassembled and slung on the ends of long bamboo carrying-poles resting on their shoulders. Even to someone accustomed to the relative informality of the American Army, they looked unmilitary. Were these the troops with which the generalissimo proposed to hold down

Manchuria against the Communists, of the Russian or Chinese variety? If they were, I decided at once that he was out of his senses. But "ours not to reason why," so having embarked the troops, we sailed for Manchuria.

It was now the beginning of autumn; the weather was cold and wet in the East China Sea; it would get colder and wetter as we went north. Most of the Chinese had no seagoing experience. These were not conditions to which they were acclimated, and my first and enduring impression of this great people was the cheerfulness with which they accepted hardships. Without this trait they never would have survived what they have had to endure over the millenia. Their meals—hot or hottish rice in big baskets—were served to them on deck, in the well between the forecastle and the bridge. I looked down on them from the bridge, amazed to see them giggling away happily all the time as they ate between dollops of salt spray. How we Americans would have complained!

As senior officer of the ship's mess—the commodore and the ship's captain dined alone in their cabins—I sat, in accordance with protocol, next to General Wang, the commandant of the Chinese troops. (There must be millions of Wangs in China.) I communicated with him through an interpreter. I never even began to learn Chinese, as I had Portuguese, but then the latter was a far easier task. In dealing with Wang I made a stupid mistake. It was one many Americans would have made, but I, as an anthropologist, should have known better. I offered him a carton of cigarettes, which I could get dirt cheap, because tax free, aboard ship. I was soon made to understand that he would not only feel obliged to accept the gift, but also, poor fellow, in order to preserve "face," to make me a return of more than equal value. He came up with a box of Chinese Victrola records. I never tried anything like that again, at least not with a Chinese.

It was my duty to accompany General Wang, who seemed rather dour as Chinese go, when he inspected from time to time the troop compartments on *Randall*. On one occasion we found some minor but obvious dirt in one of the compartments. I do not know how far Wang would have gone had I not been with him, but as it was, he grabbed by the ear the Chinese officer who appeared to be responsible for the area, and holding the ear, Wang in effect rubbed the officer's nose in the dirt. I myself had dumped a bucket of water over a hung-over cook, but I could never have gone as far with an American officer.

More ticklish was the problem of deaths among the Chinese troops. As I have said, they were not acclimatized to the cold wet weather of the East China Sea in autumn, and they certainly were not dressed for it. These conditions brought out any latent pulmonary diseases among them, and in spite of the efforts of our medical men several of them died—on the average, as I remember it, about one a day as we sailed north. The question then arose about what to do with the corpses. We ourselves held, of course, a regular religious service for Americans who died at sea, but I did not know whether this applied to the Chinese. Ought Confucian or Buddhist rites be performed? I had always heard that the Chinese were given to ceremonial. At the same time I had heard that they set a low value on human life. Through our interpreter I asked General Wang what was to be done with the Chinese dead, and he answered in effect: "No problem: just dump them overboard." But I still felt uneasy and consulted my commodore. He insisted that Chinese casualties should be treated in just the same way as American ones, and if the Chinese had no heathen ceremony to propose, we should provide a Christian one. Accordingly I arranged that every Chinese corpse should be covered with an American flag, that our chaplain, who I believe was an Episcopalian, should read over the corpse the regular service for burial at sea, that a squad should fire a volley, and finally that the corpses, adequately weighted, should be slid over the taffrail. Though he attended these services, I am sure General Wang thought we were silly. Let no one suggest that the division did not do its full duty by the Chinese, at least in the matter of ceremony.

As we went north a further incident brought intimations of things to come. We were to land our Chinese troops at Chinwangtao at the head of the Gulf of Pechili, where China proper meets Manchuria, and where, indeed, the Great Wall comes down to the sea. As we sailed along the Korean coast in cold weather and on one of those calm, dry days that bring preternatural visibility, we met a column of Russian freighters sailing in the opposite direction. They were, we were sure, loaded with machinery "liberated" from the mines and mills of Manchuria, where the Japanese had surrendered as they had elsewhere, and they were bound for Vladivostok. I was on the flag bridge when, much to our surprise, we received a message by flashing light and in perfectly good English from the Russian commodore, inviting us to dine with him in Vladivostok. I do not know whether he intended this as a heavy-handed form of Russian humor or as a genuine gesture of goodwill, but I took him at his word and said we should be delighted to accept his invitation. Naturally I could not get to Vladivostok. By this time the Russians would not have let any American ship enter the port. I am sorry, and I have not yet visited the U.S.S.R.

At Chinwangtao I could not go ashore. I had to remain on the ship, more or less in charge of the landing operation. But I could scan through my glasses the flat plain of north China, bare and treeless as far as eye could see. I could begin to imagine how hard that land had been used, to feed so many millions over so many millennia. The Chinese troops went ashore. It was cold, and they were still clad in their khaki shorts and their sneakers. Making every allowance for their national hardihood, we wondered what would happen to them in the bitter winter that would soon be upon them. Their officers assured us that our Navy had agreed to provide cold-weather gear, which would arrive immediately following the present landing. I do not know whether it ever did, or whether indeed our armed forces had a large enough supply of cold-weather gear within quick shipping distance of Manchuria. Even if it had arrived it would not have made much difference. The troops Chiang Kai-chek hurriedly sent north to hold industrial Manchuria simply melted away under the pressure of the Chinese Communists, the first step in the campaign that would give Mao Tse-tung control of all mainland China by 1949. By that time the Fourth Marine Division and other American units had withdrawn from China. In my naval career I had never taken part in a more futile operation—and I had taken part in some pretty futile ones, but in none that was more interesting. I do not blame the Navy. I suspect the China Lobby in Congress forced it to go along with the ideas of Chiang.

Our division returned empty to Hong Kong, where we picked up more of Chiang's troops. This time we took them to Tsingtao on the Shantung peninsula, the former treaty port and naval base of Imperial Germany. Here I was allowed to go ashore. Architecturally Tsingtao was still a combination of traditional China and, say, Munich, and the two went well together. I was impressed by the physical type of the North Chinese. Used to the slight, light-boned Cantonese and other southerners, who made up most of the Chinese in the United States as well as among the soldiers we had carried north, I was surprised to encounter the big, sturdy peasants of Shantung. I also met the officer I had told to go to hell at Charleston; it now seemed so many years ago. He was cordial and did not seem to hold my words in the least against me.

Here at Tsingtao on November 18, 1945, my active service in the Navy came to an end. Two events occurred simultaneously. I received a letter from Paul Buck, the then provost of Harvard and dean of the Faculty of Arts and Sciences, offering me an associate professorship of sociology, then a tenured position, presumably in the new department to be formed out of the three Departments of Sociology, Anthropology, and Psychology. This was the first I had heard that the plans Clyde Kluckhohn had sketched to me in the middle of the war were really coming to pass. I need never have asked for permission to resign from the Navy, the action for which I was most ashamed. On the other hand, Professor Ferguson's prediction that there would be no tenured position for me at Harvard if I survived the war, and that therefore I should have to seek my fortune in the academic boondocks, was proved wrong. I had been, and I have been since, luckier than I deserved.

Buck urged me to get back to Harvard as soon as I could, and I answered that I should do my best. Commodore Glutting was ready to cooperate. The job of ferrying Chiang's troops was mostly over, and Glutting was ready to release me from my status as a "military necessity" and indeed to write a letter for my file in the Navy Department certifying that I was well qualified for promotion to commander. At the end of my naval career I was beginning to become a useful naval officer. I bade the commodore an affectionate farewell and, with other officers and men released from active duty, embarked aboard the transport *Samuel Chase*, bound for San Diego. I was theoretically officer-in-charge of the naval passengers, and as such enjoyed a splendid large stateroom, but I had nothing to do, as no one was going to start any trouble just as they were homeward bound. I spent my time sketching out what I thought I had learned about the social problems of small warships. After a long but pleasant voyage, though it was late in the season, we reached San Diego, whence I flew to Boston. There on December 16, 1945, I was transferred to inactive duty, just in time for Christmas and easily in time for the opening of the spring term at Harvard.

What were my reflections as I crossed the Pacific on my way out of the Navy? First of all, I was alive, unwounded, and in good health, none of which I had expected when I had been called to active duty. But then I had taken part in no famous engagements except in the most minor way; indeed I had spent much of my time on activities whose usefulness was doubtful. Still, I supposed this had been the experience of most men in most wars. Such distinction as I had received had only been in small part of the kind expected of a seaman: it consisted mostly in talking and writing. Naturally I had seen a great deal of the sea in all its moods, except the great icy winter gales of the high latitudes. I thought of the opening lines of the *Odyssey*. Like Odysseus I had "in my spirit suffered much upon the sea," but my sufferings were largely of my own making and my worries about disasters that never came to pass. Unlike Odysseus, who never admitted he enjoyed himself at sea, I had done so often. Like him "I had seen many of the cities of men and known their customs," from Recife to Hong Kong, yet I had penetrated them only superficially, and I had seen even more of uninhabited coasts and islands. Most important and most relevant for my future career I had acquired what my old master L. J. Henderson would have called "intuitive familiarity" with a wide variety of my countrymen and with the social problems of small, isolated groups. As another of my masters, Elton Mayo, would have urged, I had done so by exercising the responsibility of command. Indeed in the end I had become a not unpopular leader of men, though I never wholly got control of my moods of mulishness or impatience. I wrote an article embodying my views on the problems of command in small warships, which was published in the *American Sociological Review*.[4] By some means unknown to me it came to the attention of James Forrestal, secretary of Defense, who wrote me a warm letter of congratulations. Call that the climax of my naval career, if you like! But remember again: it was writing that did the trick.

Above all I had taken part in the greatest event of my time. Mine had not been a central part, but at least I had been *there*. I had not stayed at home; I had not even sat out the war at a desk in Washington; like my ancestors I had commanded at sea. One of my favorite poems is Lucy Ashton's song in Sir Walter Scott's *Bride of Lammermoor*.[5] I had not taken her ironic advice to "sit thou still when kings are arming." By Mr. Justice Holmes's rule, I had thus proved that I had lived.[6] Moreover, the war I had taken part in had been a just war, so far as any war is just, and my country had been victorious. Some idiots say that wars accomplish nothing—and future wars may accomplish far less than nothing—but at least Hitler was not around when our war ended. Perhaps my feeling was best described in words those of us who took part and survived sometimes repeated to one another when we were among ourselves, for they would have shocked sensitive and "liberal" civilians: "It was a hell of a war but better than no war at all!"

NOTES

1. William Shakespeare, *Hamlet, Prince of Denmark*, act 4, sc. 4, lines 62-65.
2. Samuel Eliot Morison, *History of United States Naval Operations in World War II*, vol. 14, *Victory in the Pacific* (Boston: Little, Brown, 1960), pp. 336-53.
3. See Samuel A. Stouffer et al., *The American Soldier*, 2 vols. (Princeton: Princeton University Press, 1949).
4. George C. Homans, "The Small Warship," *American Sociological Review* 11 (1946): 299-300; reprinted in George C. Homans, *Sentiments and Activities* (New York: Free Press of Glencoe, 1962), pp. 50-60.
5. Walter Scott, *The Bride of Lammermoor*, ch. 2.
6. *The Occasional Speeches of Justice Oliver Wendell Holmes*, comp. Mark De Wolfe Howe (Cambridge: Harvard University Press, 1962), pp. 6-7: "I think that, as life is action and passion, it is required of a man that he should share the passion and action of his time at peril of being judged not to have lived."

18

HARVARD AFTER WORLD WAR II

I was reemployed by Harvard University beginning with the spring term (February to June) of the academic year 1945-46. I returned as associate professor of sociology, that is, in what was then a tenured position. I do not know how I got through the scrutiny of the *ad hoc* committee that the president of the university appoints whenever a department makes a recommendation for filling such a position. The committee is supposed to make sure that the person recommended is the ablest person in the world available for the appointment. In my opinion he or she often is not. I suppose I got by on the strength of my two published books, on Pareto and on English villagers, and a few published articles. I may well have been helped by the accidental death in the U.S. Army in Germany of my chief contemporary rival at Harvard, Edward Y. ("Ted") Hartshorne. And if Robert Merton at Columbia had been willing to come, I should have sunk without a trace. I did not consider myself the ablest person in the world available for the post—though I did not count myself any slouch either—but if others did, that was their affair.

I was getting a tenure position. But had not old Dean Ferguson, when I was called into the Navy, told me that there would be no such position for me? What made the difference was that the current dean and provost, Paul Buck, had decided to support the establishment of a new department, the Department of Social Relations, and to support it in the strongest way by allotting it two new tenured positions. One was mine. The other, a full professorship, went to Samuel A. Stouffer, who was a great statistician and had led the social science research team in the U.S. Army during the war. His group, among many other actions, had devised the "point system" for priorities in getting discharged at the end of the war: I had been one of the exceptions to the system.

The Department of Social Relations was to include all members of the Sociology Department, which was to go out of existence as such, the social anthropologists of the Anthropology Department, which left it still in existence but limited to physical anthropologists and archaeologists, and the so-called personality and social psychologists of the Psychology

Department, leaving it too still in existence but limited to the physical psychologists and the experimentalists who worked with animals (rat psychologists). The actual distribution never quite realized the plan.

The first meeting of the Faculty of Arts and Sciences I attended was the one that voted to establish the new department according to the plan the dean had approved. Professor Gordon Allport of Psychology made the motion to found it under the name of Human Relations. At once representatives of the Departments of History, Government, Economics, and no doubt others were on their feet, objecting not to the existence of the new department but to its name. Human relations was what *they* taught, and this upstart was not to stick his nose into their business, at least not with the word *human*. After the faculty had thrashed around for an hour debating this issue, and all seemed to be lost, some genius—I have forgotten whom—moved to amend the motion by calling the new department Social instead of Human Relations. The faculty adopted the amended motion by acclamation: we might be social as long as they remained human. As if it made the slightest difference! My very first faculty meeting introduced me to the enormous capacity intelligent, but intellectual, men and women command for debating the trivial, for debating about words, not things. As someone said later, the town meeting of Sherborn, Massachusetts, can handle business more effectively than the faculties of either Harvard or M.I.T.

As I have mentioned earlier, the idea of the Social Relations Department had emerged out of a series of informal discussions carried out during the late war by a group whose central members were Professor Talcott Parsons of Sociology, Professor Gordon Allport of Psychology, Dr. Henry Murray, also of Psychology, and Professor Clyde Kluckhohn of Anthropology. I returned to Cambridge for only a few days during the war; I took no part in the discussions; I heard little about them and that mostly at second hand. Accordingly my history of the founding may well be biased.

The founding fathers always stressed later the shared intellectual interests that brought them together: these were first a fascination with what were then considered the "softer" sides of the social sciences, especially the relations between personality, culture, and society, and second, the need to develop a theory that would link all three. But there was a second force that brought the founding fathers together, a force that cannot be wholly separated from the first. That was dissatisfaction with their personal situations in their own departments. The department gave a dinner at the Harvard Club of Boston to celebrate the tenth anniversary of the Social Relations Department. Professor Parsons, as chairman, spoke of the high intellectual ideals, the yearning to build bridges between disciplines—Talcott was always "building bridges" even if there were not always two abutments to build them between—that had brought the department together. Provost Buck, following Parsons, said: "Now, Talcott, it wasn't that way at all, and you know it." He did not tell us then, nor did he later, what the real way was. I suspect, had he not wished to remain tactful, that he would have said more about the personal interests of the founding fathers.

As the first chairman of Sociology, Professor Pitirim Sorokin, though possessing other great qualities, had acquired the continental European tradition—which he did not find uncongenial—that the head of a department had the right and duty to be an autocrat. As such I am sure he made life difficult for Talcott Parsons. By founding and then becoming chairman of the new department, Talcott got out from under Sorokin, whose long chairmanship came to an end.

In Psychology, Professor Gordon Allport specialized in the fields of personality and social psychology, considered soft or unscientific by both the physiological psychologists like S. S. ("Smitty") Stevens and the behaviorists like Fred Skinner. For a time, I am told, Allport and the chairman of the Psychology Department, Professor Edwin G. Boring, could not bear to talk to one another face to face and wrote memoranda instead. Joining the new department meant that Allport no longer had to worry about the Borings, Stevenses, and Skinners. He brought some bright younger men, such as Jerome S. Bruner, into the department with him.

Dr. Henry A. ("Harry") Murray was an old friend of my family's. I had met him when I was an undergraduate through our common, though somewhat different, interests in the novels of Herman Melville. For many years Harry carried out psychoanalytical research on the life and writings of Melville, only part of which unfortunately he ever published.[1] I am not sure that he was even a regular member of the Psychology Department. But he was independently wealthy and used his money to support the "Psychological Clinic" in an old-fashioned, rambling wooden house on Plympton Street in Cambridge. The clinic was certainly affiliated with the department, though despised by many of its members. There Murray and his young associates pursued Freudian and neo-Freudian research, which was definitely "soft" psychology. Joining the Department of Social Relations would bring Harry too from the periphery to the center. He eventually was appointed professor.

Clyde Kluckhohn may have been less alienated from his department, Anthropology, than the others were from theirs, and he always retained membership in both his old department and his new one. Still, he was a social, not a physical, anthropologist and, even as a social anthropologist, rather on the "soft" side compared with his former or current colleagues such as Lloyd Warner, Carleton Coon, and Eliot Chapple. He had been psychoanalyzed or at least studied Freudian theory in Vienna; he was close to Harry Murray; and he was much interested, among other things, in the field, now largely abandoned, called "culture and personality." Its adepts tried to apply Freudian ideas to explaining the differences between cultures and between the "modal personalities" they were supposed to produce.

If the founding fathers had fully understood how different, in some ways, though not in all, my ideas were from theirs, I doubt if they would have shown themselves so ready to welcome this viper into their bosoms. But then I had been away for a long time, and my ideas had been changing. Socially, moreover, I always got along well with them, except for occasions like Christmas parties, when I felt juniors might be allowed some license in what they said about seniors. I enjoyed writing skits, which portrayed, for instance, Gordon Allport as a bit of an old woman. (I suppose such things would damn me as sexist today.) "Remember," I would tell the graduate students, "Gordon Allport is *not* your mother." Mild enough, but Gordon did not take this sort of thing in good part and put an end to our skits. He should have taken them as compliments, for his fussiness, which was really conscientiousness, made him, with the stern help of his secretary, Mrs. Eleanor Sprague, a great administrator of our graduate program. I got along even better with junior members of the department, some of whom in later years had also been students of mine: Jerry Bruner, Oscar Handlin, who later went into history with great distinction, Florence Kluckhohn, Barrington Moore, Jr., Robert White, Richard Sheldon, David Aberle, David Schneider, Hank Riecken, Joe Kahl, Chuck Tilly, Kim Romney, Dan Rosenblatt, and many others. My problems with the department were never personal.

The new department had the advantage for me of exposing me to new influences, particularly methodological ones. The "old" Sociology Department was strong in alleged "theory"—especially in classical theory: Durkheim, Weber, Pareto, etc.—but weak in statistics, especially statistics as applied to survey (questionnaire) data, which was becoming a more and more important tool in both sociology and psychology. Sam Stouffer and later the much younger Fred Mosteller were brought in to remedy this deficiency. Sam, a congenial man and a great entrepreneur of social science, always scurrying around like a terrier sniffing out holes, never made the big substantive contribution to sociology that his real originality in statistics entitled him to. Whenever he did tackle such a problem, it either turned out to be uninteresting or he got nowhere near solving it.

Second, the social psychologists brought into the new department the experimental tradition in psychology, in their case the experimental study of human subjects. The experimenters tried to make a change in an independent variable: for instance, they had some subjects carry out a task under what was called "autocratic" leadership, others under "democratic" supervision, etc. Then the experimenters scored along various dimensions the ways in which the subjects performed the task under the various conditions of leadership, and if, for instance, the average differences in productivity between the autocrats and the democrats could have occurred by chance less than five out of a hundred times, then the hypothesis of a relationship between style of leadership and productivity was said to be confirmed or at least "supported."[2] Unlike my friends such as Fritz Roethlisberger at the Business School or the social anthropologists, the social psychologists in their eagerness to carry on the experimental tradition in psychology seemed to do little field research.

My problems with the department were intellectual rather than personal or social. I could sympathize with its general aims. I agreed that the different disciplines of social science would each be strengthened by unification, for I believed, as I still do, that the sciences of human behavior are a single science, in the sense that they share the same general principles, though I was not yet sure what these were. I believed in what is called cross-disciplinary teaching and research. Was not that what I had been doing with Mayo? Indeed if the sciences were a single science, need the teaching and research even be called cross-disciplinary? The different departments of social science were administrative conveniences, supported, it was true, by different intellectual traditions, but these I felt, and still feel, were not irreconcilable.

I could sympathize with the general aims of the department but not with the ways in which the founding fathers proposed to carry them out. I did not myself have to go along with their plans, and they certainly never tried to make me do so (in fact they thought for a while that I *was* a conformer), but I could not help hearing about the plans, and to hear was to be vexed. The social science disciplines were not, I felt, to be integrated by the study of personality in the manner of Freud, of culture in the manner of, say, Ruth Benedict, or of sociology in the manner of Durkheim. (Of course I speak crudely.) Of Freud, the later theorist as distinguished from the earlier clinician, I had already, as a result of my work with Mayo, become thoroughly skeptical. I had also become skeptical of the culture-vultures, one of whom, Clyde Kluckhohn, was a founding father. The approach by way of the classical theorists, represented in the department by Talcott Parsons, I shall have much to say about later. But I already knew that the Durkheim who claimed society to be an entity *sui generis*, something more than the resultant of the actions of individual human beings, was, on the evidence, it seemed to me, simply *wrong*.[3] And I meant *wrong* in the strongest sense of the word, that is, untrue. Fortunately for Durkheim's reputation he made many other statements of a different sort.

As for the methodological program, I was thoroughly in favor of introducing a more sophisticated statistics to the new department, though I never became even a passable statistician myself. I began to appreciate the temptation to choose problems because a sophisticated statistics could be applied to solving them rather than because they were important in their own right. Yet good statisticians did not give way to the temptation, and I began to understand, thanks to the teachings of "Munya" Postan in England, what statistics could contribute to one of my own fields, medieval social and economic history. Statistics now have a respectable place in historical research, though under the fancy name of "cliometrics." In my youth many historians considered history to be statistics-proof, not even a social science but a humanity. A humanity it still may be, but it is certainly also a science, as any field of investigation must be that claims to rely on evidence to support its statements.

My willingness to accept the importance of a more sophisticated statistics did not prevent my savoring a certain *Schadenfreude* when Sam Stouffer, with characteristic enthusiasm, perpetrated a temporarily famous *gaffe*. Allport had asked him to give a guest lecture on survey techniques in the first term of the introductory course in the department. This was Social Relations 1a, which concerned itself with personality and social psychology. (I myself was in charge of the second term, Social Relations 1b, concerned with sociology and social anthropology.) By chance, Stouffer gave his lecture on the day before the presidential election of 1948 in which the candidates were Harry Truman and Tom Dewey. Stouffer told the large class of about seven hundred students something like this: "Our methods for predicting the results of an election by polling in advance a carefully selected sample of voters are now so well developed that you need have no doubt that Thomas E. Dewey will be elected the next President of the United States!" What a flurrying in the statistical dovecotes followed upon the immediate election of Truman! Naturally the pollsters wanted to know what had gone wrong, and set up a useful investigating committee.

The experience was healthy for them as it was for all of us, though perhaps in somewhat different ways. I had no general prejudice against the use of questionnaires. Still, I believe they often revealed how people thought they ought to behave rather than how they really would behave when faced with similar decisions under the more precise and compelling pressures of real life. The reason that the pollsters often came so close to being correct in predicting the results of presidential elections—and they got better after the great Dewey *débâcle*—was that the conditions facing a person answering a question in a poll were much the same as those he or she faced in a real voting booth. Elsewhere, in my view, questionnaires were most valuable when used together with other methods, especially for the purpose of nailing down formally what one already knew intuitively from field research.

As for laboratory experiments on human subjects, which the social psychologists introduced me to, I wondered about their relation to human behavior outside the laboratory, in what we were pleased to call "real life." In manipulating the independent variables, the experimenters were seldom able to offer their subjects rewards or punishments nearly as powerful as those that swayed them in real life. The subjects did not much care what they did, one way or the other, which did not make for clear-cut results. Or the experimenters tried so hard to control rigorously everything that entered their experimental design that they succeeded in destroying in the laboratory the conditions in "real life" that gave rise to the hypotheses they wished to test. As for the dependent variables, when the experimenters dichotomized their subjects into groups that had scored high and those that had scored low in some dimension, they did not emphasize that the average difference between the two groups might be "significant" statistically but absolutely quite small. For instance, a study of the effects of different supervisory practices on the productivity of workers might show that the differences between "high-producing" and "low-producing" groups was less than 15 percent of total production.[4] Fifteen percent would mean a great deal if it could be extended to all of American industry, but it was not going to be. Was all the effort put into the training of foremen as a result of such experiments to make as little difference as this?

These features of experimental and survey research in social psychology meant that its results were often weak or ambiguous. When two experimenters reached apparently contradictory results, they did not search carefully enough to discover whether they had really performed their experiments under identical conditions. If the conditions were not identical, the experiments might well produce contradictory results. Finally, the social psychologists piled up thousands of their studies, so many that no single mind, certainly not mine, could encompass them all; and the worst textbooks, of which there were many, consisted of utterly unreadable abstracts of one study after another, their authors making little or no effort at achieving the economy of thought and teaching that would have come from showing the different findings followed from a few general principles.

Still, I was prepared to think well of some studies in social psychology, especially when they seemed to me to reproduce "real-life" conditions fairly well—indeed some experiments could be carried out in the real world itself and not in academic laboratories—and especially, of course, when they seemed to confirm conclusions I had already reached from field research, my own or that of others. Though I myself never performed an experiment or carried out a survey, I was eventually to provide an intellectual framework into which the findings of such research might fit.

Perhaps the most important point to be made about the social psychologists was that they were better at testing hypotheses than at finding good ones to test. Theirs were what I called at best "experiments of proof" rather than, in Francis Bacon's words, "experiments of light."[5] One got one's ideas about human behavior from field research, nondirective interviewing, from the messy data of history, even from good novels. Above all, one got them from taking responsibility for the behavior of others. These were the kinds of experience that provided us with "intuitive familiarity" in our field. The social psychologists did not seem to be able to draw on these resources, and apparently their experimentation was no substitute. True, none of us can live as social beings without acquiring at least a smattering of intuitive familiarity with social behavior, but I often felt the social psychologists kept their smattering well compartmented from what they did in their laboratories.

Let me illustrate. The question of distributive justice, of whether rewards are divided fairly among persons or groups, has aroused fierce passions throughout history. Aristotle, the first great social scientist, had considered the question at length in his *Nichomachean Ethics*.[6] Had modern social psychologists ever made an experimental study of this monumental problem, which obviously lay within their field? They had not. Most of them were good liberals in politics and as such regularly clamored for "social justice," but they had not allowed their political interests to spill over into their research. In theory they were not against letting them spill: in practice they kept the real world well apart from the laboratory. In sociology Bob Merton and Alice Kitt had recently made a good study of the kindred problem of "relative deprivation,"[7] through an analysis of some of the data Stouffer's group had gathered during World War II. Yet I think it is fair to say that it was I who brought the problem of distributive justice fully home to social psychology. I had had my nose rubbed in it, in the form of an issue in wage differentials, in the course of my research, carried out by field observation and nondirective interviewing, without any experiments or surveys, in the Customers' Accounting Division of the Boston Edison Company.[8] My hypothesis about distributive justice, which turned out not to be mine but Aristotle's, came to me by induction from observations and interviews. I had not entered Boston Edison with any hypothesis I wanted to test. I had not then even read Aristotle's *Ethics*. I just wanted to study a group of clerical workers, hoping that something interesting would turn up. In my experience, it always does. Since then, social psychologists have made an industry of research on distributive justice. By making their experimental controls too elegant and rigorous, some have even succeeded in showing that the phenomenon does not exist. But it does and will not go away. At least as far as the record shows, the study of distributive justice began in the field and not in the laboratory.

In the early days of the new department, when, except for the founding fathers, most of us did not know one another well, either personally or intellectually, we made heroic efforts to "integrate." For one thing, we held for a year or more a seminar on methods, in which each of the staff gave at least one lecture on the methods of research he or she considered appropriate to the study of social relations. I talked of the necessity, at least in the early stages of research, of taking what I called a "natural history" approach to sociology. Remember that years before I had begun my informal scientific career as a field naturalist, a conchologist. I used to give my "red-billed duck" lecture. At some point in his career a sociologist should simply observe human behavior as a naturalist does, when, sitting in a blind, he or she listens and watches through glasses the behavior of red-billed ducks, drakes, and ducklings, and then simply records what they do. (As far as I know there is no species actually called the red-billed duck.) To observations of this sort we owe the foundations of ethology, the study of the social behavior of nonhuman animals. I also gave a lecture on the use of quantitative methods in history. The case I used was the tendency for Puritans in sixteenth-century England to come predominantly from counties given over to the woolen-cloth industry.[9] (Contemporaries had observed the same thing.) I am sure that Sam Stouffer found my use of historical statistics to be utterly without rigor, as I am sure it was. The methods seminar did nothing to integrate the department methodologically; we all kept on using the methods we felt comfortable with. It was soon abandoned. But at least it served to inform me about methods that had only been names to me before.

More ambitious was the effort to integrate the department theoretically. This project was dear to the heart of Professor Talcott Parsons, and as chairman he took the lead in organizing it. There were to be two committees on theoretical integration, a senior and a junior. The senior consisted of full professors in the department, together with at least two visitors, the psychologist E.C. Tolman from Berkeley and the sociologist Edward Shils from Chicago. Richard Sheldon, of junior rank, served as secretary. The junior committee consisted of persons below full professor in rank, such as Jerry Bruner and I.

The senior committee met about once a week for the better part of one academic year, trying to hammer out by discussion what should be the nature of a general theory in the field of social relations. Though naturally I was not present, I am sure that Parsons dominated the discussion. Later I came to the conclusion that one could not argue with him, at least I could not. After I thought I had him convinced, what he wrote down later always turned out to represent his original position. In discussion, too, he had a turn of speech which I am sure he had not deliberately adopted but was nonetheless vexing. When one thought he had finished his remarks—and my wife claimed one of his sentences took fifteen minutes to pass a given point—and that therefore one might take the floor oneself, he would, after a pause, start talking again as if he had never stopped, and so shut one off.

From time to time the seniors sent down to the juniors memoranda on the current state of their deliberations, on which we were supposed to comment and provide them with what was already being called "feed-back." As I remember it, the seniors never paid any attention to our reactions, and the junior committee withered away, but not until we had reached with some pleasure a scientific generalization: the number of boxes (categories) in Parsons's theoretical scheme increased weekly as the square of 4. Our meetings stopped when he reached 256. It was spineless of us not to wait and see where the series would, if ever, end.

Much research can be effectively carried out by teams, but I do not believe that theories, good or bad, can be developed so. When the final report of the senior committee came out in 1951 in the form of a small paperback entitled *Toward a General Theory of Action*[10] and popularly referred to as the "Yellow Book," it turned out to be largely the work of Parsons and Shils and represented their views. They gave little more than lip service to the views of the other participants, who must by then have been too exhausted to argue further. The secretary, Richard Sheldon, wrote a chapter very discreet as befitted a junior member of the staff. Still, reading between the lines, one could detect the skepticism. Almost immediately afterwards he left sociology for business, a great loss to the science, as he was one of the brightest among us. I suspect he has had the consolation of making more money than most of us who remained in academia.

I too thought little of the "Yellow Book," because I was beginning to suspect that the authors' view of what constituted a theory was bound to lead their "approach" up a dead-end street: it would not even begin to move towards a theory of action. I shall pursue this issue no further now but take up the whole problem of theory, which I first encountered as the "Parsons problem," in a later chapter. Parsons himself laid the "Yellow Book" before a meeting of the whole department, including both tenured and nontenured members, urging us all to read it and implying, though without quite saying as much, that it ought to be adopted as the official doctrine of the department to guide future teaching and research. I was going to have none of that, if I could help it. Accordingly as soon as I was really satisfied that Parsons had finished, I spoke up and said in effect: "There must be no implication that this document is to be taken as representing the official doctrine of the department, and no member shall be put under any pressure to read it." Indeed there can be no official theoretical doctrines in science. A dreadful silence followed my attack, and I thought no one was going to support me. But finally Sam Stouffer, a tenured professor and a member of the senior committee, spoke up. He was always a fair-minded man—which did not mean he always agreed with me—and much to his honor but, I felt, somewhat reluctantly, he declared that the "Yellow Book" ought not be treated as departmental doctrine. There the matter dropped. Afterwards many of the junior members thanked me for what I had done. My seniors at last realized I was a bit of a rebel. No further official effort was made to integrate theory for the Department of Social Relations. Practically, for some years the structural-functionalism of Parsons was the dominant school of thought among our graduate students in sociology.

Though we failed to "integrate," the new department was not for that reason a failure. Like other universities, Harvard was full of veterans returning from World War II. They were more serious minded and mature than most peacetime undergraduates, and their experiences in the war, including the very fact of the war itself, taught them that something was much amiss with the world and that its problems could be solved only by a new approach, especially one that centered on "people." The new department, they felt, might supply what they were seeking. Accordingly many students took the courses the department offered. While Allport and I were teaching the introductory course, some seven hundred students enrolled and many of them majored in our department. (Harvard calls majoring "concentration.") In the early 1950s the department was offering one of the largest courses and enrolled one of the largest number of concentrators in the undergraduate part of the university, "Harvard College." As the number of veterans declined, so did our majors. And as the years went by, people perceived—and rightly so— that the sciences represented in the new department did not have the answers to the problems of the world. This did not mean that what we taught was not often interesting and useful in itself. The largest number of our concentrators became those interested in the field of personality: they joined us in part in order to get some grip on their own personal problems. Fewer were those interested in the ills of the world as represented by our other three disciplines.

Besides teaching the second half of the introductory course for some years, I was further responsible for undergraduates, especially our concentrators, by serving as chairman of the Committee on Undergraduate Instruction. I was, so to speak, a "chairman of the board." The detailed administrative work was done by a head tutor, analogous to a "president." What fun it was working with such lively and intelligent head tutors, so full of a sense of humor, as Hank Riecken and Joe Kahl! What splendid flaps we got into! By my definition a flap is an emergency that bothers someone else more than it does oneself. I should love to tell about some of them, were I not crushed by lack of space.

Over the years the Department of Social Relations gradually disintegrated as a department, though not for disreputable reasons, until in 1970 it formally dissolved into something like its original components. Sociology, under my chairmanship, became a separate department again. Social Psychology, the remains of Personality Psychology, and other odds and ends rejoined the "old" Psychology Department. The social anthropologists went back in membership if not in physical presence to "Peabody," which is what Harvard calls the Department of Anthropology, after the Peabody Museum, which contains its offices, library, and museum. Social Relations fell rather than was torn apart.

After the formal efforts to integrate the methodology and theory of the department had failed, what had we left to hold us together? The founding fathers had died or retired, and with them had gone the shared personal interests and antagonisms towards outsiders that had originally driven them together. Harvard had built a building to hold all of us and Psychology too, a fifteen-storey skyscraper by Cambridge standards, in the style referred to, after its Japanese architect, as "Shinto Gothic." But William James Hall, with its many floors, slow elevators, and dreary corridors, tended rather to divide than unite us. True, we had organized a single undergraduate field of concentration; but an undergraduate major is not enough to hold a large department together, especially not a department like ours which was a "general education" department, that is, one most of whose undergraduate majors did not continue in the field but dispersed as graduate students to medicine, law, business, etc.

Not undergraduate education but graduate education and research, in which professors and students collaborate, intimately it is hoped, hold a department together. But here from the beginning the department was divided in ways no amount of intellectual integration could overcome. We never dared offer a single graduate Ph.D. degree in social relations as such. We felt we could not place a person holding such a degree in a university post, especially as most other universities did not imitate the plan of the department. Instead we offered from the beginning four different graduate degrees: in clinical (really personality) psychology, social psychology, social anthropology, and sociology. The persons responsible for administering these degree programs developed their own special requirements for each, perpetuating for good or ill the previous traditions of their disciplines. As the years went by, the original subfields of the department began more and more to act as if they were departments in their own right. They even acquired the name of "wings."

There were no general departmental requirements for graduate students, at least no requirements that were not born sickly. One was in foreign languages, which the department, to its shame, soon gave up. Another was in statistics, which the department also gave up, though only for a time. At first, all graduate students took a single "integrative" seminar, usually offered by Professor Parsons and other members of the department whom he invited as guest speakers. Eventually it was given up under pressure from the students themselves. I am far from saying that the individual graduate programs were weak, though Clinical Psychology gradually withered away because the tenured members of the department never could find someone who was willing to carry out for a long enough time the work of building up opportunities for students to get clinical experience and providing supervision for their work. The problem was not, for the most part, that the individual "wings" were weak.

The original design for the department had called for the founding of a "Laboratory of Social Relations," whose first director was Sam Stouffer. It was not a laboratory in the original sense of a place where scientists conducted experiments, but rather a holding company to collect monies for research, to distribute them to members of the department for their varied projects, and finally to account for the expenditures. As such, the laboratory was a useful administrative device, for it relieved researchers of much paperwork they would otherwise have had to perform themselves. The founding fathers and Provost Buck had hoped that the new department would be cross-disciplinary not only in its theory but in its research, and the laboratory was especially interested in funding and supporting such research. I myself took part in joint research with anthropologists. The laboratory was not divisive, but neither was it a strong force for integration.

In these years, 1946-70, American universities expanded rapidly and especially in the behavioral sciences, both in number of academic positions and in the amount of research. Harvard itself quadrupled, I believe, the number of its professors and has lived to regret it. Social Relations took part fully in this growth. The number of staff members in each "wing" increased, and thus the ability of the wing to act independently. In the early days of the department, when its members were few, the tenured professors, gathered to make a recommendation for a permanent appointment, knew the work of most of the possible candidates and could compare their abilities. By 1970, though, when it was a question, for instance, of making an appointment in the field of personality psychology, the sociologists and others would simply have to take the word of the psychologists as to which of the candidates was really able. They themselves would not even have heard their names and were quite unable to judge their published works. This condition is thoroughly unhealthy. The department had simply grown too large.

Yet, as many will argue, history departments in some universities, though often as large or larger in membership than Social Relations became, are able to agree on recommending good scholars for appointment, in spite of the fact that the medieval historians may not even have heard of the candidates in the field of American history. The reason, I believe, is that all historians share an old and strong tradition, which may now be weakening. They all think that they can recognize the difference between good and bad history in any field.

For the reasons I have given, the Social Relations Department would have fallen apart sooner or later, but the actual event had to have a precipitating cause. That turned out to be the student rebellions, which, beginning at the University of California, Berkeley, in the earlier 1960s, reached Harvard in the years 1969 and 1970. I myself particularly disapproved of the way the then leaders of the department, otherwise good men, allowed the establishment of a famous student-organized and radical course called Social Relations 129. It came to the point at which I could not bear to listen in department meetings to the bleatings and wafflings of the foolish, hypocritical, and self-righteous "liberals." It seemed to me then that there were more of them—though only a few more—among the psychologists and anthropologists than among the sociologists. I wanted out, and one of the purest pleasures I have enjoyed from no longer being a member of the Department of Social Relations is my freedom from ever having to pay the slightest serious attention to such people again. If they will stick to their business, they are often good fellows, but as academic statesmen they make me puke.

Let me not give the impression that I was the chief mover in the breakup of the old department. That was my colleague in sociology, Harrison White, who put forward the theory that sociology would be able to wangle more new appointments out of the dean of the faculty if it were an independent department rather than a mere "wing" of Social Relations. He turned out to be quite mistaken, since his proposal came just at the time when Harvard, like so many other universities, began, as a combined result of inflation and previous overexpansion, to run a large deficit at least in the Faculty of Arts and Sciences. There were no new appointments to be had, though old ones could be filled when they became vacant.

Harrison White was more Machiavellian and nailed my own agreement down, when he suggested that I should become chairman of a revived sociology department. Nobody in his right mind would become chairman of a department, when chairmen have as little power as they do at Harvard. They have much responsibility without commensurate authority. Yet being a chairman was a normal part of an academic career. Though I had long held enough seniority, the members of the Social Relations Department had never been willing to make me chairman. I was too much of a rebel. I was, to use the current term, too abrasive. For me, being abrasive was simply telling the truth, naturally in as downright a manner as possible, but nothing is more abrasive than naked truth. I wanted to show the others what fools they had been, and that I could handle the job of chairman at least as well as they. And I did. Only Talcott Parsons, the last of the founding fathers who was still active, defended to the end the continuation of sociology within the Department of Social Relations. After all, he had been its chief founder. With the agreement of the dean of the Faculty of Arts and Sciences, at that time John Dunlop, later secretary of Labor of the United States, and by vote of the faculty, the new Department of Sociology came into existence, with me as chairman, on July 1, 1970.

Let me not be hard on the Department of Social Relations. As we say, it was a good try, and a life of twenty-four years is a long one for a noble experiment. As far as I was concerned, the department offered me a rich intellectual environment, just at the time my old environment in the Business School of Henderson and Mayo was disappearing. Though I did not always agree with them, the department put me into contact with many ideas, both theoretical and methodological, that were new to me. It allowed me to teach not only sociology but anthropology and social psychology, and did not object, though it might well have, to my teaching medieval English history to boot. It put me in touch with many good and interesting men and women—as well as with some consummate asses. Some of them were both interesting and asinine at the same time. The department constrained me not at all, and ended at the right time. From my own point of view—and here I can take no other—this seems a pretty good record. Let us shed a tear or two for the passing of the department, but not a flood.

Just as I found upon my return from the war the Faculty of Arts and Sciences much changed for me by my appointment to a permanency and membership in the new Department of Social Relations, so I found in the Business School an almost unrecognizable environment. Henderson had died in 1942; Mayo was to retire in 1947 and go to live in his beloved England, where he himself died in 1949. The Western Electric and Yankee City researches had come to an end—though not the flood of writing about them.

Before he retired Mayo did me one last good turn. He arranged that I should spend some days at Dartmouth College with Professor Adelbert Ames. Ames belonged to a well-known New England family. He had begun his adult life as a sculptor but had then turned himself into a psychologist as an expert in human perception. After all, a sculptor's or painter's first concern is with perception. Ames did not teach by lectures or experiments but by what can only be called a series of visual demonstrations of the following doctrine. An infant is born with few percepts, but well endowed with the means of acquiring new ones by learning. He learns how to perceive the world. Put it more strongly: he learns the perceptual world and does so by acting on it. Those ways of perceiving associated with rewarded actions, for instance, being able to move around without always bumping into things, he is apt to retain. Indeed he is apt to retain them for some time even if the physical environment in which he learned them has changed. Or he will make some compromise between what he has learned to perceive in the past and what, in changed circumstances, he perceives now. Ames was an adept at arranging such changes and showing how his subjects' past perceptual experiences affected their reaction to them. Ames fully persuaded me that perceptions are learned and maintained much as other actions are. Though I was not conscious of it at the time, this insight later helped me escape the false dichotomy some psychologists try to draw between behavioral and cognitive psychology. But I am getting ahead of my argument.

With Henderson dead and Mayo retired, the senior member of what was called the "human relations" group at the Business School and the man who did most to carry on and develop its traditions became Fritz Jules Roethlisberger, ably assisted by George F. F. Lombard. I must write about Fritz not only because for a time I worked closely with him and became very fond of him—and that in spite of our frequent disagreements—but also because his own autobiography[11] contains the only outsider's account of my own style and character and not just my work. I myself am the only person who can write as an insider on this subject.

Fritz was Mayo's first and, in many respects, ablest student. He became the chief field investigator in the Western Electric researches and the senior author of the best book about them.[12] In the course of my association with Mayo and Henderson before the war, I had often met Fritz but had never known him well. He was twelve years older than I. After the war I revived and maintained an informal association with the "human relations" group, attended many conferences with them at the Business School, and even served for a term, to my great pleasure, as a visiting professor there. In these years I could not help, nor did I wish to help, becoming more than just an acquaintance of Fritz's.

Indeed with two junior partners, Abraham ("Abe") Zaleznik and Roland ("Chris") Christensen, we carried out a research project together. After the war we both came to feel that, in our field studies of small working groups in American business, we kept on reaching the same intuitive findings over and over again. Might we not therefore, perhaps with a theory I was on the way to developing, be able to predict what we should find in some group new to us? Was not prediction one of the jobs of a science? We chose a group and set our junior partners to work making a field study of it, while Fritz and I, kept from all knowledge of the group except for what could be obtained from accounts of the technology, the physical layout, and standard personnel information, made predictions about the social behavior and organization of the group. Our junior partners would check these predictions against the information they obtained by observation and interviewing in the field.

Our work on the prediction study was great fun, but we had been too ambitious. We had made so many predictions that a large number of them might have turned out to be correct, as they did, simply by chance. And some of the findings turned out to be not easily reconcilable with any of the theories (sets of hypotheses) with which we had tried to make our predictions. It fell largely to Abe Zaleznik to make such sense as he could—and it was quite a lot—of our results. For my part I still feel some guilt because I got out of my responsibility to help write up the report by running away to England and a visiting professorship at Cambridge University in the academic year 1955-56. I shall say no more about the prediction study. After all, Fritz has written about it in his autobiography,[13] and the report of the study has been published.[14] I learned much about the difficulties of applying a theory. I also learned much about Fritz and Fritz about me.

Fritz was a rather small man, usually looking up at me from under his eyebrows with his skeptical but kindly, deep-set, little eyes, a most engaging but timid grin wrinkling his whole face. He was an excellent, even a master teacher, at least when using the "case discussion" method, which had become part of the ideology of the Business School, though that allowed many variations in practice, including Fritz's own. (I was never any good at using the "case method".) Fritz was also an excellent writer: all his books make good reading, which is high praise indeed for a social scientist. Above all, he was a superb interviewer, building on Mayo's example. It was he who developed the rules for nondirective interviewing employed in the Western Electric researches. Whether as interviewer or observer, he was the best field researcher I have known. Though we often disagreed about other matters, I never questioned for a second any clinical generalization he had reached about individuals or groups he had studied at first hand.

These skills required a high degree of tact. One of his criticisms of me, which of course he never expressed to my face, was that I utterly lacked it. He wrote: "George in his personal style was forthright and direct. No one had any question where he stood: he never seemed to care upon whose sensitive toes he trod. . . . Although I felt that George had about as much intuitive skill in dealing with these social phenomena as Henderson (which as I have said earlier was not much), I never felt that he sloughed them off as too trivial or unimportant to be reckoned with intellectually. I never heard George 'pooh pooh' my clinical findings as such or the method by which they had been obtained."[15]

I will plead guilty to the charge of tactlessness, though I confess it is painful to be found equal with Henderson on this score. Of course, Fritz knew little about my background. From both my Adams and my Crowninshield ancestors I had inherited a tendency to use strong language, a tendency the endless bickering between two able sisters and myself had further strengthened in our childhood: we practiced telling home truths about one another in the most unflattering way. And had not "Ba" Barlow, what we should now call my role model, "dared speak the truth and shame the hypocrites"?[16] In fairness to myself I must also insist that I was ready to take as good as I gave: a number of men came to call me "the pachyderm" because my skin was thick enough for me to take almost any kind of insult without getting angry. Nor had Fritz observed me in my own bouts of doing fieldwork by interviewing and observation. Then I could be tactful enough, indeed become as good an investigator as the next man—though never in a class with Fritz himself.

Fritz himself did not seem to me without faults—but who is? Besides his native temperament some of them I thought I could ascribe to a "trained incapacity." A good interviewer must not exert authority over his interviewees, and I felt that Fritz, even outside the interviewing role, had become reluctant to exercise authority, especially that side of authority which consists in the ability to reach decisions quickly: I had no doubt that Fritz could reach wise decisions if given enough time. But even in the process of research, decisions sometimes have to be made quickly, and I found myself, in the course of working with Fritz in a team, making more and more of such decisions. It is also true, as my history in the Navy shows, that I am apt to reach decisions all too quickly. But at least I am able to make them, while Fritz, in this respect, could never have become a good naval officer. Luckily he never had to become one.

For the most part Fritz and I agreed on how the enterprise of social science ought to proceed. Following Mayo, Henderson, and also, I believe, our own instincts, we felt it ought to begin by the investigator's acquiring intuitive familiarity with a body of data—that is, not just a number of isolated facts—and acquiring it, if possible, while holding responsibility. Social scientists still do not often follow this rule. Only then should the investigator try to develop a conceptual scheme: a classification of the principal kinds of data, grouped as concepts or variables, together with some notice that the variables are related to one another, though not necessarily just how they are related. Such a conceptual scheme allows the investigator to develop not just intuitive familiarity with, but systematic knowledge of, his body of data. It organizes the data and helps him think further about them, provided he treats it only as a convenient walking stick to be discarded when he is ready to take the next step.

So far so good, but what was the next step? For me—though I am again getting ahead of my argument—it was to develop a theory of the phenomena embedded in the data. A theory consisted of general propositions, general in the sense of applying to the whole body of data, from which, under different given conditions, lower-order, empirical, or clinical findings might be deduced, and thus explained. The theory of a phenomenon is an explanation of it.

In theory, so to speak, I believe Fritz accepted my notion of theory, but he never practiced it. He himself never stated or used in explanation any proposition I considered general, though he was prepared to play with mine. Again, I think part of the trouble was that he suffered, as I did too in a different way, from the defects of his virtues. A good clinician, which Fritz certainly was, must remain close to the data and he may therefore have difficulty with broad generalizations.

Another part of the trouble I attribute to Fritz's social and intellectual environment at the Business School. At the Business School both teaching and research were, almost necessarily, oriented towards action, towards what ought to be done in a particular situation and how to do it. The problem of applying a theory to action is always a difficult one, and especially difficult in social science. Fritz had to worry about it. On the other side of the Charles River, in the Social Relations Department, I did not have to worry about action unless I wanted to. I could concentrate on theory simply as explanation.

The Business School also was, and still is, full of types who produced theories of organization, manufacturing, or whatever, from which the behavior of real men and women seemed to have disappeared. Fritz felt he had to keep up a long battle, not so much to bring people back into such theories as to deal with "human relations" as if they too could be treated as isolated phenomena. I sometimes felt he was perpetuating the same error as the organization theorists only in the opposite direction. I felt this situation tended to trap him into false dichotomies—if something is not black it must be white—such as the distinction between logical and nonlogical behavior, from which I thought I had escaped when, long ago, I began not just to admire Pareto but to criticize him.

At any rate, I find rather sad Fritz's efforts in the later chapters of his autobiography to escape from the toils he had netted for himself: he only managed to entangle himself further.[17] I wish I had had the chance to discuss those chapters with him, but his autobiography was published only after his death. My diagnosis may well be wrong, and it is not fair that I should thus have the last word. Whether he was being right or wrong, he was always both a good and an intelligent man, for of course one may be wrong for perfectly good reasons. Like the saint he was, he bore my tactlessness so well that it did not prevent his listening to my ideas. I miss him.

I turn next to my struggle to cope with just those issues on which Fritz and I did not so much disagree as fail to reach a full meeting of minds.

NOTES

1. Herman Melville, *Pierre; or, The Ambiguities,* ed. Henry A. Murray (New York: Farrar, Straus, 1949).
2. Kurt Lewin and Ronald Lippitt, "An Experimental Approach to the Study of Autocracy and Democracy: A Preliminary Note," *Sociometry* 10 (1938): 292-300. Reprinted in A. Paul Hare, Edgar F. Borgatta, and Robert F. Bales, *Small Groups: Studies in Social Interaction,* rev. ed. (New York: Knopf, 1965), pp. 648-55.
3. See especially Emile Durkheim, *Les Règles de la méthode sociologique,* 8th ed. (Paris: Alcan, 1927).
4. Michael Argyle, Godfrey Gardner, and Frank Cioffi, "Supervisor Methods Related to Production, Absenteeism, and Labor Turnover," *Human Relations* 11 (1958): 23-40.

5. Francis Bacon, *Novum Organum,* aphorism LXX.

6. Aristotle, *Nichomachean Ethics,* bk. V.

7. Robert K. Merton and Alice S. Kitt, "Contributions to the Theory of Reference Group Behavior," in *Continuities in Social Research: Studies in the Scope and Method of "The American Soldier",* ed. R.K. Merton and P. Lazarsfeld (Glencoe, IL.: Free Press), pp. 40-105.

8. George C. Homans, "Status among Clerical Workers," *Human Organization* 12 (1953): 5-10, and "The Cash Posters," *American Sociological Review* 19 (1954): 724-33. Both reprinted in George C. Homans, *Sentiments and Activities* (New York: Free Press of Glencoe, 1961), pp. 61-102.

9. George C. Homans, "The Puritans and the Clothing Industry in England," *New England Quarterly* 13 (1940): 519-29. Reprinted in George C. Homans, *Sentiments and Activities* (see n. 8, above), pp. 182-91.

10. Talcott Parsons and Edward A. Shils, eds. *Toward a General Theory of Action* (Cambridge: Harvard University Press, 1951).

11. F. J. Roethlisberger, *The Elusive Phenomena,* ed. George F. F. Lombard (Boston: Harvard University, Graduate School of Business Administration, 1977).

12. F. J. Roethlisberger and William J. Dickson, with the assistance and collaboration of Harold A. Wright, *Management and the Worker* (Cambridge: Harvard University Press, 1939).

13. Roethlisberger, *Elusive Phenomena,* pp. 291-47.

14. A. Zaleznik, C. R. Christensen, and F. J. Roethlisberger, with the assistance and collaboration of George C. Homans, *The Motivation, Productivity, and Satisfaction of Workers* (Boston: Harvard University, Graduate School of Business Administration, 1958).

15. Roethlisberger, *Elusive Phenomena,* p. 243.

16. See ch. 13.

17. Roethlisberger, *Elusive Phenomena,* bk. 2.

19

THE HUMAN GROUP

When I returned to Harvard after World War II, I had lost, except for sheer experience in the ways of men and ships, about five of the potentially most productive years of my professional life. I wanted to catch up. Above all, I wanted to write, and knew that I should not gain further academic advancement unless I published—but I really believe that "publish or perish" was a secondary motive with me. I wanted first to put flesh on the conceptual scheme for the study of social organization that I had been turning over in my mind for years.

I have already described how it originated largely through my reactions to the work of Eliot Chapple and Conrad Arensberg in the later 1930s. The first printed version of it appeared in the last chapter of my *English Villagers of the Thirteenth* Century,[1] where it took the form of three main classes of variables: *interaction, sentiment,* and *function,* which were mutually interdependent, but just how I did not say. During my first years in the Navy I am sure my unconscious was working on it. Consciously I did not take it up again until my ship was laid up for repairs in Willemstad, Curaçao, in 1943. Then in two weeks I revised the whole scheme and wrote it out in the form of a sketch.

In my Willemstad sketch, I kept my three classes of variables: interaction, sentiment, and function. But I had sense enough to drop the name *function* and change it to *activity*. What I added was a distinction between the *internal* system and the *external* system. An intellectual boundary might be drawn around any social system, such as a group. Within this boundary the three classes of variables were mutually dependent in the behavior of the members. This set of relations formed the *internal* system. But there were also influences across the boundary, between the internal system and its social or physical environment. Thus the pattern according to which the management of a factory laid out the physical equipment of a department might well affect the interpersonal relations within it. Besides cross-boundary influences, I assumed that the three classes of variables would be mutually dependent outside the boundary as well as within it, and so I referred to them as the *external* system. This was a mistake. Beyond the boundary the variables need not be mutually dependent. I learned later that what I called the external system might better be referred to, in the conventional way, as the given or boundary conditions, or as the parameters, of the internal system. Working with biological systems, Henderson had concluded that, in a system, a change in the value of any variable would produce change in the values of all the others. As I changed my mind about the external system, so I came slowly to the conclusion that human social systems were much less organic, less systematic, than what Henderson had in mind.

When I returned to Harvard I published a revision of the Willemstad sketch as "A Conceptual Scheme for the Study of Social Organization."[2] This was the only one of my papers Mayo really disliked. He thought I had become, like so many sociologists, a scholastic, a mere word-monger, which indeed I had it in me to become. Yet I believe I have escaped. At the same time I was beginning to become less a disciple, more independent, of Mayo, and his strictures did not bother me much.

I was not content with merely publishing a sketch. I wanted to apply it to a complex body of data. I originally intended to expand it by writing a general book on social organization, that is, on the organization of whole societies. After all, my readings in social anthropology and my research for *English Villagers of the Thirteenth Century* had given me some capacity for this kind of work.

But once again chance took a hand. I must record another of those accidents that have made so much difference to the course of my life, and always for the better. I was going, still by railroad train in those days, to a convention of the American Sociological Society in Chicago at the end of, I think, 1946. Connie Arensberg, coming from Columbia, was on the same train. We met and naturally fell into conversation, in the course of which he let fall the remark that he planned to write a general book on social organization. On the spot I decided not to reveal that I had planned to write one too. I had a high opinion of Connie's abilities and of his knowledge of comparative social organization. I would not try to compete with him in this field. But what, then, should be the subject of my own book, for I was determined to write one?

Before many hours had passed I had made up my mind that, if I conceded Connie the large, I should lay claim to the small. I would apply my conceptual scheme to a number of excellent field studies of small groups that had appeared before and during the war. This decision made me henceforward a "small group man," a micro- rather than a macro-sociologist. The irony of my decision was that Connie never did write his general book on social organization. At North Hatley, Québec, our summer home, I wrote out in longhand and at top speed a draft of the whole of what was to become *The Human Group*. But unnerving incidents had not yet ended. I read in some publishing advertisement that Ed Shils, of the University of Chicago and co-author of the "Yellow Book," was getting out a book to be entitled *The Small Group*. Horrors! Had I escaped Arensberg only to fall into the claws of Shils? I had a high opinion of the abilities of both men. But by now it was too late to change my mind a second time. What is more, I had no place to go. Again irony showed its cheerful face. Shils never published his book on the small group. Ah, the unpublished books that have helped my published ones!

Although as it turned out I need not have made my decision not to write about social organization at large, I have never regretted it. The big subject would have turned out to be too much for me. Moreover, I came later to believe that the decision made good sense intellectually. As I came slowly to understand what a theory was and to choose the kind of theory I would use for my social science. I became more and more strongly convinced that its power, at least in a first approximation, would initially have to be demonstrated in explaining the familiar phenomena arising from the face-to-face interactions between human beings, what I called the elementary features of social behavior, before it would ever be accepted as explaining large-scale social phenomena, though I did not despair that in the long run it would prove acceptable even there.

The Human Group appeared in 1950.[3] It had been turned down by Alfred Knopf, who had published *An Introduction to Pareto*, or rather by his social science editor. I am sure Robert Merton, advisor in social science to Harcourt, Brace & Company, persuaded that firm to publish it. But the firm must have been nervous about the choice, for it brought it out with no less than two laudatory introductions, one by Merton and the other by my old teacher and friend, Benny DeVoto, though he had no clue to what I was talking about. Harcourt Brace, now Harcourt Brace Jovanovich, has never had any reason to regret publishing *The Human Group*, which has been by far the most successful financially of all my books. It has also been the favorite with both students and teachers. It is not mine. I certainly will not disown it, but I think my later *Social Behavior*[4] is the better of the two. *The Human Group* came out when I was forty years old. Was it my oracle, Mr. Justice Holmes, who said that no one who had not made his mark by the age of forty was likely to make it at all? I had just gotten in under the wire.

In *The Human Group* I chose to analyze five closely observed, concrete field studies of small groups. (Some of them were not all that small.) Aside from an introduction to the book and other general material, I devoted at least two chapters to each of the groups, a procedure I feared would make the book fatally dull but did not seem to do so. The first chapter of each pair provided a shortened version of the original investigator's account, though not shortened so much as to omit anything essential, and, above all, adding nothing of my own. In the second chapter I applied my conceptual scheme to the original account, describing what data might be classed under each of my variables, what under the external system and what under the internal system, and showing that the variables and systems were related to one another. The purpose of this exercise was to allow the reader to check for him- or herself how an abstract scheme could be related to concrete data.

In one of the earlier chapters I made a bad mistake, which none of my critics has ever picked up.[5] I had intended my category, *sentiments,* to comprise expressions of interpersonal feelings. I included them in the chapter, but I also included *motives,* partly to help me show the mutual dependence of sentiments and activities in the external system. Now motives (values) are not identical with sentiments. Sentiments may be motives for action, but they are not the only ones. There are many motives that have nothing to do with sentiments, at least as I had defined sentiments, and I ought not to have lumped them together. Still, the appearance of motives in *The Human Group* is the first hint of what was to figure so prominently in my later work: the use of psychological propositions to explain social behavior. From this experience I learned how uncritically most people, even those with so-called trained minds, read books. I myself am my own best critic, though I usually keep my mistakes to myself.

In *The Human Group* I meant to apply my conceptual scheme to a body of data on five small groups. But the phrase "conceptual scheme" breeds, like so many terms in metascience, confusion. Following Henderson I meant it to mean a list of the variables I intended to use in the analysis of a set of phenomena, together with their definitions, operational or other, statements that some of the variables were related to others, though usually not how or why they were related, and finally a sketch of the given conditions within which the phenomena were to be analyzed. I believe this notion of a conceptual scheme resembles what others, such as Robert Merton, would call a *paradigm.* But some scientists go further and use "conceptual scheme" to mean a full-blown theory. Though I had heard the word *theory* often enough, I was not yet sure what it meant.

As I got into writing *The Human Group,* I began to feel, rather than to think, that I ought to try to do more than just show how to apply my conceptual scheme to concrete data. It was not enough to show that two variables were somehow related. Sociology was full of such statements. They were often good guides to research: I have come to call them *orienting statements.* But if the examples of other sciences were any guide, it was necessary sooner or later to go beyond them and show *how* the variables were related. Such statements I have come to call, following an old tradition, *propositions*. They did not have to state a precise relationship between two or more variables, such as $x = \log y$. Henderson had taught me that one often had to remain content with a first approximation. But a proposition had at least to say, for instance, that as x increased in value, so did y, even if one did not know by just how much. In writing the book I began to state, almost by inadvertence, some of the propositions that seemed to stare at me out of the data. One example was: the more frequently two persons interacted, the more apt they were to like one another. This was a proposition relating my variables interaction and sentiment.

It did not bother me, though it certainly bothered some others, that the proposition did not hold good in all circumstances. Indeed if the two persons were competing with one another, the relationship might reverse itself and frequent interaction be associated with disliking rather than liking. This kind of lesson should be among the first a young scientist learns. All I might claim for such propositions was that, if they did not hold good in all circumstances, at least they did in the circumstances obtaining in some of the groups I studied. My decision to state propositions relating some of the variables in my conceptual scheme was one of the most important intellectual steps I ever took: I began to wonder whether what I was creating, or what I ought to try to create, was something more than a conceptual scheme.

I also added a few more or less interesting digressions, such as the discussion of what I called the Social Contract and the Social Mold theories of social behavior.[6] They are not real theories but sets of orienting statements. The distinction came out of my old efforts to reconcile the theories of magic advanced by Malinowski and Radcliffe-Brown. To put it briefly, the Social Contract theory looks on society as the creation of millions of individuals acting over time, often wholly without coordination, indeed often at odds with one another, and collectively achieving results, including institutions and social structures, which none of the individuals may have intended. The Social Mold theory, which Radcliffe-Brown and his master, Emile Durkheim, seemed to hold, was less interested in the creation and change of societies than in their results, once created. This theory was concerned with how the institutions and other structures of a society affected the behavior of its members. In the Contract Theory the behavior of individuals provided the independent variables; in the Mold Theory, the characteristics of institutions and structures did. This difference in emphasis still exists among sociologists, and I shall return to it later.

The favorable reception of *The Human Group* led to my offering for many years a course entitled, first, "An Introduction to the Study of Small Groups," and later and more accurately, "Fundamental Social Processes." I used to say that small groups were not what we studied but where we studied it—the "it" being the fundamentals of social behavior. In preparing myself to teach the course I had to make myself familiar not only with field studies of small groups, in which I had long specialized, but with the growing number of survey and experimental studies the social psychologists had made. I had to go still further in this direction when my friend Henry Riecken and I undertook to write the article on group phenomena for the first edition of the *Handbook of Social Psychology*[7]—a "handbook" two heavy volumes long. My teaching and my study of the literature in social psychology gave me further reason to consider whether the scheme I put forward in *The Human Group* for organizing intellectually the findings on fundamental social processes was really adequate. Other intellectual issues I had to face in the early years of the new department were driving me in the same direction, especially the issue of theory.

NOTES

1. George C. Homans, *English Villagers of the Thirteenth Century* (Cambridge: Harvard University Press, 1941).
2. George C. Homans, "A Conceptual Scheme for the Study of Social Organization," *American Sociological Review* 12 (1947): 13-26.
3. George C. Homans, *The Human Group* (New York: Harcourt. Brace, 1950).
4. George C. Homans, *Social Behavior: Its Elementary Forms* (New York: Harcourt, Brace & World, 1961); rev. ed. (New York: Harcourt Brace Jovanovich, 1974).
5. Homans, *Human Group,* pp. 37, 99.
6. Ibid., pp. 316-21.
7. Henry L. Riecken and George C. Homans, "Psychological Aspects of Social Structure," in *Handbook of Social Psychology,* ed. Gardner Lindzey, 2 vols. (Cambridge: Addison-Wesley, 1954).

20

THEORY AND EXPLANATION

In *The Human Group* I had intended to show how my conceptual scheme, in my sense of that term, could be applied to a complex body of data. Before I had finished the book I wondered whether I had not begun to do something more: create a theory. *The Human Group* had described the characteristics of a theory as I then understood them. They were sound as far as they went, but I was to discover that they did not go nearly far enough.

In my undergraduate and graduate years, from Whitehead to Henderson, people had been talking to me about theory and had proclaimed so often as to make me puke that "nothing is more useful than a good theory." Some even knew they were well on their way to creating one. Talcott Parsons, the chairman of my new department, seemed the most sure of it. Yet one fact began at last to astonish me. No one, at least in the social sciences, had defined what a theory *was*, not even Henderson, though he was the most sophisticated philosopher of science in the Harvard of his time. Perhaps they did not define theory because they took it for granted that everybody knew: it was some form of what came to be called the "covering law" view of theory. But that was not the sort of theory the social scientists were creating. Accordingly the next intellectual question I wanted answered, though as usual I did not know I wanted it until I had the answer in my hand, was: What *is* a theory? Many sociologists, while still mouthing the word *theory,* have not gotten the answer yet.

The first step I took was not intended to answer the question, but helped unintentionally. While at sea during World War II, with plenty of time on my hands, I refurbished my calculus, so that I was able to understand the mathematical reasoning that lay behind classical physics, before Einstein and quantum mechanics. When I got back to Harvard I continued to attend the dinners of the Society of Fellows, where I became a friend of Tom Kuhn's, a member new since my time, a physicist who later became a famous historian of science.[1] Simply for the good of my soul, I asked Tom to suggest books for me to read that treated classical physics rigorously. He first suggested Ernst Mach, *The Science of Mechanics*,[2] a history of the oldest branch of physics, and later Max Planck, *Treatise on Thermodynamics*.[3] Reading these books was hard work, because I made sure I understood the steps in the mathematical reasoning and did not just take them for granted.

Mach's book was the more interesting to me, because it was a history. It showed scientists over the centuries groping for the concepts and propositions that would allow them to present their findings most consistently and powerfully. Through his treatment of D'Alembert's Principle, Mach also showed me how physicists formulated and used propositions concerning equilibrium. At last I was fully able to understand what Pareto meant by it. Mach persuaded me that the concept could not be of much use in sociology until that subject was far more fully developed. Kuhn, through Mach and Planck, helped me appreciate what physicists had certainly recognized as good theories for their times, though no theory is forever. At his urging I read other classic works of science, notably D'Arcy Thompson, *On Growth and Form*.[4] It is full of entrancing material, though not a unified theory.

Nor was Tom Kuhn the only influence on my reading. Sometime in the early 1950s, at the Salzburg Seminar in American Studies, I had met Ralph Turvey, then an economist at the London School of Economics and now a prominent British civil servant. Again for the good of my soul, I had long wanted to make myself familiar with the basic principles of economics, if there were any. I was catching up with subjects I ought to have studied as an undergraduate—which did not mean that I have ever come to despise, as my great-uncle Henry Adams professed to do, the literary and historical studies that filled my college years. Turvey put me through some readings on neoclassical microeconomics, notably George Stigler, *The Theory of Price*.[5] Stigler is now a Nobel laureate. Microeconomics was to have its effect on my later book *Social Behavior*.

Though my reading provided me with good examples of theories, I did not study them with the deliberate purpose of discovering what a theory was. That question was precipitated for me by contact with, and reading the works of, Talcott Parsons. In 1946 Talcott became the first chairman of the Department of Social Relations, of which I was now a member. A graduate of Amherst College, Talcott had gone on to the London School of Economics as a graduate student and then to Heidelberg, where he came under the spell of the works of Max Weber, though Weber himself had died. Weber had converted Talcott from economics to sociology, and when I first met him in the 1930s, he was a junior member of the then Sociology Department at Harvard, and I was still a Junior Fellow. Talcott took me to be an ally of his. I had written a book on Pareto, and Talcott himself was working on a big book, in which he would try to show that

Pareto, Durkheim, Weber, and Alfred Marshall, star of the great Cambridge, England, group of economists, had independently worked out what were, in Talcott's view, essentially similar theories of social action.

Talcott asked me to read and criticize the manuscript of this book, which was to be published as *The Structure of Social Action.*[6] I conscientiously read it, but did not criticize it, I hated it so much. It was another book of words about other persons' words. Rarely did it make contact with actual human behavior. In such a book it is easy to claim one has demonstrated whatever one wants to demonstrate. Social science bulges with books of this sort. I did not think Talcott had come even close to proving his thesis. Perhaps I ought not to have been so critical, since my own book about Pareto had been one of the same kind. Yet in my view there was so much wrong with the book that, were I do to justice to my disapproval, I should have to write a book equally long. That I was certainly not going to do; I had my own fish to fry. So I returned the manuscript to Talcott with very general, pusillanimous, and hypocritical words of approval, accompanied with only enough objections to show that I was independent minded. I did not disabuse him of his conviction that I was at heart an ally.

Though gruesome, that was my only possible policy. Later I learned that any effort to criticize Talcott's work would be wasted anyway. He would never meet arguments head on. He would only dismiss his critics as "unsympathetic" and never ask himself whether they had anything to be unsympathetic *about*. My hypocritical answer had the further advantage of not losing me Talcott's friendship, and I am sure he was one of my supporters when I became a candidate for a tenured post. (A reader will have no trouble discovering that I do not put myself forward as a *moral* academic.) As chairman of the new department, Talcott always treated me fairly. Only with the publication of the "Yellow Book" was it fully revealed to him that I was a member of the opposition.

My trouble with Parsons centered on his notion of theory as expressed in a flood of publications. Implicitly I was sure it was not mine, but I could not yet make explicit in what ways it was not. Like Marx, Talcott wrote so much and so turgidly that one can find almost anything one wants to find in him. By the same token, one can hardly avoid occasionally doing him an injustice. Curiously enough, he was sometimes a good concrete sociologist. When he wrote about matters, such as the medical profession, that he had studied at first hand, his observations were often shrewd. His tragedy was that he did not want to be known as a concrete sociologist. There was more prestige in being a theorist, and that, he always insisted, was what he was.

No doubt my description of Talcott's "theory" will be found partial and unfair. He was always insisting that it was changing and developing. He was always hailing a new "breakthrough." To my mind, the more breakthroughs he made, the more his theory remained essentially the same. He started with a basic social situation: two persons, the actions of each of whom "sanctioned," that is, rewarded or punished, the actions of the other. This was a very good place from which to take off. I myself started from it when I later began to develop my own theory. To be sure, Talcott did not state the propositions that describe how the sanctioning takes place, that is, how rewards and punishments shape behavior. That would have gotten him into behavioral psychology, the last school he would have wished to find himself associated with. Some people seem to have a sixth sense that tells them when they are stepping into danger. Then, and now, behaviorism is intellectually dangerous. In psychology, Talcott held with psychoanalysis and even had himself put through a didactic analysis.

In any event, Talcott never did much with the basic social situation. Instead of building up from, and elaborating it, he usually jumped at once to the social system, embodied in a society as a whole. In order to survive or remain in equilibrium, a society had to be imbued with certain values, which were embodied in institutions. The function of these values was to maintain the system. I was back with functionalism, though in a slightly new form. Indeed Talcott's was usually called a "structural-functional" theory. The values, sometimes referred to as the "pattern-variables," were four in number. They had to be embodied at each level of the social system from the highest down, thus increasing in number in their downward progress as the square of four, a law we junior members of the department had discovered in the course of studying the drafts of the "Yellow Book." If the four values (functions) had to be met at the level of the United States as a whole, so they had to be met at the level, let us say, of The Country Club of Brookline, Massachusetts, though at the level just above The Country Club, that institution might be contributing to only one of the values, let us say the one called "pattern maintenance." Thus Talcott's theory looked like a set of internesting Chinese boxes, which fitted into one another and into which all sorts of social behavior could in turn be fitted. Fitted—but what else could be done with them?

Mine, of course, is a caricature, though one that allows me to accent what disturbed me most about Talcott's "theory." First, it raised again the question of functionalism, about which I had long been a skeptic. Second, it fully raised the issue of the nature of theory. Each of the boxes (categories) in the alleged theory was supposed to be related to the other three boxes at its own level and to the appropriate boxes below and above it in a hierarchy of levels. But just how were they related? What particular change in the material in one of the boxes (variables) would produce a change in another, and in what direction? Talcott did not say. If there was one thing I had made up my mind about it was the maxim: "No proposition, no theory!" A proposition had not only to say that at least two variables were related but also how they were related, at least to the extent of stating, for instance, that an increase in the value of one would be accompanied by an increase in the value of the other. Though I cannot swear that an exhaustive search of Talcott's writing would have unearthed no propositions, I am sure it would have unearthed damned few. His "theory," therefore, was at best another conceptual scheme or paradigm. One might concoct as many paradigms as one pleased. I was sure that a theory would have to face more searching tests.

Parsons's notion of a theory was obviously so different from the one I instinctively held after reading Mach and Planck that I decided to pursue the matter further and discover what the philosophers of science had to say about theory. In the course of my path so far, I had also made up my mind that, though the concrete propositions of theories in different sciences were bound to be different, and that good theories were certainly more easily attainable in some fields than others, nevertheless the general characteristics of a theory must be the same in all sciences, physical, biological, or social. Accordingly, what the philosophers had to say about theory, if it were otherwise reasonable, must hold good of all theories.

I shall have no space here to consider the prolonged visits I made to English universities in the years following the war: to Manchester in 1953, to Cambridge in 1955-56 and again in 1972, and to Kent (Canterbury) in 1967. I enjoyed each visit enormously and made many good friends. In England I first began to read what the philosophers of science had to say about theory.

In 1953, when I was at Manchester, Meyer Fortes, professor of social anthropology at Cambridge, whom I had first met through the Kluckhohns, invited me to talk to his seminar at King's College. Born a South African, Meyer had become more British than the British and was fond of trying to put Americans down when there was any question of comparing the achievements of the two nations. I treated these remarks, which were no more than teasing, with the indifference they deserved: to try to put a man down on an issue is to show you have some doubts about your own position. Superiority should be effortless. On this occasion R. B. Braithwaite, professor of philosophy at Cambridge, had just published a book entitled *Scientific Explanation.*[7] Meyer asserted, "You Americans could never have produced a book as good as that!" Of course we could and did, but that did not prevent my reading Braithwaite's book, which was indeed excellent. Later I read American books on the subject, especially those of Nagel[8] and Hempel.[9] Eventually I offered a graduate seminar in my department on "Explanation in the Social Sciences" and even wrote a little book on the subject.[10]

These philosophers seemed to be saying much the same things about theory, and I accepted what they had to say, because it corresponded with the characteristics of the real theories I had studied. They had nothing to say about how a theory is constructed. We know how to construct a house but not a theory. Though intuitive familiarity with the data certainly helps, it is never enough. What the constructor of a good theory also needs is a leap of the imagination, and alas! he or she cannot summon that up at will.[11] Henderson used to say that a good theory may be reached by some of the damnedest methods. What the philosophers were talking about was what a theory looks like *after* it is constructed, though no theory is ever more than provisionally completed.

A theory of a phenomenon is an explanation of the phenomenon— hence the title of Braithwaite's book. But *explanation,* like *theory* itself, is just another word. What do we mean by it? We "explain" to someone how to drive a car, but that is not what we mean by scientific explanation. A scientific explanation, for most but by no means all scientists and philosophers of science, consists of a set of propositions, and I have already said what I mean by a proposition. At the extreme it may simply say that if x is present, y also is present. The terms of a proposition are *empirically,* not, as some ignorant theorists in social science were fond of saying, *logically* related. What is logically related are the propositions themselves, not their terms.

The set of propositions forms what Braithwaite called a *deductive system.* At least one of the propositions in the set is the one to be explained, the *explicandum.* It is explained when the theorist shows that it follows in logic from the other propositions in the set: this is where logic comes in. At least one of the propositions in the set is more general than the others, in the sense that it cannot be deduced from the others, though the *explicandum* can be deduced from it together with the others. From the requirement of a general proposition or propositions, this view of explanation is often called the "covering law" view. In the course of time and the development of science, any current general proposition may be shown to follow from, or to converge under special conditions with, others still more general.

Besides *explicanda* and general propositions, various other kinds of propositions may enter deductive systems. First, we may make some of our deductions with the help of the equations of pure mathematics. Such propositions themselves derive from deductive systems of a different

kind from those we have been considering so far. The general propositions of these systems, usually called *axioms,* we assume *a priori*. The kind
we have been considering so far Braithwaite calls *contingent,* because fact,
evidence, data, are relevant to our accepting them as true or false. This is
not true of mathematical propositions.

Second, some of the propositions must state the givens, initial or
boundary conditions, or parameters—call them what you will—to which
the theorist must apply his general propositions if he is to make the
deductions from which his *explicanda* follow. Many idiots sound as if
they believed general propositions by themselves can explain. Not so,
they must be applied to given conditions, which may themselves be
explainable by their own deductive systems. This is notably true of
historical explanation. Where one chooses to cut off such subsidiary
explanations may be a matter of convenience or depend on whether or
not information is available. It is often not available for so-called *divergent*
phenomena, in which small initial differences spiral over time into
enormously larger ones. Divergent phenomena occur often in history. I
think I can explain why William the Conqueror, duke of Normandy,
decided to invade England in 1066. I do not think that I, or anyone else,
can explain why he won the very close-run battle of Hastings, though his
victory made over time a great and reverberating difference to English
history. Never fear: there are some phenomena, and important ones at
that, we shall never be able to explain.

Usually what we call a theory does not consist of a single deductive
system but a cluster of such systems sharing some of the same covering
laws. Such is the science of mechanics. The larger the number of
explicanda we can show to follow, under a variety of given conditions,
from a few covering laws, the more confidence we have in a theory.

To sum up much in a small example: we explain why in most places
there are two high and two low tides in a little more than twenty-four
hours by showing that this proposition follows from Newton's laws of
motion, including the law of gravity, when applied to such given
conditions as that the earth is largely covered with water, that it rotates
daily on its axis, and that the moon orbits the earth in something like a
month. I do not know whether modern astronomers can explain why
these given conditions should be what they are. I take a seaman's interest
in the tides.

Lately some philosophers have argued that the "covering law" doctrine
of explanation is unacceptable.[12] But they have failed to agree on what
would be a better one. Until they do, I shall cleave to the "covering law"
view, because it seems to me to correspond to what great scientists have
created and their followers have acknowledged to be theories.

Now let me confess. The covering-law view of theory is an ideal. Even those of us who accept it have seldom lived up to it fully. Our logic has not been tight, often because our propositions themselves have been only first approximations. We have left out steps in deduction, either because they seemed obvious, or because they took up too much space, or because we could only guess at the given conditions. Still, we know what our ideal is and we have taken some practical steps to live up to it. I am told that this is true of the hard sciences as it is of sociology, though not to such a degree.

Let me now return to Talcott Parsons and illustrate with an anecdote, which I believe to be true, the difference between his view of theory and the one I had accepted. In a lecture which he gave at Cambridge, England, of all places, where John Maynard Keynes was then the God of economics, Talcott asserted that Keynes's theory was "an interesting special case" of Talcott's own theory of action. In real theories, a special case is one in which the general propositions are applied to only a few of the given conditions to which they may be applied. Thus the theory of the tides is a special case of Newtonian mechanics. To argue that a phenomenon is a special case of a theory is certainly to argue that it can be deduced from the general propositions of the theory. But Parsons had not deduced Keynes's theory from his own. What he had done was something quite different. As we have seen, Parsons's conceptual scheme contained four categories at every level. He thought he had found in Keynes's theory four categories that corresponded in some way to the four of his own but were less comprehensive in scope. This is not deduction, for Talcott stated no propositions relating the categories to one another. The finding of correspondence between categories is something anyone with a little imagination can always succeed in doing. I was told that when Talcott made his statement a member of the audience shouted, "Shit!"

I was now satisfied that for practical purposes I knew what a theory was. But answering one question always raises another. However useful it was in some ways, *The Human Group* was not a theory, but perhaps on the way to becoming one. What should I have to do to create a real theory of social behavior? How was I to practice what I preached?

If the philosophers of science were correct, the chief problem in constructing a theory was the invention or choice of appropriate covering laws, the most general propositions, at least for the time being, of a theory. The greatest scientists had had to invent their own covering laws, and that required what Einstein thought of as a leap of the imagination. Not only did I not possess the scientific muscle to make such a leap, but I had a shrewd idea that I should not have to invent my own covering laws but could borrow those of somebody else and just apply them in a new area. What a parasite have I been! Not only have I borrowed the findings of field and experimental studies made by others, I have also appropriated other persons' laws.

One conclusion I had reached before World War II as a result of my readings in social anthropology. There was a single human nature, single in its general characteristics, which did not mean that every individual human personality was like every other. Therefore my general propositions would have to be propositions about this human nature. And they would have to be psychological rather than sociological, propositions not about groups as such but about what human beings have in common as members of a species. If this were not so, I could not explain why individuals so far separated in time and space that they could not have borrowed from one another had invented, under similar conditions, similar institutions. Of course in the societies I had studied there often were enough persons, living under similar conditions, to produce such norms of behavior. As I looked back I realized that both I and other social anthropologists had in fact used psychological propositions to explain these social phenomena.

The position I now adopted explicitly as others had implicitly is sometimes called by the ghastly phrase *methodological individualism*. It was not a new idea either to sociology or to the human race. John Stuart Mill had summed it up well: "The laws of the phenomena of society are, and can be, nothing but the laws of the actions and passions of human beings united together in the social state. Men, however, in a state of society are still men: their actions and passions are obedient to the laws of individual human nature. Men are not, when brought together, converted into another kind of substance, with different properties: as hydrogen and oxygen are different from water. . . . Human beings in society have no properties but those which are derived from, and may be resolved into, the laws of the nature of individual man. In social phenomena the Composition of Causes is the universal law."[13] By the "composition of causes" Mill was referring to the fact that social phenomena are the, usually unintended, resultants of the actions of many individuals. The trouble with Mill's statement was not that it was untrue, but that it did not specify what "the laws of the nature of individual man" were. It was only what I call an "orienting statement," though an especially important one. By itself it was not enough for explanation. What I needed were general propositions describing the characteristics of human nature.

Unfortunately there were by this time a number of theories of human nature that might be, but were not always, stated in the form of explicit propositions. One of them was psychoanalysis, but a large part of that I would not, as we have seen, accept. And what I would accept could readily be cast into the language of other psychologies. Then there was Jean Piaget, to whom Mayo had introduced us, but his was a theory of the intellectual and moral development of children, whereas I wanted a theory that accounted not only for development but for behavior when developed. And so on for a number of other psychologies.

Yet from my new colleagues in the department I had heard a great deal about "learning theories," which seemed to resemble one another in many respects. At this point I bethought me of my old friend Fred Skinner, who was back at Harvard as professor of psychology. Though his work obviously fell within that class, Fred did not call his work "learning theory." Indeed he refused to claim for his work the status of a theory. Here I think he was being silly. His propositions, when applied of course to appropriate given conditions, explained not only much of the process of learning but also the characteristics of a person's behavior after it was learned. I reread two of Skinner's books, one on his experimental work, *The Behavior of Organisms*,[14] and another, meant for a more popular audience, *Science and Human Behavior*.[15]

I decided to use Skinner's propositions, which were not stated as such but nevertheless stood out clearly in his writings, as the "covering laws" of an explanation of elementary social processes. Perhaps the strongest reason for my choice of Skinner was that he made fewer unnecessary assumptions than did his rivals, such as Clark Hull. (He also failed to make some assumptions that *were* necessary.) Since Skinner's propositions were not limited to learning, I referred to them as the propositions of behavioral psychology. In accordance with Henderson's *dictum* that it was good to begin with approximations, I used only as many of Fred's propositions as I needed for my purposes, and I used them in stripped-down form, without any of his extra rigors and subtleties, important though these were in other respects. Nor, after a time, did I confine myself to Skinner. I learned much from reading the work of Albert Bandura[16] and from both reading the work of, and long conversations with, Richard Herrnstein, who had been a student of Skinner's, became in turn professor of psychology, and added crucial, indeed revolutionary, experimental ideas to Skinner's work.[17] Revolutionary additions are not always welcomed by the person subject to the revolution. The following chapter will be devoted to my attempt to use the propositions of behavioral psychology to explain human social behavior.

NOTES

1. For example, Thomas S. Kuhn, *The Copernican Revolution* (Cambridge: Harvard University Press, 1957).
2. Ernst Mach, *The Science of Mechanics*, trans. Thomas J. McCormack (La Salle, IL: Open Court Publishing, 1942).
3. Max Planck, *Treatise on Thermodynamics*, trans. Alexander Ogg (New York: Dover Publications, 1945).
4. D'Arcy Wentworth Thompson, *On Growth and Form* (Cambridge: Cambridge University Press, 1948).
5. George J. Stigler, *The Theory of Price*, rev. ed. (New York: Macmillan, 1952).
6. Talcott Parsons, *The Structure of Social Action* (New York: McGraw-Hill, 1937).
7. Richard Bevan Braithwaite, *Scientific Explanation* (Cambridge: Cambridge University Press, 1953).
8. Ernst Nagel, *The Structure of Science* (New York: Harcourt, Brace & World, 1961).
9. Carl G. Hempel, *Aspects of Scientific Explanation* (New York: Free Press, 1965).
10. George C. Homans, *The Nature of Social Science* (New York: Harcourt, Brace & World, 1967).
11. See especially Gerald Holton, *The Scientific Imagination* (Cambridge: Cambridge University Press, 1978), pp. 84-110.
12. Frederick Suppe et al., eds. *The Structure of Scientific Theories* (Urbana: University of Illinois Press, 1974).
13. John Stuart Mill, *A System of Logic* (New York: Harper, 1881), p. 608. Originally published 1843.
14. B. F. Skinner, *The Behavior of Organisms* (New York: Appleton-Century, 1938).
15. B. F. Skinner, *Science and Human Behavior* (New York: Macmillan, 1953).
16. Especially Albert Bandura, *Principles of Behavior Modification* (New York: Holt, Rinehart & Winston, 1968).
17. Richard Herrnstein, "Quantitative Hedonism," *Journal of Psychiatric Research* 8 (1971): 399-412.

21

SOCIAL BEHAVIOR

I had thought of *The Human Group* as a work of induction: in the course of working on my case studies of small groups, certain low-level or empirical propositions simply seemed to pop out at me. *Social Behavior,* on the other hand, I intended to be a work of deduction, that is, of explanation. I wanted to show how the propositions of *The Human Group,* together with others I had later encountered in my own research and in reading about new field studies, survey research, and experiments in social psychology, followed from the more general propositions of behavioral psychology. Notable among the new field studies were those of Peter Blau on working groups in bureaucracies.[1] My project first took the form of an article, "Social Behavior as Exchange,"[2] and then the form of the book itself, *Social Behavior: Its Elementary Forms,* in 1961. A revised edition appeared in 1974.[3]

Scholars often forget that no general propositions explain anything by themselves: they must be applied to given conditions; and applied to different givens, they explain different phenomena. Though I did not fully understand the reasons at the time, I did not, in *Social Behavior,* try to apply the general propositions to market situations, though they certainly can be and often are so applied, usually only implicitly. In classical markets the participants need not have repeated interactions with one another. I was interested in situations in which they do, at least for some period of time, and in which different phenomena appear from those that appear in classical markets and are treated by microeconomics. My conditions were met in relatively enduring small groups, such as those in industry. I wanted to explain the appearance of such common and familiar features of social behavior as conformity to norms, status systems, distributive justice or the lack of it—more generally the appearance of social structures. As I have said, I thought that we had to be able to explain such things before we went on to more large-scale or more idiosyncratic examples of social behavior. Hence the subtitle: *Social Behavior: Its Elementary Forms.*

My book is not a textbook of behavioral psychology, and in any event I do not want to repeat much of what I said there. To speak broadly, the propositions of behavioral psychology connect features of the environment of a higher animal, including man, with the actions the animal takes upon the environment. Behavioral psychology assumes that these connections are mediated by the nervous system and other physiological features of the animal, but it has nothing itself to say about the nature, for instance, of the brain that makes the connections possible. Scientists now know something about the nervous system, and will eventually know much more. But behaviorists believe that even then their own propositions will still hold good in a first approximation, and in the meantime they are the most general propositions available to us for explaining behavior.

The general propositions relate four main classes of variables to one another: the frequency with which a person performs an action (in B. F. Skinner's language an *operant*); the frequency with which an action is followed by a reward, a punishment, or nothing at all (in Skinner's language, the frequency with which an action is *reinforced,* positively or negatively); the degree of reward or punishment experienced by the actor (in my language, not Skinner's, the *value* of the reinforcement); and finally the environmental conditions, *stimuli,* that attend a person's action. Note that a person need not get a reward *because* he performed a certain action. The reward may be the result of wholly different causes. To serve as a reinforcer, it is enough that it follows the action, which leaves an opening for superstitious behavior.

Some of the propositions that relate the variables to one another are, in a first approximation, the following. The more often a person's action is rewarded, the more likely he or she is to perform it. Also, the more valuable the reward, the more likely he is to perform the action, but if it rewarded too often, the value of the reward tends to decrease (satiation). If conditions (physical, social, personal) similar to those that attended a rewarded action recur, the more likely the person is to repeat the action. To these I added propositions about emotional behavior, because it is so important in real life. The interesting feature of emotional behavior, such as aggression, is that, like a reflex but unlike an operant, a stimulus alone, such as a frustrating situation, can originally produce it, but a person can also learn to use it as an ordinary operant. Thus a person can learn to use aggressive behavior as an action that may bring him reward, and if it does, he may repeat it.

Under most circumstances a person usually has more than one action open to him or her to perform. He tends to perform the action for which the value he expects from the reward, multiplied by the probability he expects of obtaining it, is the larger. This rule, while useful, certainly does not hold up rigorously at the extremes, and in any event we can estimate the value of a person's expected reward and his expected success in obtaining it only very crudely in comparison with those of an alternative. *Expectation* may sound as if it were a new variable, but it is not, for it depends in turn on a person's past experience with actions and their alternatives: his past success in obtaining rewards, their value to him, and the attendant stimuli both past and present.

The expectations for the alternative action, the one not performed, the path not taken, we behaviorists call the forgone rewards, or costs, of the action the person does perform. Economics speaks of these as opportunity costs. The need to take alternatives into account was brought home to me by microeconomics, by Herrnstein's experiments[4]—and by common sense. Curiously, Skinner had not treated alternatives explicitly. His pigeons could either peck a key and get a pellet of food or indulge in some random behavior, such as scratching their backs. He did not present them—and Herrnstein did—with two keys, pecking of which was rewarded at different rates. The notion of alternative actions is essential to understanding human and indeed animal behavior.

Behavioral psychology is an historical science. It is concerned with behavior repeated over time. It explains the present and predicts the future behavior of a person by his past experience and present circumstances. Its heart is what we now call a "feedback loop," in which the results of a person's actions feed back to affect his future behavior.

Obviously my interest lay in social behavior. Though the propositions of behavioral psychology are stated as if they applied to a rat or pigeon acting alone (actually in the presence of an apparatus that rewards or punishes the animal when he acts on it), I was sure that they also applied to the social situation, that is, one in which the action of an organism is rewarded by the action of another organism and vice versa. The behavior of a man acting alone on the environment, as, for instance, when he is fishing, is not to be explained by propositions different from those needed when he is interacting with another person. Because the given conditions are different, naturally the results are different, but no new general propositions are needed to explain them.

In adapting behavioral psychology to my project, I had to modify the conceptual scheme of *The Human Group*. *Interaction* was easy; it remained what it always had been, the frequency with which reciprocated action between at least two persons took place. In behavioral psychology, *sentiments* and *activities,* though somewhat different in kind, were both *operants* or, in the case of emotional behavior, might become such. I lumped both kinds of behavior together under the name of *activities*. I might just as well have called them *actions,* with a gain in brevity and no loss of meaning. The *value* (positive or negative) of a reward was explicitly new to the scheme. I finally abandoned the *external system*, at least under that name. It became the set of given environmental conditions, whether physical or social, including the stimuli attending persons' actions, to which the general propositions had to be applied in order to explain concrete behavior.

With this conceptual and propositional apparatus, I wrote the first draft of *Social Behavior: Its Elementary Forms* in the academic year 1958-59, when I had leisure as a Fellow of the Center for the Behavioral Sciences in Palo Alto, California. Before I started writing I was again alarmed by the possibility that I had been scooped. When I arrived at the center and told the managers what I planned to do, they referred me to a manuscript, which ultimately became a book, in the library of the center, written by the social psychologists John Thibaut and Harold Kelley, who had been Fellows of the center the year before.[5] The managers suggested that their manuscript sounded much like the one I planned to write. My fears were groundless, first, because I had published the guts of my theory in my article "Social Behavior as Exchange" the year before, and second, because Thibaut and Kelley turned out to be only partly in competition with me, since they asserted they were not going to be concerned with "sequential effects." As a behaviorist I had to be concerned with sequential effects, for the propositions of behaviorism refer to a sequence of events over time. What I did get from Thibaut and Kelley was the useful expository device called a "choice matrix," which they had taken in turn from what is called "decision theory."

I cannot and need not review here what I said in *Social Behavior* and its revised edition. After all, the book is still there to be read. My general intention was, of course, to explain how small groups, given half a chance, tend to develop social structures, that is, relatively enduring patterns of interpersonal behavior. Specifically, I tried to explain such phenomena as the following: Why members of a group who are similar in one respect, tend to become similar in other aspects of their behavior also; under what conditions the members of a group exercise power over other members, so that their behavior conforms to a group norm, and under what conditions they fail; how a status system tends to arise and become congruent, that is, how a member who ranks high on one dimension of status tends to become of high rank on other dimensions too; how and why the members of a group develop rules of distributive justice, that is, justice in the distribution of rewards; how leadership emerges and what amount to regular channels of communication tend to converge on the leader; how the status system tends to become stratified, with "social" interaction, in the special sense of leisure-time activities, tending to be especially frequent between members who are roughly equal in status. I have already described how my work on distributive justice, which I had taken straight from Aristotle because I had observed my Americans behaving exactly like his Greeks in this respect, has given rise to a large research industry in social psychology, now called "equity theory."

At the end of *Social Behavior* I turned my argument around. Once the members of a group have by their actions created and are maintaining a social structure, that structure in turn becomes one of the set of environmental contingencies affecting their further behavior. For instance, it makes a difference to a member's behavior where he finds himself in a developing status system. If, because the other members of the group judge his behavior to be "bad" by their standards and so put him at the bottom of the system, no worse behavior can lower his status further. As John Bunyan's shepherd in *Pilgrim's Progress* sings:

> He that is down needs fear no fall,
> He that is low, no pride.

Because for him the costs of behaving badly are thus reduced, he becomes even more likely to behave badly. That confirms him in his low status, and to that extent helps maintain the structure of the group. But note that the mechanisms by which structure has this further effect are still those of behavioral psychology, one of whose principles is that the reduction of the cost of an action, relative to an alternative, makes a person more likely to take the action.

In explaining, that is, deriving such propositions about behavior in small groups from the general principles of behavioral psychology, I must confess that my logic was usually pretty sketchy. The reason was that the data I had to deal with were usually sketchy too. For instance, one had to deal with "lesses" and "mores" rather than with precise quantities, and this condition may give rise to all sorts of fallacies, though there is no rule that says it *must* do so.

In neither of its editions has *Social Behavior* been as well received as *The Human Group,* though I myself believe it is the better, because more general, book of the two. It has given rise to much misunderstanding and controversy, which in the long run may turn out to be good for sociology.

Let me first consider a rather minor problem in the use of language. Scientists, including sociologists, have gotten into the habit of calling any subject by the name of X-theory if it has gone beyond the most empirical form of research. Thus in the social sciences we have decision theory, dissonance theory, equity theory, and others. I began by considering the fundamental social situation in which the actions of one person reward the action of another and vice versa. This sounds much like an exchange of rewards, and indeed I had called the paper in which I had first sketched my theory "Social Behavior as Exchange." As I might have anticipated, my theory therefore got stuck with the name of "exchange theory." This was too bad, not only because the theory is not limited to social behavior that looks like exchange but also because it suggested that the theory was a special kind of theory, whereas it is a general behavioral psychology, admittedly applied to a limited range of social situations. This in turn diverts attention from what I have come to believe, namely, that the propositions of behavioral psychology are the general propositions of all the social sciences.

Some critics thought I was trying to show how originally isolated individuals had come together to form groups, just as the early theorists of the social contract, such as Hobbes, had tried to do, and my critics would have none of that. They were right, but I was making no such attempt. I assumed that humanity had always evolved under social conditions. But whenever one had the requisite information, one could always show that a change in a social structure or the development of a new one could be explained according to the principles of behavioral psychology, which are individualistic in the sense that they refer to what individuals have in common as members of the same species. But this is very different from assuming that human beings have ever lived in isolation from one another. I had not studied history for nothing.

Social Behavior and some of my other writings of the time vexed many sociologists because in them I proclaimed myself, perhaps too stridently, a "psychological reductionist," in the sense that the very marrow of my argument lay in showing that sociological propositions, which I take to be propositions about social aggregates, groups, and institutions, could be shown to follow from psychological propositions. No doubt reduction has a bad name. In its vulgar form, it asserts that some phenomenon, taken for some reason to be "higher" or "nobler" than another, is "nothing but" that other, taken to be "lower" or "baser." Naturally it insults a person who thinks he has been working on the "nobler" to be told that he has been dealing with the "baser" all along. The problem may lie simply in the way we rank phenomena. Reverse the ranking and the antagonism towards reduction might disappear.

To speak more accurately, reduction is often the process of showing how the propositions of one named science follow in logic from the more general propositions of another named science. The problem may lie not only in the way we rank sciences but also in the fact that we draw lines between them and give them different names. It was not as if scientists in some disciplines were not making reductions, in this sense, all the time without arousing any indignation. The classic case was thermodynamics, which Henderson used to describe to me. William Gibbs had shown that the propositions of thermodynamics, at least as far as they concerned a gas in an enclosed space, followed from those of statistical mechanics, provided one made some assumptions defining the variables of the former in terms of those of the latter. Thus *temperature* in thermodynamics was defined as the *mean kinetic energy* of the molecules of the gas in statistical mechanics—a definition no one seemed to find unreasonable. True, reduction was often of greater theoretical than practical use. It increased the intellectual unity of science: but an engineer continued to use thermodynamics in designing heat engines. I did not see what it was about the psychological reduction of sociology that aroused such moral indignation.

Of course I was being silly and I knew it. The reduction of thermodynamics to statistical mechanics had an emotional impact far smaller than the reduction of sociology to behaviorism. For many years humanists had accused behaviorism of robbing human beings of their humanity. Ted Spencer, professor of English, a friend of mine and usually intelligent to boot, had announced that the mild Fred Skinner was "the most dangerous man in Cambridge." Nor was the issue dead. Jim Coleman, a famous sociologist, argued that, in adopting behaviorism, I had robbed human beings of their "purposes," obviously one of their most precious prerogatives.[6] But behaviorism does nothing of the sort: it only says that purposes do not come to a person out of the blue; they have histories. He or she learns them as he does other actions, for carrying out a purpose is an action. If one's purpose is to go to a postbox to mail a letter, one must previously, for instance, have been told by one's mother to take the letter to the box, and perhaps still earlier have found compliance with one's mother's suggestions rewarding. And if one's letter actually reached its addressee—a contingency admittedly less and less likely in the U.S. Postal Service—one would have been rewarded and therefore go to the postbox under similar circumstances again. One would have learned a purpose. Coleman had simply not thought enough about purposes or behaviorism. He was one of many who still believe that human purposes can be accounted for only by teleological or final-cause types of explanation. Behaviorism accounts for them easily by efficient causes, especially by the feedback loop according to which a person's success in earlier actions leads him to repeat similar actions in the future.

It was not as if persons holding my beliefs denied that there were truly sociological propositions, which I take to be propositions that are not merely statistical summaries of the behavior of individuals belonging to a particular category. Among such fully sociological propositions are those that relate institutions to one another. One example might be: nations with freely elected legislatures are apt to possess independent judiciaries. True, the reduction of such propositions to psychology was not made as easy as the reduction of thermodynamics to statistical mechanics with the help of defining the variables in the former in terms of variables in the latter. All we behaviorists claim is that the institutions themselves and their relationships are the resultants of the actions of many persons, acting often, as in this case, over a long period of time, some acting in concert, some at cross-purposes, some with more power than others, etc., and that the resultants are often, though not always, those not intended by any of the participants. All of the participants still act in accordance with behavioral principles, but to demonstrate that fact we need a lot of history. For primitive societies we do not have the history, and in the case of some others, at some point, the supply simply runs out. But for short-lived structures in small groups we can see the process at work.

One reason for the antagonism to reductionism in sociology was that some of the most prestigious men in the field had been against it too. Sociologists are much more ready than other scientists to take the writings of their classic writers as gospel. Chief among the opponents of reduction was Emile Durkheim, who had been one of the influences on Radcliffe-Brown and much of whose work we had read with Mayo. He had written some important books, but also at least one, *Les Règles de la méthode sociologique,* in which he had made silly statements. (I suppose we are each entitled to write one such book.) In it he discussed what he called "social facts." He wrote: "Since their essential characteristic consists in the power they possess of exercising, from outside, a pressure on individual consciousnesses, it follows that they do not derive from individual consciousnesses and that, accordingly, sociology is not a corollary of psychology."[7] In fairness to Durkheim one must recognize that he did not possess an adequate psychology. I construe "consciousnesses" (about which we know very little) as "behavior" and "a corollary of psychology" as "a proposition that can be derived from those of psychology." I have refuted Durkheim's statement elsewhere, and I shall repeat myself as little as possible here. All one has to do is to ask *how* a social fact, such as, to take a simple example, a red light at a traffic intersection, exerts its power from outside, as it certainly does, on the behavior of the drivers of cars. One cannot answer a question like this, one cannot explain the behavior, without bringing in at least one proposition of psychology.[8]

Again, Sir Karl Popper seems to believe that, if interaction between two persons has results neither of them desired, these results *ipso facto*

cannot be explained psychologically. No sillier fallacy—nor one more easily shown to be such—has ever, to my knowledge, been perpetrated by an otherwise great philosopher. But then I suppose it would be boring if intellectuals were sensible all the time.[9]

My efforts to explain empirical propositions about social behavior brought me back in new ways to issues I had first pondered in the course of my reading during the 1930s. Some of my critics pointed out that the small groups I studied existed within larger social structures, such as formal organizations, which were much more persistent than their constituent groups and therefore more important in determining micro-social behavior. These structures are certainly important, for they provide many of the given conditions within which social behavior develops. Yet the structures themselves arose and are maintained by persons acting in accordance with the same psychology that accounts for behavior in small groups. In fact my main effort in *Social Behavior* was to show how many small groups themselves create structures, which have many of the characteristics and effects of organizations.

The question of structure raised another new issue, which was also an old one. Sociologists do not often realize that they pursue two related, but often distinguishable, subjects for empirical research. Most sociologists pursue one far more often than they do the other; a few pursue both. The first, which I shall call *individualistic* sociology, is concerned with the way in which individuals in interaction with one another create structures, and the second, which I shall call *structural* sociology, is concerned with the effects these structures, once created and maintained, have on the behavior of individuals or categories of individuals. In the empirical propositions of the former, the behavior of individuals is treated as the set of independent variables and the characteristics of structures as the set of dependent ones. In the latter, the process is reversed: the structures are treated as the set of independent variables, and the behavior of individuals as the set of dependent ones.[10]

The latter process indeed feels as if the structures were exerting from outside a pressure on individual consciousnesses (behavior). And it seems to me, perhaps mistakenly, that sociologists have devoted more research hours to the latter than to the former. Durkheim himself made a classic study of the correlations between various kinds of social conditions (structures) and the suicide rates among individuals exposed to these conditions.[11] And modern American sociologists study, for instance the effects of school segregation on the educational achievements of various categories of students. It is, by the way, usually easier to study the effects of social structures than to change the structures themselves.

To the other, the individualistic side of the picture, sociologists devote

far fewer research hours, and therefore many of them are biased towards the structural approach to sociology. Indeed they are apt to abandon to the historians the study of the creation and change of large and long-lasting structures. Most of them are illiterate in history, though this condition seems to be changing for the better. At a lower level, the study of the creation and maintenance of structures such as status systems in small groups, though more easily observable and filling a much shorter span of time than the great historical changes, sociologists leave to what may be a shrinking number of persons who carry out field studies at first hand.

But it is not just a question of empirical approaches: it is a question of explaining their results. Both the individualist and the structural type of empirical propositions require psychological propositions for their explanation, for structures do not act on individuals automatically. They do so because they establish some of the contingencies under which persons act: their stimuli, rewards, and punishments; and the explanation why and how these contingencies affect behavior requires psychological general propositions. I suspect, though, that structural sociologists find this especially difficult to remember, and therefore find it especially difficult to accept *methodological individualism*[12] emotionally, for methodological individualism implies a psychology whose propositions refer to the behavior of individuals as members of a single species. Yet in our tradition of seeking the truth I am sure they will accept it in the long run. The run may be very long.

Empirically the two approaches differ; theoretically the type of explanation needed to account for their results remains the same. So let sociologists recognize the validity of each type of approach, even if they do not all practice both of them. I had, in effect, practiced both when, in *Social Behavior,* after showing how members of small groups could create relatively enduring social structures, I then turned around and showed how these structures themselves provided contingencies in which members developed still newer forms of behavior, though still in accordance with the propositions of behavioral psychology.[13]

What I now call individualistic sociologists who are interested, among other things, in how individuals create social structures, are the descendants of what I called in *The Human Group* adherents of the Social Contract theory; those who are interested in how social structures, once formed, affect individual behavior, descendants of adherents of the Social Mold theory.[14] To attain intellectual integrity sociology must fuse the two.

I found myself coming back over and over again to old preoccupations in new forms. As I struggled with the nature of explanation in sociology, I

found myself thinking again about functionalism. Long ago I had decided that theories called functionalist also took at least two different forms, corresponding to the differences between Malinowski's and Radcliffe-Brown's explanation of magic.[15] I made up my mind that pure or societal functionalism, towards which Radcliffe-Brown leaned, does have general propositions and thus meets one of the conditions for being a real theory. They take the general form: If X is a society that is surviving, or maintaining its structural continuity, it must possess institutions of a certain class, let us say, procedures for settling disputes between members. (It must also possess institutions of other classes. Together, these are often called the "functional prerequisites" of a society.) Let us suppose we can take this proposition as generally true, which in fact we cannot. Then if it is known that X is a surviving society (the minor premise), it must possess institutions of this class, whose presence in the society is thus explained. So far as it goes, this is a deductive system, a theory.

The trouble with societal functionalism is not that it does not possess a deductive system, but that among other defects, the system does not go far enough to satisfy the mind. We are not often interested in explaining why a society has some method for settling disputes: we are interested in specifics. Why, for instance, do the legal procedures of English-speaking nations include trial by jury? By what methods did these nations acquire it? Pure societal functionalists cannot answer questions like this; they leave them to the historians if there is any historical record on the matter. Do institutions compete with one another, so that only the fittest survive? There may be something in this argument, in that, if a large number of members of a society believe that a change in their institutions would preserve or increase something like their safety or their wealth, they may be able in time to secure the change. But to advance this sort of argument is to change a societal functionalism into an individualistic one, since the mechanism by which the institution becomes functional for the society is that many of the individual members of the society expect it to be rewarding for them.[16] Upon experience with the institution, their expectations are, of course, often defeated.

The format of what I have called societal functionalism need not be applied to societies alone. It may also be applied to institutions within a society, such as its government. Some Marxists, for instance, might advance arguments of the following general form:

1. For a capitalist state to survive, it must maintain a certain amount of unemployment.
2. X is a surviving capitalistic state.
3. Therefore X maintains a certain degree of unemployment. Q.E.D.

In fact this explanation is mixed, for its advocates are rightly dissatisfied with the syllogism given above. They further assert that capitalists (who control the capitalist state) maintain unemployment because unemployment renders more credible their threats of firing workers, and so allows them a greater degree of control over the latter. But this again turns the argument from a functional into an individualistic one, because it implicitly assumes that persons, in this case capitalists, take certain actions because they find them rewarding. Unlike many arguments of the type represented by societal functionalism, this addition does at least put forward a mechanism for the appearance of the institution (unemployment). Unfortunately we know a great deal about the causes of unemployment, and I think it fair to say that the known facts would not bear out this kind of Marxist explanation.

In his presidential address in 1959 to the American Sociological Association, Kingsley Davis asserted that we were all functionalists now.[17] Were it so, it was because we used the same word and not because we all thought in the same way. Some self-proclaimed functionalists used arguments that were nearer to the Malinowskian or individualistic type than to the societal one. Take Robert Merton of Columbia, who had done so much to get my books published. He certainly called himself a functionalist. At least he had published a famous "paradigm" of functional analysis. Remember that, in my language, a paradigm is usually not a theory.

Merton honestly and rightly went beyond the paradigm and provided a real example of what he meant by functional analysis. It concerned the functions of the old-time American city bosses and their political machines, such as Tammany Hall. The bosses had performed many services for the newer immigrants to this country, helping them to get what they needed for life in an unfamiliar environment and to deal with unfamiliar bureaucracies. In return, the immigrants rewarded the bosses by voting as the bosses asked them to. With these votes, the bosses themselves or their henchmen could get themselves elected to political office and thus hold a measure of political power. Many businessmen needed the help of politicians in the legislatures to secure franchises such as, in those days, streetcar routes, which were at the disposal of the government, and they rewarded the politicians' favors not only, doubtless, with cash but also with jobs for the politicians' clients. Finally, the politicians could use these resources to provide quick and effective help for the immigrants; and thus the ring was closed.[18]

There was no question here of the survival of a society, but there certainly was one of the survival of a system. How was that accomplished? Each category of persons in the system rewarded by its actions the behavior of another category, and thus made that behavior more probable. (Remember that, if some of the categories were also organized groups, the members of an organization are still individuals.) The proof that the system was maintained by mutual reward is easy, for if any category failed to provide its characteristic rewards, the system tended to break down. Thus when the federal government under the New Deal undertook to provide for the poor many of the services hitherto provided by the bosses, the system tended to wither away.

Merton spoke, for instance, of the functions the bosses served for the immigrants. He might also have spoken of the functions the politicians served for the businessmen. But the word *function* here can be translated without any loss of meaning into *reward*, as I have done. And that mere change of a word reveals that the explanation of the system does not depend on a special theory called functionalism, in this case of the "individualistic" sort, but on our old friend behavioral psychology. For if, as in Merton's example, the provision of reward by one person or group for particular activities by another renders the other more likely to perform the activities, the implied proposition belongs to behavioral psychology. Functionalism of this sort is "nothing but" behavioral psychology.

Societal functionalism, though it may not satisfy the mind by accounting for enough details of social behavior, at least possesses general propositions and a deductive system of a limited sort. The condition of much so-called theoretical work in sociology is more seriously deficient. We are riven into a series of coteries, each treasuring its name and thereby hoping to maintain its beloved identity: symbolic interactionism, phenomenology, ethnomethodology, even my own, badly misnamed, exchange theory. My belief is that they are all individualistic and psychological sociologies, but it is difficult to tell because they do not make their general propositions explicit. Indeed they talk about theory and explanation without stating what they mean by these words, and therefore fail to recognize the importance to both of general propositions. Instead they rely on what Mr. Justice Holmes used to call "unstated major premises." In the language of philosophy their theories are *enthymematic*. Because they do not make their propositions explicit, one cannot be sure whether the propositions of one school can be translated into those of another, much less whether they can all be translated into behavioral psychology, or indeed, whether the schools have any real theories at all. I am not arguing that one should put at the head of every deductive system (explanation) its most general propositions. Since they would appear in many explanations in sociology, they would make texts highly repetitive and thus boring. But until we can take our general propositions for granted, and that time seems far off, I urge that at least once in every publication the author make his own propositions explicit. Until its many current schools change their behavior in this respect, sociology will not regain whatever small degree of unity it once had.

Towards the end of my academic life, I had to put my mind on another new problem in explanation which was at the same time an old one: the relation between genetics and behavior in humans and animals. Many biologists had revived the problem at about the same time. What especially brought it home to me were two books written by Professor E. O. Wilson of Harvard: *Sociobiology*[19] and *On Human Nature*.[20] Of course the characteristics of animal behavior itself, as described by behavioral psychology, had evolved genetically. But that was not the chief issue. No one doubted that physical differences between species or between individuals of the same species were inherited. The question was whether behavioral differences were inherited too. No doubt some were, since human beings simply did not have, for instance, the physical equipment to enable them to fly, while birds did. But what about behavior they *could* learn? Were, say, father and son in some respect similar in their behavior because the son had inherited some of the father's genes, or because, to take the crudest case, the father had taught the son what he himself had learned? This was the old issue of nature versus nurture.

Some behavioral psychologists, who talked that way inadvertently because their minds were on other matters and not because they did not really know better—and these included me—left the impression that, given the physical equipment that enabled them to do so and suitable contingencies in the way of reward and the like, human beings could learn all kinds of behavior with equal ease. They were *tabulae rasae*, on which the external environment could write whatever behavior it chose. This is, of course, not true. Genetically, for instance, humans can learn a language, at least their first language, much more easily than they can, for instance, learn to swim. Indeed learning a first language comes so easily to them that it looks as if not even reward were needed to help them, though of course it is.

Following Wilson, I decided that the real problem was not one of choosing between nature and nurture but of how the two interacted. Suppose a boy was big and strong (in large part a genetically determined characteristic). Then he was likely to find rewarding certain kinds of behavior, let us say physical aggression, that a boy of puny build would not, and therefore the social behavior of the two would be markedly different. On the other hand, the big and strong boy might become an unlikely target for the aggression of others; therefore his own aggression might seldom be aroused, and his temper, if it were sweet in the beginning, might remain so. But in either case genetics and learning interacted to produce behavior. At the extreme, a person who possessed a genetically determined potential for a certain kind of action, but had no occasion to perform it, could receive no reward for it, and so it might not appear outwardly in his repertory of behavior.

One of Wilson's examples I particularly liked because it aroused few emotions.[21] People are apt to be born either right- or left-handed: the difference seems to be genetic. It is much easier at first for a right-hander to learn to use his right hand than for a left-hander to do so. According to perfectly sound behavioral principles the latter can be taught to use his right hand, but it takes extra time and practice. Again, genetics and learning interacted.

The issue becomes more emotional in the case of traits, which people often call intelligence, which may not be identical but overlap, and which can be measured in various ways. Told that intelligence is to some degree genetically inherited, which it is, some social scientists are driven to fury. In my experience, they are particularly apt to come from the ranks of the structural sociologists. If they believe that human beings are *tabulae rasae* on which a benign social structure can write what behavior it wishes, such as equality of intelligence or its results, and that they, the sociologists, will have a hand in designing such a structure, and then, after all this, discover that everyone possesses something of the genetic Old Adam, extremely difficult though perhaps not impossible to change, their plans must to some degree be defeated, and that experience is never pleasant. Remember that here I am speaking about individual, not ethnic, differences in intelligence. Of one thing I have become sure: genetic as well as environmental differences must be taken into account among the given conditions under which psychological principles operate to determine behavior. It is true that we still know much less about the genetic contingencies than about the environmental ones.

NOTES

1. Peter M. Blau, *The Dynamics of Bureaucracy* (Chicago: University of Chicago Press, 1955).
2. George C. Homans, "Social Behavior as Exchange," *American Journal of Sociology* 63 (1958): 597-606.
3. George C. Homans, *Social Behavior: Its Elementary Forms* (New York: Harcourt, Brace & World, 1961); rev. ed. (New York: Harcourt Brace Jovanovich, 1974).
4. Especially Richard Herrnstein, "Quantitative Hedonism," *Journal of Psychiatric Research* 8 (1971): 399-412.
5. John W. Thibaut and Harold H. Kelley, *The Social Psychology of Groups* (New York: Wiley, 1959); for "sequential effects" see pp. 18-19.

6. James S. Coleman, "Social Structure and a Theory of Action," in *Approaches to the Study of Social Structure*, ed. Peter M. Blau (New York: Free Press, 1975), pp. 76-93.
7. Emile Durkheim, *Les Règles de la méthode sociologique*, 8th ed. (Paris: Alcan, 1927), pp. 124-25.
8. George Caspar Homans, "Contemporary Theory in Sociology," in *Handbook of Modern Psychology*, ed. Robert E. L. Faris (Chicago: Rand McNally, 1964), pp. 970-71.
9. Karl R. Popper, *The Poverty of Historicism* (New York: Harper, 1964), p. 158.
10. See Viktor Vanberg, *Die zwei Soziologien* (Tübingen: Mohr, 1975), and Karl-Dieter Opp, *Individualistische Sozialwissenschaft* (Stuttgart: Enk, 1979).
11. Emile Durkheim, *Le Suicide* (Paris: Alcan, 1897).
12. For this term, see J.W.N. Watkins, "Historical Explanation in the Social Sciences," in *Theories of History*, ed. Patrick Gardiner (Glencoe, IL: Free Press, 1959), pp. 503-514.
13. Homans, *Social Behavior*, rev. ed., pp. 319-39.
14. George Caspar Homans, *The Human Group* (New York: Harcourt, Brace, 1950), pp. 317-19.
15. George Caspar Homans, *Sentiments and Activities* (New York: Free Press of Glencoe, 1962), pp. 192-201.
16. See the interesting discussion in Richard A. Posner, *The Economics of Justice* (Cambridge: Harvard University Press, 1981).
17. Kingsley Davis, "The Myth of Functional Analysis as a Special Method in Sociology and Anthropology," *American Sociological Review* 24 (1959): 757-73.
18. Robert K. Merton, *Social Theory and Social Structure*, enl. ed. (New York: Free Press, 1968), pp. 104-138.
19. Edward O. Wilson, *Sociobiology* (Cambridge: Harvard University Press, 1975).
20. Edward O. Wilson, *On Human Nature* (Cambridge: Harvard University Press, 1978).
21. Ibid., p. 61.

22

SUMMARY: MEDFIELD

When I find myself coming back, although in new forms, to issues I faced in my first years as a sociologist, it must be time for me to bring this venture to an end, and try to sum up what I think I have learned about social behavior and how I learned it. Remember that this has been an intellectual autobiography: it has been concerned with ideas. I have talked of my life in the everyday world only enough to show that I never quite became a disembodied mind. Remember also that, though this was certainly not the intent of an early teacher of mine like Mayo, I have not studied social science in order to help change the world for the better—though I am sure my studies have done no harm—but to understand its intellectual problems and perhaps resolve some of them. I am sure I have described the progress of my ideas as more straightforward, in the sense of one idea's leading naturally to another, than it really was. Instead it was marked by turns up blind alleys, by doubts and backslidings, by the abandonment of positions once taken and their later recovery, right up to the present. It was heavily influenced by chance, which means only that some highly improbable, yet not undetermined, events made a difference to it. Above all, it was marked by a dialogue with myself that seldom rose into consciousness but, when it did, showed me that it had not been standing still.

None of us can help beginning our study of human behavior without acquiring intuitive familiarity with it. Some of us never get any further, and our familiarity remains unconscious. I was brought up in an environment that was to a high degree "socially conscious," in the broadest sense of those words. It was also, particularly in its interest in ancestry, an environment imbued with history. Lastly, it was an environment that put me into early and intimate touch with good literature. Good literature is no substitute for direct experience as a way of acquiring intuitive familiarity with human behavior, but it the next best thing.

When I became, quite by chance, a sociologist and began to think seriously about my subject, I was lucky to have to study Pareto first. He did not so much add anything positive to my thinking as get rid of much that was negative; he cleared my mind of cant, at least some kinds of cant, much more rapidly than I should otherwise have been able to do. I believe I should have reached the goal on my own hook, but it would have taken me much longer. At the same time I began to ask myself a question that Pareto certainly did not mean me to ask. Unless one wants to improve human behavior in some way, instead of simply describing it as it is, what purpose is served by asking whether it is rational or irrational (in Pareto's terms logical or nonlogical)? Is it not more important simply to ask what determined it? Of course the fact that it is sometimes rational in the sense of being known to achieve a particular purpose, like the action of a skilled carpenter in building a house, may be one of its determinants. I have not always gotten from my teachers or my reading just what I was supposed to get. Instead I have reacted against them.

My next insight came from my reading, through Mayo's influence, many good field reports on so-called primitive societies. They persuaded me that there was much to be said for Henderson's notion of a social system in which every institution of a society was related to every other, though much more loosely than Henderson implied. This provided me with the model for my own researches on, and later book about, English rural society in the High Middle Ages.

Much more important than those concerning the relations within a society were the intuitions to which my reading led me about relations across societies, cross-cultural relations as we call them. I discovered that certain relationships between institutions seemed to hold good in so-cieties so far separated in time and space that their members could not have borrowed them from one another. Instead human beings must have invented and developed them independently over and over again. This insight did not refute the culturalists' assertion that every culture was unique, but it did imply that when persons were placed in the same circumstances they tended to produce the same kinds of actions. Of course no society was placed in just the same circumstances as another, only some of them, and only then did the cross-cultural generalizations tend to appear. How much have I owed to that hoary anthropological figure, the mother's brother! This insight certainly implied that human nature was the same the world over, and it freed me at once both of culturalism and what I have called societal functionalism, which was the attempt to explain the institutions of a society by arguing that they existed because they helped the society to survive. Perhaps they did, but the functionalists could point to no mechanism by which they had acquired this interesting property other than that human beings had made them so. Even if one granted that human nature was the same the world over, one could still ask what were the characteristics of this human nature. For a long time I did not get a halfway satisfactory answer to this question. But at least I had become, without realizing it, what is now called a methodological individualist.

My next problem did not come from reading anthropological field reports but from asking how one should organize the findings that were coming out from good studies of small groups in the Western Electric and Yankee City researches. Here the problem was how to devise a conceptual scheme: how should the data be measured and classified and what classes were related to what other ones? Here again my insights came from reactions against those of others, in this case Eliot Chapple and Conrad Arensberg. They seemed to me to insist not only that a class of data called interaction could be operationally defined, which I was prepared to accept, but also, which I was not, that in social behavior interaction provided the eternal independent variable whose changes caused the changes in other aspects of the behavior. My first reaction was to add two further classes of data, sentiments and activities, to the scheme and to insist that changes in them were not simply caused by interaction. Instead, all three classes of variables were in mutual dependence with one another. In my Willemstad sketch I added the quite standard notion of drawing a line between a social system and its environment, and I insisted that the classes of variables were mutually dependent not only within the line (the internal system) but also across the line (between system and environment) and within the environment itself (the external system). This last assumption was both unnecessary and often incorrect. Other than insisting on their mutual dependence I did not specify how the classes were related.

After World War II I wrote *The Human Group*[1] in order to show how my conceptual scheme could be applied to five good concrete studies of small groups. Though my decision to limit myself to small groups was the accidental result of a conversation with Conrad Arensberg, I have since concluded that it was wise for more general reasons. I had first to show how my scheme and its later theoretical development could be applied to the familiar features of small groups before others or myself could use it for less frequent, larger-scale, or more complicated social phenomena.

In the course of writing *The Human Group* I found staring up at me from the data, when organized in my conceptual scheme, several propositions of low generality which implied not only that some of the variables were mutually dependent but also how they were, at least to the extent, for instance, that an increase in the value of one was accompanied by an increase in the value of another. I was sensible enough to try to state some of these propositions explicitly.

Should I carry this process further and, if so, how? Although I had heard about theory and its virtues for many years, no one had ever told me what a theory was. I now think people like Henderson assumed that every scientist knew what a theory was, though as far as he went in writing was to use strong language about "the final task in the scientific study of cases": "This is the clear, explicit, and logical formulation of all relevant observations, analyses, and conclusions. *In scientific work the final task must be invariably performed* [Henderson's emphasis]. This is an induction from experience. It is a judgment from which there can be no appeal."[2] This is vintage Henderson: one can hear the pile driver, but it is still not very specific.

My membership in the new Department of Social Relations and participation in efforts to "integrate" it forced me as never before to consider Talcott Parsons's notion of theory or at least the kind of theory he proposed to work toward. From the first I was intuitively sure that this was not what I meant by theory, and I took steps to decide what I did mean. I was also sure that the general characteristics of a theory, though naturally not its specific content, were the same in the physical as in the social sciences, and under the influence of Tom Kuhn I had studied carefully what had been accepted as theories in the physical sciences. The fact that both Newtonian mechanics and thermodynamics had been superseded by more general theories did not prevent their being good examples of the genre. The philosophers of science had also begun to be interested in the nature of theory. I read what some of them had to say, and it seemed to correspond with the features of my examples.

Of course theory is only a word. One can define it in any way one chooses, provided one makes the definition consistent and does not change it once chosen. From my examples and from the arguments of the philosophers I decided to adopt what has come to be called the "covering law" view of theory. The theory of a phenomenon is an explanation of it. What is to be explained are low-level or empirical propositions stating how at least two variables are related to one another. They are explained when they can be deduced from more general propositions under specific given conditions. These general propositions are the "covering laws": a "covering law" view of theory was also a "deductive system" view.

Note that this is a description of a theory after it has at least been tentatively constructed. It is not a description of how it was constructed. The methods by which theories are constructed—if one can call them methods at all—are far more varied and far less easily described.

Adopting this view of theory raised for me the question what should be the covering laws, the general propositions, of the theories in social science. One had to remember that, on the evidence, no set of covering laws remained the most general forever. One had to work with what one had at any given time, either propositions one invented oneself or those one borrowed from others. I decided that for me the most useful covering laws were those of what is sometimes called "learning theory" but is much more accurately called behavioral psychology, since it applies both to the process by which a person learns actions and to the way he uses them after he has learned them. I decided to use them in the forms in which, as first approximations, B. F. Skinner, Richard Herrnstein, and others had stated them. Like other general propositions, they were unlikely to remain the most general propositions of psychology, but they were the best on hand now.

They were propositions that held good of the behavior of individuals as members of the human species, propositions about human nature. They were not propositions—though Parsons thought they were—about the idiosyncrasies of particular personalities. Indeed they could be used to explain these idiosyncrasies, provided one knew enough—and one seldom did—about a particular person's past history, including his genetic past, and the circumstances he faced at present. These were the given conditions to which the propositions about a shared human nature were to be applied.

In any event I did not wish to explain the idiosyncrasies of individual personalities. I wished instead to use these propositions, couched as holding good of the behavior of individuals as members of a species, to explain the social behavior that seemed to emerge repeatedly in small groups, both those I had analyzed in *The Human Group* and others I had encountered in my own research and in further reading, and had brought to my notice in the course of membership in my new department. I believed that the propositions were currently the most general in all the social sciences, but in fact I limited my application of them to a particular set of given conditions: those in which a fairly small number of persons were in repeated contact with one another over a fairly long period of time. The classical market did not meet these conditions, and accordingly the general propositions applied to markets could not explain the same empirical findings as they could when applied to small groups. Persons interacting with one another in small groups tended to create interpersonal relationships, and these relationships tended to persist. That is, small groups tended to produce what sociologists call social structures. Findings about the characteristics of these structures—not a series of isolated findings but a connected body of findings—were what I wanted to explain. I tried to do so in the two editions of my book *Social Behavior: Its Elementary Forms*.[3] I will confess that the logic of my explanations is not wholly airtight, but at least I made my general propositions explicit.

Having done this work, I was condemned for being—as indeed I was quite prepared to admit—a "psychological reductionist," since I had explained what were thought of as being sociological propositions using more general psychological ones: I had tried to "reduce" sociology to psychology. Intellectually, though not emotionally, I consider reductionism to be a largely bogus issue.

Much more important, as I was working on *Social Behavior*, I made a discovery which, as is usual with me, was that of an object in plain sight. Once the members of a group have begun to create a relatively enduring social structure, that structure itself produces new forms of behavior in the members by changing the contingencies under which they act. Both the creation of the structure by individual members and the back effects of the structure on their behavior require the propositions of behavioral psychology for their explanation. But, in gross, the dual process tends to create two types of social scientists: those who concern themselves largely with the effects of the behavior of individuals in producing social structure, who treat, so to speak, the behavior of individuals as their independent variable, and whom I call the individualists; and those who concern themselves with the effects of structures on the behavior of individuals, who take the structure as their independent variable, and whom I call, perhaps infelicitously, the structuralists. I believe the structuralists in sociology to be more numerous than the individualists, and that it is their misunderstanding of their relationship with the individualists which creates for them the problem of reductionism. We need both kinds, indeed both embodied in the same persons, if we are to heal the rifts in sociology. Both kinds of interests are wholly legitimate. Indeed I see no reason why any particular person should concern himself with theory at all. But if he does so, he should try, at least once, to make his theory explicit, particularly its major premises. Otherwise we shall never be able to tell whether and in what way his theory differs from other theories.

I do not consider any of these views original with me. Indeed I often feel that all I have done is to try to bring sociologists back to what might be called the common sense of science. At the end, think of the following: the crucial importance of intuitive familiarity with human behavior, as embodied, for instance, in field research; the organizing usefulness of a conceptual scheme; the covering-law view of theory; in social science theory, acceptance of the unity of human nature and methodological individualism as embodied in the propositions (covering laws) of behavioral psychology; the creation by individuals of relatively enduring structures of interpersonal relations; and the back-effects of these structures once created upon the further behavior of individuals. Both the structures and their back-effects consist of the behavior of individuals.

In order to keep a sense of proportion, I must return at last from these increasingly attenuated abstractions to regain strength from the earth that I share with the woodchuck and the snapping turtle. The earth I belong to, and my ancestors have belonged to, is Massachusetts Bay, not Massachusetts as a whole, but to the sea and coast that lie between Cape Ann and Cape Cod and to the woods that lie inland from the coast. I belong between the sea and the woods. I have spoken of the sea: now I must get back to the woods. I call them woods, because that is just what they once were. In one of the most heroic efforts of history my collective Yankee ancestors, with the help of axes, oxen, and stone-boats, cleared the woods and fenced in their fields with the innumerable rocks that the glaciers had left behind them and the frost heaves replenished every spring. For a time they successfully mined the thin soil. But Massachusetts Bay is not meant for agriculture, and as soon as the Middle West was opened up for settlement, many of the farmers simply took off. The woods have returned, though now filled with ranch houses, and with the woods their original wild inhabitants, notably the white-tailed deer and no doubt soon after them the beaver and black bear. Mine is one part of America where, I believe, the ecosystem has, since my childhood, mostly changed for the better.

Massachusetts Bay is a shy and secret land, of small, meandering rivers, small hills with outcroppings of granite ledge, but also of much swamp and marsh, both salt and fresh. It has no bold features or long vistas. But it is an easy land to hide in, to snuggle into.

What kept me in touch with the earth was my parents' purchase at about the time of their marriage in 1907 of some forty-seven acres of abandoned farm lying along the Charles River in the upper part of the town of Medfield, some twenty miles west-southwest of Boston. Besides its other charms, Medfield keeps me in touch with the past. No doubt it got its name partly from its great marshes, which the English colonists valued highly because, when ditched—and the clogged ditches are still there—they made excellent meadows of natural hay, and partly from Metfield (originally Medefield), Suffolk, England, which I have visited and of which nothing remains but a church. More Puritan immigrants came from Suffolk than from any other English county. And in the graveyard of our Medfield there is a memorial to one of our early settlers who had served as a colonel under Oliver Cromwell. On our own land there is a shady spring, called according to local legend King Philip's Spring, because around it the braves of King Philip, chief of the Wampanoags, are supposed to have camped before making a bloody attack on Medfield in 1675 during King Philip's War. Medfield then lay on the wilderness frontier.

My parents had originally planned, as so many of their kind had done, to build a regular country house on their Medfield land, but they never did so. Instead my mother settled for a small, unwinterized cottage, where we could spend weekends in the spring and fall. Before we sited the cottage, our carpenter thought it necessary to employ a dowser (water witcher) to locate water for a well. He taught me the principles of dowsing. I never believed a word he said, but I followed it nevertheless, and he said he thought I had it in me to be good at the trade. Remember that, though I am a skeptic, I am also a certified magician.

From my earliest youth my parents took me out to Medfield on most weekends, taught me how to use an axe and how to light a brushfire in the snow even in the depths of winter. Since the death of my father in 1934 I have been responsible for the land—and that will soon be for fifty years. When I first remember it, it was largely old pasture, except for some enormous spreading white oaks, coeval with the settlers who had first cleared the land. It was already growing up into grey or "poverty" birch and what we call cedar—really a species of juniper. Oh! the pungency of the thick cedar groves in autumn. The grey birch is, luckily, not a long-lived tree, and the cedars gave shelter to pine and hardwood seedlings, which in time betrayed their protectors, so that the woods consist now of mixed pines and hardwoods, largely oak, beech, and red (or "swamp") maple. The white pines, which together with the white oaks if they are given time and room to spread, are the noblest of New England trees, have reached about the same age as I and, like me, are ripe for harvesting. I do not know that our woods have yet attained what botanists call their climax, their natural equilibrium.

Throughout this process I have worked, usually alone, for other visitors come only to see the sights, to keep some paths through the woods clear and some parts of the old pastures open. Of course I could not preserve it as real pasture, but I could at least see that it grew up to no more than sheep laurel and lowbush blueberries, from which my neighbors gather an abundant and savory harvest every summer. I have kept it clear, not by using chemicals but by going over it nearly every year with a brush-scythe, which has a shorter and broader blade than the scythe used for mowing hay. With a good whack, it can cut through a stout shoot. Of course the shoot will grow up again, so that I shall have to keep up my bushwhacking as long as I can.

This work has kept me in touch with much that a bookish man forgets at his peril. Formulas of words have no effect on wild nature, and less than we think even on human nature. They have no effect on the great gales of winter, or the black squalls on the edge of a cold front coming through, on the occasional hurricanes of late summer, that uproot great pines or snap them off like matchsticks. They have no effect on the deer, showing their white tails as they leap away in the distance, on the blacksnakes head down in mouse-holes intent on their prey. (We sometimes called the Medfield land our snake-ranch.) They have no effect on the huge female snapping turtles lumbering up from the river in spring to lay their clutches of eggs on higher ground, nor on the hen partridge, who, when I surprised her with her chicks on the ground and not yet able to fly, flew straight at me, in order to startle me enough to let her brood scatter and escape—not that I meant them any harm. They have no effect on the red-tailed hawks, circling, often in pairs round and round one another high in the sky. These taught me something of the unappeasable strength that lies in what psychologists call drive.

Though these things recurred every year, I saw that nature also changed according to much longer cycles: everything flows. I noted this especially in the changing mix of our species of birds. In my childhood I had never seen cardinals or Canada geese at Medfield. Now some of the geese even nested hereabouts instead of flying north, and in the autumn I could hear them honking as they came in to land on a reach of the river for the night. My beloved bluebirds disappeared, but tufted titmice increased. Only last year I saw the first pileated woodpecker I had ever sighted in Medfield. It is surely the most spectacular of New England birds. Fairly constant in numbers has remained the bird which has been my companion in rummaging in the underbrush—the chestnut-sided towhee.

The seasons in Medfield with their varying colors do most to keep me gay. I use "gay" deliberately to help prevent its falling wholly into the mouths of a special-interest group. At the end of February the pussy willow and the skunk cabbage bring to winter its first signs of new life. How homely are these harbingers! Yet if the skunk cabbage comes, can spring be far behind? The answer is that it can, often very far behind. In the meantime the pink flowers of the swamp maple and the little yellow-green ones of the spicebush do their best to keep up our spirits. When spring does come and "sea-winds pierce our solitudes,"[4] it comes, except for the golden cowslips (as we call marsh marigolds) by the brook, in a rush and in wreaths of white: shadblow, wild plum, windflowers (wood anemones) on the banks of the Charles from which the floodwaters have just retreated, and further inland starflowers and whole lawns of lilies of the valley and false Solomon's seal. Most virginal of all are the dogwood, loveliest of our trees, and its tiny, shy relative, the bunchberry or dwarf cornel. Later not all is white, not the sheep laurel or the blueberry, and for a few years a pinxter (wild azalea) briefly flowered under conditions less than encouraging. We end the spring with the tropical and most un–New-Englandly opulence of the lady slippers in the pineneedles. A lady slipper is a Zenobia at Brook Farm.[5]

We purchase all good things at a cost. With the withering of the lady slippers, spring ends and the curse of Medfield begins. The great marshes of Medfield and Dedham act as huge sponges, buffering the floods of the Charles that would otherwise swamp cities as far downstream as Cambridge. They also produce just the right environment for breeding millions of aggressive and virulent mosquitoes. How could my ancestors bear them without even any escape to screened houses? I suppose that for them, as for all of us, needs must. . . . For myself I get away to Canada, where the beasts are few and positively tame.

Like a migratory bird, I come back in the fall. Everyone knows about our autumn foliage. As my mother used to say, hell would be fine in October. It is not just the big trees that are beautiful. Beside goldenrod and asters, I love the deep magenta of the highbush blueberries. And our berries, though fewer, are even gayer with red than our leaves: the barberries, the winterberries, and hidden under their leaves on the forest floor, the partridgeberries. Just when all seems lost, at the end of October and the beginning of November flower the twisted, golden threads of that ancient understory tree, the witch hazel. The "witch" is a folk-etymology, for the Anglo-Saxon *wych* from which it comes does not mean that. But real witches took over the thing from the word, and my master in the craft taught me to use forks of the witch hazel in dowsing. In the last of a set of verses honoring the little tree, I wrote:

> *This poem has a thought behind it:*
> *The hazel's tangled threads of gold*
> *Tell us that spring is where you find it,*
> *Even in age, even in cold.*[6]

Goethe wrote, "Grey is all theory." The witch hazel stands for his contrast, "the golden tree of life."[7] Medfield, except just before snowfall at the beginning of winter, is never gray. If theory is gray, nature there is bright with color. And I need the riot of color to nourish the sobriety of theory.

NOTES

1. George C. Homans, *The Human Group* (New York: Harcourt, Brace, 1950).
2. *L. J. Henderson on The Social System: Selected Writings,* ed. Bernard Barber (Chicago: University of Chicago Press, 1970), p. 148.
3. George C. Homans, *Social Behavior: Its Elementary Forms* (New York: Harcourt, Brace & World, 1961); rev. ed. (New York: Harcourt Brace Jovanovich, 1974).
4. Ralph Waldo Emerson, "The Rhodora."
5. See Nathaniel Hawthorne, *The Blithedale Romance.*
6. "The Witch Hazel," *Harvard Magazine* 72 (1970): 15.
7. Johann Wolfgang von Goethe, *Faust,* part 1, lines 2038-39.

INDEX